THE BEST OF THE
CORVETTE RESTORER

1953 - 1967   VOL. 1 – VOL. 5

Michael Bruce Associates, Inc.
Post Office Box 396
Powell, Ohio 43065

© Michael Bruce Associates, Inc., 1980. All rights reserved under Pan American and Universal Copyright Conventions by Michael Bruce Associates, Inc. Reproduction without permission is prohibited. Text portions appearing on pages 7 through 235 are reprinted courtesy of The National Corvette Restorers Society, © 1975, 1976, 1977, 1978, and 1979, N.C.R.S.
Front cover design and illustrations by Dick Yoakam.

The NCRS and the Corvette Restorer...
a brief history

The National Corvette Restorers Society was founded in March, 1974, by seven men, John Amgwert, Dick Campbell, Joe Chess, Tom Essig, Sam Folz, Jay Kellogg, and Gary Mortimer. Soon after the organization got rolling, another Corvette enthusiast, Noland Adams, joined the small group. By the time of their first official meeting on June 1st of the same year at the Wapakoneta, Ohio, Holiday Inn, membership had grown to 100. By 1979, the 100 became 3500. And it continues to grow, making the NCRS the largest organization of its type anywhere.

Along with the growth of the NCRS went the growth of the **Corvette Restorer**, its excellent quarterly member magazine. In initial format, the "Restorer" contained just sixteen pages, with typewriter copy and a very non-pretentious format. But even a glance at the first issue, reproduced in its entirety in **The Best of The Corvette Restorer**, reveals a harbinger of great things to come. And come they did. In the five year period covered by Volume One through Volume Five of the **Restorer**, the NCRS and its magazine grew in more than just membership. They grew in prestige. The NCRS became the "in" Corvette organization. Its members were the purists, the experts, the pros...the best.

To understand how it happened can best be accomplished by understanding the very reasons the NCRS was founded and by whom it was founded. The organization states its purpose as the preservation, restoration, and enjoyment of early Corvettes. To accomplish this, the NCRS stresses study of the Corvette's history...how it was conceived, how it has changed, and especially how it was built.

But what is it that makes the Corvette such a likely subject for such scrutiny? Is it really a unique automobile? Yes. The Corvette was not the world's first modern sportscar, but it was America's. The story of its rush into production by Chevrolet's Ed Cole, a feat of timing that probably will never again be equalled in the industry, created an assembly line scenario that changed with practically every unit built during the early years. Under such conditions, even the most refined data records systems would have been difficult to maintain. To make matters worse (or better, depending on your viewpoint), General Motors didn't try very hard. Putting it simply, GM did not document the construction of Corvettes well.

To someone in the process of restoring a Corvette, this lack of information from the car's manufacturer can be maddeningly frustrating. But to the founders of the NCRS, it was more like a delightful challenge. A challenge that, by their own admission, can never be fully met. The reason the NCRS was founded? A lack of information regarding the car they loved. And who were these Corvette lovers? Well, they weren't enthusiasts temporarily enthralled with Corvettes, not part of the fluid group which rolls in and out of whatever is fashionable. These were men who had been around awhile, long enough to have developed a binding affection for Corvettes. More than that, they were car men, meaning that they loved many breeds of automobiles. But for them, the Corvette was special. Maybe they'd grown up with it.

The NCRS was born and bred by men of dedication and purpose. But another ingredient of its success cannot be overlooked...timing. Remember that the NCRS was founded in 1974. Remember what the new automobiles of the era were like? It was the era of battering-ram bumpers, of catalytic converters that set the leaves in your driveway on fire. It was the era of increasing weight and decreasing performance. It was the era of terrible fuel mileage on ever higher priced fuel. There were people who remember what great cars had rolled out of the St. Louis Corvette plant (and Flint for the '53) just a few years previous.

The men who founded the NCRS remembered. And the timing couldn't have been better because a lot of other people remembered too. The success of the NCRS isn't at all difficult to understand. For many enthusiasts, the thrill of new car ownership was gone, because of what many new cars had become. The solution was to restore the cars of the past.

There are of course many other reasons for the success of the NCRS beyond the timing of its inception. The timing may partially explain the tremendous growth, but most agree that the new cars of today have regained at least some of yesterday's excitement, and yet the NCRS continues to grow in popularity.

The **Corvette Restorer** grew with the NCRS. In the twenty issues which constitute the magazine's and the society's first five years, the **Corvette Restorer** published more hard-facts information about 1953 through 1967 Corvette models than most enthusiasts even dreamed existed. **Corvette News**, the in-house GM publication for Corvette owners, said this about the **Corvette Restorer**. "The magazine has been acclaimed as one of the finest single-marque club publications in the old car hobby class being published today."

But the **Corvette Restorer** and NCRS members do not know all the answers. If they ever did, the need for the organization would lessen. In preparing **The Best of the Corvette Restorer**, we were faced with a decision. Should changes, corrections and new information be inserted into the articles, or should the material be reproduced exactly as it first appeared? We did the latter, though text corrections are grouped on page 236.

Now, relax and enjoy **The Best of the Corvette Restorer.**

CONTENTS SOURCE PAGE

VOLUME ONE

FRONT JACKET Volume 1, Number 1   7
Bob Donohoe, Joe Pike, Becky Bodnar, and Sam Folz

NCRS DIRECTORS Volume 1, Number 1   8
The founders and the officers start it off

EDITOR'S PAGE Volume 1, Number 1   9
Apologies for the old Smith-Corona

SOME PEOPLE CALL IT JUNK! Volume 1, Number 1   10
Interchangeable Corvette Parts

WAPAKONETA MEET Volume 1, Number 1   12
The NCRS is off and running

A LETTER FROM NCRS PRESIDENT Volume 1, Number 1   14
Gary Mortimer speaks

TECH SESSION Volume 1, Number 1   15
Mufflers and transmission conditioners

IREC REPORT Volume 1, Number 1   16
Data, data, and more data

BACK JACKET Volume 1, Number 1   22

FUEL INJECTION PRODUCTION FIGURES Volume 1, Number 3   23
1957-1965

SUPERCHARGED Volume 1, Number 4   26
McCulloch blowers on early Corvettes

FEATHERWEIGHT CHAMPION Volume 1, Number 4   28
The fiberglass story from General Motors World

VOLUME TWO

A VISIT WITH TONY KLEIBER Volume 2, Number 1   34
He drove the first Corvette off the assembly line

CORVETTE SALES LITERATURE GUIDE Volume 2, Number 1   36
A listing of GM showroom and Motorama literature

TECH SESSION Volume 2, Number 1   43
Sam verifies a 1955 model 6-cylinder installation

1956 ASSEMBLED CORVETTE Volume 2, Number 3   44
Yes, it belonged to Zora himself

RESTORATION TIPS Volume 2, Number 3   46
Door hinge rebuild, Y-50 mirrors, paint removal

CORVETTE FUN QUIZ Volume 2, Number 3   48
Fifty questions to strain your brain

LITERARY REVIEW Volume 2, Number 4   50
A much needed book misses the mark

RESTORATION TIPS Volume 2, Number 4   52
New crossmembers, old weatherstripping

CORVETTE FUN QUIZ RESULTS/ANSWERS Volume 2, Number 4   54
Now we know who knows

1956/1957 VALVE COVER USAGE Volume 2, Number 4   58
Nine fins, seven fins, and piezometer rings

CONTENTS | SOURCE | PAGE

VOLUME THREE

AVANTI MOTOR CORPORATION *The sort of operation a Corvette buff admires*	Volume 3, Number 1	59
TECH SESSION *So maybe a few '62 models had gold grills*	Volume 3, Number 1	62
RESTORATION TIPS *Park and license lamps, tach drives, mirrors*	Volume 3, Number 1	64
1956/1957 HEAD IDENTIFICATION *An explanation of the pyramid and tower symbols*	Volume 3, Number 1	68
RESTORATION TIPS *Side trim, tach drives, wide-base wheels*	Volume 3, Number 2	69
TECH SESSION *Paint codes courtesy of PPG Industries*	Volume 3, Number 3	72
PAINT SELECTION AND BODY PREPARATION *A great overview by Ray Halsey*	Volume 3, Number 3	74
1953-1962 CORVETTE PARTS SURVEY *The parts restorers need most*	Volume 3, Number 3	76
RESEARCH PROJECT 1956/1957 *Vehicle Identification Numbers*	Volume 3, Number 3	78
1957 ENGINE/VIN SERIAL CORRELATION *What all those numbers really mean*	Volume 3, Number 3	80
RESTORATION TIPS *Imron, wide wheels, tire covers, plexiglass*	Volume 3, Number 3	81
SIX CYLINDER FUEL PUMPS *They're there if you know where to look*	Volume 3, Number 3	84
RESTORATION TIPS *Aluminum, door handles, headlamps, wide wheels*	Volume 3, Number 4	86
TECH SESSION *Seat coatings, paint codes, 1962 wheel colors*	Volume 3, Number 4	89
RESEARCH PROJECT 1956/1957 *A 1956 Corvette "coop"*	Volume 3, Number 4	90
CHEVROLET PRODUCES 500,000th CORVETTE *Corvette reaches the half-million mark*	Volume 3, Number 4	91
MICHIGAN TO CALIFORNIA IN A 1954 CORVETTE *Joe and Gertrude recall a memorable trip*	Volume 3, Number 4	92

VOLUME FOUR

RESEARCH PROJECT 1956/1957 *1957-58 engine production statistics*	Volume 4, Number 1	94
EARLY CORVETTE JACKS *The two jack types used through 1962*	Volume 4, Number 1	96
RESTORATION TIPS *Side trim, tools, crossover pipes, clocks*	Volume 4, Number 1	98
RESEARCH PROJECT 1956/1957 *1957 price and production figures*	Volume 4, Number 2	100
RPO 684 DUCTING ON 1957 CORVETTES *Crude but effective and just 51 were made*	Volume 4, Number 2	102

CONTENTS — SOURCE — PAGE

RESTORATION TIPS — Volume 4, Number 2 — 104
Fender scoops, flat Imron, door hinges, pedals

STING RAY QUIZ — Volume 4, Number 2 — 107
Another brain strainer for '63–'67 lovers

TECH SESSION — Volume 4, Number 2 — 108
Brake fluid

TECH SESSION — Volume 4, Number 1 — 109
Leaking Carter YH Carburetors

ROBERT S. MORRISON — Volume 4, Number 3 — 110
An incredible fiberglass story

1953-1954 AFFAIR — Volume 4, Number 3 — 114
The editor attempts a body pull

TECH SESSION — Volume 4, Number 3 — 118
VIN plates, phony and real

1953-1967 CORVETTE HOSE CLAMPS — Volume 4, Number 3 — 122
Another finishing touch for correct restoration

1956/1957 GAS CAPS — Volume 4, Number 3 — 127
$50 and more for the correct units

RESTORATION TIPS — Volume 4, Number 3 — 130
Radiator mounts, stripped screws, manifolds

STING RAY FUN QUIZ ANSWERS — Volume 4, Number 3 — 132
Now you know

TECH SESSION — Volume 4, Number 4 — 133
Don't junk it, sit on it!

1956-1962 HARDTOP IDENTIFICATION — Volume 4, Number 4 — 134
They may look the same, but...

1961-1962 MATURED MACHINE — Volume 4, Number 4 — 135
The dating game...interpreting the date codes

RESTORATION TIPS — Volume 4, Number 4 — 138
Clamps, air cleaners, washer pumps, fuel bowls

1956-1962 OIL FILLER CAPS — Volume 4, Number 4 — 140
The correct numbers and their histories

FUEL INJECTION UNIT #7017380 — Volume 4, Number 4 — 142
Details of the '64 and '65 FI units

1965 CORVETTE GAS DOOR LID — Volume 4, Number 4 — 145
Subtle changes through the model run

VOLUME FIVE

TECH SESSION — Volume 5, Number 1 — 146
Correct winter storage practices

RESEARCH PROJECT 1956/1957 — Volume 5, Number 1 — 147
Fuel injection distributors

1961-1962 MATURED MACHINE — Volume 5, Number 1 — 150
Detecting a genuine fuel injected model

THE FLINT CORVETTE PLANT — Volume 5, Number 1 — 154
The inside story of the Corvette's birthplace

BODY PANEL ALIGNMENT 1963-1967 — Volume 5, Number 1 — 165
What to check and how to fix it

BASIC ELECTRONICS — Volume 5, Number 1 — 169
The V=IR refresher course

CONTENTS

	SOURCE	PAGE

1953-1967 CORVETTE RADIO IDENTIFICATION
Usually unique to Corvette usage — Volume 5, Number 1 — 172

STRANGE 1953 CORVETTE ENCOUNTERS
Some serious questions about E53F001003 — Volume 5, Number 2 — 174

1956-1962 CORVETTE IGNITION SHIELDING
The numbers and the changes — Volume 5, Number 2 — 178

1953-1960 GRILL TEETH REPLACEMENT
My, but your bicuspids are lovely — Volume 5, Number 2 — 182

PART ONE: THE HISTORY OF EX-122
The 1953 Corvette Motorama car lives again — Volume 5, Number 2 — 184

1963-1967 INDEPENDENT SUSPENSION
Mr. Duntov's masterpiece explained — Volume 5, Number 2 — 188

CORVETTE MODELS
Cute little critters — Volume 5, Number 2 — 191

1958-1962 CORVETTE WINDSHIELD WASHER TANKS
Application variations — Volume 5, Number 3 — 193

RESEARCH PROJECT 1956/1957
Fuel injection distributors update — Volume 5, Number 3 — 194

1965 PRODUCTION
Option and usage percentages — Volume 5, Number 3 — 195

1966 PRODUCTION
Option and usage percentages — Volume 5, Number 3 — 196

1967 PRODUCTION
Option and usage percentages — Volume 5, Number 3 — 197

1963-1967
Finding your Corvette order copy — Volume 5, Number 3 — 198

FUEL INJECTION DISTRIBUTOR RECONDITIONING
Lessons learned on a ruined trip to Billings — Volume 5, Number 3 — 202

PART TWO: THE HISTORY OF EX-122
The conclusion of the story — Volume 5, Number 4 — 206

POWER TOP RESTORATION
A rare article on a rare option — Volume 5, Number 4 — 211

TECH SESSION
Triple carb synchronization — Volume 5, Number 4 — 214

RESEARCH PROJECT 1956/1957
The birth of the air box — Volume 5, Number 4 — 218

1956-1965 CORVETTE RADIATOR CAPS
Ed Gurdjian spills the facts — Volume 5, Number 4 — 220

FINAL SERIAL NUMBERS BY MONTH
Find out when your '58-'67 model was made — Volume 5, Number 4 — 222

1961-1962 MATURED MACHINE
Rear end identification — Volume 5, Number 4 — 224

1963-1967
Vehicle Identification Plates for Sting Rays — Volume 5, Number 4 — 227

7017380 FUEL INJECTION UPDATE
Plenum chamber stamp locations — Volume 5, Number 4 — 230

CORVETTE MODELS
Duntov's SR-2 in miniature — Volume 5, Number 4 — 232

CORRECTIONS — 236

NCRS MEMBERSHIP FORMS — 237

The CORVETTE RESTORER

THE OFFICIAL NEWSLETTER OF THE NATIONAL CORVETTE RESTORERS SOCIETY

VOLUMN ONE NUMBER ONE   SUMMER 1974

The societies first meet at Wapakoneta, Ohio was a big success which included a visit from the staff of CORVETTE NEWS. Pictured (L to R) are; Bob Donohoe, Joe Pike(CN), Becky Bodnar(CN), and Sam Folz.

The CORVETTE RESTORER

THE OFFICIAL NEWSLETTER OF THE NATIONAL CORVETTE RESTORERS SOCIETY

The NCRS Direstors (Gary Mortimer, Jay Kellogg, Tom Essig, Dick Campbell, Joe Chess, Sam Folz, and John Amgwert) have approved the following list of officers and chairmen to serve in their respective areas throughout the remainder of this year.

President- Gary Mortimer, 6978 River Rd., Harrison, Oh. 45030

1st Vice President-Jay Kellogg, 10007 Frederick, Vandalia, Oh. 45377

2nd Vice President-Tom Essig, R#5, Goshen, Indiana 46526

Secretary-Treas.-Joe Chess, Box 591, Houghton Lake, Mich. 48629

Technical Chairman-Sam Folz, 3824 Coventry Ave., Kalamazoo, Mich. 49007

Meets Chairman-Dick Campbell, 4021 Chamberlain SE, Grand Rapids, Mich. 49508

Publicity Chairman-Jay Kellogg

Membership Chairman-Tom Essig

Judging Chairman-Charles Sagonek, 2254 Gorno Dr., Trenton, Mich. 48183

Parts Chairman-Dora B. Pence, 5719 E. Jackson, Elkhart, Ind. 46514

Awards Chairman-Steve Hero, 264 W. National Rd., Vandalia, Ohio 45377

Publications and Historian Chairman-John Amgwert, 3600 "L" St., Lincoln, Nebr. 68510

Membership in the National Corvette Restorers Society is open to persons interested in the restoration, preservation, enjoyment, and history of the early Corvette from 1953 to 1962 and all related material. Dues are $8.00 per year payable to the NATIONAL CORVETTE RESTORERS SOCIETY. Dues and membership information should be mailed to NCRS Membership Chairman: Tom Essig, R.R. 5, Box 13, Goshen, Indiana 46526. Articles and other items for inclusion in the quarterly publication "The Corvette Restorer" should be mailed to NCRS Publications Chairman: John Amgwert, 3600 "L" Street, Lincoln, Nebraska 68510. Publication dates of "The Corvette Restorer" are January 1st, April 1st, July 1st, and October 1st.

EDITOR'S PAGE

The above artwork is quite adapt for this first edition of "The Corvette Restorer" (come to think of it, I've taken a bath in my '54 on rainy occassions), as it seems like when I took the post of N/L Editor I was very worried about how to get information to fill it's pages. Well, Volum One-Number One is done and although it may never be as prized a possession as the first copy of PLAYBOY, it is the beginning of our new organization for many of our members (those who missed Wapakoneta, missed a good one).

The Newsletter to me, and others, is a very important part of the Society, as it is the only contact many (about 87%) of the members have that can't, or don't, attent the meets. Restoration has its complicated problems and it will be this editor's intension to focus on those problems. But I can't do it alone. So I guess you could say this is a call for HELP! Help from you members in terms of articles, photos, tips, news articles, historical data, anything. If it's of interest to you, it will be of interest to others. All material will be returned. Your suggestions will be appreciated on content of the newsletters. LET'S HEAR FROM YOU.

The Newsletter in terms of production has been uncomplicated in several ways. The Society has an Address-o-graph machine which is a life-saver in terms of addressing. The printing is all being done commercially, and the "parts-pages" are being done by Dora Pence. Ads, of course, are free to members and you should direct your ads to her. Address: Dora Pence, 5719 East Jackson, Elkhart, Indiana 46514.

There are, of course, many areas to be conquered. Hopefully in the future we can expand the size, and have the type-set. I apologize for the old Smith-Corona. These expenses may be able to be covered by the inclusion of paid advertisements by businesses offering restoration services. These are down the road a bit I'm sure.

I've got a few ideas, and I'm sure you do to. Make them known, and I'll see you next issue.

John Amgwert
Editor

P.S. We need an idea for a Society Emblem.

EDITOR'S NOTE: NCRS Secretary/Treasurer Joe Chess has asked me to relay to the membership that your first year's dues checks are being delayed slightly pending the setting up of a club account, with the establishment of NCRS as a non-profit organization, and the subsequent filing of such organization with regard to revenue status. So, please be patient.

SOME PEOPLE CALL IT JUNK!

Anyone who is restoring an old car usually spends a good amount of time rummaging through the local junk yards. They are virtual museums of automotive history and an education can be gained in an afternoon.

But one thing that most all junk yards don't have is a supply of Corvette "parts cars". Corvette wrecks are generally stripped of parts or rebuilt(?) long before they make it to a yard, and dealers are interested in wrecks for the metal not fiberglass. This is not to say that junk yards cannot be a great source for the Corvette restorer. Many parts can be replaced, or at least substituted on early Corvettes from these mounds of rust and broken glass.

Unfortunately there is no quick reference source we can use to tell which Corvette parts had _other_ applications, or which parts can _be modified_ for a perfect match. So, it will be the purpose of this column to begin collecting and informing the Corvette restorer of suitable replacement parts that hopefully will be more readily available than the original. With help from members and the use of photographs we can surely turn someone's headache into an easily solvable situation.

While rambling through many parts wanted lists in the various Corvette publications, I notice at least several people in need of a windshield washer set-up for their early Corvette. Owning a '54 that was without one, I headed for a junk yard.

I brought home about six brackets and pumps, and two good jars. These items can be found on '50-'55 Cadillac, Buick, Olds, Pontiac, and _some_ '55 Chevys. The '53 and '54 Chevy bracket is _not_ correct. Out of three '55 Chevys with washers, only one had the correct bracket, indicating the use of two types of fluid containers.

If you find a '55 Chevy with a W/W bracket, get it, regardless of type, as it has a small extension piece that holds the bracket out from the inner fender.

1955 Chevy washer bracket extension

The '53-'55 Corvette also has a similar piece attached to the inner fender, and this piece can be made from the '55 Chevy part for a perfect match. This part must be shortened, bent in a different angle, and two new holes drilled.

This extension piece is the only part that is unique to the '53-'55 Corvette. Brackets can be found by the dozens*. The jars are also easy to come by. At last check Chev. still services the part (#3692419), and they're also in junk yards unless broken by water being left in them during winter.

This brings us to the pumps. Pumps with dash mounted controls (late '53s and '54s) are still serviced by the original manufacturer. The part number is #AWS-2 and can be ordered @ $7.20 each from Trico Products Corp., 817 Washington St., Buffalo, NY 14203.

For pumps with foot operated controls (early '53s and '55s) you'll have to do some looking. I believe this was also used on another car, and rumor has it that some early Chevy or GMC trucks would be a good place to start looking for this foot control and jar lid unit. Hopefully in the near future we can present a solution for this style pump.

Bracket location on the '53 and '54 Corvette is on the right side inner fender, on the '55s it is on the left side inner fender near the firewall. If the washer assembly has been removed, you should be able to see the three holes where it was located.

I have attempted to cover the washer for the '53-'55 Corvette but I am sure there is also a problem with owners of the '56-'62 in this area. I feel at this point that there must be a suitable replacement and after we are able to collect some more data from members we will publish the findings.

NOTE: Ken Hooley, 404 Colorado Dr., Goshen, Ind. 46526, recently sent a note saying he is having the W/W bracket extension made. They are excellent at $3.00 post paid.

NATIONAL CORVETTE RESTORERS' SOCIETY
WAPAKONETA MEET
JUNE 1 & 2, 1974

Delores Kellogg talks with honored guest Joe Pike, Editor of CORVETTE NEWS, who was present Friday and Saturday to see the societies first meet.

About 150 people were present at the first meet with the parts swap showing about 15 vendors.

The societies first meet was held June 1 and 2, 1974 at the Holiday Inn in Wapakoneta, Ohio, with a very high percentage of the membership participating. There were 33 early Corvettes present with a large variety of parts being offered by vendors.

The society was honored with a surprize visit from Joe Pike, Editor of CORVETTE NEWS, and several members of the staff, who viewed the cars and interviewed many of NCRS members present for a possible future C/N story on the meet.

Judging during the Concourse consumed most of the afternoon for the four judges because of the large turnout, and in the final tally, Jay Kellogg's '54 was awarded Best-of-show. Jay has now retired his car from competition for one year.

There was quite an unusual event staged in which a navigator and blind-folded driver had to maneuver their car thru a maze of balloons. The winners were Don Benz and Frank Kallem.

The awards banquet Sat. night was attended by 54 members and the program consisted of a society business meeting and several Chev. promotional movies loaned by Joe Pike were shown.

Several meet sites were discussed for the rest of the season. The next meet will be July 26, 27, and 28 at Goshen, Ind., and the third meet will be held in Sept. at either South Haven, Mich. or possibly St. Louis, Mo. with a special tour of Chevrolet's Corvette Plant. Many members expressed a desire to expand some of the meet locations for the convenience of some of the more distant NCRS members.

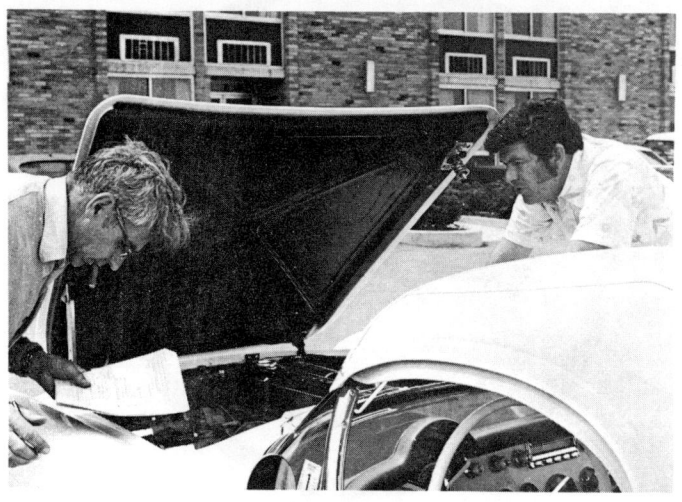

Bob Donohoe and Gary Mortimer during judging of concourse.

Some of the 33 early Corvettes that were present at the meet.

1st place, Sen. class; E53F001091 owned by Sam Folz, Kalamazoo, Mich.

1st place, 61-62 class owned by Don Benz of Milford, Ohio.

Tom Steiner and Larry Riggle were forced to repair Tom's '54 on the spot.

Out of the 33 early Corvettes present at the meet, there were 19 cars in the '53-'55 catagory.

A LETTER FROM NCRS PRESIDENT

Dear NCRS Member,

I am confident that our club is off to a good start. We have well over 100 members and our first meet is now behind us. This is the first issue of our newsletter and you will receive three more with your years membership. We will also be publishing a membership roster soon. Our publishing dates for the newsletter will be July 1st, October 1st, January 1st, and April 1st.

There are seven founders who will serve as Directors thru the first year. The Directors have elected officers for the club and appointed members to act as Chairmen. We are in the process of finalizing a Constitution and By-laws to present to the membership.

Our purpose as written in our Constitution shall be "the preservation, restoration, and enjoyment of early Corvettes and related material as well as to encourage and publish studies and research pertaining to their history. An additional purpose shall be to conduct meetings, tours, and programs of any sort relating to the development and history of Corvettes.

We certainly appreciate the kind letters and phone calls that accompanied many membership applications. These words of encouragement and offers of assistance have certainly been appreciated.

There will be two more meets this summer. The next will be in Goshen, Indiana on July 26,27, and 28. The second will be decided by the membership. We have two possibilities; Grand Haven, Mich. and St. Louis, Mo. with a club tour of Chevrolet's Corvette facility.

I'd like to take this opportunity to invite the members who have never attended a meet to come to Goshen and receive your full membership benifits by meeting fellow members and viewing their cars.

Sincerely

Gary Mortimer

Gary Mortimer, President

TECH SESSION
WITH SAM FOLZ

Have a question of authenticity or a problem that needs an answer? Most likely Sam can help. Send return, stamped envelope to: Sam Folz, 3824 Coventry Av. Kalamazoo, MI 49007.

Since Chevrolet no longer services mufflers for early Corvettes, you'll be glad to know that there's an easy solution to the problem.

MIDAS #M3D795M, which they stock for 2-passenger T-Birds is an excellant replacement. The MIDAS unit will not have the integral inlet pipe like the Chevrolet part, so if yours is bad, they'll have to bend you one, an easy job. The price is right and the part is guaranteed, including labor, for the time you own the car. They also can match most any Corvette exhaust and tail pipes.

I have used GM Transmission Conditioner with good results (Gp. 8.800, Part #1050008). This product is a dispersant and seal-swelling agent designed to stop or reduce dripping from automatic transmissions with old leaking seals.

Prior to using this product, I always was troubled by a "clunk" when the unit dropped back to low range upon stopping. This was a "standard feature" of mine and other old Corvette Powerglides when hot.

Since using this conditioner, I find that the "clunk" has dissappeared and the performance is like a new car. Dripping has virtually stopped. This may not work in all cases as it did in mine, but at the cost, it's worth a try.

On the following pages is Report #1 of the International Registry of Early Corvettes. This study is being conducted and sponcered by George Campbell of Corvallis, Oregon, a member of NCRS. IREC, as reported in this issue, represents a tremendous effort, both past and ongoing, by George.

The data in this report is consistant with other known efforts along this line and is especially interesting regarding the 1955 model, which to this time was showing a far smaller "survival rate" than the '53 and '54 models. It now appears that its survival will compare with '54 models, but both '54 and '55 will continue to show lower survival percentages than the '53 units. This may be due to the fact that GM placed the rare '53s with people of renown and financial substance and possibly those, generally older persons, were less likely to expose the car to the rigors of the drag-strip, road course, and "hop-up".

We thank George for giving NCRS permission to publish this report and will follow up with subsequent reports in future issues of "THE CORVETTE RESTORER".

REPORT NO. 1

POST OFFICE BOX 666

CORVALLIS OREGON 97330

In Pursuit Of An Objective.......With the passing of twenty years the Chevrolet Corvette has become universally recognized as a collector's car, and is increasingly subjected to preservation and restoration by devoted fans and auto historians. It has taken its place in auto collections next to the cars that bear the historic names of Packard, Mercer, Duesenberg, Bugatti and Pierce-Arrow. With its increasing recognition as a car with a great past and a greater future has come the recognition that the early development of a comprehensive registry of the early production of the cars can provide a valuable contemporary historical perspective of the marque, and can benefit those dedicated to the study and preservation of the car in several practical ways:

1. The accumulation of prior ownership historical data on individual cars.
2. Assistance in the authentication of production details as the cars were made.
3. Provide a continuing tracer on cars to discourage theft.
4. Provide data concerning production volume---rarity of existing cars--- to assist in appraisal of value for insurance purposes and as a guide to the buyer or seller of the car.
5. Provide past and early Corvette data for the greater enjoyment and broadened knowledge of owners and aficionados of the car everywhere.

With these and other similar objectives in mind, IREC has made a beginning, and this constitutes the first of a series of reports based on data now being accumulated from hundreds of individually contacted owners throughout the Northamerican continent and wherever they may be found around the world. To those who have taken the time to make their data available, our thanks for their cooperation and enthusiastic response. For the unreported owners, our invitation to join in the study of our automotive marque by writing IREC at P.O. Box 666 in Corvallis Oregon 97330 to request an Inquiry Sheet and become part of the contemporary history of the first editions of "America's only true production sports car."

A Progress Report........When a 1953-1955 Corvette is reliably reported to still exist, through information provided by Corvette clubs, responsible individual reporters, or from other acceptable sources, it is noted in the basic Registry. This is even true of cars identified by serial number with ownership information incomplete or indefinite, and cars identified by owners where the serial number is not yet known or verified. It is from this basic entry that contact is made by the forwarding of an Inquiry Sheet for greater detail about the car, together with information to introduce the function and purpose of IREC. When the Inquiry Letter is returned, the information is tabulated and becomes part of the permanent file of the ownership for that car. Additional data on specific cars is obtained by follow-up correspondence in those cases where special information might be of value. How is IREC doing in accumulating the data on the 4640 cars made between 18 and 20 years ago? Here is our current progress report:

	1953 NO.	%	1954 NO.	%	1955 NO.	%	1953-1955 NO.	%
Car Fully Accounted For	114	38.0	665	18.3	139	19.9	918	19.8
S/N & Name W/O Addr;Addr W/O Name;Unable to Contact	34	11.3	42	1.2	7	1.0	83	1.8
S/N Verified, No Name/Addr.	7	4.3	0	0	0	0	7	0.2
S/N Unknown or Questionable	2	0.7	94	2.7	15	2.1	111	2.4
S/N & City, No Name/Addr.	1	0.3	0	0	0	0	1	---
S/N Possibly Accounted For	0	0	4	0.1	2	0.3	6	0.1
Verified S/N Destroyed	1	0.3	2	---	0	0	3	---
Total	159	53.0	807	22.2	163	23.3	1129	24.3

These figures represent the basic entries currently shown in the IREC listing as of September 1, 1973. The second column figures represent the per cent of total original production for each of the years and for all three years combined. We have used as a base a production of 300 for 1953, 3640 for 1954, 700 for 1955, or a three year total of 4640 cars.

That nearly one-quarter of the original production has entered the IREC data in one form or another is an indication of the "staying power" of the early Corvettes. Last year one of the foremost automotive magazines featured an article concerning the attrition rate of cars following their initial production. An example of the manner in which registrations indicate the declining existence of a given car was cited in the case of the 1956 Plymouth. The writer concluded that by 1970 less than 10% of the original production could be expected to remain, and the survival rate of 1% could be extrapolated by 1978. Further, using a sample group of 15 cars manufactured between 1953 and 1959 the level of 1% survival averaged 18.5 years after production, and was down to 0.1% after 23.2 years. The writer also recognized, however, that the survival rate would be affected by interest in the preservation of an old car and the accuracy of such attrition projections would be countered somewhat by collector interest.

The figures which have emerged from the preliminary IREC analysis would indicate that the 1953-55 group of Corvettes could well set some sort of record for their persistence both before and after the influence of "collector interest" was felt. For nearly one-fourth of the original production to be accounted for, between eighteen and twenty years after their production origin, and after a period of less then three years being devoted to the accumulation of such information, is nothing short or remarkable. From the point of view of IREC, at this still early date, it would seem that 50% of the total production of 4640 might still be accounted for eventually. Only time and the continuing enthusiastic response of the early Corvette owners will provide the answer to such speculation, but a long stride has been made in the direction of confirming the suspicions that many of us share. And with the growing interest in the preservation and restoration of the marque, we can expect that the rate of attrition has tapered off markedly, and the condition and quality of the cars which remain will tend to rise steadily. What this means in the area of economics as well as aesthetics is not lost on many of today's owners, nor is it lost on the awareness of those who seek future ownership of the car.

The effort of IREC has only just begun. The validity of the information made available to early Corvette owners will be strengthened as time goes by and a greater participation is achieved. For that reason, this series of reports may be considered only <u>preliminary</u> at this early date. Already, however, some fascinating information is emerging from the mass of data accumulated. This first report will concern itself with two points about which considerable interest has been expressed: 1) an engine report, and 2) a mileage analysis. Subsequent reports will deal with other topics such as condition, term of ownership, color selection, etc. We also hope to share wil you the story of some of the cars with an unusual past history, and the interesting stories told by some of the current owners in the acquisition and restoration of their cars. From these reports we hope a greater understanding and appreciation of the 1953-55 Corvettes will emerge for the greater enjoyment of all who find fascination with the story of "America's only true production sports car."

First Fruits........The Engine Compartment

A common question raised among early Corvette owners concerns the sequence of numbers appearing on the engine blocks and whether they parallel the serial numbers assigned to the cars. IREC research indicates there is an inconsistent parallel as revealed in the following representative sample:

----------1953------------		----------1954------------		----------1955------------	
Serial No.	Eng. Block No.	Serial No.	Eng. Block No.	Serial No.	Eng. Block No.
E53F001026	LAY10039	E54S001231	0273233F54YG	VE55S001008	0092860F55FG
E53F001065	LAY494733	E54S001306	0299141F54YG	VE55S001050	0118322F55FG
E53F001089	LAY425223	E54S001328	0670747F54YG	VE55S001055	0118328F55FG
E53F001091	LAY341018	E54S001602	0342427F54YG	VE55S001278	0246153F55FG
E53F001093	LAY505454	E54S001609	0374576F54YG	VE55S001319	0188985F55FG
E53F001145	LAY549382	E54S002267	0515430F54YG	VE55S001325	0246544F55FG
E53F001173	LAY537522	E54S002268	0515811F54YG	VE55S001347	0262986F55FG
E53F001214	LAY517164	E54S004165	0643677F54YG	VE55S001366	0262796F55FG
E53F001276	LAY567023	E54S004167	0643822F54YG	VE55S001453	9288352F55FG
E53F001278	LAY567031	E54S004408	0958399F54YG	VE55S001494	0175010F55FG
E53F001284	LAY567014	E54S004409	0958378F54YG	VE55S001575	0363464F55FG
E53F001300	LAY566991	E54S004594	0647546F54YG	VE55S001596	0362212F55FG

It can be seen from this sampling that the engine block number generally rises as the serial number rises, but the sequence of the numbers is not precise. This would seem to indicate that the 6 cylinder engine blocks were delivered from the engine plant to the production area in groups, and then were drawn from stock as they were encountered in the holding area. At the end of the 1954 production run, it appears they were working their way back into some of the engines that had been delivered earlier, since there are a number of instances where block numbers used in the last 200 cars are similar to those appearing early in the 4000 series of serial numbers. The least consistent sequence is found in the 1955 series, although the pattern of ascending numbers is still evident.

A further study of the engine information reveals the ravages on originality exerted by the passing of the years. Engines wear out and are replaced rather than rebuilt. Race enthusiasts discard original blocks for something more productive on the track. Accidents cause the disposal of a doubtful engine and transmission arrangement in favor of a safer replacement engine. With the study of this engine data we can begin to grasp the relative prevalence or rarity of the stock and original motive equipment at this two decade passage of time. Of those reported on Inquiry Sheets as of September 1, 1973, this is the picture:

	1953 Corvette	1954 Corvette	1955 Corvette
Original Engine	64%	56%	41%
Replacement 6 Cyl.	16%	16%	2%
Replacement V-8	---	9%	41%
No Engine	10%	4%	6%
Unknown/Not Rept'd	10%	15%	10%

When evaluating the relative rarity of an original car, it helps to have a valid reference point for such basics as how many cars still around have the original engine configuration. If we accept the premise that as many as 50% of the original 1954 production still remains, and if we accept 56% as a representative figure for how many of those cars still have the original engines, then we might believe that the number of existing cars which meet the first test of originality--that of the engine--would not exceed 1,019 (3640 x .50 x .56). How many of those cars fall short of originality because of other alterations can only be left to the imagination at this time. Perhaps the number of qualifying cars is even smaller than anyone has previously imagined. Only time will help pin down the accuracy of that 50% assumption and verify the reliability of the 56% figure which now asserts itself.

Examination of the 1953 group might reveal another 50% potential in car originality adjusted downward by a 64% engine factor, for a result of 96 cars (300 x .50 x .64); and for the 1955s the same assumptions would indicate a total of 143 cars (700 x .50 x .41). How many such cars have you seen lately? It makes food for thought, doesn't it?

How Far Have They Gone? .... A Mileage Analysis:

What constitutes a low mileage early Corvette? What is a typical odometer reading for the 1953-1955 cars? This study produced a few surprises to ponder. Summed up simply, an unexpectedly large number of the cars are still "low mileage" cars, as reported by the responding owners of today. Here's the picture:

Mileage	1953 Production	1954 Production	1955 Production
Under 20,000 Miles	2.7%	1.5%	1.8%
20,000 - 39,999	8.1%	7.5%	8.8%
40,000 - 59,999	18.9%	15.9%	19.3%
60,000 - 79,999	13.6%	21.4%	10.5%
80,000 - 99,999	2.7%	16.4%	12.3%
100,000 - 149,999	5.4%	10.4%	15.8%
150,000 - 199,999	---	1.5%	1.8%
200,000 & Over	2.7%	1.0%	---
Questionable	8.1%	.5%	---
Unknown or Not Reported	37.8%	23.4%	29.8%

By the very nature of its being a "specialty" car we would expect these Corvettes would be the lessor used of two or more cars in most families. But consider that a 1953 car with just 60,000 miles means an average of 3000 miles per year. That's low miles!

The spread between the lowest and highest 1953 mileage is a mere 276,200 miles. One 1953 is reported in at 8,800 original miles, while the record holder is an impressive 285,000 miles. The 1954s range from 15,000 original miles to a high of 257,000 miles. Low mileage honors at this time go to a 1955 which claims actual mileage of 6800, and the high end for that year is a modest 162,000 miles.

Obviously IREC is not in a position to verify the mileage claims made by its participants. But, the additional data provided usually tends to corroborate the claims and we trust such information is as accurate as the owner can provide. The emerging picture is one of a disproportionate percentage among the early Corvettes which qualify as low mileage cars. If mileage of 10,000 annually is typical among all cars, then a 20 year old car might expect to have either 200,000 miles on the odometer, or to be so worn out that it has been exiled to the junk yard. Remember that some of the reported cars exceed that figure; some are so high in mileage that the true figure is unknown today; and remember that the majority of the cars produced in the 1953-55 era are not yet registered, and may never be, because they have indeed gone the way of tired automobiles, to their final resting place. Those that are left though, seem to be in good shape to face the next 20 years, and with the continuing effort by restorers to defend the marque from further attrition, we can expect to see an improving level of quality even though the quantity will continue to be fixed by the fortunes of vehicular fate. On that positive note, we conclude our story of "How Far They Have Gone" with the expectation that the survivors still have a long way to go as they wend their way into automotive history.

IREC Epiloge:.........Comments regarding this IREC data are welcome. Participation by all previously unregistered 1953-54-55 Corvette owners is solicited. We extend our thanks to the many who have already become a part of this effort. We are particularly grateful for the cooperation and encouragement received from John Hutchins of the Classic Corvette Club in Alma Michigan, Ed Thiebaud of the Vintage Corvette Club of America in Fresno California, Jim Prather of the publication Vette Vues in Atlanta Georgia, and the excellent work done by a number of "regional reporters" whose sharp eyes and unbridled enthusiasm have turned up many cars which would otherwise have languished unknown for some time to come. Their efforts will be recognized individually in a future issue of the IREC Report.

Permission is granted to any Corvette publication to reproduce in whole or in part any of the data provided in the IREC Report, as long as the source of that data is identified as coming from the International Registry of Early Corvettes, P.O. Box 666, Corvallis Oregon 97330. Written requests for permission to reprint by other publications will be appreciated. IREC is a non-profit educational effort to accumulate and disseminate information about early Corvettes and the people who own them. IREC is not affiliated with any other Corvette organization or publication, and provides its information on a non-exclusive basis.

George F. Campbell
IREC Registrar

Fuel Injection Production Figures

By John Amgwert

Recently, while reading my December 16, 1974 copy of OLD CARS Newspaper, I ran across an article by Wally Wyss on the early Corvette V-8. In the article, Wyss mentions the "fact" that only 240 Fuel Injected Corvettes were built in 1957. This took me back to the December, 1971, issue of MOTOR TREND and a retrospect article on the '57 Corvette, which was also written by Mr. Wyss. In that article, Wyss quotes Ed Thiebaud (who's '57 Corvette was featured in the article) as saying that 240 '57s were produced with fuel injection. Can we summize that Wyss is using Ed Thiebaud as his source? If so, where did Thiebaud get his information?

Karl Ludvigsen, a highly respected automotive author, also uses the figure of 240 '57 Fuel Injected Corvettes in his book CORVETTE-AMERICA'S STAR SPANGLED SPORTS CAR. The book seems well documented, but how did he arrive at that figure?

Some research into this subject has been conducted by NCRS member Mike Hunt of Madison, Wisconsin, and it is the subject of this article to present the data that has surfaced as to fuel injection production figures, not just for 1957 Corvettes, but for all years and models.

Mike has also heard that figure of 240 and he questions it. He felt he should go to the original sources of production so he started writing letters. In 1966 he received a reply from Joe Pike of Chevrolet saying that "approximately 1100" injected units were produced in 1957. In a reply from Mr. Thiebaud (mentioned earlier) some 4 years ago, he stated that Rochester had informed him that something like 2000 injection units were produced in 1957. The 240 figure suddenly changes! Still not satisfied, Mike did some more inquiring.

A letter that Mike sent out came back from a anonymous GM source recently. The figures were penned on his original letter and this is what they showed.

1957 Corvette	#7014360-	182 units
	#7014520-	713 units
	#7014800-	102 units
	#7014900-	43 units
	Total -	1040 units
1957 Passenger Car-		1530 units
1958 Corvette-		1504 units

Fuel Injection Production Figures

Suddenly the production figure gets larger. Mike seemed pretty excited, although an anonymous source couldn't really be true documentation. He decided to get in touch with NCRS Technical Chairman Sam Folz to see if he could help in his search for the truth as a back up to the information he had just received. Sam agreed that an anonymous letter was not sufficient, although very interesting.

Sam contacted a mutual Corvette enthusiast, Jon Blanchette, who just happened to work for Rochester Products. In October, 1974, Jon compiled the list you see here, which is the only data on fuel injection available at Rochester. This data is complete, and it took Jon some time to compile, check and recheck. It lists units, years and vehicle applications, as well as service quantities.

Model Year	Model Number	Production Quantity	Service Quantity	Vehicle Application
1957	7010250	5	0	Cadillac
1957	7014360	604	7	Corvette
1957	7014370	447	0	Pontiac
1957	7014520	1060	0	Chev. Pass.
1957	7014538	0	0	(63) units- School
1957	7014800	1623	131	Corvette
1957/58	7014800R	57	0	Corvette
1957/58	7014880	511	0	Pontiac
1958/59	7014900	1867	2	Corvette
1958	7014960	326	2	Corvette
1959/60/61	7017200	238	4	Corvette
1959/60/61	7017250	76	1	Corvette
1960	7017300	5	0	Corvette
1960/61	7017310	0	6	Corvette
1960/61	7017320	2308	54	Corvette
1961	7017355	16	0	Corvette
1962/63	7017360	2131	16	Corvette
1962	7017365	0	22	Corvette
1962/63	7017370	0	47	Corvette
1963	7017375	3022	91	Corvette
1964/65	7017380	2114	67	Corvette

ROCHESTER FUEL INJECTION PRODUCTION DATA

Compiled by JON BLANCHETTE

It is a fact that this data is documented from current Rochester records. But I'm sure that after you study the data and make some comparisons with information from Chevrolet, you can see that there are some contradictions. Example: The vehicle application does not match for the #7014520 unit, as Rochester shows it as a Chevrolet Passenger Car unit. I personally have knowledge of at least eight examples of this unit on '57 Corvettes. To add to the confusion, the chart showing carburetor and injection usage for the '53-'62 Corvettes taken from the Corvette Servicing Guide ST-12 is also shown in this article. It shows the #7014520 unit's application on the '57 Corvette, as do past Chevrolet Corvette Parts Catalogs that I've checked with.

Another discrepency is in the model year usage. No units are shown in the Rochester data as being used on the '58-'59 Chevrolet Passenger Cars. It was offered as an option! Possibly the '57 units were "held over" for the '58s and '59s and the data just doesn't show it. Also the fact that it lists the #7014960 unit as a '58, when specification lists from Rochester show it as a "57.

YEAR	HORSEPOWER	CARBURETION
1953	145—6 Cyl.	YH-2066-SA
1954	150—6 Cyl.	YH-2066-SA
1955	150—6 Cyl.	YH-2066-SA
	195	WCFB-2366-S
	210	WCFB-2366-SA
1956	225	Front WCFB-2419-S / Rear WCFB-2362-S
	220	WCFB-2655-S or 2366-SA
	245	Front WCFB-2626-S / Rear WCFB-2627-S
1957	250	Fuel Injection
	270	Front WCFB-2613-S / Rear WCFB-2614-S
	283	F.I. 7014360, 4520, 4800

YEAR	HORSEPOWER	CARBURETION
	230	WCFB-2668-S or 2669-S
	245	Front WCFB-2626-S / Rear WCFB-2627-S
1958	270	Front WCFB-2613-S / Rear WCFB-2614-S
	250	F.I. 7014800, 4900, 4960
	290	F.I. 7014900R
	230	WCFB-2669-S
	245	Front WCFB-2626-S / Rear WCFB-2627-S
1959	270	Front WCFB-2613-S / Rear WCFB-2614-S
	250	F.I. 7017200, 7300, 7310
	290	F.I. 7017250, 7300R, 7320

YEAR	HORSEPOWER	CARBURETION
	230	WCFB-2669-S
	245	Front WCFB-2626-S / Rear WCFB-2627-S
1960	270	Front WCFB-2613-S / Rear WCFB-2614-S
	275	F.I. 7017200, 7310
	315	F.I. 7017250, 7320
	230	WCFB-3059-S or 2818-S
	245	Front WCFB-3181-S / Rear WCFB-2627-S
1961	270	Front WCFB-3182-S / Rear WCFB-2614-S
	275	F.I. 7017200, 7310
	315	F.I. 7017250, 7320
	250	WCFB-3191-S
1962	300	AFB-3269-S
	340	AFB-3269-S
	360	F.I. 7017355, 7360

FUEL INJECTION MODEL	7014360	7014520	7014800	7014900	7014900R	7014960	7017200	7017250	7017300	7017300R	7017310	7017320	7017355	7017360	7017365	7017370
Power Stop @ .5" H₂O (±.1 Hg.)	2.4	2.2	2.0	1.4	1.6	2.2	2.6	2.5	2.5	2.2	2.6	2.7	2.2	2.2	2.2	2.7
Economy Stop @ .5" H₂O (±.1 Hg.)	1.2	1.2	0.9	0.7	0.7	0.9	1.2	0.9	0.9	0.9	1.2	0.9	1.0	1.0	0.9	0.9
Fast Idle Speed (RPM—Hot Engine)	1800															
Throttle Valve Clearance	.0045"															
Enrichment Diaphragm Clearance (Min.)	.040"															
Cold Enrichment Housing Cover Index	1½R	1½R	1½R	1½R	1½R	1½R	3½L	1½R	3½L	1½R	1½R	3½L	3L	3L	3L	3L
Cranking Signal Valve—Vacuum to Apply (" Hg Max.)		1"	1"		1"	1"		1"	1"	1"	1"	1"	1"	1"		
Enrichment Diaphragm—Vacuum to Apply (" Hg) Economy Stop	9" Hg															
Power Stop	3" Hg															
Main Signal Diaphragm—Vacuum to Apply (" H₂O)	½" to 30" H₂O															
Float Level	2⁹⁄₃₂"															
Float Drop	2²⁷⁄₃₂"															

CHART FROM ST-12 CORVETTE SERVICING GUIDE

In checking the ST-12 chart, you will note that the units listed with an "R" do not match the Rochester data. Jon Blanchette says that records only show one unit with the "R" (#7014800R). The "R" stands for Recalibration, and possibly some units were logged out of Rochester without regard to the "R".

One other check, is with existing unit serial numbers. All seperate units were numbered starting with 1001. In the example of the #7017300 unit, the total number produced, according to Rochester, is Five. This would mean that the highest serial number you should be able to find would be 1005. Sam Folz came up with unit #7017300, serial 1481. We can conclude that a lot of units must have went out of Rechester with no record through their production control.

I've done this with other units that I have knowledge of though, and the numbers did fall into the proper quantities for the various units listed, except #7017300.

In summary, I will try and state some facts, as this is what the research is all about. Don't take all the figures presented here and believe they are complete and correct. I can see that some can and will be challenged. I also don't feel that the material is all incorrect, because of the confusions. On the contrary, it is correct, according to the Rochester records. That is what is important. We should all be able to see that the figure of 240 1957 Corvettes produced with fuel injection, mentioned in the beginning, is not necessarily a fact. The numbers pretty much had to be higher.

We can all be assured that more research will be done, especially trying to get some documentation from Chevrolet. One of these days we'll wonder what all the fuss was about. Until then, we'll keep digging.

SUPERCHARGED

Setting the Record Straight

by John Amgwert

The question was raised during the tech session at the St. Louis meet last October as to the possibility of Chevrolet ever developing and using a supercharger on the early Corvettes. Two examples were brought up for discussion.

Don Peers of Omaha, Nebraska, related that when he bought is 1953 (#99) back in the early 60s, it had a "SUPER-" emblem in place of the factory side "CHEVROLET" script, and an unusual air cleaner attached to the right inner fender on the engine side. He has always thought that at one time the car might have been supercharged, although he does not know the car's complete history.

Mike Hunt of Madison, Wisconsin, also saw a 56-57 model in 1963 that had chrome "SUPERCHARGED" script located front and rear above the standard emblem and bezel. Mike was not able to find the car's owner to ask questions and see the engine compartment. Vette Vues magazine ran Mike's picture of this car in the Oct. '74 issue.

This discussion also brought to mind a photo that appeared in the Feb./Mar. '72 issue of Corvette News showing a close-up of the same "SUPERCHARGED" script above a 53-55 front emblem. The article did not however elude to that photo.

Sam Folz, NCRS Technical Chairman, and George Campbell, IREC Registrar, who were conducting the tech session at St. Louis could not enlighten the group on how these cars came to be supercharged. Sam was of the opinion that these cars were modified through the use of an after-market installation kit.

Shortly after the meet I received several photos of a 1953 Corvette (E53F001060) owned by Fred Neff of St. Paul, Minnesota, which is supercharged. The engine is a stock 235 c.i. six (#LAY 494499) with a McCulloch blower that incorporates the three standard Carter side-draft carburetors. The car also has "SUPERCHARGED" script located above the hood emblem and rear license plate compartment. The only other visible changes from the stock configurations are different exhaust extensions and wire wheels of the Dayton or Kelsey-Hayes type which were sold by many Chevrolet dealers as an accessory to the factory wheels and caps.

The McCulloch blower mounts on the right side of the engine and is driven by a large belt and idler pulley. An air cleaner canister is mounted inside the right wheel well with ductwork going through the right inner fender to the blower. From the blower, the ductwork is directed forward through the front right fender skirt, crossing from right to left between the grille and radiator reentering the engine compartment through the left front fender skirt. The pressurized air is then distributed to each carburetor.

Fred has restored the car and does not currently have the supercharger unit mounted on it. The pressurized atmosphere of the supercharger has a tendency to blow carburetor gaskets and he doesn't want to ruin his carbs.

The installation of this unit is very professional according to Fred who has felt that the car could possibly have been modified by Chevrolet. This is not the case. This type of installation should be considered a "contemporary modification" that definatly enhances the car and its value. It should not, however, be considered a Chevrolet factory item.

Karl Ludvigsen, in his book "Corvette America's Star-Spangled Sports Car", has two photos of a 1954 Corvette with a supercharged six engine and the script. In the book he mentions that McCulloch developed a supercharger kit for the early Corvettes in search of more power. Fred said that the installation of his unit is almost identical to the one pictured in the book.

The supercharger division of McCulloch was sold to Paxton Products, Inc., back in the 50s and I wrote them a letter inquiring about the supercharger unit on Fred's car and other installations they may have made on Corvettes. I received a letter from Mr. Frank Distaso, president of Superchargers and Kits, Inc., of Los Angeles, California.

Mr. Distaso wrote that the original installation on Fred's 1953 Corvette was done in their plant. The company has been the sole distributor and manufacturers for Paxton supercharger installation kits for some 20 years. All installations are custom fabricated and the car must be in their possession. The chrome "SUPERCHARGED" script was hand made by Mr. Distaso. The company also made all the supercharger installations on Studebaker Avantis, and early 1950s Kaisers. He added that no superchargers of this type were ever installed by the General Motors Corporation.

So, for all of you who have wondered about these supercharged early Corvettes, there it is. In case you're interested, Superchargers and Kits, Inc., still installs units on these early cars as well as late models.

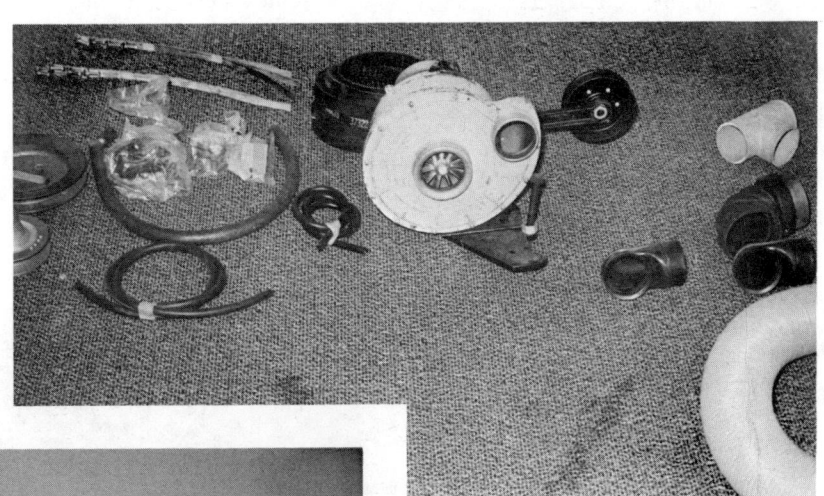

diet of plastic in Corvette trims pounds off

featherweight ch

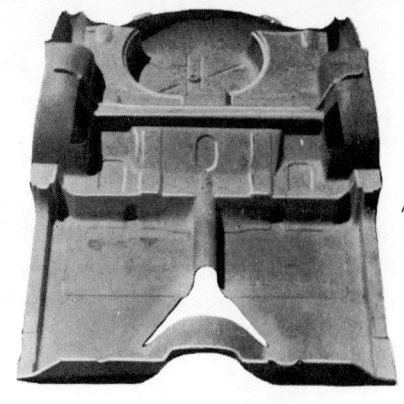

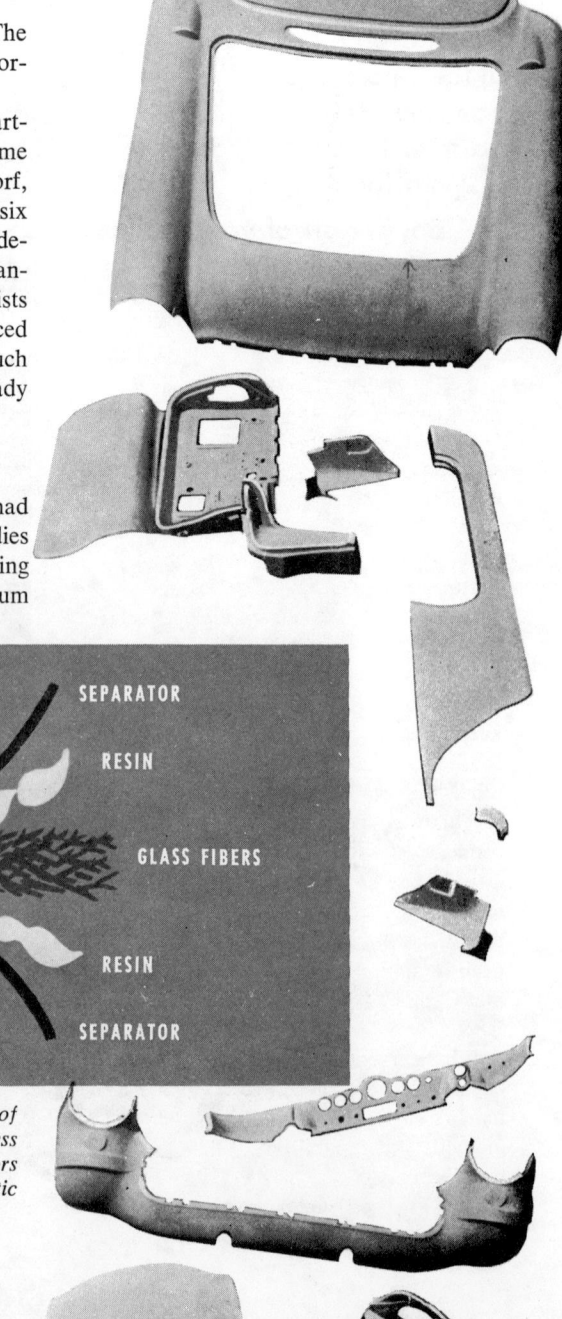

In St. Louis there is a Chevrolet assembly line that is unlike any other in the United States, Chevrolet or otherwise. Many of the sights and sounds associated with putting automobiles together are missing. You normally expect to find swinging overhead fixtures carrying body panels, welding guns blazing sparks, and rubber mallets thumping. Not so on this St. Louis line. Some people wear space helmets. Others squirt chocolate icing from large paper cones. The clank of steel is missing because the product is made of plastic. One has the impression of being in a large toy factory, but these are no toys. They are sturdy, substantial sports car bodies for Chevrolet Corvettes.

The Corvette is the only production sports car made in the United States. That alone sets it apart, but it has an additional distinction in its fiberglass reinforced plastic body.

Back in 1951, Harley J. Earl, G.M. Vice President in Charge of Styling, set a group to work designing a two-seater sports car. He felt there was a spot in the domestic market for such a unit.

By June of 1952 the Corvette, as it was called from the first, was ready for consideration by the Engineering Policy Group, not as another dream car but as a production car. After seeing the prototype the Policy Group approved. E. N. Cole, present General Manager of the Chevrolet Motor Division and at that time Chief Engineer for Chevrolet, asked for the job of developing a production version. The Corvette became the Chevrolet Corvette.

The Chevrolet Engineering Department determined to develop it in time for the New York show at the Waldorf, January 17, 1953. That left about six months to come up with a chassis designed for the performance and handling of a true sports car. Body stylists were to produce a fiberglass reinforced plastic body. With the aid of much midnight oil the Corvette was ready on time.

Limelight on Plastic

Three other G.M. Divisions had dream cars at the show, all with bodies of plastic. This material was proving to be a quick and economical medium

Reinforced plastic is a laminate of glass fiber and resin in thickness as needed for strength. Separators may be oil or a suitable plastic

Chevrolet's...
Champion

Assembled plastic body is painted and trimmed in conventional way, as if it were of steel. Here a Corvette body is dropped onto its chassis for bolting, connecting of electric wiring and final finish and inspection

for experimental body making. In fact, a special plastic development group to study these materials had been set up in the Engineering Staff at the G.M. Technical Center. As expected, the "sports car with the plastic body" created a great deal of interest. What was unexpected was the large number of people who came forward with check in hand and asked "How much?" and "How soon?"

Corvette production planning called for a steel body using kirksite molded tooling. The first units were to be produced during the 1954 model year. But to meet the public response, it was decided to start building 300 units with plastic bodies in June of '53. Serious thought was given to scrapping the steel body plans and studies were begun to determine the practicability of such a course. Building a single show unit of plastic is one thing; keeping an assembly line supplied with fabricated plastic parts is quite another.

This was not General Motors' first production experience with plastics. At the close of World War II, Cadillac made some replacement fenders of plastic because the original dies had been scrapped. It is interesting to note that Cadillac's chief engineer then was E. N. Cole.

Engineers of the Corvette project began visiting plastic manufacturing plants to learn first hand the problems, methods and capabilities of the industry. Four methods of forming fiberglass reinforced plastic were studied; hand lay, vacuum bag, pressure bag, and matched metal dies. Any of these methods will give satisfactory quality. Choice among them is usually dictated by the type product to be made, the volume or rate of production and the money to be spent on tooling.

Hand Lay—The hand lay method requires the least amount of tooling and is particularly adaptable to low production items or pilot models. It needs only a single mold, not a pair. After a parting agent has been applied to the mold, resin and a fiberglass mat are laid up by hand and allowed to dry or cure. The operation is simple but slow.

Vacuum Bag—This process also uses a single mold. However, after the resin and the fiberglass layers have been laid up, a plastic bag is placed over them and sealed to the edges of the mold. Air trapped under the bag is exhausted. The resulting effective surface pressure, of about 12 pounds per square inch, causes an even distribution of the resin.

Pressure Bag—Stronger and more expensive molds are required. The method has been successfully used in making plastic boats. A male and female mold are used. The bottom or

featherweight champion

female mold is coated with a parting agent and then sprayed with a gel coat (a thick layer of resin). Fiberglass mats cut to shape are laid on top of this and are impregnated with more resin. When the mold is closed, a rubber bag clamped to the upper male mold is inflated, exerting about 50 psi on the fiberglass reinforced plastic. The resin is evenly distributed and any excess is forced out of the mold.

Matched Metal Dies — This is the most expensive method. It calls for two metal molds or dies, usually iron castings or high carbon plate steel. They are made so that when placed together a space remains between them, establishing the thickness of the part to be produced. Curing of the resin is accelerated by the heating of the molds, with electric or hot water coils.

Method Chosen

Matched metal dies have the highest production capability. Accordingly, the Corvette body panels were designed for this method. Dies were to be cut on Kellers and hand finished, exactly as if intended for pressing steel panels, but tooling for the plastic parts was simpler. One pair of dies would suffice where steel pressing would have required compound or series dies to manufacture the same part. In fact, at relatively low volumes the dollar advantage of producing the Corvette body in plastic lies in the saving of tool costs. This advantage is considerable—in the millions of dollars.

The non-tooling cost of a plastic body is higher than it would be for a similar body in steel. Thus as the total production increases the dollar advantage gained in tooling is gradually decreased. At this stage of the art, it would seem that plastic bodies are destined for limited production models only.

Working with plastic does have other important advantages. For example, a flange can be continued around a curved surface without wrinkling as it would in steel. Complex shapes and large single pieces with compound angles tend to pucker in steel but not in plastic. As a result plastics allow a greater freedom for

Following the contours of a plastic model, the Keller machine shapes a rough casting to form the female metal die of a rear upper panel assembly

Chopped fiberglass thread is blown onto a pre-form screen the size and shape of the panel being made. Simultaneously, resin is sprayed to hold the threads together

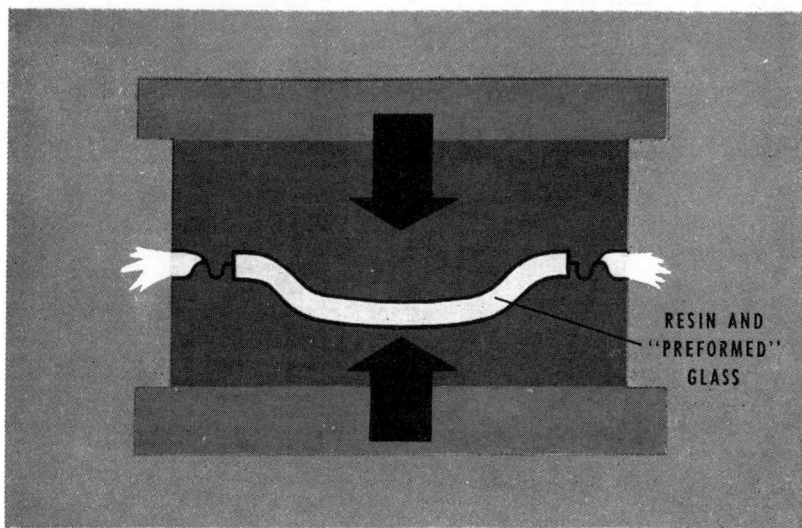

Glass fiber is roughly pre-formed to hold it in place in matched metal dies

the designer, cheaper tooling and simpler assembly operations.

Die making for the Corvette was begun, to be ready for use in 1954. A few prototype cars were made by the Engineering Parts Fabrication Department at the Technical Center using the hand lay method. It was at first planned to produce the 300 units scheduled for 1953 by the vacuum bag method. Actually components for over a thousand units were made this way at the plant of Lunn Laminates at Huntington, Long Island and assembled by Chevrolet at Flint.

Dies Cast and Spotted

As metal dies were finished they were put into operation at the Molded Fiberglass Company's factory in Ashtabula, Ohio. Production at Huntington tapered off and by July 1954 the entire Corvette body was being built at Ashtabula.

In the hand lay and vacuum bag methods the heavy resin gel coat produces smooth surfaces on finished parts. Drying time for the gel coat is too slow for volume output. Instead a surface mat of extremely fine fiberglass filament is used. It weighs only four ounces per square yard.

Material pressed between the dies is partially pre-formed. Fiberglass thread, called roving, is chopped up and blown onto a screen the size and shape of the panel to be made. At the same time resin is sprayed on the screen to hold the threads together. The preforms are heated and semi-cured in an oven.

The surface mat is then cut to shape and laid in the metal die. The preform is placed on top of the mat and a measured amount of resin is spread over it. Heated dies close for about three minutes and when they automatically open the finished part can be taken out. Edges are filed or sanded to remove strands of fiberglass not pinched off by the die and the part is shipped to the Corvette assembly plant in St. Louis.

Rendezvous in St. Louis

In general, plastic body panels, like steel, nest well. This conserves space in shipping and in storage at the assembly plant. Here the largest single part, the underbody, is drilled with bolt

Plastic body panels nest well and even the large single piece underbody can be stored without wasting space

The pre-form is passed through an oven. Here it is heated and semi-cured in preparation for the matched metal die mold

The pre-form is then placed in the die on a fine textured fiberglass mat and a measured amount of resin is spread over the entire surface

A finished body panel is removed from the die. The edges must now be filed or sanded to remove the strands of fiberglass

featherweight champion

holes before it goes on the conveyer.

The conveyer takes the plastic parts into an enclosure where the men in space suits dwell. They blast the edges and joining areas of the panels with steel shot, roughing them for bonding.

Assembly begins when plastic and aluminum reinforcements are added to the underbody, and body sills are bonded and clamped in place. The plastic bonding medium, which looks very much like thick chocolate icing, is squirted from paper cones. Aluminum rivets are used to hold some production parts firmly together while the bond is curing. After it has cured, the rivets are unnecessary, because the bond is stronger than the panels themselves.

Each underbody goes on a dolly, which is both a conveyer and an assembly jig. Front and rear body assemblies, built up on feeder lines are bonded to the underbody by the squirt gun men.

Bonded joints are sanded smooth. Because plastic panels are exact replicas, no adjustment in fit or clearances is necessary in a carefully assembled body. When an adjustment is necessary, for example, if the clearance of a trunk lid is not exact, it can be corrected with a few passes of a sanding wheel.

Five Coats and a Lustre

Bodies move to the paint shop where, after dry sanding and hand rubbing with clay, they get two coats of primer, three coats of lacquer, and are sanded between coats.

Next comes the trim line and body drop as on a conventional line. The unit is driven off the line, the top is installed, and then follow the usual water spray, final spot finish, and spin around the test track.

Five years ago plastic Corvettes came off the Flint assembly line at the rate of three per day. Today in St. Louis one drives off the line every ten minutes, six an hour, forty-five a day.

Four Hundred Pounds Lost

The final proof of a product is, of course, how well it performs. Just how does fiberglass reinforced plastic stand up against steel? To be more specific how does 20 gauge steel, the thickness usually used in manufacturing automobile bodies, compare with .1 inch reinforced plastic used on most Corvette body parts? The plastic is almost three times the thickness of the steel and yet a comparable steel structure would be nearly twice as heavy. In the Corvette this means a weight reduction of almost 400 pounds. This results in a very favorable power to weight ratio, and contributes to fine handling qualities and high acceleration.

How about strength? It would not be correct to say categorically that plastic is stronger than steel. It is possible to say that in a great majority of accidents you would be as safe in a fiberglass body and your repair bill, if any, would be less.

Corvette body panels have a high impact absorption which gives them a stiffness equivalent to corresponding steel panels. Greater thickness of plastic parts also provides a bending rigidity almost exactly equivalent to the thinner steel panels. In boxed sections such as a hinge pillar the steel part has the advantage.

No Dents or Wrinkles

An important characteristic of fiberglass reinforced plastic is that, unlike steel, it does not have a point of yield. Steel, under impact lower than its yield point, will spring back to its original shape. If the impact is great enough to pass this point, permanent deflection results: a dent in your door or a crinkled fender. Fiberglass reinforced plastic cannot be dented. It can be fractured, but the force necessary to do this is greater than the force needed to dent an equivalent steel panel.

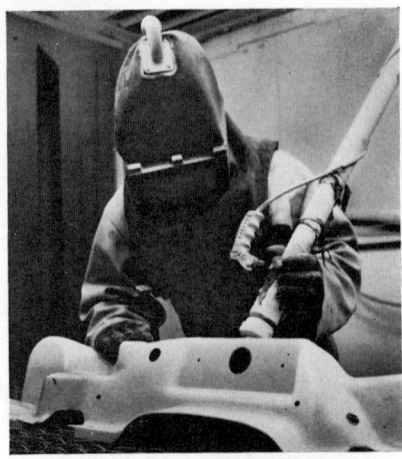

First step of the car assembly is shot blasting the joining surfaces roughing them for bonding

This means that in most minor accidents the plastic Corvette would be undamaged. If the plastic should fracture, damage would tend to be localized. It would not be transmitted through the body causing, as might be the case with steel, a sprung hood or a jammed door.

Repairing a damaged plastic body is relatively easy and cheap. It can be done by the dealer. A small crack is filled with resin and chopped fiberglass. More severe damage is repaired with a patch of fiberglass cloth wetted with resin. If necessary, an entire body panel can be replaced.

The plastic body will not rust or corrode, and the material is inert to any chemicals it may be exposed to in service.

When the Chevrolet Corvette first

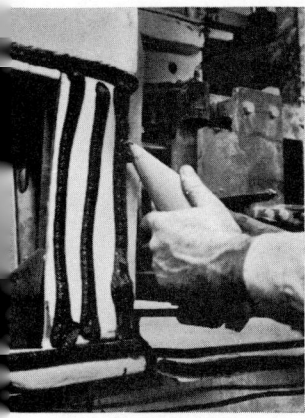

"cake decorator" tube spreads the fiberglass bonding material. When the panels are joined a chemical heating reaction creates a rock-like bond

The front body panel is fitted into position on the assembly line. Note lack of overhead fixtures

The rear body panel is held in position while the bonding material cures, and the body keeps moving along the assembly line

appeared on the road a car with a fiberglass reinforced plastic body was quite a novelty. Even today, a steel minded general public is still apt to knock on the fenders and say, "Yup, that's plastic." But after five years in the greatest proving ground of all — actual service in owners' hands — fiberglass reinforced plastic has earned equal acceptance with steel as a basic body building material in its special field.

The light frame is easily jockeyed into place at the body drop of the St. Louis plant

the road the plastic body proves its worth providing an attractive appearance and enhancing the car's fine handling qualities

Under the bright lights of the paint spray booth the body is sprayed with special acrylic high luster lacquer

Trim

A VISIT WITH TONY KLEIBER

"The first Corvette completed at Flint, was driven off the line June 30, 1953 by Tony Kleiber, a body assembler, as press photographers' flash bulbs popped to record what turned out to be a high point in Detroit's automotive industry." These were the words used in a General Motors news release to describe the famous photo taken as Corvette #1 was completed.

What happened to #1? We know through close inspection of the window sticker in the photograph that the car went the Chevrolet Engineering. Where is it now? This famous photograph may be all that is left of #1. But what about Tony Kleiber, the man that drove the car off the line? Your Editor, with the help of Mark French of Flint found Tony, and with Mark's help and assistance, a two hour interview was conducted.

Tony Kleiber, now 69 years old, is in ill health having suffered a stroke that has left him bedridden. Tony, however, remembers much about the original Flint Assembly Plant.

He was a foreman in the Passenger Car Plant in 1953 and was assigned to the Corvette Plant as an overseer of production. Production of the '53 Corvettes was slow at first and Tony attributes this to general lack of know how in assembling this new type of car. There was no problem with a delay in parts used in production. Tony says that the quality control at the Flint Corvette Plant was good and the cars were not "thrown together" as has sometimes been attributed to early Corvette production. Doors, trunk, and hood were aligned on the line, cars were tuned before shipment, they were checked for water leaks, and finished cars were all test-driven.

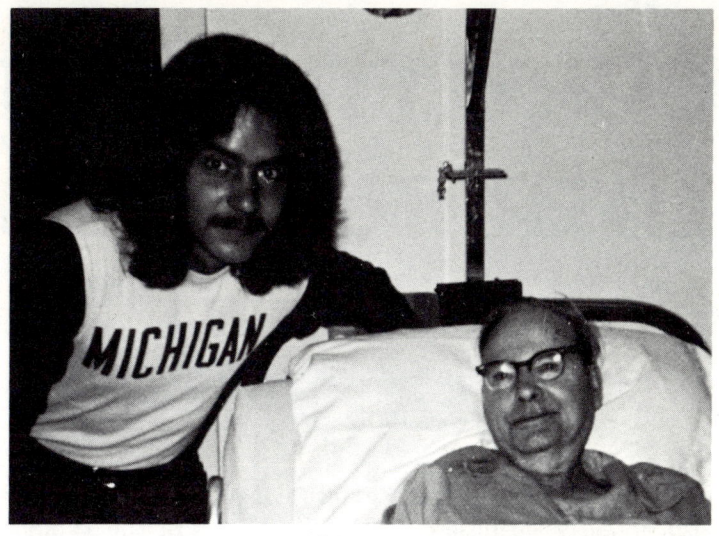

Mark French and Tony Kleiber.

Being an overseer at the plant, Tony was very conscience of how production techniques could be improved upon, and occasionally he got his hands into some of the actual work. Tony recalls that Chevrolet was very concerned about problems that might arise, and he was flown out to New York, Delaware, Maryland, as well as Michigan to check over cars that had been delivered to customers. One of the owners of a 1953 that Tony recalls is Du Pont's son.

We have long believed that the '53 Corvettes were produced at a rate of three cars per day. Tony says that although production was slow at the start, full production saw six Corvettes coming off the line per day. Some question has also been related to the total number of 1953 Corvettes produced. Tony recalls that the serial number sequence ran from E53F001001 through E53F001300, a total of 300 cars.

In the photo of #1 coming off the line, the car has 1953 Passenger Car wheel covers installed. Tony says that approximately the first 25 Corvettes were equipped with these covers, but he doesn't know if they were later taken off and replaced with the Corvette items.

All 1953 Corvettes were produced with the radio and heater options installed, however, Tony says some cars left the factory with blackwall tires as opposed to the standard whitewalls. He also said that owner's manuals were placed in the door pocket at the factory. Although he doesn't remember any specifics, every 1953 Corvette was pulled from the production line for special outfitting and testing. He doesn't recall any cars being produced in other than the Sportsman Red interior and Polo White exterior, but he does state that the engine compartments were painted with gloss black paint.

The workers followed the car down the line, having various jobs, and the publicity photos taken at the plant were not staged. The assemblers were actually working, however, the line did stop and workers would finish whatever they were doing as the photos were taken.

What happened to the first two serial numbered cars? Tony states, "The first two cars were thoroughly tested, were never shipped. Was told they were destroyed, but did not actually see them destroyed."

When the original Flint Corvette Plant (located at Bristol Road and Van Slyke in Flint) was closed and converted to Passenger Car Assembly, production of the Corvette was transferred to St. Louis where it remains today. Tony was transferred to St. Louis and continued in Corvette production work.

As I said, Tony Kleiber is very ill and we all hope for his recovery. If members would like to send him a note of encouragement, please send them to Mark French, 2416 Altoona, Flint, MI 48504, and Mark will forward them to Tony.

Few people can say they own or have owned a 1953 Corvette, even fewer can say they drove number one, but Tony Kleiber can.

CORVETTE SALES LITERATURE GUIDE
by George Riehl

George Riehl is a lifelong auto enthusiast. Traditionally a collector of the Packard automobile, he was also an early enthusiast for the sports cars of the 1950s and early sixties, several of which he owned and drove at that time.

Bitten by the Corvette bug, which he caught from several friends with whom he shares the delights of Corvallis, Oregon, he bought his first car of that marque in 1971, a 1954 roadster now under meticulous restoration.

George is well qualified to tackle the project of assembling for NCRS what we hope will become a comprehensive bibliography of Corvette literature. He owns an extensive automobile research library, including a large library of automotive magazines dating back to the beginnings of Motor Trend, Road & Track, Car Life, Automobile Quarterly, etc. To this he has added an impressive collection of automotive magazine advertisements, covering the entire spectrum of American cars, since their beginnings.

As his interest in Corvettes developed, so did his concurrent collection of Corvette literature. With his own library to draw upon, as well as the Corvette literature collections of several friends, he has developed the beginnings of the bibliography, to serve as a reference guide to others, in their search for appropriate literature. And, as a service to those getting a late start in their accumulation of such items, he has also made note of those pieces which he has knowledge of having been reprinted, so the buyer can take special care to know whether he is buying a copy or an original with his money. George hopes that others will contact him with information about those items known to exist but for which he does not have the detailed description, and about those items not previously accounted for in the bibliography. Periodically he plans to provide an updated list of items until our knowledge of Corvette literature is complete. Those wishing to contact him with additional contributions to the list should send them to George A. Riehl, P. O. Box 1183, Corvallis, Oregon 97330.

— George F. Campbell

This listing has been compiled for exclusive publication in "THE CORVETTE RESTORER" by George Riehl with the assistance of George Campbell and Barry Baker. You are encouraged to send any additions or corrections to George Riehl, P. O. Box 1183, Corvallis, Oregon 97330.

A COLLECTORS GUIDE TO CORVETTE SALES LITERATURE

This is a listing of sales literature available at the local dealers show room and/or sent out by him through the mails. Also included are pieces given to persons attending the G. M. Motorama shows. The appendix lists closely related pieces not always found at the local dealers' showrooms. Not included are salesmen's data books, owners manuals, shop, body, tune up and other service manuals, etc. We hope to develop a listing of these items along with magazine articles and advertisements in the future as separate projects.

Explanation and definition of column headings and listings.

Model Year — Indicates model year of car and not necessarily calendar year in which piece appeared. An asterisk (*) below denotes that there is a reprint of this piece on the market. Most of these are very high in quality and *not* always marked as being a reprint. There is nothing wrong with reprints as they help to fill some important gaps but care should be exercised to make sure that one does not pay the price of an original for a reprint.

Type — Catalog;
Two or more sheets of paper folded and usually stapled together in book form.

— Folder;
A single sheet of paper that has been folded one or more times.

— Mailer;
Can be either a catalog or folder that has a space on it for an address and postage.

— Sheet;
A single sheet of paper that has not been folded.

— Card;
A single sheet of stiff paper.

— Post Card;
A single sheet of stiff paper that has a space on the back for an address and postage.

Pages or folds — Number of pages includes each side of each leaf plus the front and back covers. By this definition no catalog would have less than eight pages. Number of folds indicates how many times the piece has to be unfolded from fully closed to fully open.

Abbreviations used:
P. = Pages
F. = Folds

Size in Inches — First line gives size of piece when fully closed or folded. Second line gives size of folders when fully open. The horizontal dimension is always listed first for each type. The actual size can vary as much as plus or minus 1/8 inch. All pieces should be checked to make sure they are not substantially under size due to trimming off rough edges, or folds that have worn through and thus part of the piece is missing.

Copyright date — Indicated by a © or the word copyright before the date. Does not necessarily indicate the model year.

Printing date — Indicates the month in which the piece was issued. Does not necessarily indicate the model year.

Number — Used by the manufacturer to identify the piece. Often contains the word revised or abbreviations such as Rev., R-1, R-2, etc., to identify subsequent revisions.

Color — Abbreviations used:
B. = Black
W. = White

Illustration and/or "title" on cover. Remarks in ( ) — Describes color and body style of car illustrated plus all or part of the title or other copy.

Model Year	*Type*	*Pages or Folds*	*Size in Inches*	*Copy-right date*	*Printing date*	*Number*	*Color*	*Illustration and/or "Title" on Cover. Remarks in ( )*
1953	Post card	None	3¼ x 5½	None	None	None	Full Color	Motorama Stage Show. (Schedule of show dates and cities)
1953	Folder	2 F.	9¼ x 5½ 27¾ x 5½	None	None	None	Blue & W. Color Inside	Small line drawings of 3 cars. "Once Again Chevrolet . . . . . " (1953 Motorama, Corvair, Nomad, Corvette)
1953 *	Folder	2 F.	7½ x 4 7½ x 12¼	None	2-53	None	B. & W. Brown & Gray	Corvette Emblem. "The Thrilling New Chevrolet Corvette" (Prototype Car)
1953 *	Folder	2 F.	7½ x 4 7½ x 12¼	None	8-53	None	B. & W. & Turquoise	White Roadster. "The Thrilling New Chevrolet Corvette"
1953	Folder	2 F.	7½ x 4 7½ x 12¼	None	9-53	None	B. & W. & Turquoise	White Roadster. "The Thrilling New Chevrolet Corvette"
1953	Post card							
1954	Folder	1 F.	9¼ x 5½ 18½ x 5½	None	None	None	White & Blue	Silhouette of 2 cars (very small). "Once Again Chevrolet . . . . . " (1954 Motorama, Corvair, Nomad)
1954	Folder	2 F.	7½ x 4+ 7½ x 12¼	None	None	None	B. & W. & Red	White Roadster. "Chevrolet Corvette for 1954 First All American Sports Car"
1954 *	Folder	2 F.	7½ x 4+ 7½ x 12¼	None	None	None	B. & W. & Green	White Roadster. "Chevrolet Corvette for 1954 First All American Sports Car"
1954	Folder						Navy Blue	
1954	Folder						Turquoise	
1954	Folder						Tan	
1954	Folder	2 F.	11 x 5½ 33 x 5½	None	None	None	Full Color	White Roadster. "Just for Fun"
1954	Post card	None	5½ x 3¼	None	None	None	Full Color	White Roadster. "1954 Chevrolet — The Corvette"
1955 *	Folder	2 F.	7¾ x 4 11¾ x 8	None	None	None	B. & W. & Green	Roadster. "New 195 H.P. Chevrolet Corvette V/8"
1955 *	Folder	2 F.	7¾ x 4 11¾ x 8	None	None	None	B. & W. & Orange	Roadster. "New 195 H.P. Chevrolet Corvette V/8"
1955	Post card							

Year	Type		Size	Date	Code	Color	Description
1956	Folder	2 F.	11 x 5½ 33 x 5½	©1955	None	Full Color	Bronze Convertible. "A New Corvette By Chevrolet"
1956 *	Folder	2 F.	7 7/8 x 4¼ 11 x 8½	©1955	None	B. & W. & Magenta	Convertible. "The New Corvette By Chevrolet"
1956	Folder	2 F.	11 x 5½ 33 x 5½	©1956	None	Full Color	Bronze Convertible. "A New Corvette By Chevrolet"
1956	Folder	2 F.	7 7/8 x 4¼	©1956	None	B. & W. & Magenta	Convertible. "The New Corvette By Chevrolet"
1956	Folder Mailer	2 F.			None		Convertible. "The New Chevrolet Corvette Comes To Town!"
1956	Post card				None		
1957	Folder	2 F.	7¼ x 11 21¼ x 11	©1956	None	Full Color	Red Convertible. "Chevrolet's New Corvette Fun!"
1957	Folder	1 F.	11 x 8½ 22 x 8½	©1957	None	Blue & W.	SS Sebring. "An Exciting New Experimental Corvette . . ."
1957 *	Card	None	5½ x 7½		None		
1957	Post card				None		
1958	Folder	3 F.	8 x 6¾ 24 x 12¼	©1957	None	Full Color	White Convertible. "Chevrolet Corvette 1958"
1958	Folder Mailer	2 F.	9 x 6 18 x 12	©1958	SC58-1	Full Color	Red Convertible with White Cove. "For '58 This Two Seater Got Sweeter."
1958	Post card				None		
1959	Folder	3 F.	10¼ x 8 1/8 33 x 8 1/8	©1958	None	Full Color	Blue-Black Convertible. "Chevrolet Corvette — America's Sports Car."
1959	Folder Mailer	3 F.	8 x 6¼ 24 x 12¼	©1959	SC59-1	Full Color	Red Convertible. "Corvette — America's Sports Car."
1959	Folder	2 F.	3¾ x 8½ 11 x 8½	None	None	B. & W. & Orange	Convertible With Hardtop. "1959 Corvette by Chevrolet Standard and Optional Equipment."
1959	Post card				None		
1960	Folder	2 F.	12¾ x 5 1/8 25½ x 10¼	©1959	None	Full Color	White Convertible. "Corvette for '60 by Chevrolet."
1960	Catalog Mailer	8 P.	8½ x 11	©1960	SC60-1	Full Color	5 Convertibles, various colors. "How To Be A Corvette Owner; 1960 Edition!"

Model Year	*Type*	*Pages or Folds*	*Size in Inches*	*Copy-right date*	*Printing date*	*Number*	*Color*	*Illustration and/or "Title" on Cover. Remarks in ( )*
1960	Folder	2 F.	3¾ x 8½ 11 x 8½					No Car Illustrated. "Standard and Optional Equipment, Corvette by Chevrolet 1960"
1960	Post card	None	5½ x 3¼	None	None	None	Full Color	Red Convertible. "1960 Corvette by Chevrolet."
1961	Folder	2 F.	8½ x 10¼ 25½ x 10¼	© 1960	None	None	Full Color	Red Convertible. "Corvette '61 by Chevrolet"
1961	Post card	None	5½ x 3¼	None	None	None	Full Color	Red Convertible with White Cove. " '61 Corvette by Chevrolet . . . . . " (Title on reverse side)
1962	Catalog	8 P.	8½ x 11	None	None	None	Full Color	Red Convertible. "Corvette for 1962."
1962	Post card	None	5½ x 3¼	None	None	None	Full Color	White Convertible. " '62 Corvette by Chevrolet."
1963	Catalog	8 P.	12½ x 9¼	© 1962	None	None	Full Color	Black Coupe. "New Corvette."
1963	Catalog	8 P.	12½ x 9¼	© 1962	None	R-1	Full Color	Red Coupe. "New Corvette."
1963	Post card							
1964	Catalog	8 P.	8¾ x 12¼	© 1963	None	None	Full Color	Red Coupe. " '64 Corvette Stingray"
1964	Post card	None	5¼ x 3¼	None	None	None	Full Color	Tan Convertible. "1964 Corvette Stingray Convertible." (Title on reverse side)
1965	Catalog	16 P.	8¾ x 11½	© 1964	None	None	Full Color	Red Coupe. "1965 Corvette Stingray"
1965	Post card							
1966	Catalog	16 P.	8½ x 11	© 1965	None	None	Full Color	Red Coupe. "The 1966 Corvette Stingray by Chevrolet . . . . . "
1966	Post card	None	5½ x 3¼	None	None	None	Full Color	Do not know car color "1966 Corvette Stingray Coupe"

Year	Type	Pages	Size	Date	Number	Color	Description
1967	Catalog	12 P.	8½ x 12	© 1966	None	Full Color	Maroon Coupe. "'67 Corvette by Chevrolet"
1967	Post card				D-35080		
1968	Catalog	12 P.	8¼ x 10 7/8	© 1967	None	Full Color	Silver Coupe. "1968 Corvette — The True Sports Car . . ."
1968	Catalog	12 P.	8¼ x 10 7/8	© 1967	None	Full Color	Silver Coupe. "1968 Corvette — The True Sports Car . . ."
1968	Post card	None	5½ x 3¼	None	D-49490	Full Color	White Coupe. "Corvette Stingray Convertible by Chevrolet"
1969	Catalog	12 P.	9 x 11	© 1968	None	Full Color	Yellow Coupe. "1969 Corvette Putting You First, . . ."
1969	Catalog	12 P.	9 x 11	© 1968	None	D-49490 R-1	Full Color	Yellow Coupe. "1969 Corvette Putting You First, . . ."
1969	Sheet	None	18 1/8 x 10 7/8	© 1969	D-67141	Full Color	Blue Coupe. No Title
1969	Post card	None	5½ x 3¼	None	D-67141 R-1	Full Color	Yellow Coupe. "Corvette Sport Coupe by Chevrolet"
1970	Catalog	12 P.	9 x 11	© 1970	D-78776F	Full Color	Red Convertible. "People Have The Idea . . . "70 Corvette"
1970		(Do not know if there is a first version of the Catalog and Sheet for 1970)			None		
1970	Sheet	None	17 7/8 x 11	© 1969	D-78775 R-1	Full Color	Red Convertible. "Chevrolet Corvette"
1970	Post card				D-78776F R-1		
1971	Catalog	12 P.	9 x 11	© 1970	None	Full Color	Green Coupe. "Corvette 1971 Stingray Coupe/Convertible"
1971	Sheet	None	18 1/8 x 11	© 1970	1143	Full Color	Red Coupe. "Corvette"
1971	Post card	None	5½ x 3¼	None	1145G	Full Color	Blue Coupe. "Corvette Stingray Coupe by Chevrolet"
1972	Folder	3 F.	8½ x 11 34 x 22	© 1971	Sept. 1971	1617	Full Color	Orange Coupe and Instrument Panel. "Sports Car Buyers Guide; 1972 Corvette"
1972	Sheet	None	17 1/8 x 10 7/8	© 1971	Sept. 1971	1620G	Full Color	Orange Coupe. "Corvette Chevrolet Building A . . ."

Model Year	Type	Pages or Folds	Size in Inches	Copyright date	Printing date	Number	Color	Illustration and/or "Title" on Cover. Remarks in ( )
1972	Sheet	None	17 1/8 x 10 7/8	© 1971	Jan. 1972	1620G R-1	Full Color	Orange Coupe. "Corvette Chevrolet Building A . . ."
1972	Post card	None	5½ x 3¾	None	None	None	Full Color	Red Coupe and White '53 in background. "1972 Corvette Coupe"
1973	Catalog	8 P.	8½ x 11	© 1972	Sept. 1972	2227	Full Color	Yellow Coupe. "1973 Corvette Building A Better Way . . ."
1973	Sheet	None	11 x 17	© 1972	Sept. 1972	2230G	Full Color	Red Convertible and Yellow Coupe Inset. "1973 Corvette"
1973	Post card	None	5½ x 3¾	None	None	None	Full Color	Yellow Coupe. "1973 Corvette Coupe"
1974	Catalog	8 P.	8½ x 11	© 1973	Sept. 1973	2675	Full Color	Orange Coupe. "Building A Better Way To See The USA"
1974	Post card	None	5½ x 3¾	None	None	None	Full Color	Orange Coupe and Instrument Panel. No title.
1975	Catalog	8 P.	8½ x 11	© 1974	Sept. 1974	3015	Full Color	White Coupe. "'75 Corvette — Chevrolet Makes Sense For America"
1975	Post card							

APPENDIX

Model Year	Type	Pages or Folds	Size in Inches	Copyright date	Printing date	Number	Color	Illustration and/or "Title" on Cover. Remarks in ( )
1953	Vending Machine Card	None	5 5/16 x 3 1/16	None	None	None	B. & W.	White Roadster. "Chevrolet Corvette American Sports Car General Motors Corp."
1953	Post card	None	5½ x 3¾	None	None	None	B. & W.	White Roadster Ex. 122 Prototype Corvette. (From 1954 Brussels Auto Show) (Title might be in various languages)
1957	Catalog		11 x 8½	None	1-1956	None	Blue & White	Convertible. "1956 Chevrolet Corvette Engineering Achievements." (2 Versions)
1968	Catalog	12 P.	8½ x 5½	None	None	None	White & Brown	Astro 1. "The Chevrolet Technicians Dispatch . . ."

TECH SESSION with SAM FOLZ

In March of this year I was able to inspect and authenticate the existance of a 1955 six-cylinder Corvette. The car is owned by Mark Ziegert of St. Joseph, Michigan and since a 1955 six-cylinder is such a rarity I will give you some of the identifying marks that make this car a true 1955.

The serial number is E55S001320 (note there is no "V"). Engine number is 0492555 F55 Y(G). The last character is uncertain as it is covered by the octain selector. It should also be noted from the photo that the "F", and "Y" characters are hand scribed on the block as opposed to the use of a machine die.

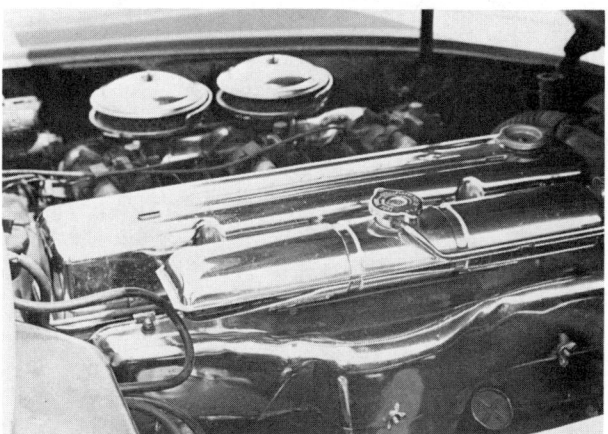

This car is identified and titled as a 1955 six-cylinder Corvette. The engine is typical of a late six-cylinder car in all respects. Voltage is 6 volts. W/S washer is a jar-type mounted on the right side. Rocker cover and ignition shields are chrome plated. Air cleaners are second type and the cleaner-duct unit now on the car is chrome plated throughout. However, a second unit with the car also the second type, is painted in a light apple green as seen on some 1955 V8 parts, such as the distributor base and plug wire holders.

The side curtains have vent window locks and there is a folding top instruction decal as on all 55s. The larger inside rear view mirror is vertically adjustable with a 1955-type pedestal and thumb screw adjuster.

This car originally had been Gypsy Red with a tan top. Upholstery originally was white with red stitching. Window bag is white. Steering wheel has red rim. Colors of the lower instrument panel and carpet are uncertain.

The frame is also that of a six-cylinder car as there is no recess in the right frame rail, typical of 1955 V8s, to clear the fuel pump.

Wheels are typical 1955-style, and the spare could be an original. Fibre panel in trunk is black, typical of a 1955 model. Trunk mat was not seen.

This appears to be a complete, correct, and (except for interior colors) an unmodified car. There is no doubt that it is really a 1955 six-cylinder Corvette.

1956 Assembled CORVETTE

COVER CAR   By JAMES J. DALESANDRO

CHEVROLET MOTOR DIVISION
General Motors Corporation   ☐ 30003 Van Dyke   ☐ Warren, Michigan 48090

June 6, 1973

Engineering Center

Mr. James Dalesandro
100 Forest Avenue
Riverside, IL 60546

Dear Mr. Dalesandro:

Yes, I was the original owner of your car. At the time it had a 283 cu. in. F.i. engine, equipped with ram-horn exhaust manifold.

The car had a 4-speed transmission, and the rear axle was 3.7 or 4.11.

The exterior color was silver, but the interior color, I don't remember. It may have been yellow. It was a pretty car.

Your car is not the 1955 Corvette used at the Arizona Proving Grounds that went slightly over 160 mph. The car I used in Arizona had a 3-speed transmission.

The above is the extent of the information I have on your car.

Yours truly,

Zora Arkus-Duntov

Zora Arkus-Duntov

ZAD:jep

    The car I own was originally owned by Zora Arkus-Duntov between 1956 and 1962. The car was sold out the back door of Chevrolet and titled a "1956 Assembled Corvette" without a serial number. The car has many 56-57 features such as steering wheel, rear convertible top hold-down clips, all dash knobs, hub caps, rear view mirror (57), hood release, shift console, and cowl-vent knob. When owned by Zora the car was painted silver with a blue stripe down the center and, as stated in the accompanying letter, it had a four-speed transmission, 283 horsepower fuel injected engine, and other non-stock '55 items. It is also interesting to note that, through a copy of an original Michigan registration, the car was titled to Alfi Arkus-Duntov, Zora's wife.
    In 1962 the car was sold to Chuck Schank, a neighbor of Zora. From conversations I have had with Chuck it seemed that Zora had a definite liking for the car and it took over a year of bugging before Zora finally decided to sell. In Zora's letter he still commented that it was a "pretty car". Chuck owned the car until 1968 and left it in much the same shape when bought from Duntov, except for an engine change resulting in the loss of the original early type fuel injection unit.

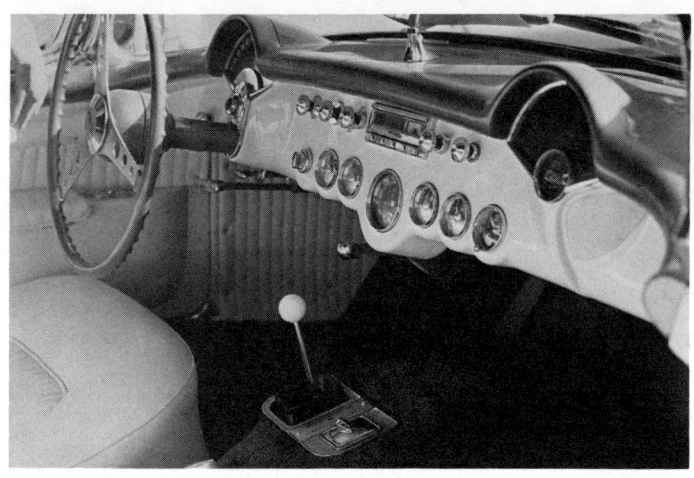

Photos by John Amgwert

The car was then sold to Mike Casey who owned the car from 1968 to March of 1972. When owned by Mike the car received a complete face lift- a custom paint job of pearl white overshot with candy apple red and webbed with pearl white. A new top was added and the interior dyed black. Mike used the car on the drag strip which again resulted in another engine change.

I bought it in 1972 and decided to return the car to its original condition. The trick paint job was removed with varnish remover and after stripping off the many coats, I discovered that the original finish was Harvest Gold. I then removed the black vinyl dye from the interior and found it to be yellow and green with white stitching.

Should I have painted the car Harvest Gold.... or silver with the blue racing stripe? In deciding which way to restore the car I may have made a mistake, bringing up all kinds of questions that need to be researched.

Where did the Harvest Gold body come from? What is the serial number on the frame? Is it a '55, or a '56?

There are other obvious changes on the car, such as a hole in the firewall that lines up with a stud on the brake pedal as if there was at one time an auxillary brake system. There is special sheet metal attached to the frame area around the engine compartment and front wheels, probably used for air-flow. The car still has '57 fuel injection ignition shielding. The cut-out for the shift lever in the floor is of the '56 design, and the front bumper extension brackets have also been modified, lowering them to allow more air to the radiator.

These various notable changes most surely were done by the Engineering Department. The quality of the workmanship, the materials used, and the techniques involved show that they were not add-on features at a later date, not to speak of its original owner!

Because of the lack of complete information, I seem to have a car without a real identity. I will continue my efforts to find out more about the car's history. I am trying to do my best to make it an automobile worthy of its heritage.

RESTORATION TIPS

Beginning with the next issue of The Corvette Restorer, this article will be penned by Martin Ball of San Leandro, California. Martin owns a 1957 Corvette which he purchased in 1969 and refers to it as a "project car". Martin says that the car was in need of much work when he got it (how familiar that sounds) and restoration has been progressive, a little at a time.

Since Martin has always done all his own work on the car, he is very adept at sharing his many projects with other NCRS members. Things we can look for in future issues will be tips on detailing the engine, installing trim, plating of parts, paint, refurbishing the dash, door jambs and trunk, installation of weatherstripping and general clean-up.

All NCRS members are invited to send their own tips, projects and so-forth to Martin so they can be shared with all.

The following restoration tips were submitted by Dave Stufun, 4812 Yucca Way, North Highlands, CA 95660

DOOR HINGE REBUILDING- Before disassembly of hinges have them glass-beaded as this makes the aluminum look like new again. To remove the hinge pin, support the hinge in a vise, heat it lightly with a propane torch (nothing hotter or you'll melt the hinge). Drive the pin out with a hammer and punch. Better yet, use a hydraulic press if possible. Use '56-'57 bushings and pins. The part number of the hinge bushings is #4110660, as these are brass instead of nylon. No drilling or reaming should be necessary.

GM BLACK RECONDITIONING PAINT is available in one gallon (#1050104), five gallon (#1050105), or 19 oz. aerosol cans (#1051688). No thinning necessary, clean-up with lacquer thinner. Works well on rubber too! If you buy the 19 oz. aerosol, replace the spray tip as the one it comes with has a large hole and sprays very fast. A tip with smaller hole will produce a much finer finish. This paint works exceptionally well if the surface is glassbeaded or sandblasted first. Otherwise, make sure the surface is really clean. The paint won't stick unless the surface is clean and grease-free. This paint produces the satin-black finish necessary for starter, generator, underside of hood, firewall, frame, etc.

THE GUIDE Y-50 OUTSIDE DOOR MIRROR can be safely taken apart (mirror head and pedestal separated). Heat the connection area lightly (pot-metal melts easily) and pop the two apart. The chrome shops can do a better job (and usually cheaper) if the two parts are separated. To mate them together again, ream the hole out one size larger and epoxy the mirror head to it. If the glass is broken almost any glass shop can install a new mirror which should look as good as the original (this is also true of the inside mirror glass).

REMOVING PAINT FROM PLASTIC- The dash board on my '55 had been spray painted black once upon a time, and every knob, lense, etc. had black over-spray on it (my hood-pull was solid black-even the chrome). Trying to come up with a paint remover that would not harm the plastic was something else! Lacquer thinner would work great on the paint, but not so great on the plastic. Rubbing alcohol didn't hurt the plastic, but it also didn't take off much paint. I tried various other methods and found that Formula 409 household cleaner works great. Just wiping the knobs with it produced good results—so I soaked the various items in it over night, then just wiped the paint right off. It even shined the stainless steel parts. This should work well for removing weathered paint from emblems.

'56-'57 SOFT TOP LATCH LOCATING TEMPLET by Martin Ball

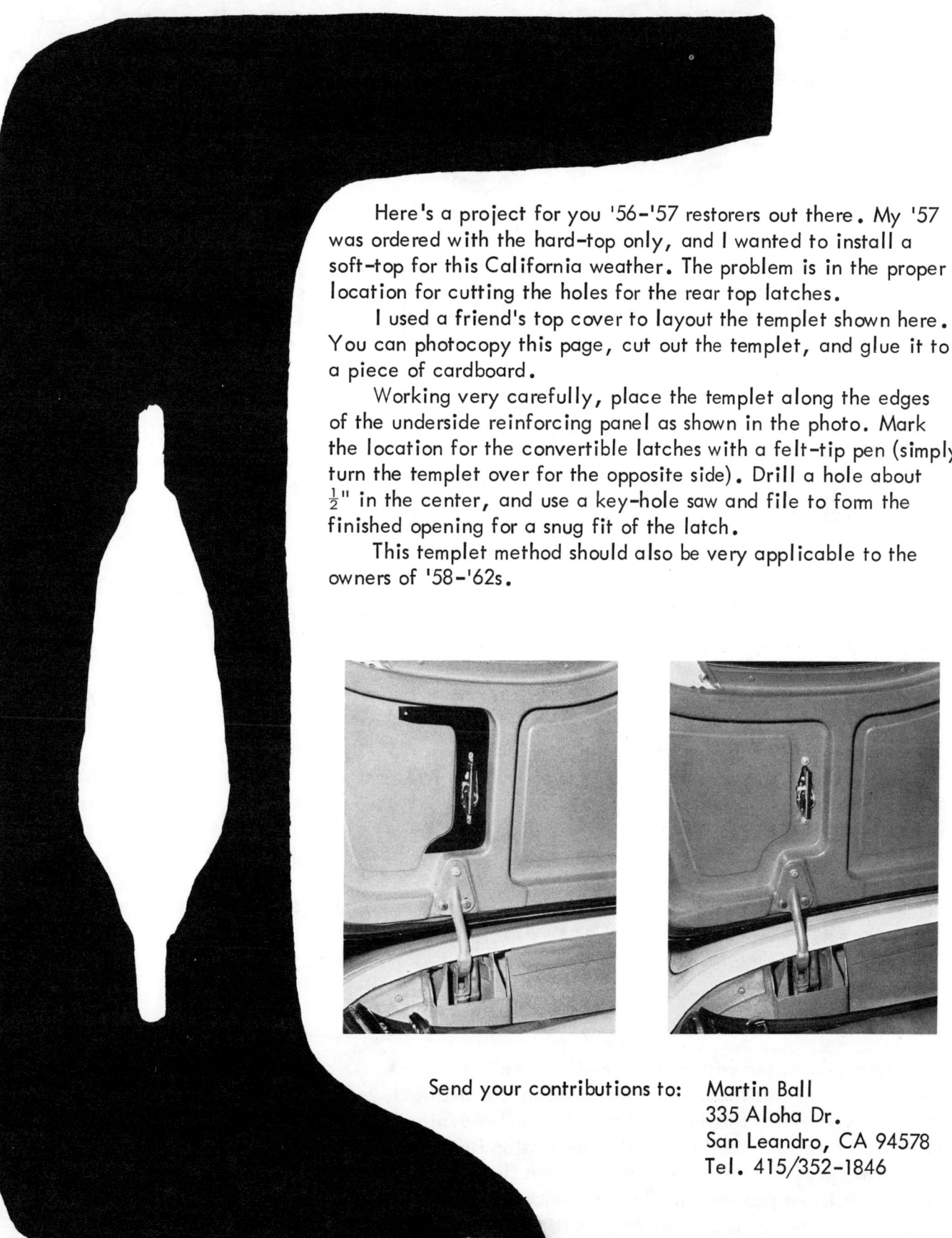

Here's a project for you '56-'57 restorers out there. My '57 was ordered with the hard-top only, and I wanted to install a soft-top for this California weather. The problem is in the proper location for cutting the holes for the rear top latches.

I used a friend's top cover to layout the templet shown here. You can photocopy this page, cut out the templet, and glue it to a piece of cardboard.

Working very carefully, place the templet along the edges of the underside reinforcing panel as shown in the photo. Mark the location for the convertible latches with a felt-tip pen (simply turn the templet over for the opposite side). Drill a hole about $\frac{1}{2}$" in the center, and use a key-hole saw and file to form the finished opening for a snug fit of the latch.

This templet method should also be very applicable to the owners of '58-'62s.

Send your contributions to: Martin Ball
335 Aloha Dr.
San Leandro, CA 94578
Tel. 415/352-1846

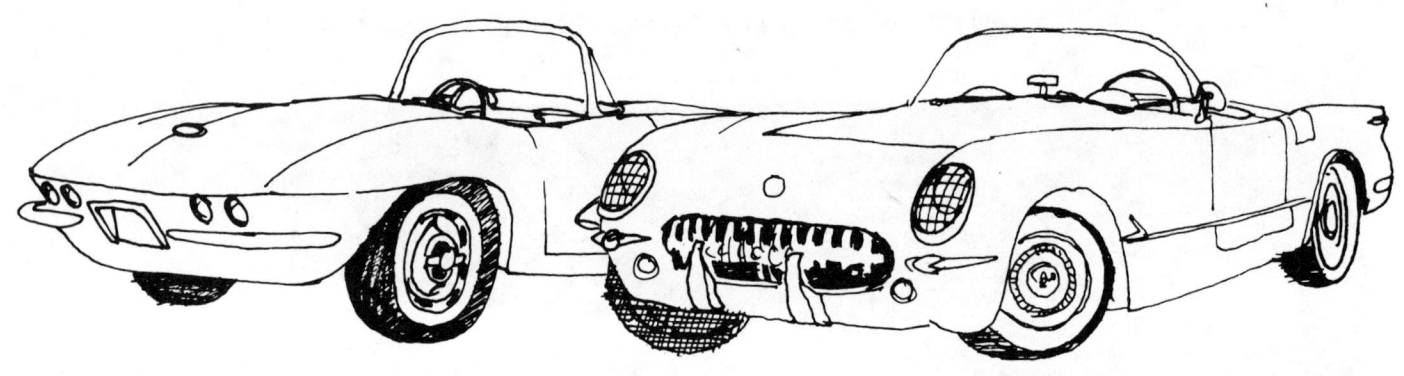

CORVETTE FUN QUIZ

The following Corvette Fun Quiz has been devised by Noland Adams, John Amgwert, and Sam Folz as a means to stimulate your knowledge of the early Corvette. This quiz concerns only 1953 through 1962 production Corvette models and prototypes, as well as related show cars.

As an incentive to those who try the quiz we will award a 1976 Corvette Promotional Model to the first five NCRS Members that achieve the highest number of correct answers. Correct answers to the quiz, along with the winners, will be published in the Spring 1976 issue of The Corvette Restorer, so, if you wish to participate in the quiz, have your answers postmarked no later than February 29, 1976.

It is urged that you use caution in taking the quiz. Some of the questions are based on little known facts, while others may have more than one correct or acceptable answer in which case one correct answer will be sufficient. If you wish to document some of your answers, by all means do so, as the correct answers will be documented in the next issue.

Your answers cannot be returned, so if you wish to check yourself, keep a copy of your answers before you send them.

Send your answers to: John Amgwert
3600 L Street
Lincoln, NE 68510

1. Who is credited with naming the Corvette?
2. What year was the 3-speed transmission first available?
3. What year was the 4-speed transmission first available?
4. What year was the Powerglide transmission first available?
5. What year did the 4-speed transmission first use a shifter with reverse lock-out?
6. What is the maximum number of vertical grille teeth in any Corvette?
7. What is the minimum number of vertical grille teeth in any Corvette?
8. What are the two states in which Corvettes have been built?
9. How many different types of wheelcovers (full) came on 53-62 production Corvettes?

10. Tube-type tires were last seen during which model year?
11. Black-wall tires became standard on which model?
12. 7.10 X 15 tires were available from the factory on some early Corvettes. True or False.
13. Concerning Corvette engine usage:
    The 235 engine was used from _____ through _____.
    The 265 engine was used from _____ through _____.
    The 283 engine was used from _____ through _____.
    The 327 engine was first used in _____.
14. Ignition shielding was a standard item on all Corvettes. True or False.
15. In what year was the least number of Corvettes produced?*
16. In what year was the second least number of Corvettes produced?*
17. In what year was the third least number of Corvettes produced?*
18. What is the serial number of the 1953 prototype Corvette?
19. What year was the SS Corvette race car made?
20. What year was the original Sting Ray racer made?
21. The 1953 prototype Corvette had a word in chrome trim on its front above the grille. What was it?
22. There were several other fiberglass bodied sports type cars by various companies about '53-55.
    A show car by Oldsmobile was the _____.
23. The Pontiac show car was called the _____.
24. The Buick show car was called the _____.
25. The Plymouth show car was called the _____.
26. The Kaiser made it into production, it was called the _____.
27. How many ribs were in the 1954 radiator auxillary tank?
28. What year Corvette sales brochure was first to be in full color?
29. What is the visual difference between the two radios used on 1954 Corvettes?
30. Name a part common to all '53-'62 Corvettes (there are several). _____
31. The recirculating-air heater (non-fresh-air type) was last seen during which model year?
32. The 6-volt electrical system was last used during which model year?
33. What year was the Positraction rear axle first available?
34. What company assembled the 1953 Corvette bodies, and where was the plant located?
35. Who designed the basic chassis layout which was used through the 1962 production Corvette?
36. What was the code-name of this project?
37. Tachometer with engine revolution counter was last used on which model?
38. What year were seat-belts made standard equipment?
39. What was the last production Corvette model to use a two 4-bbl. set-up?
40. What year did the Warner T-10 4-speed transmission receive an aluminum case?
41. What was the first year for the aluminum Powerglide?
42. Aluminum pistons were first used in what year and on which horsepower engine?
43. Aluminum cylinder heads were briefly tried in what year?
44. Aluminum radiators were were first used in what year?
45. Aluminum intake manifolds were first used in what year and on what horsepower engine?
46. 1956 through 1962 Corvettes equipped with a factory installed radio had the antenna mounted on the left rear fender. True or False.
47. 1962 Corvette grilles are what color?
48. What was LPO 1625 (Limited Production Option) ?
49. A Corvette equipped with LPO 1625 could not be equipped with what other option?
50. What horsepower engine had the ignition coil mounted on the firewall, as opposed to to being mounted on the engine?

*Question refers to "model year production", not "calendar year production".

LITERARY REVIEW

By John Amgwert

With this and subsequent issues I will attempt to report on Corvette related books, magazines, and articles. Members are asked to bring to my attention material which may, or may not, be of interest and merit to others.

THE REAL CORVETTE, An Illustrated History of the Chevrolet Corvette by Ray Miller
Published by Evergreen Press- $22.95

Since it was published last year, there has been a rash of statements (made mainly by those selling it) that well overestimates the book's limits. To say it is "the best on the subject" (which is probably true as there is nothing to compare it to), "A must item for all serious restorers", "Just the book for the '53 to '67 Corvette restorer" ('53 owners are in for a surprise here), or "(it) will enable appropiate renovation of cars into showroom condition" (Old Cars Newspaper should have known better) is stretching the truth just a bit. I find none of these statements to be accurate as the book will certainly keep one hopping trying to distinguish fact from fiction.

The book itself says at the outset that the author (Miller) has "attempted" to locate "unrestored" cars wherever possible or restorations "believed to be of the highest quality". It is also quick to point out that "there may well be items of incorrect data or style on a given automobile", and "cars may well have been modified to suit the convenience of an earlier owner". Concerning incorrect material that may appear, the book says "We have attemped to screen the inaccuracies; we trust that we have succeeded in the effort. This book was intended to be what it is, a compendium (brief summary) of information which will enable an observer to identify, and to classify, both cars and parts. If there are errors, they are not to our knowledge." This disclaimer is all important to what follows in the book.

The format of The Real Corvette tries to cover each model year in a seperate chapter with many photos of distinguishing features of an example car(s). However, Miller begins with a miniscule reference to the 1953 Corvette, subsequently "lumping" it into the 1954 catagory. He does this saying "Despite variations of relatively minor nature, (almost invariably the result of "running" type changes), the principal difference between the so-called "1953 Corvette" and the "1954" model is the serial number plate." It appears to me that Miller never compared a 1953 and 1954 Corvette as there are no less than 15 "differences" between the two that were not "running" type changes, the biggest being the engine which is far from "relatively minor nature." He goes so far as to show us a 1953 engine in the engine section and labels it as a 1954-55 and in the same breath says that the 1955 version received 12-volt accessories which is completely wrong.

This is a small example as many of Miller's statements throughout his book indicates to me that he was lacking in research and technical assistance of the various models. He stumbles into the 1954 model by first listing the specifications from a 1955 Corvette sales brochure (the 1954 specs show up in 1955 section). On the next page he lists "Corvette Copper" as being available on the 1954 Corvette when it was a 1955 color and states that early 1954 tops were black in color when actually all '54 tops were tan. The 1954 Corvette with a black top used as an example has an incorrectly shaped rear window indicating that it is a replacement. From there he proceeds to show us the top instruction decal never pointing out that only about the last 600 1954s used them, an incorrect 1954 gas cap, an incorrectly painted steering wheel, a pair of shots of a 1955 dash (we're still in the '54 section), an incorrect description of the turn-signal knob (they did not have ribs), a statement indicating all later 1954 valve covers were chrome and they were not (used randomly on a small percentage of the '54 production), ending the section with a picture of a hole in the windshield casting which is described as being used to hold a pin on the forward edge of the side curtain assembly (which doesn't exist) when the hole pictured is actually used to secure the soft-top.

In the 1955 section (other than listing the specs that should have showed up in the 1954 section) Miller shows us a car with incorrectly upholstered seats, states that white wall tires were "standard" and they were not, lists the 1955 steering wheel colors and omits the most common combination of red and white, and mentions the 12-volt electrical with reference to the radio and light bulbs never pointing out that 6-cylinder '55s used a 6-volt system...... the list goes on and on.

The many inaccuracies that appear and the lack of complete details on numerous important features of the various models in the book in my opinion drastically hinders its use and value. Restorers using Miller's book as a guide will most likely be very confused when comparing many of the photos and text to their own car. I certainly hope no one changes the tachometer in their 1957 Corvette to match the one Miller shows.... or installs a 1957 inside rear-view mirror backwards and upside down as the one shown in the book... or installs "cross-flag" emblems on the fenders of their 2-4 bbl. equipped 1957 because Miller says they were there.... or scours the country for a pair of high-priced nine-ribbed valve covers only to find out later that the optional engines in 1957 didn't necessarily use them throughout the model which Miller failed to mention.... or fails to reinstall the ignition switch position identification bezel because Miller says 1957s didn't use them. Sadly enough, these types of inaccuracies are present throughout the book, in virtually every model section.

Noland Adams wrote to Miller shortly after the book was released pointing out the many errors that he initially found in the early section. Over six months and other correspondence later, Noland has never received any kind of a response from the author. However, a recent review of the book in Old Cars Newspaper mentioned that "some Corvette historians" have noticed some errors, to which Miller retorts he has documented proof that the cars photographed are authentic. My only comment to this is that if all the numerous incorrect and improperly installed items pictured, and the erronious statements in The Real Corvette can be authenticated, I'll eat my copy!

One NCRS member recently wrote to Sam Folz suggesting that we have a contest to see who can find the most errors in the book. While the idea of a contest is a bit on the extreme side, it might be more feasible to compile and publish the inaccuracies for those who have questions. I personally have had questions asked concerning the book's engine specification table listing the 1955 V-8 engine as having a 2 bbl. carburetor, and one member wondered if the exhaust pipes really do exist "ahead" of the rear wheels on a 1962 as the book states. Would our publishing the known inaccuracies be of value?

Miller undoubtedly did much preparation to complete the book, and a publication of this "type" has been needed for some time. The many errors, unfortunately, cause this book to fall far short of the marque, over-shadowing its better points. The book will give you a brief summary of the features on the various models he selected as examples. I only hope that the errors in The Real Corvette do not take years to correct as I envision.

RESTORATION TIPS

WITH MARTIN BALL

What I hope to do in this and future issues will be to outline some of the procedures that are used in restoring and replacing parts on the early Corvettes produced during the years 1953 thru 1962.

I would like to remind all NCRS members, if you have any tips or projects that you think would be of interest to the members you are encouraged to send them to me so they can be included in this article. I know they will be appreciated by all.

53-62 REAR FRAME CROSSMEMBER REISSUED BY GM

The rear frame crossmember Group 7.014, part number 3744337, is back in the part's book. This part was discontinued for a short time. This part is known to rust out on some cars that are exposed to the elements and I would advise members to inspect theirs. This part fits all '53-'62 Corvettes and can be ordered through your local Chevrolet Dealer Part's Department.

CLEANING OLD WEATHERSTRIPPING

Overspray, grease and dirt can be removed with acetone. Be careful not to get any on the painted surface of the door. Work a small section at a time, wipe it on, but do not soak the rubber.

Weatherstrip fasteners ('56-'62 Corvette, part number 4653672) are still available through your local dealer at the time of this writing.

If you are lucky enough to find some new old stock weatherstrip, check the manufacturer identification marking (see photo) to see if it compares with your old strip. Just like the weatherstrip itself, there are many types of adhesives or glue on the market and the choice is yours. I have found the brush type of contact cement to work the best for me.

To add the final touch, go over all the rubber with a good dressing; Rubber Wax, Armor All, etc. Paint is not the way to go, it might look good on a show car but it drys out the rubber, chips, and you're back where you started.

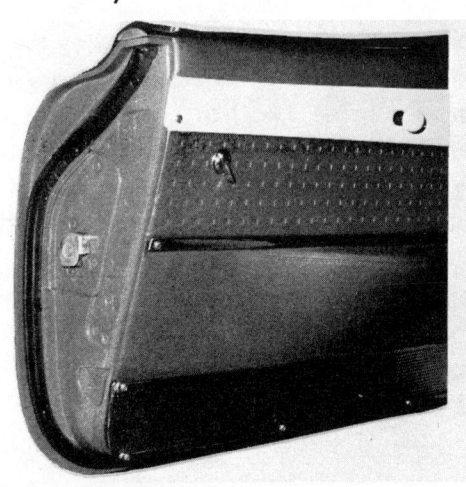

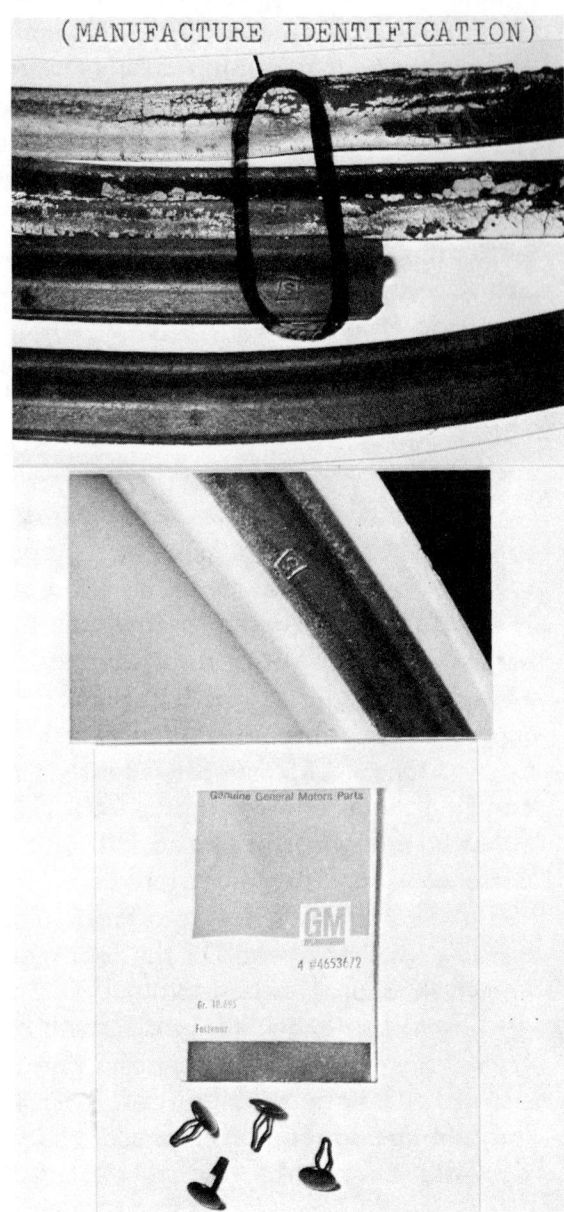

(MANUFACTURE IDENTIFICATION)

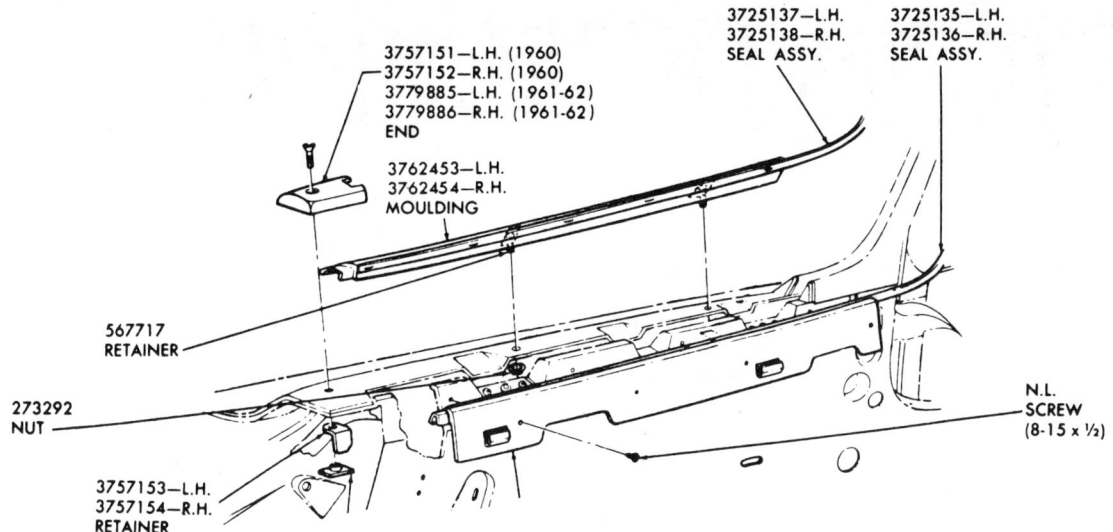

REPLACEMENT OF SEAL ASSY. (window felt) ON 56-62 CORVETTE DOORS

GM part numbers- 3725135, 3725136, 3725137, 3725138, Group 10.710, available through you Chevrolet dealer. Refer to the Corvette Servicing Guide ST-12 for details on removing door-panels, window glass, and moulding.

I found that the new seal is not drilled for mounting. GM used wire staples to mount the seal to the moulding and since they are made of steel will rust out in time as mine were.

I used 1/8" aluminum pop rivets. Grind off each side so you have a "T" shaped rivet. Line up the new seal on the moulding and drill new 1/8" holes through the seal and moulding about 5 inches apart. After attaching the seal, paint the head of the rivets with flat black paint.

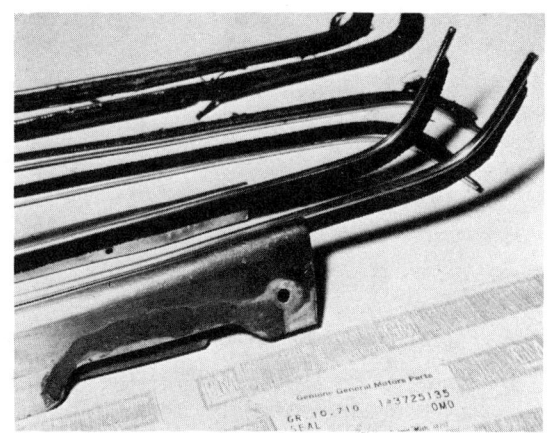

I will include part numbers whenever possible for the General Motors parts. Many of these parts will still be available from Chevrolet on a "special order" basis only, meaning your local dealer will not have them in stock. It is known that some dealers are not always cooperative with regard to parts for older Corvettes so the part numbers will hopefully be a big help.

In some cases there may be other sources for Corvette parts such as after-market manufacturers, antique car and Chevy swap meets and wrecking yards, which are often overlooked by restorers of Corvettes. When sources and interchangability are known, I will present them to you. Your help in this regard will be appreciated.

The 1953-62 Corvette Servicing Guide ST-12 referred to in this article is available from:

Helm, Inc.
P. O. Box 07130
Detroit, MI 48207
Ph. 313/871-6606

It is priced at $6.50 post-paid (Michigan residents add 4% Michigan sales tax) payable to Helm, Inc. This manual is quite extensive and will be indispensable to any restorer. Helm will also supply you with a list and order form for other Chevrolet service publications.

SEND YOUR RESTORATION TIPS OR CONTRIBUTIONS FOR INCLUSION IN THIS ARTICLE TO:

Martin Ball
335 Aloha Drive
San Leandro, CA 94578
Ph. 415/352-1846

CORVETTE FUN QUIZ
RESULTS

The Corvette Fun Quiz published in the last issue only brought responses from 27 NCRS members. The quiz was a tough one and possibly discouraged many members from sending in their answers. The best score achieved was 45 correct out of 50 questions and the average score was 35 correct answers.

The top five members in answering the questions in order of highest scores and those that receive the 1976 Corvette Promotional Models used as prizes are:

E. Bernard Lewis, Jr.
Demascus, Maryland

Paul Welsh
Clarksburg, Maryland

Dan Smith
Imperial Beach, California

Al Solis
Fresno, California

Chip Miller
York, Pennsylvania

Our congratulations to these five members, and to all who participated in the quiz. This "Fun" quiz was just that, or at least some of those who responded said it was fun, and challenging.

We present now the answers to the quiz and a few comments that are appropriate. Some of the questions were specifically asked because of incorrect information that has appeared in Corvette articles, magazines and books. It is hoped that all members will find this quiz interesting.

1. Q- Who is credited with naming the Corvette?
   A- Myron Scott — No one answered this question correctly, and the most common answer was Ed Cole and Harley Earl. Mr. Scott was a Chevrolet public relations man who originated the annual Soap Box Derby, and this answer comes from the Dec. 4, 1972 issue of Sports Illustrated.

2. Q- What year was the 3-speed transmission first available?
   A- 1955 — The '55 received the 3-speed transmission toward the end of that model and an original is very rare.

3. Q- What year was the 4-speed transmission first available?
   A- 1957 — The original Warner Gear T-10 4-speed transmission entered production during the '57 model run. This option sold for $188 and is documented in Karl Ludvigsen's book, Corvette, America's Star-Spangled Sports Car.

4. Q- What year was the Powerglide transmission first available?
   A- 1953

5. Q- What year did the 4-speed transmission first use a shifter with reverse lock-out?
   A- 1959 — Ludvigsen's book is quite clear on this, however, did "all" '59 4-speeds use the T-handled shifter?

54

6. Q- What is the maximum number of verticle grille teeth in any Corvette?
   A- 15   Here was a trick question that caught only a few. 15 grille teeth were used on the Corvette SS experimental car.
7. Q- What is the minimum number of verticle grille teeth in any Corvette?
   A- 9 ('58-'60 model)
8. Q- What are the two states in which Corvettes have been built?
   A- Michigan and Missouri
9. Q- How many different types of wheelcovers (full) came on 53-62 production Corvettes?
   A- 5 (would accept 6)   This question was not answered correctly by anyone. The most common answers were 3 and 4. The first wheelcover used in production of approximately the first 25 1953s was the '53 Bel Air domed cover. Photographs and a reference in the 1953 owner's manual attest to their use. The second cover was #3706488 used on the remainder of '53s and '54s. The third cover (and apparently elusive to all but Chip Miller) was the '55 cover #3716754 which was changed by moving the perimeter gripper teeth to align with the four small rim ridges used on the 1955 wheels for a better "hold". The forth cover was that used from '56 through '58, and the fifth one used from '59-'62. We would have accepted a sixth cover, that being a variation of #3706488 with the spinners aligning perpendicular to the "bow-tie" emblem. Several examples exist and many photos of '53s equipped with these covers have appeared. This last example should not be confused with the "prototype" five-piece cover.
10. Q- Tube-type tires were last seen during which model year?
    A- 1954   Tubeless tires were advertised as standard on the 1955 Corvette. Possibly some of the later '54s were also equipped with them, but tubes were last seen in 1954.
11. Q- Black-wall tires became standard on which model?
    A- 1955   Contrary to popular belief, and Ray Miller's book, The Real Corvette, 1956 was not the first year. The 1955 Corvette pricing bulletin #6-1955 shows white wall tires listed as RPO 290B costing $25 extra.
12. Q- 7.10 X 15 tires were available from the factory on some early Corvettes. True or False?
    A- False   The only tire size listed in sales brochures and Finger-tip Facts books is the 6.70 X 15. While the $5\frac{1}{2}$ X 15 optional wheels were designed to accept the 7.10 X 15 tires, they were available only from tire manufacturers.
13. Q- Concerning Corvette engine usage:
        The 235 engine was used from (1953) through (1955).
        The 265 engine was used from (1955) through (1956).
        The 283 engine was used from (1957) through (1961).
        The 327 engine was first used in (1962).
                (No one missed this question)
14. Q- Ignition shielding was a standard item on all Corvettes? True or False?
    A- False (only those equipped with a radio)
15. Q- In what year was the least number of Corvettes produced?
    A- 1953 (300)
16. Q- In what year was the second least number of Corvettes produced?
    A- 1955 (700)
17. Q- In what year was the third least number of Corvettes produced?
    A- 1956 (3467)

18. Q- What is the serial number of the 1953 prototype Corvette?
    A- EX-122   Several answered this with E53F001001 which was a production serial number. EX-122, although modified by GM, still exists.
19. Q- What year was the SS Corvette race car made?
    A- 1956 and 1957   Karl Ludvigsen's book has an extensive section on this car indicating that building began in '56 and was completed in '57.
20. Q- What year was the original Sting Ray racer made?
    A- 1959   Again, Ludvigsen's book has an extensive section on this car, which used the chassis of the Corvette SS.
21. Q- The 1953 prototype Corvette had a word in chrome trim on its front above the grille. What was it?
    A- CORVETTE
22. Q- There were several other fiberglass bodied sports type cars by various companies about 53-55. A show car by Oldsmobile was the (F-88).
23.   The Pontiac show car was called the (Bonneville Special). The Firebird Turbine car was not a Pontiac project.
24.   The Buick show car was called the (Wildcat). The F-88, Bonneville Special and Wildcat cars all appeared in the 1954 GM Motorama show and all have striking similarities to the '53-'55. We will present these three cars in a future issue.
25.   The Plymouth show car was called the (Belmont).
26.   The Kaiser made it into production, it was called the (DKF-161 or Kaiser-Darrin)
27. Q- How many ribs were in the 1954 radiator auxillary tank?
    A- None (very early) or Two
28. Q- What year Corvette sales brochure was first to be in full color?
    A- 1954   Reference: "Corvette Sales Literature Guide" by George Riehl (Corvette Restorer Vol. 2, #1)
29. Q- What is the visual difference between the two radios used on 1954 Corvettes?
    A- Conelrad or Civil Defense marks added to the dial face during '54 model run.
30. Q- Name a part common to all '53-'62 Corvette (there are several).
    While many correct answers were possible, the most common answer was the Guide Y-50 outside mirror. Some of the incorrect answers were: front park light bezel, cardboard trunk liner, and exhaust valves.
31. Q- The recirculating-air heater (non-fresh-air type) was last seen during which model year?
    A- 1956 (early production) Only three got this one correct. Early '56 examples exist with the recirculating-air heater and the Chev. publication "56 Corvette Engineering Achievements" bares this out.
32. Q- The 6-volt electrical system was last used during which model year?
    A- 1955 (6-cylinder)   Ray Miller's book, The Real Corvette, says '55 6-cylinder cars used 12-volt accessories which is incorrect. Reference Corvette Servicing Guide ST-12 and examples that exist.
33. Q- What year was the Positraction axle first available?
    A- 1957   Ludvigsen's book says the positraction rear axle, made by Spicer, was available with ratios of 3.70, 4.11 and 4.56.
34. Q- What company assembled the 1953 Corvette bodies, and where was the plant located?
    A- Chevrolet Motor Division/Flint, Michigan   Many gave the answer of Molded Fiberglass Body Company (MFG) in Ashtabula, Ohio. MFG fabricated the body panels, Chevrolet assembled the body.
35. Q- Who designed the basic chassis layout which was used through the 1962 production Corvette?
    A- Maurice Olley   While Robert F. McLean layed out the basic car, Olley (under Ed Cole) designed the car's chassis. A sketch by Olley dated June 12, '52 will be presented in a future issue.
36. Q- What was the code-name of this project?
    A- OPEL

37. Q- Tachometer with engine revolution counter was last used on which model?
    A- 1958   While Ludvigsen's book says that the 1960 Corvette introduced the new 7000 rpm tach minus revolution counter, it was actually introduced on the '59 model. The 6000 rpm tachs used in '58 were the last to use the rev counter, however it should be noted that the 8000 rpm '58 tach did not have this feature.

38. Q- What year were seat-belts made standard equipment?
    A- 1958   Ludvigsen's book and '58 Corvette sales brochures attest to this.

39. Q- What was the last production Corvette model to use a two 4-bbl. set-up?
    A- 1961   Here's a question that tripped up no one. The Corvette Engine Series Number and Suffix Chart (published in many parts catalogs) lists a 1962 Corvette engine with dual 4 barrel carburetors designated "QB" and most surely it is in error.

40. Q- What year did the Warner T-10 4-speed transmission receive an aluminum case?
    A- 1961   Ludvigsen's book and the 1953-62 Corvette repair manual by Chilton bear this out.

41. Q- What was the first year for the aluminum Powerglide?
    A- 1962   Reference: Service manuals and Corvette, America's Star-Spangled Sports Car by Karl Ludvigsen.

42. Q- Aluminum pistons were first used in what year and on which horsepower engine?
    A- 1953/150 hp   This one tripped up several!

43. Q- Aluminum cylinder heads were briefly tried in what year?
    A- 1960   Available for a short time on FI equipped cars, these were discontinued early in production, according to Karl Ludvigsen, due to casting flaws and damage through possible engine overheating. 1960 engines with these heads are designated "CY" or "CZ".

44. Q- Aluminum radiators were first used in what year?
    A- 1960   Included on engines equipped with Hi-lift camshaft. Aluminum radiators became standard with the 1961 model.

45. Q- Aluminum intake manifolds were first used in what year and on what horsepower engine?
    A- 1953/150 hp   Like question #42, this one tripped up several.

46. Q- 1956 through 1962 Corvettes equipped with a factory installed radio had the antenna mounted on the left rear fender. True or False?
    A- True   Ray Miller's book, The Real Corvette, says the 1958 Corvette antenna was mounted on the right rear fender. The example he shows has obviously been tampered with as it sports a non-Corvette antenna. Additionally, at least one of the early Corvette owner's manuals (1960) also states that the antenna was mounted on the right rear fender, but in actuality they show up on the left side in production cars. Regardless, as this question reads, the only acceptable answer, and the way this question was most often answered, is true.

47. Q- 1962 Corvette grilles are what color?
    A- Black   There is not supporting evidence indicating anything but black grilles were used.

48. Q- What was LPO 1625 (Limited Production Option)?
    A- 24 gallon fiberglass fuel tank.   Reference: 1961 Corvette Sales brochure and AMA specs.

49. Q- A Corvette equipped with LPO 1625 could not be equipped with what other option?
    A- 1) Soft top, or 2) power assisted mechanism for soft top.   The 24 gallon fuel tank option necessitated the hardtop as the soft top could not be lowered into its well.

50. Q- What horsepower engine had the ignition coil mounted on the firewall, as opposed to being mounted on the engine?
    A- 195 hp (1955)   The 1955 ignition coil is mounted on the firewall, horizontally, between the brake master cylinder and the wiper motor on the V-8 car.

56/57 Valve Cover Usage

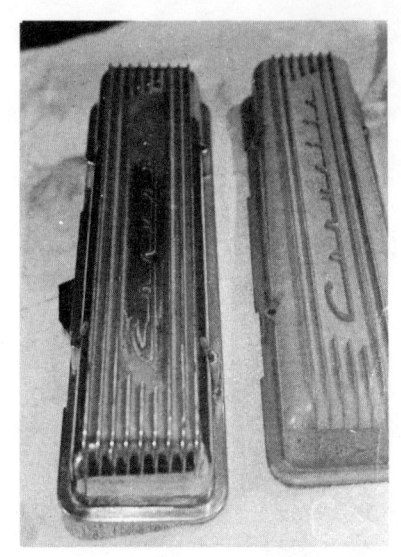

BY MICHAEL HUNT

As increasing numbers of 1956 and 1957 Corvettes undergo restoration, the question of correct rocker covers arises. The problem does not involve base engines, because they uniformly used stamped steel covers during both years. But the optional engines came equipped with both 9-fin or 7-fin cast aluminum covers, and the trick is knowing which version belongs on a given vehicle.

All optional 1956 Corvette engines had the 9-fin variety covers, which simplifies matters for owners of that model. But a "running change" from 9-fin to 7-fin on the optional 1957 engines clouds the issue. With the Chevrolet Motor Division either unwilling or unable to pinpoint the moment of change, restorers must examine remaining "original" cars, and draw their own conclusions.

Probably the most reliable guide at this point is the research done by Richard G. Robinson of Fort Washington, Pennsylvania. Dick "theorizes" the following breakdown for the optional 1957 engines. The vehicle serial numbers are approximate!

E57S100001 to E57S102000: 9-fin
E57S102001 to E57S104500: 9- or 7-fin
E57S104501 to E57S106339: 7-fin

This second category initially bothered me, as one would expect a running change to occur and be over, as opposed to a 2500 unit fluctuation. Yet my own research tends to support Dick's ideas. We have found 7-fin covers on apparently unaltered cars as early as E57S102558, while the 9-fin covers are retained on E57S104329, a vehicle which I personally traced back many years. After additional cars are surveyed, I may be able to refine the Robinson data somewhat-- but at the present, it's the best data going.

To further complicate matters, the 9-fin covers on the fuel injected engines show a $4\frac{1}{2}$" gap in the uppermost fin, directly beneath the piezometer ring on the driver's side. Perhaps the need for this additional machining caused the mid-year switch to the 7-fin covers. Surprisingly, both the 9-fin and 7-fin covers share the same casting number; #3726086.

I will touch upon this topic again at a later date. But in the meantime, my advice is to stick with the Robinson breakdown, and you'll be fairly close. I would most certainly appreciate any comments on this, particularly related to vehicle serial number and engine serial number. Please direct your remarks to: Michael Hunt, 903 Swarthmore Ct., Madison, Wisc. 53705.

Avanti MOTOR CORPORATION

Story by NCRS President GARY MORTIMER
Photos by NOLAND ADAMS

Three bus-loads of NCRS members attending the Goshen Meet enjoyed a special tour of the Avanti Motor Corporation on Friday, April 30th.

I first became interested in the Avanti when my family demanded a four passenger car. We had two children and a pair of Corvettes (a '63 and a '54). My wife felt our six year old was developing a permanent fastback that exactly matched our '63 Corvette.

I vaguely remembered Studebaker introducing a fiberglass car the same year I bought the '63 Corvette so I started investigating the possibility of purchasing a '63 or '64 Avanti.

continued......

Stockpile of original Studebaker frames.

Frames (still left from Studebaker stock) receive several modifications and are readied for body.

Body goes through extensive hand finishing prior to painting.

Painted bodies are baked in infrared oven.

The more I found out about the Avanti, the more certain I was that this was the car we needed. The last Studebaker Avanti was built December 31, 1963 and the first Avanti II's in the Spring and Summer of 1965. Nate Altman and Leo Newman (life-long friends and former Packard, Edsel and Studebaker Dealers) purchased one of the Studebaker buildings along with all Avanti tools, dies, jigs, and part's inventory. Avanti Motors was headed by Nate Altman until his untimely death two weeks before our NCRS visit to the plant. Arnold Altman, Nate Altman's brother, now heads up Avanti Motors.

If you're interested in the Avanti you'll want to visit South Bend, Indiana where they are still being produced today with a similar fiberglass body using the Chevrolet 400 C.I. engine and the Turbo-Hydramatic Transmission.

The plant employs about 90 workers, many of them picked from the reservoir of Studebaker employees who wanted to stay in South Bend and continue to build cars.

Installation of window glass

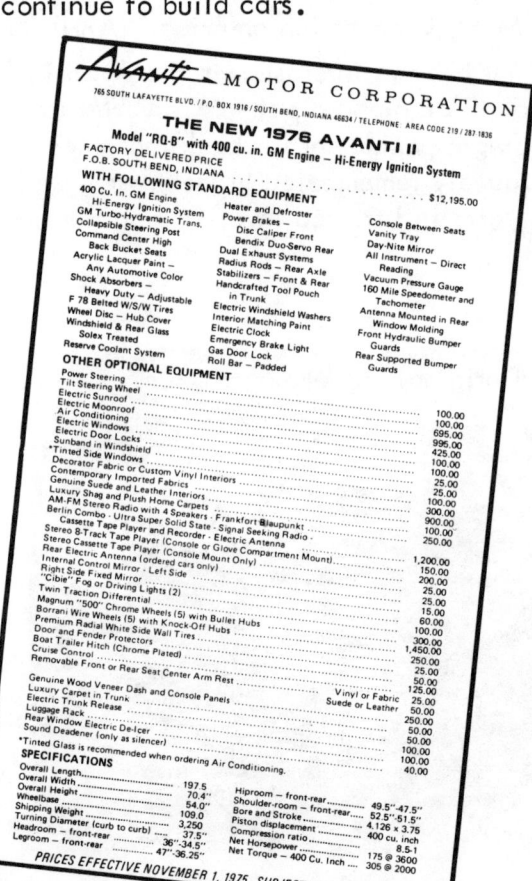

Chassis and body lines converge.

Driveline is 400 ci Chevrolet mated to a Turbo-Hydramatic transmission. Ignition shielding is strictly Corvette.

There's no assembly line; the cars roll through the old Conestoga wagon plant on four-wheeled dollies. The trip takes 10 weeks from the time the fiberglass pieces of the body are taken from their crates until the finished car is through the doors for personalized delivery. By the way, the fiberglass panels are produced by Molded Fiber Glass Body Company in Astabula, Ohio, the company that produced so many of the Corvette panels.

Avanti Motors builds approximately 200 cars annually. The basic car sells for $12,195 but the factory offers $9,000 in options. The most expensive Avanti to go out the door so far was in the neigborhood of $19,000. Lead time on your order is about 16 weeks.

The complete area devoted to Avanti manufacture, parts and service is roughly the size of a medium to big Chevrolet dealer service department. Sales are handled primarily through the factory and with representatives in various parts of the country which respond to inquiries with a demonstrator. The plant itself also operates as a dealer service dept. with anything from tune-ups to complete interiors to overall paint jobs available for customer service.

At the time of our visit there were about 10 new Avanti II's in stock, with another 10 '63 and '64 Studebaker Avanti trade ins out back waiting to be refurbished when time permits. Also out back are several stacks of chassis frames. Budd Company made the frames for Studebaker and Nate Altman bought 20 carloads 12 years ago. Avanti Motors only has enough left for one more year's production and then they must find a source.

A rusting Packard remains as a reminder of the Studebaker Packard Plants at South Bend.

Body line work is slow with more attention paid to finish detail than to speed.

TECH SESSION

With NCRS TECHNICAL

CHAIRMAN, SAM FOLZ

WHERE I'M COMING FROM

From some of the questions I am asked regarding features and specifications of 1953 through 1962 Corvettes, I think that a little personal or biographical information is in order.

I have always been more than just casually interested in cars in general, and Corvettes in particular. Since 1960, when I was lucky enough to have my '53 find me, I have actively sought all of the printed matter relating to Corvettes that I could find. Many generous friends aided the search.

In 1960 I started a subscription to Corvette News which I've collected from that time without interruption, and that same year I joined a local Corvette Club which was affiliated with the National Council of Corvette Clubs.

My son, Joe, who is also a car fancier, helped me immeasurably with his own collecting skills that included all the promotional models of Corvettes and kits that came along from about 1957 to date.

In addition, Joe, at the ripe old age of four or five years, formed a friendship with a local Chevrolet salesman who saved for him the annual editions of "Finger-Tip Facts", and the large, full color, master sales books that show colors, paint chips, fabric swatches and the like.

In addition to all those goodies, we've saved all the sales pamphlets that normally are given to customers in showrooms or at auto shows, and we've accumulated appropriate parts and accessories catalogs from 1953, 1955, 1957, and 1962, as well as some other related material such as engineering specs, identification, color specs, photos, articles, etc. This, then, constitutes the "library" from which I research the answers to your many questions. I try to keep some of it near one telephone so that long-distance calls (which are received in increasing numbers) are not unnecessarily delayed in searching for answers.

If you have attended one or more of the Tech Sessions in conjunction with one of our meets, I'm sure you've heard me explain that we are not oracles. There are some questions which I cannot answer, but I don't like to guess and I won't deliberately "snow" a questioner because I, like you, want to see these cars restored correctly.

Occasionally a reader or correspondent disagrees with an opinion provided in the Restorer, or by me in person, or by letter. Some of these challenges are interesting and cause me to dig harder for more information.

In the Fall 1975 issue of the Restorer we printed some GM color and paint spec charts for all model years, with the notation that there probably were errors in the charts. Several readers pointed out such errors and we later noted such verified corrections.

I am troubled, however, not because someone may disagree with me, but when such person chooses to assume an adversary position and forward improper or incorrect information or criticism to another Corvette publication, rather than direct that disagreement to me. This practice not only risks the publication of bad data, but promotes hard feelings.

In a particular instance, an individual claimed that grilles used on 1962 Corvettes were color-coded to optional engines, with top horsepower engines receiving gold grilles and others receiving black grilles and, further, that there was a similar correlation between paint in 1962 rocker panel mouldings to engine horsepower. A check of all appropriate factory catalogs, books, brochures, etc. in the "library" indicates that 1962 grilles were black, period. However, I did spend time locating and speaking with three people who knew and know these cars, both in 1962 and now. One presently owns such a car. Two were very active with NCCC in 1962-63. One owned a 360 HP 1962 as a new car. Opinions of all three agree with the "library" information that 1962 models had black grilles. Further, there is only one part number assigned to rocker panel trim. No option keyed to engine.

This brings up a few interesting points, i.e.: (1) In the models years 1953 through 1962, the only cars which had external identification revealing engine type or power were the 1955 8-cylinder jobs with the gold "Vs" and 1957 through 1962 models carrying "fuel injection" nameplates. (2) Service parts were not necessarily as good quality as original-equipment parts of the same part number. In some cases they are not even supplied to GM by the same suppliers. We see this in variations in die-castings and in painted plastic parts such as emblems, horn buttons, dash pads, etc. Conversely, if there has been a problem, service parts may be better than original parts. (3) On a "low-volume" car, such as Corvette, running changes can be made on an "in and out" basis. Examples are the use of chrome rocker arm covers and shields on 1954 models. No known blue-print or engineering change documents this, yet we know that it did occur. There are many such examples over the model years that we recognize- not the least of which is the '76 rear bumper changes.

It is, therefore, entirely possible that for whatever reason, such as to prevent a line shut-down, some 1962 cars might have been fitted with some other grilles. The need to protect production schedules could explain some of the apparent sightings of 1962 cars with gold-anodized grilles.

Those of you who were fortunate enough to attend our 1974 NCRS Meet in St. Louis may recall the story told of the "sexy", big-block hood panels with scoops, being installed on base engine cars due to a shortage of the proper hood, while at the same time, dealers who were trying to have such a deviation installed as a factory option on special orders were told that this was unavailable.

So, that's what makes this job interesting. I do this for fun. I am not, nor have I ever been employed by GM as some people have surmised. The data is very good and specific in some areas; very hazy and mixed-up in others. It keeps me on my toes. I need your continued help and cooperation so that I may do a better job of helping you.

For technical assistance write: Sam Folz, 3824 Coventry Ave., Kalamazoo, MI 49007. Don't forget to include a self-addressed-stamped-envelope.

RESTORATION TIPS

WITH MARTIN BALL

Included in this issue are several rebuilding tips for parts manufactured by Guide Lamp Division of General Motors. I have also tried to include some interesting parts interchanges that many of you may not be aware of. These are projects that do not require any special skills, except for some plating work, all can be done with ordinary tools.

(GUIDE) PARKING LAMP RESTORATION 53-62 CORVETTE

Replacement parts: These assemblies with the correct "F-57" molding lenses and the rounded edge chrome bezel for the 53-57 model can be found on at least several other cars. Try the 47-50 GMC pickup truck and the '47 and '48 Cadillac park light assemblies. Better yet, try some early '50's Cadillacs equipped with back-up lights. These assemblies will mount through the trunk and will usually be in perfect condition. Be sure to get the hollow screws used to attach the chrome bezel as these (like clutch-head screws) were a GM exclusive and can be hard to find. These hollow screws can be found on most any Cadillac park light assembly regardless of type so screws should be easy to come by.

The parking lamp assembly on the Corvette come apart easily for clean-up and restoration.

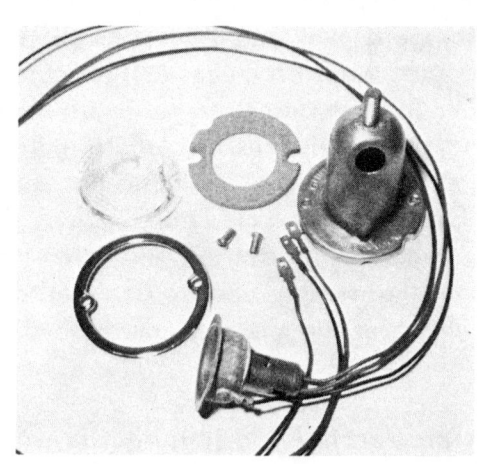

The housing is plated, not chrome, but Cadmium (or "Cad."). There are two variations of Cad plating on the Corvette that I have found. Cad-I is silver in color as on the gas cap, radiator cap, carb linkage and arm, etc. Cad-II has a heavier iridite wash which gives parts like these Guide lamps a gold tint. Cadmium plating is no where as expensive as chrome as there is none of the buffing required.

55-61 GENERATOR TACH DRIVE ADAPTER

There has been a number of persons in need of this part recently. While Chevrolet still services the driven gears (2) the adapter that mounts on the back of the generator was discontinued by them in July of 1970. However, it appears that it can be ordered through any Delco Dealer. The part number is #1930846 and is still listed in the Delco book selling for about $35 list new. It is a factory order meaning that the factory makes them as they are ordered so you may have to wait for some time (maybe six months?). Rumor has it that this part runs an hour meter on some farm related agricultural engine as this is the reason it is still serviced by Delco. I understand that two sources have begun reproducing this part, which could be in jest if the original manufacturer is still in production of it. I would like to hear from anyone who gets this part through Delco.

It should also be pointed out that for those that also need the generator with the longer armature shaft, you should try the passenger car generator that also drove the power steering pump on mid 50's Chevrolets as they work.

(GUIDE) LICENSE PLATE LAMP 56-60 CORVETTE

This part is overlooked by most Corvette owners. It is an assembled part manufactured by Guide, diecast housings (cast) LH and RH part #5947393 and #5947394. Plastic lens (molded) Guide LIA-56 part #5947392 gasket and backing plate (stamped) Guide LIA-56 made in U.S.A. (steel) plated in Cadmium with a heavy iridite wash riveted together.

This is not as hard as it might look to disassemble. Make a center punch mark in the middle of each stud, using a 1/4" drill, remove the head of the rivet. Be careful and not go too deep, pot metal is soft! Using a screw driver, pry the backing plate off, removing the gasket lens.

My chrome housings were pitted and the lenses were in very poor condition. After ordering a pair of repro lenses and having the other parts plated, the parts can be reassembled with epoxy glue by placing a drop in each stud.

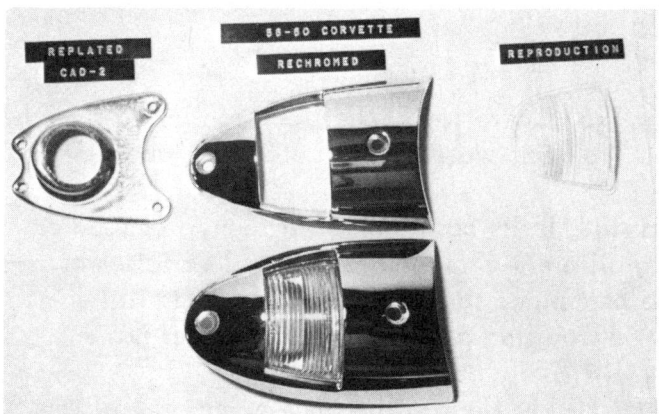

REBUILDING THE GUIDE Y-50 OUTSIDE MIRROR

As mentioned in Vol. II, number 3 of the Restorer, the Guide Y-50 mirror can be taken apart. I used a small propane torch, holding the pedestal on the bottom with a pair of Vise Grips and heating the pot metal carefully. I used a pair of pliers on the stud and pulled it straight out. In order to remove the glass without damaging the rim of the mirror, you have to break the glass. Now the mirror can be broken down into three parts.

I found alot of rust on the ball and socket retainer. You can go over it with steel wool and give it a coat of rust proof paint.

After rechroming the pedestal and outer shell (Y-50) reassemble the shell and ball and socket retainer. Epoxy the stud in the pedestal and almost any glass shop can replace the mirror glass.

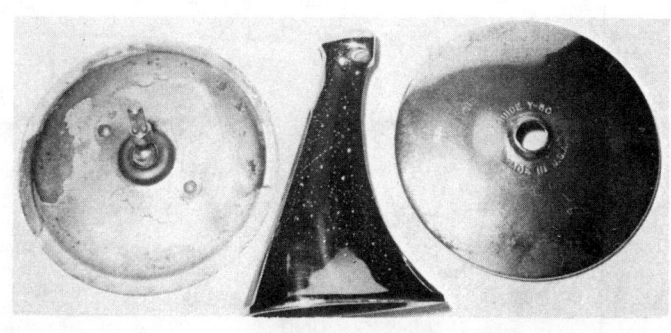

continued.....

56-57 HEADLIGHT ASSEMBLIES

Photo shows rusted remains of a headlamp from a 1957 Corvette. Fender location inside the wheel well exposes this assembly, as well as the park light, to mud, water, snow, etc. Replacement of this assembly is a simple matter.

The headlamp assy. which is stamped "Guide H-18", in its basic universal form, was used on many 1950's circa GM cars. Specific applications to different cars required several varieties of headlamp "door" attaching brackets and wiring. The best place to look for replacements is the local wrecking yard. The best car to look for is a 1956 Cadillac as this particular model has a protective inner fender and the headlamp assemblies will likely be as new.

To adapt these Cadillac items to a 56-57 Corvette simply transfer the door mounting brackets using new rivets (some new location holes may have to be drilled). You'll also want to remove the Corvette wiring and lamp socket from the old body as it is the proper lenght and has the correct electrical connectors. Lacquer thinner will work great in cleaning the wires.

You'll also want to replace the wiring loom. This should be no problem as most any Delco Dealer should have it in stock. Its called Delco Auto Loom #1204 in the 5/16" variety and will sell for about 25¢ a foot. This wiring loom was used on all Corvette headlamp assemblies from 53-62.

While I have described the 56-57 headlamp assembly I should point out that the 58-62 lamps will also be found on other GM cars with the newer quad headlight arrangement. The 53-55 headlamps will be a tough item to replace as it sat farther back in the fender and had a unique stamping to clear the tire, and its wiring harness came out through the top.

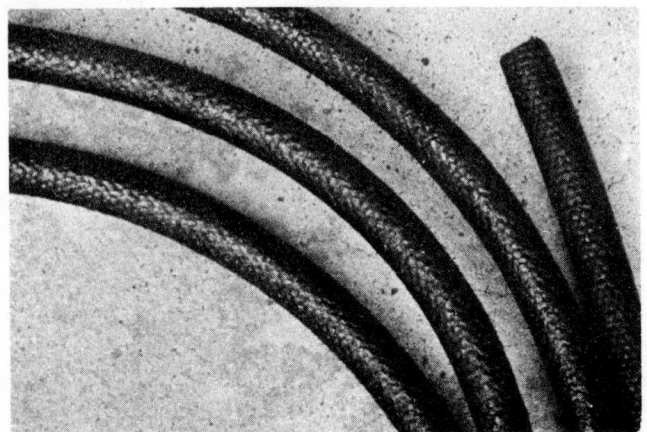
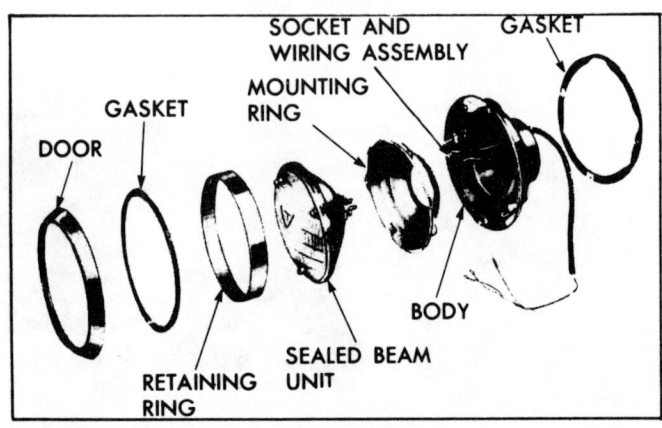

Headlamp Exploded View

53-57 HOOD SPRING SUBSTITUTE

The spring pictured on the right is from the front hood spring bracket that mounts under the hood along the side of the radiator on 53-57 models (also the same as the male hood catch on the underside of the hood panel). The spring on the left is from the front of a 1953-54 Chevrolet hood and with a little tension taken out with a torch (its a bit longer) should work fine on the Corvette.

53-55 NEUTRAL SAFETY SWITCH

The neutral safety switch pictured on the left is for the 53-55 Corvette. The one on the right is a replacement switch for a 1950-54 Chevrolet. The Chevrolet switch mounts at the base of the steering column and has a tongue that attaches to the shifting rod. This tongue can be removed and the switch will fit on the Corvette switch bracket on the transmission. The shifting pattern is the same and there are two extra connections (for back-up lights) that will have to be removed.

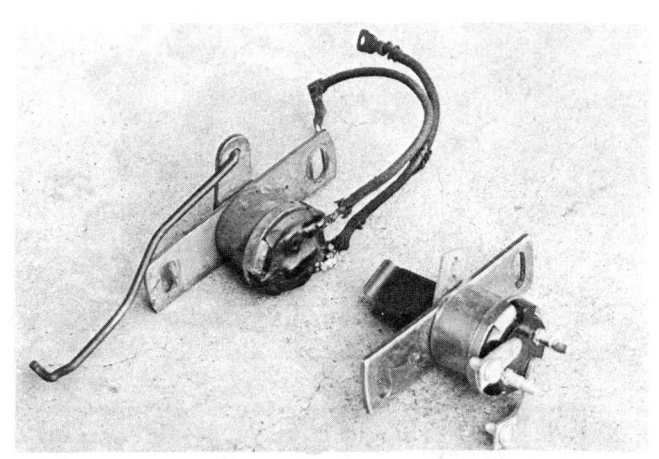

If you don't have the bracket it should be easy enough to make if you have one to go by. It should be pointed out the the switch bracket shield #3706355 for 53-60 Corvettes is still available from Chevrolet.

One last little parts interchange tip: The cowl ventilator adjuster knob part #4619984 for 1956-62 Corvettes is the same as the front seat adjuster knob on 1955-57 Chevrolet passenger cars.

The following restoration tip was submitted by James Perand of Lockport, Illinois: This is a handy tip for those who want to replace ignition switches without having new keys made. With the key in, push a straightened paper clip in to the little around the edge of the switch and at the same time turn the key to the left and pull the switch out.

SEND YOUR RESTORATION TIPS AND CONTRIBUTIONS FOR INCLUSION IN THIS ARTICLE TO:

Martin Ball
335 Aloha Drive
San Leandro, CA 94578
415/352-1846

56/7 Head Identification

By MICHAEL HUNT

Photos show single pyramid and 3731539 casting number from a 1957 283 hp cylinder head.

When 1956/7 Corvette engines are discussed, the question of "correct" cylinder heads frequently arises. The variety of casting numbers and symbols is potentially confusing for would-be restorers. However, sufficient information is now available for at least a "tentative" listing.

The following table is based upon a review of reliable printed source material, plus an on-going examination of numerous, apparently well-preserved, 1956/7 Corvettes:

YEAR	HORSEPOWER	DESCRIPTION	SYMBOL	CASTING #	PART #
1956	210 225 (early, with 2-bolt exh. mani.)	Single Pyramid	⌂	3725306	3729785
1956	225, 240 (with 3-bolt exh. manifold)	Double Tower	⊓⊓	3731762	3734029
1957	220, 245, 250, 270	Single Tower	⊓	3740997	3741459
1957	283	Single Pyramid	⌂	3731539	3739270

The above table is subject to revision! Hats off to Richard Robinson, Jerry Bramlett, Rick Kilmer, and others, for help in compiling this data.

Please direct any comments, suggestions, etc., to Michael Hunt, 903 Swarthmore Ct., Madison, Wisconsin 53705. Photocopies of any additional or contrary documentation would be appreciated.

RESTORATION TIPS

WITH MARTIN BALL

I would like to include some GM part numbers and parts in this issue that are still serviced for the early Corvette from your local Chevrolet Dealer.

56-61 CORVETTE SIDE TRIM

All side trim parts which surround the cove are still available except for 56-57 front curved pieces #3730106 and #3730105. These parts were removed from service in September of 1972.

Side trim mounting bolts, known as "T" bolts can be ordered. They come in a box of 20 and the part number is #3730104. The mounting nuts are a standard hardware store item size 6/32".

One way to keep the bolts from sliding around on the trim strips is to apply a small amount of body caulking or clay to each side of the bolt (see photo). This will aid greatly in mounting.

GENERAL MOTORS PART NUMBERS FOR 1956-1961 CORVETTE SIDE TRIM

LEFT SIDE

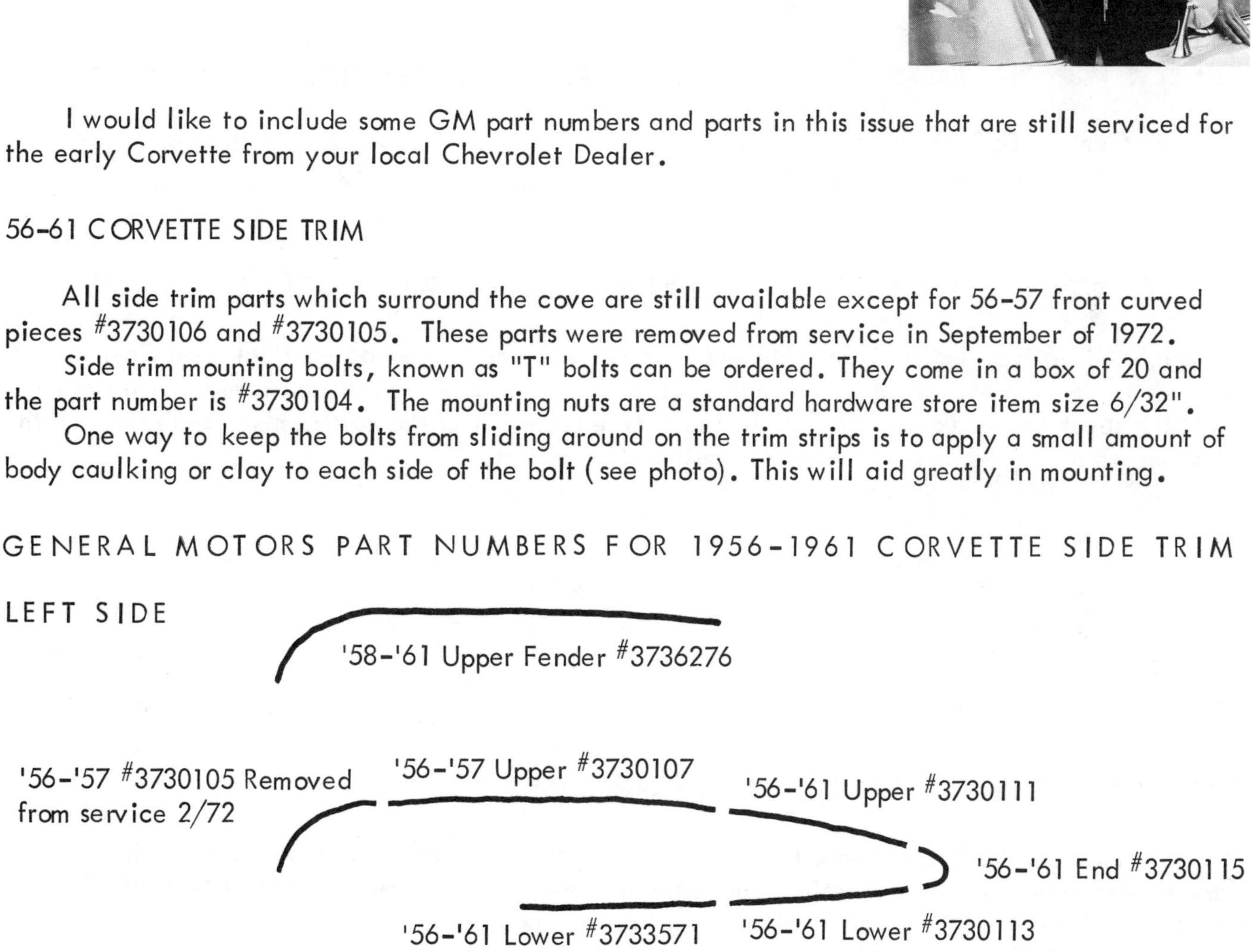

'58-'61 Upper Fender #3736276

'56-'57 #3730105 Removed from service 2/72
'56-'57 Upper #3730107
'56-'61 Upper #3730111
'56-'61 End #3730115
'56-'61 Lower #3733571
'56-'61 Lower #3730113

RIGHT SIDE

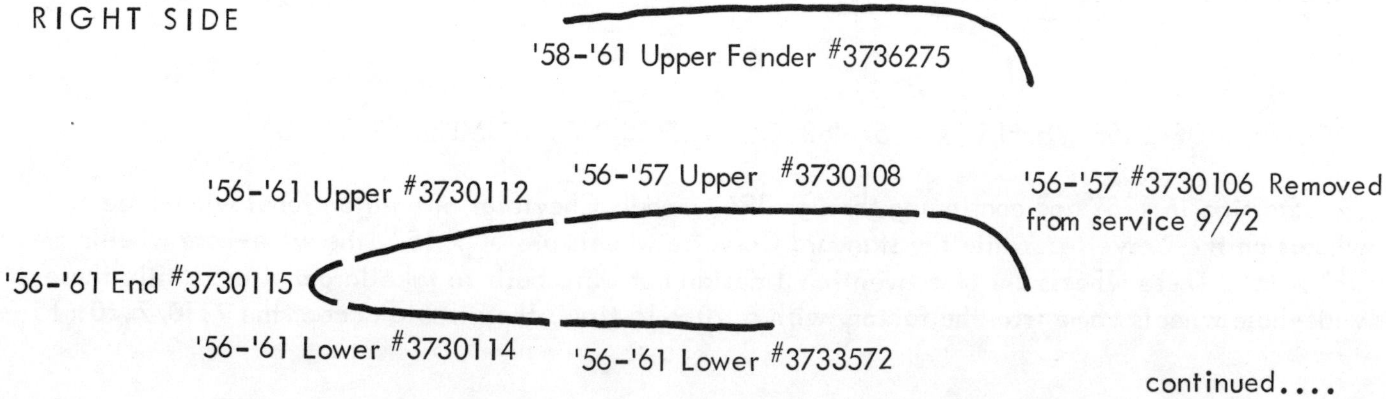

'58-'61 Upper Fender #3736275

'56-'61 Upper #3730112
'56-'57 Upper #3730108
'56-'57 #3730106 Removed from service 9/72
'56-'61 End #3730115
'56-'61 Lower #3730114
'56-'61 Lower #3733572

continued....

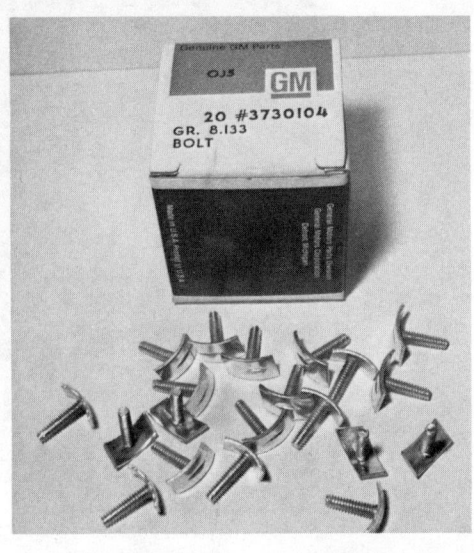

'56-'61 CORVETTE SIDE TRIM "T" BOLTS
GRP. 8.133 #3730104 BOX OF 20

56-62 IGNITION SHIELDING WING BOLTS

These come in a bag of 20 bolts. The part number is #3728415.

'55-'61 GENERATOR TACH DRIVE (CONTINUED FROM LAST ISSUE)

Erich Kilmer from Indiana, John Holmes from Pennsylvania, and Charles Heck from Connecticut all wrote to say that tach drive parts are available from Delco. Mr. Heck mentioned that his order took only about one week for delivery. Included here are a list of the part numbers and prices on the parts that were ordered and received from their Delco dealers.

Part #	Description	List	Net
1930846	adaptor	34.95 (list)	23.94 (net)
1930847	case (cover)	33.25	23.35
1930848	gasket		.11
1930852	gear	9.05	6.34
1930853	gear	5.60	3.92
1930854	shaft	not available	2.71
1930325	washer		.12

53-77 CORVETTE PARTS AND ILLUSTRATION CATALOG

This parts book is the same one local Chevrolet dealer uses and is very extensive. It includes many exploded photos and illustrations and lists all those parts that are currently still available from General Motors. This book is priced at $10.00 postage paid (several years ago it was only $3.50). It is available from: General Motors Parts Division, Publication Processing Center, GM Photographic, 465 W. Milwaukee Ave., Detroit, Michigan 48202.

RPO 276 WIDE BASE WHEELS FOR '57-'62 CORVETTES PART NUMBER #3838080

Starting in 1957 and continuing through 1962 models Chevrolet offered optional wide-base wheels on the Corvette. While the standard Corvette wheels are 5" x 15", the wide-base wheels are $5\frac{1}{2}$" x 15". These wheels are of conventional design but were built to take larger tires. While these wide-base wheels came from the factory with 6.70 x 15 tires, they would accept the 7.10/7.60 x 15

RPO 276 wide-base wheels mounted on a 1962 Corvette owned by Don Huggins of Illinois. This option was a no cost extra and the wheels (5) were painted in body color.

size which had to be acquired from tire manufacturers.

Wide-base wheels do not have the four little raised mounting lugs around the outer rim for holding the full wheel-covers in place, so these wheels came from the factory equipped with small hub caps. We will discuss the use of these hub caps in a future issue.

There was one question that came up at the California Meet Tech Session regarding the currently available wide-base wheel (#3838080) not fitting over the front brake drum hub, requiring some reaming of the hub opening to make it fit. The photo shows the wide base wheel mounted on my '57 with standard front hub and brake drum with no problem. Perhaps the finned RPO drums have a larger diameter hub? I would like to hear from anyone who has had problems in mounting these currently available wide-base wheels on their car. I hope to have more on these wheels in the next issue.

$5\frac{1}{2}$ x 15 wide-base wheels #3838080 which are currently available from GM were mounted on my '57 with no problem.

Note "15 x $5\frac{1}{2}$ K" stamped inside rim.

I appreciate your contributions and comments to this article. If you have a tip that worked for you during your restoration, take several minutes to write it down and send it to me so that I may include it in future issues. It might just help another member with the same problem. Send your restoration tips to:

    Martin Ball
    335 Aloha Dr.
    San Leandro, CA 94578
    Tel. 415/352-1846

TECH SESSION

WITH NCRS TECHNICAL CHAIRMAN SAM FOLZ

We are indebted to Mr. Lynn S. Cullens of PPG Industries for the long-needed paint color information included in his letter which we reproduce in this issue.

You'll note that this now gives information necessary to purchase modern acrylic lacquers replacing all of the 1953 through 1957 nitrocellulose lacquers in a good, commercial color-match. The lone exception, as Mr. Cullens points out, is Combination #573, Corvette Copper, which Ditzler calls "Metallic Bronze Poly". This off-set is too golden brown, and not red enough to be considered a perfect match.

Note, too, that Ditzler information has always referred to what are commonly called "metallic" finishes as "poly" or "polychrome".

I believe several questions may be anticipated in this data and I'll try to explain them.

Chevrolet used some passenger car colors on the Corvette, but sometimes by another paint-code number and name. The first example is a 1953 passenger car color called Combination #506 - Target Red. On the Corvette, this color was called Sportsman Red, Combination #569. In each case, Chevrolet approved Ditzler DAL-70418 as the correct color. That is why Mr. Cullens' letter refers to the year 1953. The 1954 passenger car did not use this red and thus Ditzler shows only model-year 1953 as a reference.

The Code #630 Harvest Gold is another example, as that name and number relate to the 1955 passenger car. The Corvette combination for this color was #632.

The model year references to the four 1957 colors in Mr. Cullens' letter should have read 1956-1957.

One other note for clarification: The first column identified as "Ditzler Code" indicates the old numbers which were prefixed "DAL". The acrylic lacquer numbers are all prefixed "DDL".

PPG INDUSTRIES, INC./P. O. BOX 5090, SEVEN OAKS STATION/DETROIT, MICHIGAN 48235/AREA 313/275-5550

October 12, 1976

DITZLER Automotive Finishes
Coatings and Resins Division

Mr. Sam Folz
National Corvette Restorers Society
3824 Coventry Avenue
Kalamazoo, Michigan 49007

Dear Mr. Folz:

Per your request, we are listing our off-sets for the Corvette colors you requested.

Year	Paint Code	Color Name	Ditzler Code	Our DDL Off-Set	
1953	506	Target Red	70418	70966	
1953-57	718	Polo White	8011	0829	
1954	570	Metallic Blue Poly	11238	13552	
1954-55	573	Metallic Bronze Poly	21207	23393	Too Golden Brown, not red enough
1955	630	Harvest Gold	80739	82171	
1955	596	Gypsy Red	70575	71903	
1957	709	Aztec Copper Poly	21295	21927	
1957	712	Cascade Green	41973	2561	
1957	713	Arctic Blue Poly	11537	13150	
1957	714	Venetian Red	70694	71708	

We hope this information will help you.

Yours truly,

L. S. Cullens

L. S. Cullens
Assistant to Market Manager
Automotive Finishes

LSC/h

PAINT SELECTION AND BODY PREPARATION
An Essay by Raymond R. Halsey

The problems of restoring a Corvette to original are many. But no matter how much blood, sweat and tears we've shed finding the correct parts or detailing an engine compartment, it can all be lost with a poor paint job! The questions that will plague you in the beginning are many. Which type of top-coat paint should be used (nitrocellulose lacquer, acrylic lacquer, acrylic enamel, or Imron)? What primers should be used and why? Should a sealer be used? And how about Feather Fill? The following methods and products are preferred by me because of the outstanding quality I have obtained with them. This is not to say that if you have found a winning combination, it is wrong.

Because all top-coats require a different use of products for their preparation, our first decision should be the choice of top-coat to be used. Corvettes were originally painted with the (old) nitrocellulose lacquers from 1953 to 1957, with the exception of a couple of colors in 1957. From 1958 to the present they were finished in the (new) acrylic lacquers. Because of these facts and the fact that acrylic enamel does not produce the desired finished results we require in restoration, it should be dropped from our list of choices.

Imron is a very high-gloss, extremely durable, chemical and solvent resistant polyurethane enamel. The only correct color it is available in is black. Therefore, most applications would have to use the acrylic lacquer paints for the correct color, then applying Imron clear (500S) as the top and final coats. Elapsed time between the application of the last coat of acrylic lacquer and the spraying of the clear Imron is very critical. So critical in fact, that DuPont no longer recommends this procedure be used as they did when Imron was first introduced. It must not be sprayed over wet acrylic lacquer as some have suggested, but it must be applied before a ten hour period has elapsed. If not, Imron will not adhere properly and can pop loose if struck with even moderate impact.

Repairing a damaged area of Imron can be very frustrating. To match or blend the color, we normally spray a little larger area than what was repaired. Because Imron is so smooth and nothing will adhere to it properly, one must remove all of the Imron by whatever means (stripping or sanding). This means whole panels could be involved and could get very costly. No one wants to think of their new paint job being damaged, but it does happen. Imagine, at this time, damage to a rear fender. You should remove Imron from both fenders, below and above the trunk lid, door-jambs, etc... Theoretically, one could end up removing Imron from everything except the doors, hood, trunk and deck lid. Removing a minor flaw such as a piece of lint can become a real chore to sand and buff out because Imron is so hard and scratch resistant. Imron cures-out a lot faster than acrylic lacquer and can make your repaired areas sink because it traps and forces the lacquer thinners down through the fiberglass.

For all of these reasons, I would not recommend the use of Imron for restoration of your Corvette except maybe on the frame and suspension parts. If you are going to use Imron on these parts, here are a few suggestions. Use the epoxy zinc chromate primer (825S) and activator (826S) as recommended by DuPont. Although you may use DuPont primer-surfacer (100S or 110S) with only a small loss of adhesion. Make sure your parts are ready before spraying! Tack rag very carefully and spray in a good dust and lint free area.

(Old) Nitrocellulose lacquer vs. (New) acrylic lacquer. I'll let the final choice be yours reminding you that pre 1958 Corvettes were painted in nitrocellulose with only a couple of exceptions in 1957 which were acrylic. Most automotive paint suppliers no longer have available the nitrocellulose thinners, primers and colors with the exception of Bill Hirsch, Judd Irish and maybe two or three others. Some of their ads can be found in *Hemmings* or *Old Cars*. Availability is not the best as you can see. I wouldn't recommend the use of lacquer primers with nitrocellulose lacquers but DuPont's 100S does work with satisfactory results.

All major paint manufactureres can supply an off-set color in acrylic to replace the nitrocellulose color used. Because pigments are affected differently in these two products, off-set colors are as close as the manufacturers can get to the (old) nitrocellulose lacquers. They may vary from Ditzler to DuPont to R & M, therefore, you will have to choose which off-set is the best match. I will recommend that someone else who has restored that same color be contacted for help in your decision. After both types have been sanded and rubbed out, it is next to impossible to tell the two apart. Nitrocellulose lacquer does not have the gloss retention that the new acrylics do and acrylic lacquers are more flexible and durable. Both of these paints can give you a very high gloss. **Availability, durability, and excellent gloss retention would be the reasons to choose acrylic lacquer for your top-coat.**

Every step in the painting process is an important one. Cutting corners of any step will affect the end quality results. For the remainder of this article I'll assume you followed the suggested top-coat choice of acrylic lacquer.

The repaired areas and bare fiberglass have to be prepared for the use of a primer-surfacer. Two possible choices are available: wax and degrease remover; or a fast dry enamel reducer. Wax and degrease removers are designed with a slow evaporation rate for the purpose of dissolving the tar, grease and wax on surface paint for spot repairs. Enamel reducers will dissolve the same foreign materials but will evaporate much faster therefore, not soaking into the fiberglass and possibly being trapped later by the primer. I would recommend the use of DuPont 3812S enamel reducer. Wipe the entire auto with a rag soaked with 3812S doing only panels at a time and wiping it dry with another clean cloth. Then use air to blow the surface clean and completely dry. Now go over the entire auto with a tack rag to remove any remaining lint and dust.

You are now ready for the next step, the one of covering body seams and repaired areas. Feather Fill, a new product on the market made by Fiberglass Evercoat, is probably the finest product now available for this purpose. It is a polyester spray putty utilizing a two-part process with a catylist and is non-reduced. So heavily bodied that it can fill 16 to 24 grinder marks with only a few coats and is easily sanded smooth. Do not use over the entire auto as that was not its intended purpose. The pot life of only 1-1/2 to 2 hours requires that all spray equipment be cleaned thoroughly before this time limit expires. I have used it very successfully with acrylic lacquers. Sorry to say, I have not yet tried this product with nitro-cellulose lacquer or Imron.

Priming of all surfaces is our next step. Primers have several functions: adhesion; sandscratch hold-outs; sandability; and film build. Several primer-surfacers are available to choose from, although my choice would be DuPont's lacquer type multi-purpose primer-surfacer 100S or 110S. The difference between the two being only color. 100S/110S offers the maximum in adhesion — far better than lacquer primers that have a tendency to flake off when struck with a strong impact. It holds down sand scratches and minor fiberglass flaws as well as enamel primers and better than lacquer primers. Film build is much faster because 100S/110S is a heavy bodied material and will require less coats than enamel or lacquer primers. This product is not the easiest to use but then all good things don't come in pretty little packages with ribbons. Because of it being heavy bodied, it is very hard to mix or pour, and after being reduced with thinner, it settles extremely fast. 100S/110S should not be left to sit in a spray gun for more than 30 minutes or it may have to be pried out with a stir stick. If this primer is not cleaned from a spray gun thoroughly, it may require disassembly of your equipment.

Ease in sanding is also not one of its more outstanding qualities. DuPont's 100S or 110S may be harder to use but the high quaility end results are far superior to other products available.

Again, we must prepare the surface using 3812S enamel reducer as previously described. The first coat of primer should be sprayed light and left to flash-dry for 30 to 45 minutes. Then the extra needed coats may be applied with proper flash time between each coat. I will mention at this point that 100S is a DuPont product but I use Ditzler 876 thinner as a reducer because of the odor that most DuPont thinners have (hint, hint, DuPont people). The first coat of primer should be reduced 200% with all remaining coats reduced at 125%.

After the last coat of 100S/110S is applied, a thin dust coat of a lacquer primer-surfacer in an opposite color should be sprayed. This will help you find the waves and imperfections that are still there when it is blocked sanded in 280 wet. This should be done no sooner than 2 to 4 hours after the last coat of primer was sprayed. After block sanding the entire car, it must be determined whether these flaws that show are too deep and should be filled with a lacquer base spot putty or glaze. The reason I have said lacquer-base is because there are plastic-base spot putties available and they swell and contract with hot and cold.

Now that the car has been glazed it is ready to be tack-ragged, primed a couple more times, dust coated and 400 block sanded for the final time. I have achieved better results when the final block sanding is done at least 24 hours after the last coat of primer. If there are any areas that are still bad, repeat the last processes but only to the areas affected. Remember, any flaw you can find, no matter how small, will show up in your top-coat!

There is still one more important step to be applied before the color top-coats. It is the one sealing. DuPont 2129S all purpose sealer works very well. It will stop or help prevent any chance of sand-scratch swelling and will give the top-coat the adhesion and chemical bonding needed. Most manufacturers recommend the use of a sealer between primers and acrylic lacquer paint and so do I. The label on the non-reduced 2129S sealer states that the first color coat should be applied within 1 hour to assure proper adhesion. DuPont's product information department says you may wait longer but it must be scuffed or 600 sanded to assure a good chemical bond. Since most of us do not have the ideal painting conditions (a $10,000.00 spray booth) and small particles of lint may appear no matter how thoroughly you've tack-ragged. These could show up in the final sanding and polishing of the color coat as little grey specks. Sealers need 15 to 20 minutes to flash dry and it takes 25 to 35 minutes to apply a complete color coat. This may not allow enough time to spray those hard to get at and hard to sand areas in the first hour. I would recommend waiting until the next day to spray your color coat and utilizing the first hour to spray those hard to get at areas.
hour to spray those hard to get at areas.

You are now ready to spray your color coats. Just a couple of last minute hints. When the color coats are metallic, spray enough clear over the top to be sanded, as metallics change color when sanded or buffed. Also, do not wax for at least 30 days as this will trap solvents under it and can cause the repaired areas to sink. Good luck.

Ray Halsey
4808 Camden Road
Madison, Wisconsin 53716
(608) 222-1182

53-62 Corvette PARTS SURVEY

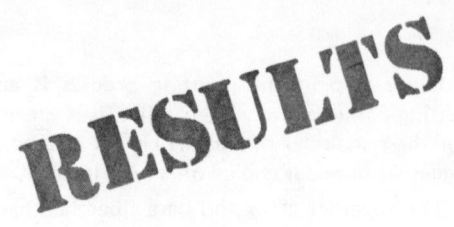

Compiled by John Amgwert

In the Spring 1976 issue of THE CORVETTE RESTORER I included a return post card for the purpose of determining which 53-62 Corvette parts are most needed to complete a restoration. Approximately 1200 cards were distributed and of those, 212 were returned, or 17.6%. It is from those 212 cards that I was able to catalog the parts onto the attached chart.

Since I asked for 5 requests for parts on each card, a total of about 1060 (5 x 212) specific requests formed the basis of the survey. In order for a part to be included in the chart, it had to achieve at least 3 requests. The chart accounts for 702 total usable requests, or 66.2%, while there were 358 (33.8%) unusable requests (2 or less requests). Those usable requests totaled 99 seperate parts and assemblies that make up the survey chart.

It is interesting to note that the majority of cards could be broken down into three basic model divisions: 53-55, 56-57, and 58-62. The majority of requests on each card stayed within one of these divisions. The requests basically fell into the following catagories:

- 53-55 - 32%
- 56-57 - 25.5%
- 58-62 - 42.5%

The survey chart speaks for itself and, where possible, I have tryed to note known interchanges, replacements that are suitable, and known applications on other vehicles. Current reproduction parts are identified with a asterisk (*).

Quantity	Model(s)	Description / Part Number
25	53-57	Frame Assy. (Grille Oval) #3706432
24	56-57	Exhaust chrome -- upper-#3725577, bezel-#3725596, lower-#3725579
23	53-55	Radio Shields (6-cylinder) -- upper-#3706399, lower-#3706400, condenser-#1926910*
22	53-55	Side mouldings -- doors-#3706385-86, #3706387-388 (6")*, fender-#3706389
19	56-57	Taillamp assy. #898097 *
15	53-55	Steering wheel (no distinction to color combinations)
15	53-55	Water pump-#3706009 Pump body-#3706013 (6-cylinder)
15	58-62	Guard assy. and license bar (front) -- guards-#3736237-38, bar-#3736263
14	56-62	Steering wheel (no distinction to color combinations)
13	56-58	Wheel cover #3725238
13	57-58	Fuel injection fuel filter ACGF 130 AC
13	53-55	Front and rear verticle bumper bars -- rear-#3706648, front-#3706628
13	53-62	Guide Y-50 outside mirror #3709299 *
12	56-57	Bumper assy. (license guards) #3724970
11	57-58	Fuel injection fuel filter bracket
11	53-55	Taillamp assy. (bezel and lens) #897731
11	53-55	Horn blowing ring #759144
11	53-55	Exhaust pipe extension (first or second design) #3711147 (2nd design) *
11	53-57	Weatherstrip (doors, trunk and hood) AUVECO supplies replacement #4731
10	56-57	Antenna #3727578
9	61-62	Taillamp assy. (outboard) left and right #899631-32
9	53-60	Jack and handle -- jack-#3706350, handle#592769 (can be modified from 60-65 Ser. 10 thru 30 truck)
9	58-62	Fuel injection air cleaner assy. #5648705
9	53-55	Front fender moulding (gullwing chrome) left and right #3706591-92*
9	59-62	Wheel cover #3759120
8	61-62	Antenna #988370
8	58-62	Bright metal dash cove trim (aluminum) behind grad rail (no distinction to color combination)
8	56-57	Air cleaner assy. (twin 4 bbl.) #1552558 *
7	58-62	Sun shades (no distinction to color combinations)
7	55-61	Tachometer generator drive unit #1930846 Partially available from Delco. *
7	55-62	Battery support tray #3725027*

Quantity	Model(s)	Description / Part Number
7	53-62	Windshield washer nozzle #3706644 Also used on 54-55 Comm. Util. (1st Ser.) exc. FFC & COE truck.
7	53-57	Grille bar (center horizontal) #3706431
7	53-55	Soft top hardware (front and rear latches) -- RH-#4154402, LH-#4154403, header-#4154404
7	53-55	Radio w/speaker vibrator (6-volt) #3706551
7	53-54	Battery support tray (6-volt) #3706318 Can be modified from early 50's Chev. passenger car.
7	56-57	Taillamp lens #5947405 *
6	57-62	Air cleaner assy. (single 4 bbl.) #5648423
6	58-61	Air cleaner assy. (dual 4 bbl.) #5645690
6	58	Chrome trunk moulding left and right #3742515-16
6	58-60	Antenna #987861
6	58-60	Rear reflex assy. (reflector) note- 58's may not have been so-equipped. #5949741 *
6	53-57	Front hood hinge spring assy. -- bracket- #3706275-76, spring-3706411
6	53-55	Powerglide transmission extension (6-cylinder) Also used on 1953 Pontiacs with Powerglide trans.
6	53-55	License bezel (chrome) #5942604
6	53-55	6-cylinder Carter YH carburetors
6	53-55	Rear bumper bar (center) #3706043
5	61-62	Door weatherstrip (right hand) #3784450
5	61-62	Door sill scuff plates (aluminum) LH-#3779762, RH-#3779761
5	58	"Pebble-grain" dash panel pad (no distinction to color combinations)
5	58-60	Exhaust pipe insulator
5	57-62	Hardtop header moulding LH-#3739310, RH-#3739310
5	61-62	Jack and Handle -- jack-#3813730, handle- #592769 (can be modified from 60-65 Ser. 10 thru 30 truck)
5	55-56	Air cleaner assy. (single 4 bbl.) #1552185
5	56-57	Door panel chrome trim (interior)
5	53-55	Rear pinion seal #3707355
5	53-55	Front fender script #3706358 *
5	53-55	Front emblem #759237 *
5	53-54	Top compartment "flipper" moulding-- LH-#4154394, RH -#4154395 *
5	53	Engine valve cover #3836135 *
5	53-55	Vent windows (side curtains) -- LH- #4154408, RH- #4154409
5	53-57	Powerglide brake pedal pad (rubber) #3706153
5	57	Windshield washer fluid container (plastic) #3740216 (Trico)
4	56-62	Door post chrome -- LH-#3762557, RH-#3762558
4	61-62	Taillamp protectors #2977446 (can be modified from 1960 Chevrolet passenger car)
4	56-62	Wheel cover ornament (spinner) #3725239 *
4	53-57	Park lamp assy. #898150 (used on many late 40's and early 50's GM cars and GMC trucks)
4	56-57	Nine fin valve covers #3726086
4	53-57	Front license bracket #3706243 *
4	53-57	Courtesy lamp (under dash) #4129371 (6-volt) (used on several early 50's GM cars)
4	57	Fuel injection air cleaner assy. #1553181 *
4	53-57	Speedometer lens
4	56-57	Front horizontal bumpers (cresents) #3725539
4	56-57	Wiring harness w/power top and power windows
4	56-57	Front fender mouldings -- LH-#3730105, RH-#3730106 *
4	53-55	Exhaust system (complete) *
4	53-55	Powerglide shifter assy.*
4	53-55	Bumper assy. (license gaurds) #3706235
4	53-55	Carburetor rebuilt kits (available from Carter Dealer, order Kit #902-118)
4	53-55	Windhield glass #4632595 (avalable from several sources)
4	53-55	Soft top assy. less canvas (bows)
4	54-55	Air cleaner assy. (6-cylinder- 2nd design)
4	53-56	Gas cap #3708440 (made by Eaton)
4	55	Ignition Shielding (V-8 distributor and coil covers) *
4	59-62	4-speed transmission shifter assy.
4	57-62	4-speed transmission shifter rods*
4	58-62	Windshield washer container #3746160
3	56-57	Heater/defroster duct (pressed cardboard heater outlet)
3	56-57	Hood release cable #1990837 (GM replacement #1990911 should work as substitute.)
3	53-57	Hood hinges-- LH-#3706267, RH-#3706268
3	53-55	Door striker plates-- LH-#4154368, RH-#4154369
3	53	Window bag (black oil-cloth)
3	53-55	Wheel covers #3716754 (still available from GM)
3	53-55	Intake manifold (6-cylinder) #3718120
3	53-54	Mirror (inside w/ fixed base) #3718120
3	53-55	Aux. coolant tank (6-cylinder, 1st or 2nd design) #3706261
3	55-56	Windshield washer fluid container (blue "Chevrolet" bag) (also used on some 55-57 pass. car and truck)
3	53-57	Male hood catch #3706663
3	57	AC 8000 rpm tachometer (column mounted) #1548680

RESEARCH PROJECT 1956/7

With MICHAEL HUNT

"VE" VERSUS "E"

As the 1956/57 Corvettes become more "collectable", owners and enthusiasts are beginning to play a veritable "numbers game" involving the Vehicle Identification Numbers (VIN#'s). From the late 1950's until approximately 1970, the topic rarely surfaced. But of late, everybody seems VIN#-conscious.

For some reason, the lower VIN#'s, representing early units in a given production run, are most sought after. Yet some collectors prefer a very late VIN#. Personally, I'd rather own 1957 Corvette E57S106339 than E57S100001. The early cars are the ones with the "bugs".

RESEARCH PROJECT 1956/7 has turned up another interesting facet: the "E" versus "VE" phenomenon. Apparently, all 1956/7 Corvette VIN# body tags and stamped frame numbers feature either E56S or E57S as the initial four digits. Yet some 1956/7 titles and Registration Certificates read VE56S or VE57S. The PROJECT has already logged-in 13 "VE" titled cars - five 1956's and eight 1957's. These are primarily Wisconsin-registered vehicles, and the several which I've personally inspected do have the expected "E" on the VIN# body tag, despite the "VE" on their respective titles. It should be noted that the use of a "V" was used on 1955 model Corvette VIN# body tags where a V-8 engine was used as opposed to a 6-cylinder, the "V" being an added stamping to the tag.

The majority of 1956/7's surveyed have been titled as "E" cars. In some cases, however, it has been possible to trace the "VE" paperwork clear back to the date of purchase. One 1956, for example, retains the original invoice, which shows "VE". And Stoughton, Wisconsin's John Hamilton, the original owner of E57S100449, has "VE" on both his old title and his original owner's wallet card, yet an "E" on his VIN# body tag (see photo). Some "E" cars are also traceable back to the beginning, with the "E" having been used all along. Note the photo of the wallet card from my E57S101927 car.

Originally, I speculated that the "VE" was just a clerical carryover from its usage in 1955. However, were this the case, one would expect consistent usage up until a specific turning point, after which the paperwork VIN#'s would consistently begin with "E". My #1927 car, for instance, started out with an E57S VIN#. Therefore, if a clerical switch from VE57S to E57S did occur at a certain point, it should precede unit #1927. Yet the 1956/7 "VE" cars I've surveyed are sprinkled at random throughout the entire range, with no discernible pattern.

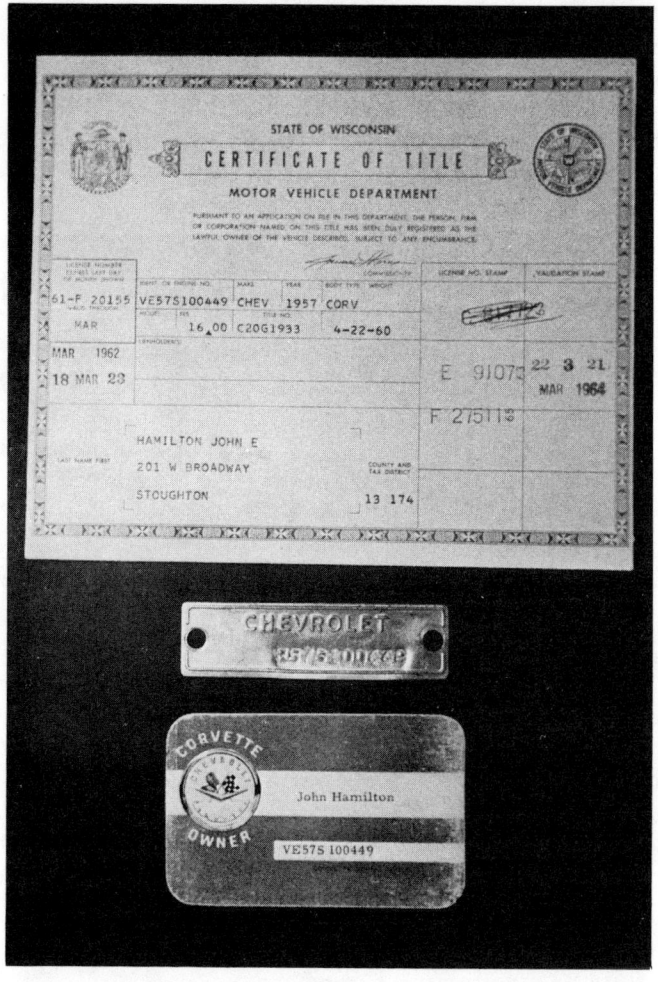

Had initial registration of the 1956/7's taken place during the computer era, one might speculate that perhaps the initial digits were occasionally cut, so that a VIN# would fit into allocated computer program field length. This little maneuver was performed on numerous Wisconsin-registered Corvettes during the 1960's, leaving the important year-identifying initial digit absent. But the 1956/7 Corvettes are definitely pre-computer.

Thus far I haven't been able to determine the exact reason for the "VE" usage. Hopefully a knowledgeable Chevrolet Motor Division employee will contact me after reading this. I suspect that both versions were taken directly off the original Statement of Origin for each 1956/7, as it arrived at the dealership. This returns us to the "clerical carryover" concept.

I'd welcome any comments or data from readers; and photocopies of wallet cards, invoices, titles, bills of sale, Statements of Origin, and the like would be appreciated. Also, a 1956/7 Inquiry Sheet will be sent to owners upon request (SASE please). The completion and return of these sheets will help advance the PROJECT.

Michael Hunt
903 Swarthmore Ct.
Madison, Wisconsin 53705
608/233-9226

1957 Engine/VIN Serial Correlation

By Fredrick Thompson

Photos by Ted Cash

Examples of information gathering and distribution have been presented in prior issues of this publication with discussions on valve cover usage and cylinder head applications on 1956/57 Corvette engines.

A related area to be explored is the correlation between vehicle identification and engine numbers. Engine blocks produced by Chevrolet in 1957 were the first not to be consecutively assigned a number propriety to each engine. The blocks contain two code sequences that can be translated into calendar dates. Those codes indicate when the engine block was cast and when the engine itself was assembled.

Engine "casting date" of F117 translates into June 11, 1957

Engine assembly source, date and type code.

The casting date of the block is located on the upper right, rear portion of the block where the bellhousing is attached. Under the coding system, the letter "A" represents the month of January, "B" February and so on through the twelve months of a year. Casting of the block photographed for this article was on June 11, 1957, which is a translation of the F117 code.

Assembly date information is located on the series number boss, located on the right side of the block, between the front of the cylinder head and water pump. A translation of the F702EL stamping in the second photograph is shown in the accompanying chart.

A complete list of all 1957 Corvette engine suffix designations was presented in the Spring 1975 issue (Volume One, Number Four) of THE CORVETTE RESTORER. Hopefully, the following serial/engine number information will be of interest to other members and encourage them to submit combinations they may know of:

E57S100101	F926FG	E57S103304	F320EG	E57S104589	F606EM
E57S100145	F925FH	E57S103567	F327EG	E57S105004	F626EF
E57S100449	F1010EH	E57S103625	F423FK	E57S105184	F701EF
E57S100903	F1109EG	E57S103853	F410FG	E57S105263	F625EH
E57S101018	F1113EH	E57F104064	F502EG	E57S105493	F510FK
E57S101675	F1123FH	E57S104232	F522EN	E57S105528	F712EF
E57S101679	F1120FH	E57S104307	F522EL	E57S105681	F725EH
E57S101927	F102EL	E57S104366	F326EM	E57S105710	F725EH
E57S102250	F131EL	E57S104435	F522FH	E57S105976	F722FH
E57S102520	F221EF	E57S104466	F522EG		

F 7 02 E L
— plant where assembled (flint)
— month engine assembled (July)
— calendar date engine built
— 283 horsepower rating (manual)
— fuel injection and Duntov cam

The above list has been compiled by me during the last year through personal inspection and correspondence with owners across the country. It can be told from the list that generally higher serial numbered cars tend to show usage of engines produced later. It is noted also that the early serial numbered cars presented here show engine production codes indicating 1956 year production which could be verified through the "casting date coding system". It appears that 1957 engine production began around September of 1956. We can assume that while engine codes and serial numbers progress rather evenly, the several engine assembly dates that don't quite follow pattern are a result of the St. Louis plant's random selection of engines for installation.

Additional contributions and comments are solicited and can be sent to my attention. Write: Fredrick Thompson, c/o Union Bank Trust Division, P. O. Box 2193 Terminal Annex, Los Angeles, California 90051.

RESTORATION TIPS

BY MARTIN BALL

In this issue I would like to include some of the restoration tips that were brought out at the last NCRS Meet in Indianapolis.

One question came up regarding wheels and wheel painting. We found out that the wheels are dipped in a black primer at the manufacturer (Kelsey-Hayes), then shipped to the Corvette Plant in St. Louis. When they are ready to be painted, they are placed on a rack that holds ten rims. Only the front of the wheel rim is painted with color, the back side is left in black except for any overspray that it may catch. This does not apply to the 1953 and 1954 wheels as these cars carried rims painted in red on both sides (the white, red, blue, and black cars carried red wheels).

"IMRON"

There were many favorable comments from some members regarding a paint produced by Du-Pont called "Imron". This is highly resistant to abrasion and also to corrosion, acids, brake fluid, etc. It is a polyurethane enamel which when used with the activator, dries to a hard finish.

Imron works great on chassis and running gear parts with best results obtained by spraying it on. You will have to use a compressor that puts out at least 50 pounds of pressure at the gun unit. If you are using a paint regulator, set it at 50 pounds.

After having my spare rim sandblasted, I sprayed it with lacquer primer-surfacer and went over it with 400 wet and dry sand paper.

Imron does have to be thinned. Mix three parts paint to one part activator. I used Jet Black on the wheel, then painted the front with the correct Venetion Red enamel.

The spray gun can be cleaned with lacquer thinner.

I found Du Pont Imron easy to work with, just follow the complete instructions on the back of the can.

RPO 276 WIDE BASE WHEELS '57-'62 (Continued from last issue)

Bill Rhodes of Georgia, wrote to say that his original 15 X $5\frac{1}{2}$ K wheels fit over the finned front hub and drum on his 1957 with no problem.

Joe Tesar of Missouri, called to say that he had just received the set of wheels he had ordered from GM and they would not fit over the front hubs on his 1962 model with standard drums.

It looks as though there are two different rims - original 57-62 and replacement 57-64. After doing some research I learned that in 1963, Chevrolet went to a $5\frac{1}{2}$" rim as standard on the Corvette. One way to tell an original 15 X $5\frac{1}{2}$ K wheel as used on the 57-62 Corvettes from that wheel used starting in 1963 is by looking at the valve stem hole. The replacement wheel has two small lugs, one on each side, of the stem hole. These small raised lugs apparently kept the '63 wheel cover from spinning.

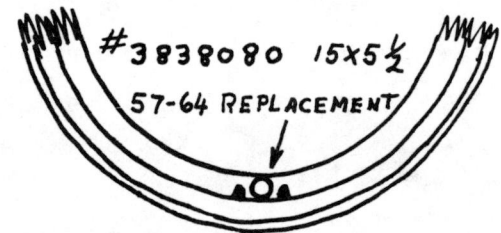

While I pointed out in the last issue that these replacement wide base wheels did fit on my '57 with no problem, some members are experiencing difficulty. One member called to say that the new wheel did fit after wire brushing the paint off the hub. The replacement 15 X $5\frac{1}{2}$ K wheel does have a slightly smaller hub opening (2 3/4") compared to a standard wheel hub opening (2 7/8"). It appears that these currently available wide wheels may require some reaming of the hub opening to make them fit on some models.

SPARE TIRE COVER FIT WITH BEDFORD TIRES

It has been brought to my attention that some members are having trouble with their spare tire board not fitting all the way down with a Bedford Brand 6.70 X 15" tire in the well. I had the opportunity to get one of these currently available Bedford wide white wall tires that had not been post inflated and the cover fit with no problem.

It seems that they inflate the tires while still hot from the mold and that expands the side wall enough to keep the spare tire board from going down to the lip on the well.

I suggest that when you order a Bedford 6.70 X 15" tire, get those that have not been post inflated at least for the spare. These tires are available from Kelsey Tire, Inc., Box 564, Camdenton, MO 65020 and from several dealers.

PLEXIGLAS--REPAIRING AND POLISHING SCRATCHES

The following product tip was submitted by Dave Stefun of Sacramento, California. The product product is called Micro-Mesh and is for surface restoration of clear plastic and plexiglass. It should work well on Corvette side curtains and license covers (53-55), and all hard top windows.

Micro-Mesh is a scientifically engineered series of cloth backed, color coded, cushioned abrasives which when used in their proper sequence with accessories, will restore the surface finish of acrylic and many other hard plastics. Micro-Mesh restores full visual transparency quickly and easily.

The product is sold in kit form with complete instructions. It's used by aircraft companies, commercial airlines and the military. For more information write: Micro-Surface Finishing Products, Inc., Box 456, Wilton, Iowa 52778.

continued.....

RESTORATION TIPS with Martin Ball

The following tips come via our editor, John Amgwert of Lincoln, Nebraska.

1955 and EARLY 1956 HEATER SHUT-OFF VALVE REPLACEMENT

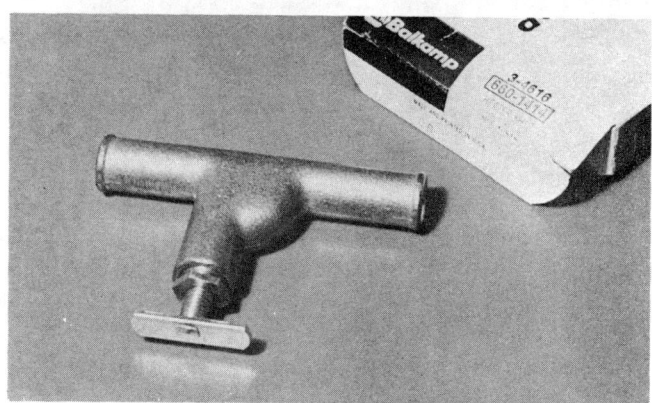

The recirculating air heater used in the 1955 V-8 and some very early 1956 models incorporated a shut-off valve in the coolant line. A good photo of this valve is pictured on page 15 of the last issue. You may note from that photo that the valve is mounted in the lower heater hose in the down position, while on 1955 models it was generally mounted in the upper hose in the upright position.

An excellent replacement for this valve is a NAPA Balkamp Heater Shut Off Valve #3-4616. It should be in stock at any NAPA parts store.

53-62 TRANSMISSION MOUNTING PARTS

As many Corvettes from 53-62 received engine and transmission changes, the original trans. support frame crossmember was removed or modified to accommodate the new drive-train. The correct frame crossmember Group 7.012, Part #3706152 is still available from Chevrolet for about $5.00 list as is the correct transmission mount retainer Group 4.083 Part #3706149, which lists for $1.75.

The problem of recent has been, however, in trying to locate the rubber transmission mounting support that bolts inside the retainer. This part #3711049 was discontinued recently by Chevrolet but since it was also used on 1950 through 1954 Chevrolet passenger cars, you can probably find a replacement at a local parts house. This mount fits all transmissions on 53-62 Corvettes.

Borg-Warner produced a replacement #31-2102 but this too has become obsolete from the factory (a parts house may still have one on the shelf).

I found, however, that the Doan #31-2102 (same number as Borg-Warner) mount is still available and in abundance. Doan Replacement Parts are made by Anchor Inductries, Inc., of Cleveland, Ohio. I paid the amazingly low list price of $1.85 for the rubber transmission mount.

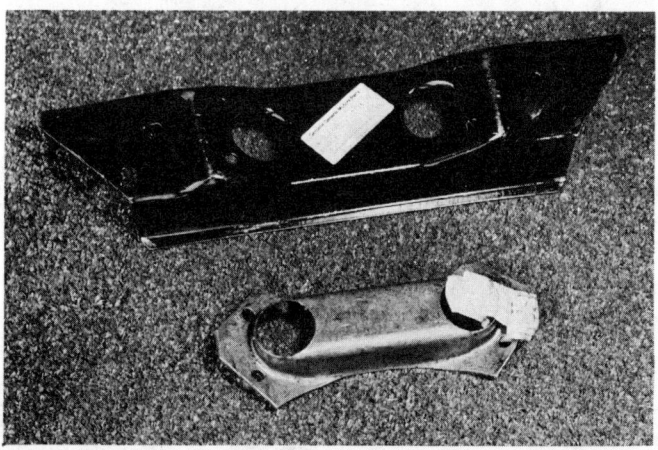 

I want to thank all those members who have sent contributions for this article. If you have a tip that worked for you, or any comment regarding restoration of your Corvette that may be of interest to the membership, write it down and send it to me so that I may include it in future issues. Write: Martin Ball, 335 Aloha Drive, San Leandro, California 94578, phone-415/352-1846.

6-cyl. Corvette Fuel Pumps

by John Amgwert

Frequent topics of discussion at NCRS Tech Sessions are the fuel pumps used on 6-cylinder Corvettes and the problem of finding replacements. Be prepared for a certain amount of heartache as original style pumps are almost non-existent and rebuild kits have been a thing of the past for many years in most parts houses.

The standard fuel pump on the 6-cylinder Corvette is most commonly called "double-action". Along with delivering fuel to the carburetors, it has a built-in vacuum pump which assures operation of the windshield wipers even under full engine throttle. We all remember the wipers that ran off of manifold vacuum — they'd speed up with deceleration and almost stop at acceleration.

A "double-action" fuel pump was offered as optional equipment on late 1952 through 1954 Chevrolet passenger cars. The pump used on the passenger car is also the same one used on the 1953 Corvette. It was made by the AC Spark Plug Division and the type number is 9797 (GM part #5592675).

To complicate matters, the pump used on the 1954 and 1955 Corvette 6-cylinder is not quite the same pump. For some reason (probably fuel pressure at the carburetors) the fuel filter for 1954 was moved adjecent to the fuel pump from its 1953 location just ahead of the #1 carburetor on the left side of the engine. Since the 9797 pump's fuel lines ran at about a 30° angle to the block, there was obviously no room for locating the filter. So, the '54 Corvette introduced the AC 4132 pump (GM part #5593235) with a fuel cover whose lines ran parallel with the block allowing for the new filter

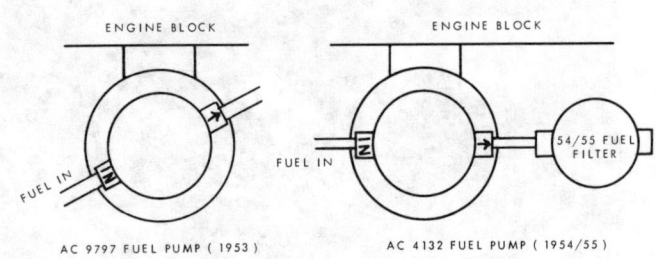

location. This is a little known fact and the reason why so many 1954 restorations appear with the incorrect pump/filter arrangement. Service manuals and even the 1954 owner's manual show the '53 arrangement with the fuel filter mounted on the left. Also, through use, many of these cars ended up with a 9797 pump, the fuel filter often being discarded altogether as the 4132 pump became harder to get.

Now to the problem of finding and/or repairing these pumps today. The AC 9797 pump is still serviced from the

AC 4132 pump body — note extra set of shallow holes cast in which can be drilled and tapped.

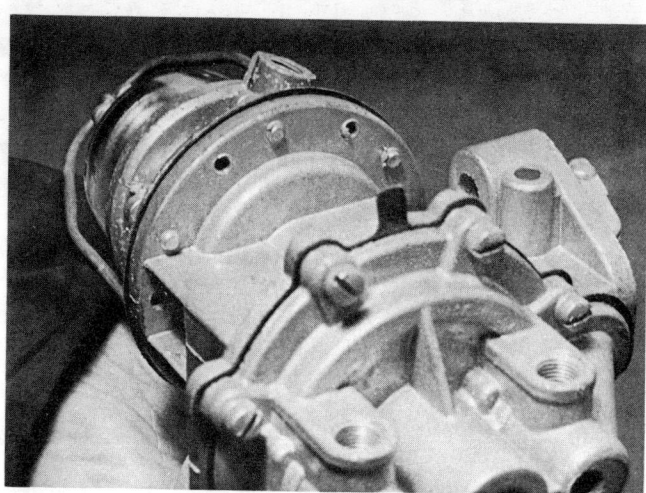

Replacement pump shown here is pre-drilled and tapped for application on either Corvette pump/filter arrangement.

AC Division. However, its top fuel cover will come with a pulsator cover and diaphragm (leveling off flow variations) instead of the original style glass bowl to catch water and sediment in the gas. You most surely could obtain this current version of the 9797 pump, adapting a glass bowl cover which would have to come from an old pump (a junk yard). All older Chevrolet 6-cylinder pumps, both single and double action, used this glass bowl cover. While this would be alright for the 1953 restorer, its use on a '54 or '55 model would require more modifying to make it correct.

The pump body on the AC 9797 pump (and the AC 4132 pump for that matter) has an extra set of partial holes cast in, for mounting the fuel cover (see photo). By simply drilling and tapping these additional holes, the fuel cover and diaphragm can be turned 30° clockwise and presto. . . a '54/'55 pump. This is the only difference between the AC 9797 ('53) and AC 4132 ('54/'55) fuel pumps.

However, in my search, I struck gold after contacting all auto suppliers in my area. In one old dingy parts house in Lincoln (known for having a lot of discontinued old stock) I found a pair of brand new 9797 pumps and while they were not AC, they have the glass bowl cover and are identical to the AC pump (except for the "AC" cast in the pump body). There was no company name on the pump or box — just "New Fuel Pump Guaranteed Replacement" and the number "9797". This replacement pump, strangely enough, was even drilled and tapped so that it could be used on the '54/'55 6-cylinder Corvette by just removing the fuel cover screws, turning the cover and diaphragm, and reinstalling the screws in the extra holes. This was just too easy! I was only charged $19 each for the old pumps compared to about $30 for a new AC 9797. While they are not quite genuine, they are of the correct configuration, and will keep my '53 and '54 drivable.

The whole search for a pump was brought about by a garage floor covered with gas after starting my '54. My original AC 4132 pump was shot! After replacing the pump with my new "find", I still had an old original which could be rebuilt and used again. The fuel diaphragm consists of several layers of treated cloth which is unaffected by gasoline and held together by two metal discs and the push-rod. The diaphragm eventually wears out. After numerous calls to local parts suppliers, I again ended up where I found the old pumps. Sure enough, on a shelf covered with an inch of dust, I found a rebuild kit. This was a AMPCO Products Kit #P-193 and included fuel and vacuum diaphragms, all check valves, oil seals, pivot pin and lever, and assorted springs and gaskets necessary to do the job. I will eventually disassemble the old pump (making notes for reassembly), have the three castings replated in cadmium, and reassemble using new parts. The old pump will be like new.

I would suggest that pumps and rebuild kits can be found a local suppliers, at swap meets (not Corvette swaps!), and there are even several firms that advertise in the car hobby magazines which offer rebuild kits for most all older Chevrolets. I have long since found out that when looking for old Corvette parts, using the word "Chevrolet" will get me more help, and probably a better price, than if I use the word "Corvette". Good hunting!

RESTORATION TIPS

By MARTIN BALL

In this issue I have included a few of the restoration tips received from some of the members, along with a few of my own. I hope that you will find them interesting.

First though, I received several comments concerning information that has appeared in past articles. Member Terry Harrison of Ohio wrote to say that after trying to order twice, his local Delco Dealer told him that the '55-'61 tach drive adapter #1930846 has been discontinued and is no longer available.

Also, Richard Ludwig of Indiana wrote me concerning a price change on the 1977 Corvette Parts Catalog we mentioned in the Fall '76 issue of the RESTORER. The price we were quoted was $10 per copy, but Richard ordered one and found that the price jumped to $12 as of Jan. 1, '77. These catalogs can still be ordered from GM by writing: General Motors Parts Division, Publication Processing Center, GM Photographic, 465 West Milwaukee, Detroit, MI 48202. They will send you a part's publication order form.

Now to the business at hand:

CLEANING AND RESTORING ALUMINUM

I recently used a product from the Permatex people called "Aluminum Jelly" on my tach drive parts and valve covers. This product is very good and so easy to use. Just brush it on, wait a while, and hose it off with water. It will work great on any aluminum part and is available at most hardware stores.

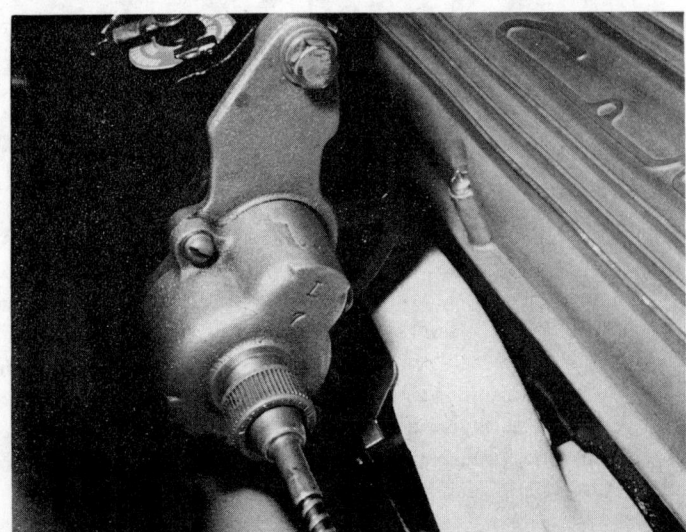

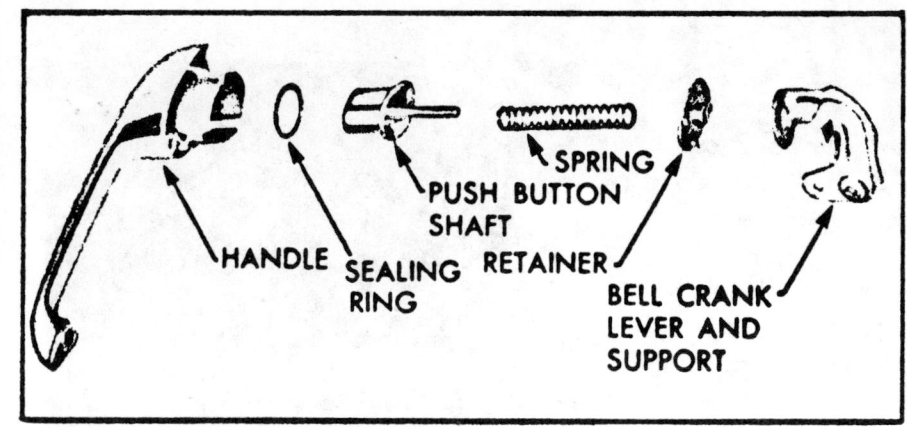 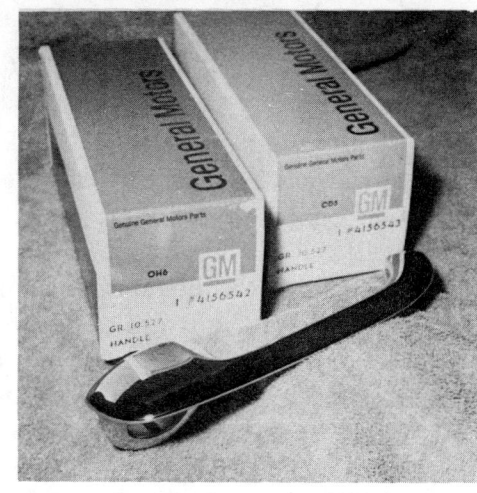

56-62 OUTSIDE DOOR HANDLES

These handles are still available from GM, order #4156542 and #4156543. It should be noted that the handles do not include the push button, spring, and various other parts. These will have to be used from your existing handles.

To remove and disassemble the door handle from the car, simply depress the retainer sufficiently to turn the bell crank lever and support one quarter turn, remove the bell crank lever and support, retainer, spring, pushbutton and shaft and sealing ring from handle. To install, simply reverse the procedure.

The following restoration tips were submitted by Rev. Michael Ernst of Bowler, Wisconsin. He writes:

I have a couple of things I've discovered that I've never seen in print, and thought maybe someone could use them.

First, on my '62, I had a couple of the seat inserts split (not the pleated ones) but the seats as a whole were excellent. It did not pay to buy all new seats, as they are fairly expensive. Also, new material next to my somewhat faded original seats didn't quite match right either.

While browsing through the local junk yard I found a '62 Impala convertible with red interior and the red top boot. The boot uses a large amount of good red vinyl material, weathered enough to match. This was just what I needed. The grain is identical, and I'm sure other years would match too.

Second, like most Corvettes, mine had door panel trim screws that pulled through the enlarged holes in the fiberglass. Reglassing would work for a little while, but opening and closing the door would pull them back through.

What I did to remedy this problem was to take a correct sized clip (pictured), commonly known as a "type A spring nut", that I got from my Chevrolet dealer, and glassed them into the door. I then drilled a tiny hole through the glass covering, and they have held the trim screws solid for a couple of years now.

56-57 HEADLAMP ASSEMBLY INTERCHANGE

Jay Price of Cadillac, Michigan submitted the following tip: Regarding 56-57 headlamps covered in Vol. 3, No. 1, Summer '76 RESTORER, it is not necessary to get "H-18" assemblies from wrecking yards, as it is still available from GMPD. Order #897161 headlamp assy., priced at $28.25 list. Its application is for the '55 to '57 Chevrolet trucks, Series 3000. It consists of a new bucket, new "T-3" lamp, new retainer and adjusters and wiring. The truck bezel can be discarded, the door mounting brackets replaced, and the wiring revised to adapt this part to the '56 and '57 Corvette.

53-62 REAR AXLE REBOUND STRAPS

These straps are still available from Chevrolet over the parts counter. The part number is #3774449 and come one to a box. The straps are precut and prepunched ready to install.

To remove the old straps, simply cut or drill out the rivets fastening the straps to the frame brackets. Remove the rebound strap loop plates and install new straps using quarter inch nuts and bolts or rivets.

These straps are very important as they restrict the bottom travel of the drive shaft, so as not to hit the "X" member.

RPO 276 WIDE BASE WHEEL OPTION (CONCLUSION)

"Yes, they did use small hubcaps!" In Vol. 3, No. 2, Fall '76 issue of the RESTORER I did mention that the '57-'62 Corvettes with the optional wide base wheels were factory equipped with the small passenger car style hub caps instead of the standard full wheel covers. This is due to the fact that the $5\frac{1}{2}$" rims are not equipped with the mounting lugs around the outer rim of the wheel to hold the full wheel covers. An added advantage was the added cooling effect around the rim.

Chevrolet did not design special caps for these wheels. All they did was use small passenger car hub caps. The '57, '58 and '59 Corvettes used the cooresponding year passenger car caps pictured. From 1960 through 1962 the 1960 passenger cap was used. You will note the 1959 and 1960-62 caps are almost identical. However, you will note from the closeup that the latter has two ridges added at the outside unlike the '59 cap which is smooth.

| 1957 Corvette & passenger | 1958 Corvette & passenger | 1959 Corvette & passenger | 1960-62 Corvette & 1960 passenger |

I want to thank all those members who have sent contributions to the article. If you have a tip that you would like to share, send it to; Martin Ball, 335 Aloha Dr., San Leandro, CA 94578, 415/352-1846.

TECH SESSION

With SAM FOLZ

Mr. George Pavlisko is the Technical Advisor to the Milestone Car Society. He also happens to be the "Super-Salesman" for the Clausen Company's line of products used in old car restoration.

When I heard George tout the merit of Leatherique at the MCS National at Carlisle in 1974, I hauled out my ready supply of skepticism and thought to myself, "Nothing could be that good."

I ran into George again at the 1975 MCS National at Dearborn. This time I personally cornered him and shot the tough questions. The problem foremost in my mind was whether I could possibly convert a nice, new, BLACK, Amco vinyl seat cover in my newly acquired MG-TD. I wanted to make it the original factory RED color so as to be able to use the good, but faded, original red on the side trim, such as the doors and wheel wells. George assured me that I could do this.

Still a little skeptical, but coming from a "What-have-I-got-to-lose-except-time-and-money" position, I forwarded a small piece of the original red vinyl from an unexposed area to Mr. Tyrus Peck at the Clausen Company and had him tint their standard red to match the exact MG color.

In short, I am most impressed with this product. It is totally unlike other "paint" type products on the market. It is not a plasticised lacquer, but rather appears to be a latex emulsion. It is water based, and tools (in my case only a nylon brush) are cleaned up with water. The coating has just the right sheen, dries quickly, has no odor, does not hide the original grain pattern, and is as flexible as the base material. The faded, but otherwise good original trim is now as fresh as new, and the formerly black seat appears to be the same color as the rest of the trim.

I see application for this product in early Corvette restoration. The '53-'55 models with their prominently exposed saddle-stitched panels pose a problem as the thread is always in a contrast color. But 1956 models all the way up to the latest jobs, whether in vinyl or real leather can be helped with careful application of this product, which has received the blessing of none less than the Rolls-Royce owner's club, and individual owners and restorers, including Richard Teague. I think those installing the recently manufactured dash pads in the '58-'62 models would be greatly helped in matching the new part to the rest of the interior.

Another Clausen product which George introduced me to is Rymplecloth. If you think a polishing cloth to rub out new lacquer or polish up a fresh wax job is just another rag, or that a cloth is a cloth is a cloth, you owe it to yourself to try Rymplecloth. A few bucks will get you a generous supply and, again, you'll be pleasantly surprised how good and different this simple product really is.

When so many products marketed today fail to live up to their promise, it's refreshing to find a couple that do. Thanks, George. Write: The Clausen Company, P. O. Box 126, Fords, New Jersey 08863

Again, with a sincere "Thank you" to Mr. Lynn Cullins of PPG Industries, we list below acrylic lacquer offsets to three original Corvette colors which were omitted from the previous inquiry:

Year	Color Name	Old Number	Acrylic Offset
1954-1957	Shoreline Beige	DAL 21054	DDL 23620
1954-1955	Autumn Bronze	DAL 21151	DDL 22819
1955	Woodland Green	DAL 41318	DDL 44413

Note that Shoreline was used on 1954 top irons and as a contrast color on 1956-1957 sidepanel depression, when specified, in place of body color on copper, green and red cars, as well as an interior trim color on 1955 Gypsy Red cars. Autumn Bronze may be the 1954 lower instrument panel color on Pennant Blue cars in 1954-55. Use caution here, as this has less metallic than the original.

Woodland Green is the contrast color used on the interior of 1955 Harvest Gold cars. Also note, as a point of interest, that the beige and bronze are also 1955 passenger car colors. The green is a 1953 passenger color.

ERRATA

With further comment on data supplied in previous articles, we can now point out that the double fan belt system described in CORVETTE NEWS, Vol. V, No. 3, and reproduced in our last issue was, in fact, factory-installed as a running change sometime after May '62 on 1962 model Corvettes with 340 HP and 360 HP engines.

IMPORTANT NOTE: 1962 CORVETTE WHEEL COLOR

As noted in the color chart from Chevrolet on the 1962 Corvette published in THE CORVETTE RESTORER, Vol. 2, No. 2, wheels were specified in body color. In the next issue we were notified that 1962 Corvette wheels should be black in color instead of body color. We now learn with authority that both prior entries are correct, but incomplete in explanation. The full story is as follows: Production figures have shown that 13,071 1962 Corvettes, or 90%, were equipped with optional white stripe tires at the factory. These cars, with white walls, had black wheels regardless of body color and had full wheel covers. Those remaining 10%, equipped with standard blackwall tires, had body-colored wheels per the chart, as did the cars with $5\frac{1}{2}$K wheels which used small hub caps.

I am most happy to try and answer your individual questions of Corvette restoration, but please include a self-addressed-stamped-envelope. Write: Sam Folz, 3824 Coventry Ave., Kalamazoo, Michigan 49007.

RESEARCH PROJECT 1956/7

With MICHAEL HUNT

A 1956 CORVETTE "COOP"

After 20 years of interest in the 1956/7 Corvettes, I recently experienced one of my most rewarding Corvette moments. Located inconspicuously on a Midwest dairy farm, I discovered a bonafide 1956 Corvette "coop" -- not "coupe", mind you, but "coop" as in "chicken coop."

Externally this dual-purpose chicken coop/tool shed looked like countless others, surrounded by chickens and geese and at least two ill-tempered farm dogs. But what rested inside may well be an intact surviving 1956 Corvette Sebring team car (see photo). If authentic, this is one of the four Corvettes seen in Karl Ludvigsen's CORVETTE, AMERICA'S STAR-SPANGLED SPORTS CAR book (pages 46-7), as they competed in the 1956 Sebring race. As the accompanying photos reveal, the car retains its distinctive side air scoops, which feed into the rear brake air ducting, and the Halibrand magnesium knock-off wheels.

The car has been in the current owner's hands since the early 1960's, a plus, since long-term ownership tends to inhibit alterations. He has made a few changes, though, painting the exterior red (the original white is still easily found upon close examination), reupholstered the seats, and installed Stewart-Warner gauges. But overall, it's relatively unmolested.

Another factor which indicated authenticity to me is the car's VIN#, which is extremely close to that of another identically equipped 1956 Corvette which I've been fortunate to survey. And both vehicles were purchased in the same area, close to the heart of Chevrolet-land.

When the feature car was decommissioned and sold through a major Midwest Corvette dealer, the original engine and transmission had been replaced with a complete 1958 driveline, including a 7014900R injector, and a T-10 4-speed, all of which it retains. This is not unusual, as all the 1956 Corvette "exotics" (SR-2's, Sebring cars, etc.) I've tracked down seem to have undergone early engine transplants. Competition is rough on powerplants. And by 1957, the 265 c.i. engine was already outdated.

Other interesting features are a 4-shock rear end (2 tube, 2 lever-action type), finned brake drums, and air scoops on the vented backing plates. The front scoops, however, are not the typical rubber "elephant ear" type equipped on 1957 and later RPO Corvettes. Instead they are metal, rather crude, and similar to the sheet metal rear scoops on a 1957 RPO car. The clutch pedal is the stiffest one I've ever encountered.

The owner stated that his car is a real performer, and had a respectable local reputation until family life called, and the Corvette went into storage some years ago. Incidentally, the owner is a strictly anonymous fellow, and is not a member or participant in any organized Corvette club or activity.

For an interesting diary-like look at Corvette team preparations for Sebring 1956, I would recommend reading Team Manager John Fitch's book ADVENTURE ON WHEELS, (G. P. Putnam's Sons, New York 1959), especially page 257. During a recent conversation, Mr. Fitch was kind enough to discuss his recollections on the 1956 race at Sebring and the vehicles used. But as far as this particular 1956 Corvette was concerned, he didn't feel prepared to attest to its authenticity. He said it sounded "good" though, especially the ivory-colored interior, a rarity on a white exterior 1956/7 Corvette.

My efforts to further document the car through Zora Arkus-Duntov, the Chevrolet Motor Division, and others, have accomplished little. So, for the present, I regard it as a "probable" 1956 Sebring team car. If any readers have information on similar 1956 Corvettes, I would appreciate hearing from you. Also a detailed 1956/7 Corvette inquiry sheet will be forwarded upon request to any 1956/7 Corvette owners wishing to cooperate with my ongoing research project. Write: Michael Hunt, 903 Swarthmore Ct., Madison, Wisconsin, 53705, ph. 608/233-9226.

CHEVROLET PRODUCES 500,000th CORVETTE

500,000th CORVETTE....gets an assist off the final assembly line at the G.M. Assembly Division plant in St. Louis from Chevrolet General Manager Robert D. Lund (at the wheel) and Plant Manager Ralph F. Hallquist. The milestone unit manufacturer's suggested retail price was $11,455.45.

St. Louis, March 15 -- Chevrolet's famed Corvette marked another milestone today in its saga as America's only authentic sports car.

The occasion was the production of the 500,000th Corvette at the GM Assembly Division plant here, which has been producing the popular fiberglass bodied sportster since it entered the Chevrolet line in 1953. The first 300 hand built models were assembled in Flint, Michigan.

Robert D. Lund, Chevrolet general manager and a General Motors vice president, said the "Corvette mystique" has grown well beyond the actual number of vehicles built and has been a key to the automaker's overall product image.

The milestone unit - a Classic White Stingray - came off the assembly line at the GM Assembly plant at 2:01 p.m. after final inspection. According to Lund, Corvette is virtually the patriarch of the Chevrolet car family. It is the oldest nameplate in the line except for the regular Chevrolet.

So went the events of March 15, 1977, a Tuesday, according to GM press release #8158 from the Public Relations Department.

While the press release mentions that the unit was built on the 15th, it should be noted for history's sake the the car was actually built on March 11th, a Friday, then after a clean-up and the 500,000th lettering painted on the windshield, the car was run down the line for the ceremony on the 15th.

The serial number of the car is 1Z37X7S426583, Classic White with red trim, equipped with L-82, A/C, tilt/telescopic wheel, TH trans., power windows, AM/FM stereo tape system, heavy duty battery, rear defogger, speed control, color-keyed mats, aluminum wheels, sport mirrors, gymkhana suspension, luggage carrier, convenience group and white lettered tires. The car was delivered to Bernie Hout Chevrolet in Mt. Clemens, Michigan where a buyer took possession.

Your editor wishes to give a sincere thank you to Fred Rinke of Ed Rinke Chevrolet in Detroit for supplying the magazine and membership with the information on the 500,000th Corvette.

I-80, the Salt Flats at 6 AM.

MICHIGAN TO CALIFORNIA IN A 1954 CORVETTE

By Joe and Gertrude Chess

Way back in January '76 we decided to take the '54 to California for the NCRS Meet last July. In preparation, the brakes were reconditioned, hoses and belt replaced, the springs replaced in the seats, and generally everything checked out and serviced that might cause a problem along the way. You see, when your '54 has over 400,000 miles on it, you know it's dependable, but not always sure!

We started out after work on June 30th in the rain and naturally we had lots of towels. With a '54 you have to take lots of towels to soak up all the water that pours in around and over the windshield and top. Benton Harbor, Michigan was the first night's stop, close enough to Chicago to go around early in the morning to avoid heavy traffic. Our CB radio came in handy for this.

The next day it was sunshine through the farmlands of Iowa. We stopped for gasoline at West Branch, the hometown of Herbert Hoover. On the CB we heard, "Breaker 1-9 for blue sports car, what kind of car is it, an old T-bird?" Shortly after that it was rain again and down the road at a gas station, while wringing out the towels a man said, "thought you were from California with a sports car, how did you keep it from rusting in Michigan?"

Across the Missouri River into Nebraska it was still raining. The rolling plains seemed to never end. We rapped with truckers on the CB that had memories of past Corvettes and some that still owned them. One asked where he could get a '54 and another broke in and said "that would take a lot of green stamps." A trucker called "Dickey Bird" heading for "Moo Town", (like in cows) or Greeley, Colorado, told us about the Smokey on our tail and a '58 Corvette he owns. At lunch an older couple were looking the car over and the man said "may as well enjoy a car like that while you're young."

At Lincoln, Nebraska, we stopped in to see John and Patty Amgwert, John is the RESTORER editor. They took us to a nice Italian restaurant for dinner and had a very enjoyable evening.

More rain the next day before Greeley, but when we wrung the towels out there, they would stay dry for the remainder of our three week trip. What a relief!

Route 34 through the Rocky Mountain National Park with the top down--what a beautiful way to see the magnificient mountain scenery.

Near Kremmling, Colorado the car started to sound like the motor was falling apart. There was a Chevrolet garage in town so we got a motel and Joe took the valve covers off and found a broken rocker arm. He was able to fix it in about 20 minutes with $6.13 worth of parts from the Chevrolet garage. Fritz Jameson, owner of the garage took us out back and showed us a nice blue '59 Corvette he is restoring.

Kremmling (population 750) was a stopping place for bi-centennial bicyclists and over 200 had stopped there. Cruising along in the '54 looked like real luxury in comparison. While working on the car a girl hiker came up and asked about the car. She mentioned that her father had several like it, and of all things, she was Mary Jo Rohner, daughter of Mr. and Mrs. John Rohner, NCRS members from Oshkosh, Wisconsin.

Kremmling, Colorado, $6.13 repair.

Devil's Tower in Wyoming.

On July 4th, heading west, five Corvettes from a Denver club on their way to the Western States convention in Salt Lake City caught up with us and started conversing on the CB's. We convoyed with them to Steamboat Springs where we all pulled off into a vacant gas station for a confab. Three more Corvettes from Wichita, Kansas caught up and stopped also. There was a nice '61 in the group. We passed out membership forms so hope some join us in NCRS. "Leadfoot" was in the lead so we dropped out of the convoy to sight-see at a slower pace.

It was very hot when we got to Salt Lake so we crossed the Salt Flats early in the morning. We got as far as Winnemucca, Nevada, and jumped into the pool to cool off.

Next day was a short run into Reno where we met Claude and Judy Mosely, NCRS members from Rochester, Minnesota, at Harrah's Car Collection. We had dinner together at Harrah's and tried our luck at the slot machines. It was a real fun evening.

We arrived for the meet at the Claremont in Berkeley the next day. It was everything the ad said; beautiful setting, large swimming pool, six tennis courts, and flowers everywhere. The hotel staff treated us very nice and what a beautiful view of San Francisco at night. We took the 5 hour tour with 40 other members and found a very exciting city and beautiful bay area. While we were at the meet, two local television stations stopped by and shot some film. We saw President Gary Mortimer on channel 6, and Joe was interviewed on channel 5.

After the meet we headed north through the redwoods. What a beautiful day's ride. There were so many giant trees that some are thousands of years old. At Fortuna the next night the motel owner said, "I saw you and your car on TV last night."

We headed on through the highest, twistiest mountain roads of the whole trip the next day in northern California and stopped in Redding to see Joe's cousin who has a ranch with walnut groves located on the Sacramento River. Then on to the high desert country of southeast Oregon. We met Tim Surgeon at Hines, Oregon, who has a '61 Corvette and he took a membership form. The next day we were in Boise, Idaho where we stopped to see Gertrude's sisters.

We headed east again through the Tetons and Yellowstone in Wyoming. Everywhere we stopped there was a group around the ole '54 eyeing the car as much as the scenery. At Yellowstone we heard on the CB, "Wow, look along side you, I don't believe I saw that. Was that a '53?" At Devils Tower in Wyoming there was a group of about 10 around the car asking questions. In Cody, Wyoming we created as much interest as the old museum they have. The paintings and statues by Russell and Remington are really fabulous there.

In Deadwood, South Dakota, we ran into a couple from our home town and had a cup of coffee with them before touring the Black Hills and Mt. Rushmore. Then on through the badlands and plains to Hawardin, Iowa where we spent the night with friends. At Dirk's Chevrolet in Dayton, Iowa we gave a salesman a membership form as he has a '58.

Now we were on the last part of our journey and anxious to get home. On Interstate 80 a trucker said, "See that '54 Corvette?" and the other trucker replied, "Ya, I won't scratch it."

All in all the whole trip was most enjoyable. It's kind of nice cruising along in a '54 with radial tires and 283 engine with overdrive. We arrived home having traveled over 6000 miles and averaged 22.3 miles per gallon of gasoline. Some day we plan on restoring the car back to original with the 6-cylinder engine (we still have it!), but for now, we really enjoy driving our '54!

Northern California Redwood country.

RESEARCH PROJECT 1956/7

WITH MIKE HUNT

1957 AND 1958 CORVETTE PRODUCTION

For the statisticians among us, in this issue Research Project 1956/7 looks at some numbers. Thanks to the recent acquisition of additional Chevrolet Motor Division documentation, accurate drive-train percentage figures are now available for 1957 and, surprisingly, for 1958.

First, a look at the 1957 fuel injection figures, a favorite sub-category of many 1957 Corvette enthusiasts. Readers may recall a related essay by Editor John Amgwert, entitled "Fuel Injection Production Figures" (Vol. 1, No. 3, pp. 7-9). In that essay, John referred to documentation which I had earlier received from a Chevrolet source, showing a total of 1040 fuel injected 1957 Corvettes. This "1040" units figure should be kept in mind, since numerous magazine articles, in follow-the-leader fashion, have cited an apparently undocumented "240" units total for the 1957 FI Corvette. Since the "1040" units figure supplied by Chevrolet remained consistent with other 1957 FI data I had obtained from additional sources, both inside and outside of Chevrolet, I have continued to regard it as probably correct.

For the readers who do not have access to Vol. 1, No. 3, the "1040 units" breakdown was as follows:

```
         A    182 units
         B    713 units
         C    102 units
         D     43 units
             1040 units (16.41% or '57 run)
```

Until very recently I had not been certain as to the exact definition of the four A-D catagories. However I have been fortunate to obtain additional documentation from a Chevrolet source, which now makes this possible. (Editor's note: At the time we originally published these A-D figures, we thought they referred to the four different injection units and presented them as such; we were wrong!) The following table shows quantity figures for the various horsepower and drivetrain combinations used with the RPO579 fuel injection option. It is based on the total model run of 6339 units.

1957 CORVETTE FUEL INJECTION FIGURES

	Horsepower	Transmission	Quantity	% of 6339 total
A	250hp (air clnr.)	3 & 4 speed	182	2.87%
B	283hp (air clnr.)	3 & 4 speed	713	11.25%
C	250hp (air clnr.)	Powerglide	102	1.61%
D	283hp (air box)	3 & 4 speed	43	.68%
	TOTAL		1040	16.41%

At this point I believe the "240 units" figure has been adequately discredited: MAY IT REST IN PEACE!!!

Note especially the total of "43 units" for the 1957 "EN" engine suffix "cold air box" (or "air intake" as Chevrolet referred to it) cars. Thanks to the subcontractor who supplied Chevrolet with the RPO 684 package components, we knew the correct total was something less than 50 units. This confirmation from Chevrolet validates the scarcity of these ducting-under-the-doors vehicles.

For a look at the overall 1957 Corvette drivetrain figures, refer to the following table. I should qualify that with an "almost overall," since this data, compiled during August 1957, represents 6136 of the total 6339 units produced. With 96.8% of the 1957 Corvettes thus represented, the table is sufficiently accurate for most needs.

Finally, we look at the 1958 Corvette production total broken by engine horsepower rating. The 1958 data is not really relevant to my research efforts, but I had the information, and thought the 1958 enthusiasts would find it of interest.

If any readers have comments or questions on the preceding, please contact me, Michael Hunt, 903 Swarthmore Ct., Madison, WI 53705, phone 608/233-9226. Be sure to enclose a self-addressed-stamped-envelope if a reply is desired. A 1956/7 Inquiry Sheet will be furnished upon request. I would especially appreciate hearing from either original owners, or owners of 1956/7's which retain the original drivetrains.

1957 CORVETTE, AUG. 1957, 6136 OF 6339 UNITS (96.79%) ASSEMBLED

Horsepower Rating	Camshaft	Fuel System	Units Produced	Percentage of total	Projected total at final assy.
220	Regular	Single 4bbl.	1528	24.90%	1578
245	Regular	Dual 4bbl.	2010	32.76%	2076
270	Hi-Lift	Dual 4bbl.	1566	25.52%	1618
250	Regular	Fuel Injection	283	4.61%	292
283	Hi-Lift	Fuel Injection	749	12.21%	774
		TOTAL	6136	100.00%	6339

1958 CORVETTE, END OF MODEL RUN, 9168 UNITS

Horsepower Rating	Camshaft	Fuel System	Units Produced	Percentage of total
230	Regular	Single 4bbl.	4243	46.28%
245	Regular	Dual 4bbl.	2436	26.57%
270	Hi-Lift	Dual 4bbl.	978	10.67%
250	Regular	Fuel Injected	504	5.50%
290	Hi-Lift	Fuel Injected	1007	10.98%
		TOTAL	9168	100.00%

EARLY CORVETTE JACKS

Story and Photos By
John Amgwert and Rev. Michael Ernst

The 1953-61 jack is on the left, the 1962 is on the right. Note that the '62 jack is symmetrical with the base welded on.

From 1953 through 1962, Chevrolet specified only two jacks for use in the Corvette. In this article, we will attempt to describe the differences in those jacks and their application.

The first design jack was #3706350 and was specified in the Factory Assembly Instruction Manual (AIM) and part's books for 1953 through 1961 Corvettes. All the major pieces of this jack are cast with the exception of the stamped lift saddle and the threaded shaft.

The base contains the casting number SJ 4653 for easy identification.

The lifting handle used with this jack is #3706351 whose tang is shaped something like a "spoon". This handle can be modified from one used in numerous Chevrolet trucks. The handle modifications would consist of removing a small section of the rod, rewelding it back together, and shaping the handle crank to match the Corvette shape.

The second design jack, and to our knowledge, used only in the 1962 model, is #3813730. This jack is basically the same as the earlier version but there are distinct differences. The base is no longer cast, but rather a stamped piece, which is welded to a lifting saddle, which now appears on both the top and bottom of the 1962 jack. If this base were missing, you would not be able to distinguish top from bottom, making the jack symmetrical. The base shows an "A" stamping which is the manufacturer's identification.

Other differences should be noted in the threaded lifting mechanism. The threads in the '62 jack resemble those of a Corvair jack as they are very coarse compared to the earlier jack. The '62 jack would lift the car with considerably less turns, but with far more effort than the early jack with fine threads.

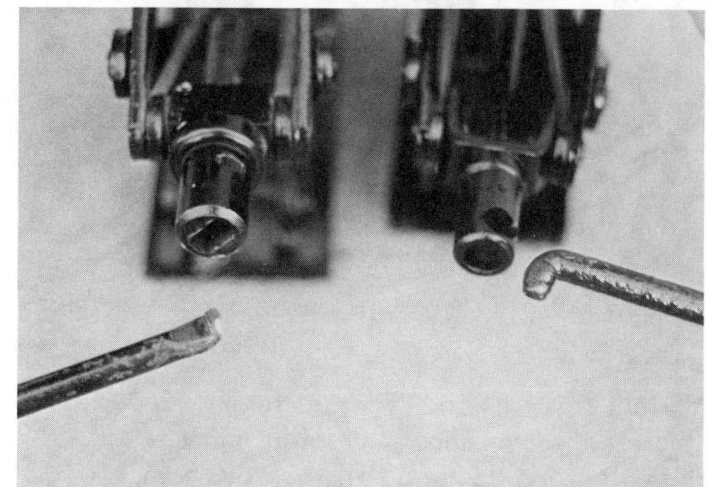

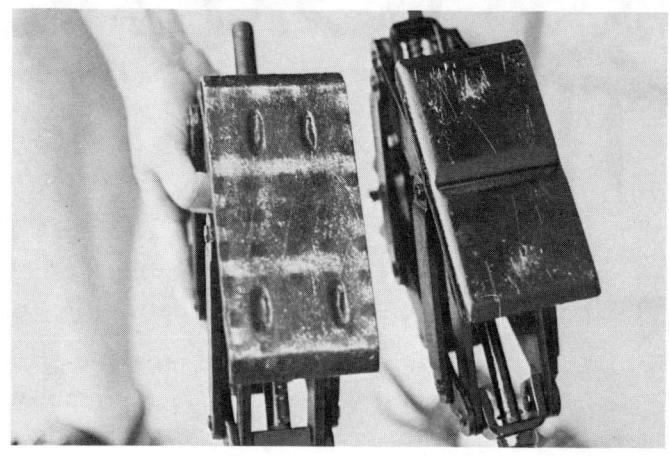

Photo shows the different appearance of the bases. 1953-61 (left), 1962 (right).

The handle used in 1962, #3815940, is different from the early handle in that the tang is now a 90° bend "hook" affair.

Both jacks were manufactured for Chevrolet by AUSCO (Auto Specialties Company) in St. Joseph, Michigan (thus the "A" stamping). Sam Folz contacted AUSCO several years ago regarding the first design jack and they said the jack was made for Corvette only and the tooling was no longer available. They did, however, manufacture a jack which resembles the original Corvette jack.

Following the NCRS Lancaster Meet, your Editor and Noland Adams visited Detroit and Fred Rinke showed us a jack he has that is identical to the '53-'61 Corvette item in every way including the SJ 4653 casting number. However, this jack was painted red (Corvette jacks were black) and it had a NAPA Auto Parts label. The NAPA part number was not readable on the label but in checking with a NAPA dealer, they no longer service a jack like this. A stroke of luck might find one on a dusty shelf in some NAPA store though.

The second design jack appears on numerous 1962 Corvettes beginning as early as the 311th unit built. It is possible that some 1961 models used it, but the part's books and the AIM for 1961 does not indicate this.

These are the only two jacks that we are aware of for the early Corvette. However, at the sake of confusing everyone, including us, two identical jacks out of two seperate 1962 models at the NCRS Lancaster Meet were different from the 1962 jack pictured here. These two examples sported a different lifting saddle and base. Your Editor, for some unknown reason, did not get a picture of this jack, so... Al Pasquine, if you're listening, we need some detail pictures of the jack in your '62. Any further comments or information from members will be most appreciated.

The stamped base is welded to the 1962 jack. Note the lifting saddle is also on the bottom.

Fine threaded shaft is '53-'61, while coarse thread and different end assembly in 1962.

RESTORATION TIPS

WITH MARTIN BALL

Included in this issue is a letter that I received from Ted Boller, Tyndall Air Force Base, Florida. Regarding the piece on Corvette side trim in Vol. Three, #2 of the Restorer, he writes:

"I have ordered and received all the correct side trim and "T" bolts for my 1960 Corvette from GMPD. My problem is that on the rear upper and lower portion of the front fender, the holes are much smaller and do not go all the way through due to the door jamb and body constructions. These holes (one upper and two lower) must take a special clip and I can't find out what they are."

Thanks for your letter, Ted! The front end moldings diagram for the Corvette Service Guide ST-12 manual shows the use of snap retainers, three on each side. These are screwed into the body and then the trim is snapped over them. We have reproduced that section of the diagram here that shows the retainer and its application. These retainers are listed in the 1977 Corvette part's book in Group 8.133, number 3730268.

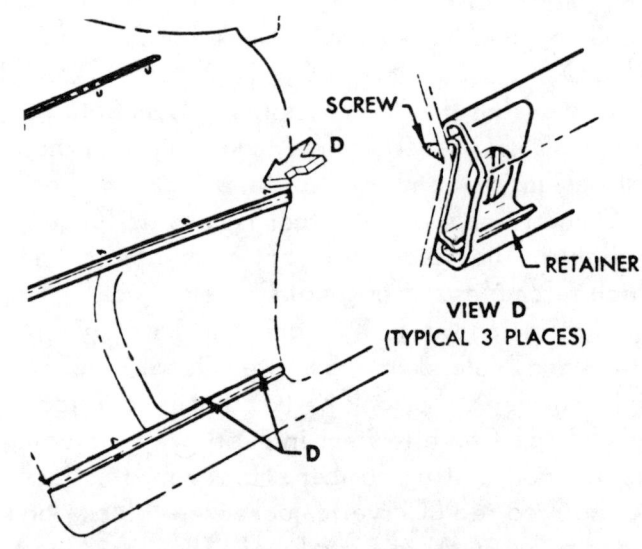

REMOVING RUST!!!

In the last issue, I reported on a product from the Permatex people called Aluminum Jelly. They also have a product called Naval Jelly for rusted metal.

Wilson Swilley of Richmond, California used it on his '63 exhaust manifolds and the finned brake drums on his RPO brake option car with great success. After applying the jelly he went over the parts with a wire brush and they came out like new.

STRIPPED DOOR PANEL SCREWS --- follow-up from last issue.

The following suggestion was sent in by Bill Neilsen of Needham, Mass. Bill found that by fiberglassing pieces of tin into the door, instead of the "spring nut" as suggested in the last issue, then drilling a hole to fit his door panel, he could control perfect alignment and not depend on the hold in a spring nut.

TOOL TIP

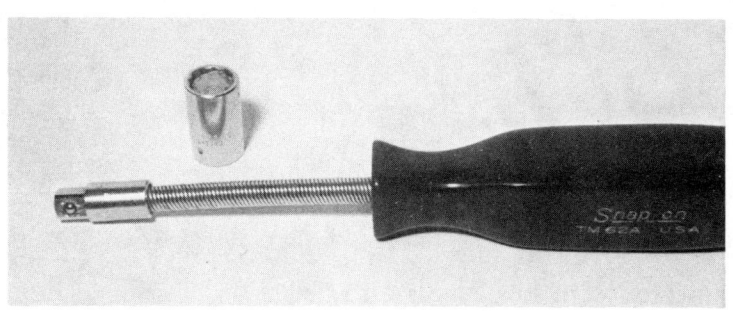

I found that by using a 1/4" drive flex spinner with a small amount of clay in the socket to hold the nut, you can replace and remove the small nuts under the dash, and in those hard to reach places on your Corvette.

57-61 EXHAUST CROSSOVER PIPES AVAILABLE!!!

Submitted by Gary Pronesti, Syracuse, New York. He writes: "I have been able to buy the 57-61 style crossover pipes at my local NAPA Parts Dealer. The list price is under $5 each. The part numbers are 41109 and 41110. The application for these pipes is not listed for Corvette, but rather 1957 Chevrolet passenger car with dual exhausts." Way to go, Gary!!

1958-1962 CORVETTE CLOCK INTERCHANGE

Rev. Mike Ernst of Bowler, Wisconsin wants to pass on that this electric Corvette clock is the same one used in the 1955 and 1956 Chevrolet passenger cars. He recently picked up several in a junk yard for about $1 each.

$5\frac{1}{2}$" x 15" WIDE BASE WHEEL INTERCHANGE

Our Editor, John Amgwert reports that the 1957-1962 $5\frac{1}{2}$K x 15" wide base wheel that we have mentioned in the past several issues was also used on another car. As you recall, #3838080 wheel, which is currently serviced by GMPD for the early Corvette application, is actually the standard wheel used on Corvettes beginning in 1963 and is detectable from the original wide wheel supplied with RPO 276. The number of the original '57-'62 wheel is #3748348 and was also used, or at least specified, for the 1962 Chevrolet Police Car, 2nd design. No earlier police models used it according to the parts books back then. Now... where do you find a 1962 Chevrolet Police car?

LOMBARD STREET LIVES!!!

I would like to report that I am now in the process of completely stripping and repainting my 1957 model (back cover, Vol. 3, #2 of the Restorer). It will be painted the original color (Inca Silver) found under the windshield frame. There we be a progress report in the next issue.

I appreciate your contributions and comments to this article. If you have a tip that worked for you during your restoration (53-67) or any of those little part's tips, write them down and send it in so that I may include it in future issues. It most surely will help another member with the same problem. Contact: Martin Ball, 335 Aloha Drive, San Leandro, CA 94578, ph. 415/352-1846.

RESEARCH PROJECT 1956/7

WITH MIKE HUNT

In conjunction with last issue's essay on drivetrain quantities and percentages, in this issue we shall examine the various other options and accessories for the total 1957 Corvette model run. For many years, fellow 1957 Corvette owners and enthusiasts have speculated over exactly how many of the various options were produced. The following table is based on an assortment of Chevrolet Motor Division documentation, including the "Check List and Index, 1957 Model and Option Price List" (10/15/56 - Rev. 10/29/56 - Rev. 4/1/57).

As noted at the bottom of the table, most of the 1957 figures were compiled at the end of the total 6339-unit model run. Those items preceded by an asterisk (*), however, reflect figures compiled during late August 1957, with only 6136 units assembled. At the end of August 1957, some 6229 1957 Corvettes had been assembled; the remaining 110 vehicles were assembled during September 1957.

Since I have never seen a single table containing FOA/RPO #'s, dealer's and recommended list prices, and quantity figures for the 1957 Corvette, I believe that this is the first time such a table has been published. Many thanks to Chevrolet Motor Division sources and cooperative NCRS members, without whose assistance this would not have been possible. Any comments or questions may be directed to Michael Hunt, 903 Swarthmore Ct., Madison, Wisconsin, 53705 (608/233-9226). Please enclose a SASE if you desire a reply.

Footnotes for chart:	F.O.A. means Factory Optional Accessory
	R.P.O. means Regular Production Option
	FOA/RPO # preceded by * indicates data after 6136 vehicles (Aug. 1957)
	FOA/RPO # not preceded by *; data after 6339 vehicles (Sept. 1957) total production.

1957 CONFIGURATION STATISTICS

F.O.A.	R.P.O.	DESCRIPTION	DEALER'S PRICE	RECOMM. LIST $$	QUANTITY	% OF TOTAL
		Model 2934 Corvette	2414.00	3176.32	6339	100.0
101		Heater (not available with RPO 684)	83.60	110.00	5375	84.8
102		Radio * w/Carb'd Engine * w/FI Engine	140.60	185.00	3626 2930 582	57.2 47.8 9.5
107		Park Brake Alarm	3.80	5.00	1870	29.5
108		Courtesy Lights	6.08	8.00	2491	39.3
109		Windshield Washers	8.36	11.00	2555	40.3
	276	15" x 5.5" Wheels	10.64	14.00	51	0.8
	290	6.70 x 15 Whitewalls	UNK	UNK	5020	79.2
	313	Powerglide Trans.	133.00	175.00	1395	22.0
	*419	Aux. Hardtop: with Softtop without Softtop	152.00 N/A	200.00 N/A	2414 1526	39.3 24.9
	426	Electric Windows	41.80	55.00	380	6.0
	*470 *470E *470F	Softtop, Black Softtop, White Softtop, Beige	N/A N/A N/A	N/A N/A N/A	1125 2386 1099	18.3 38.9 17.9
	473	Power Top	98.80	130.00	1338	21.1
	*677 *678 *679	Positraction (3.70) Positraction (4.11) Positraction (4.56) with 3-Speed with 4-Speed	34.20 34.20 34.20 34.20	45.00 45.00 45.00 45.00	311 790 22 48	5.1 12.9 0.4 0.8
	677/8/9	Positraction	34.20	45.00	1236	19.5
	684	H. D. Brakes & Sus. Fuel Injected (283) Carbureted (270)	551.00	725.00	51 43 8	0.8 0.7 0.1
	685	Close Ratio 4-Speed	UNK	188.30	666	10.5
	N/A	3-Speed (Std.)	N/A	N/A	4278	67.5

RPO 684 Ducting On 1957 Corvettes

By FREDRICK THOMPSON

Photos by Ted Cash and John Amgwert

If, as advertised in the May, 1957 issue of Road & Track Magazine (see back cover), the 1957 Corvette was a "Tiger in a Tuxedo!", a striped one was truly uncommon unless it was among the equipe whose Polo White bodies with blue markings were sponsored by Chevrolet.

Optional equipment brochures detailed the half-dozen elements comprising the RPO 684 chassis selection, available only with the 270 or 283 horsepower engines. However, few in the litter as only 51 cars were so-equipped, with the total competition package of special engine with racing camshaft and mechanical lifters, Positraction rear axle, 15 x 5.5K wheels, standard three speed, later, optional four speed close ratio Syncro-Mesh transmission and heavy-duty brakes and suspension with quick steering. All, compulsory components needed to transmute the standard production Corvette into a full-bore predator.

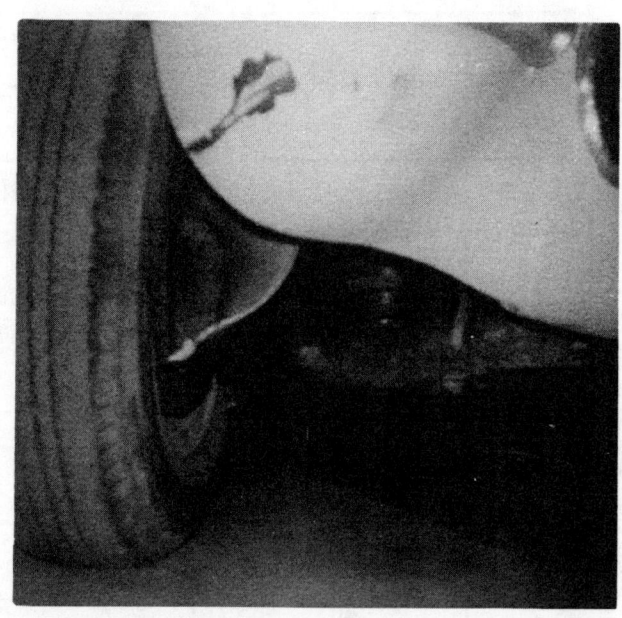

Note scoop attached to front backing plate. Scoops were shipped in trunk and were owner installed.

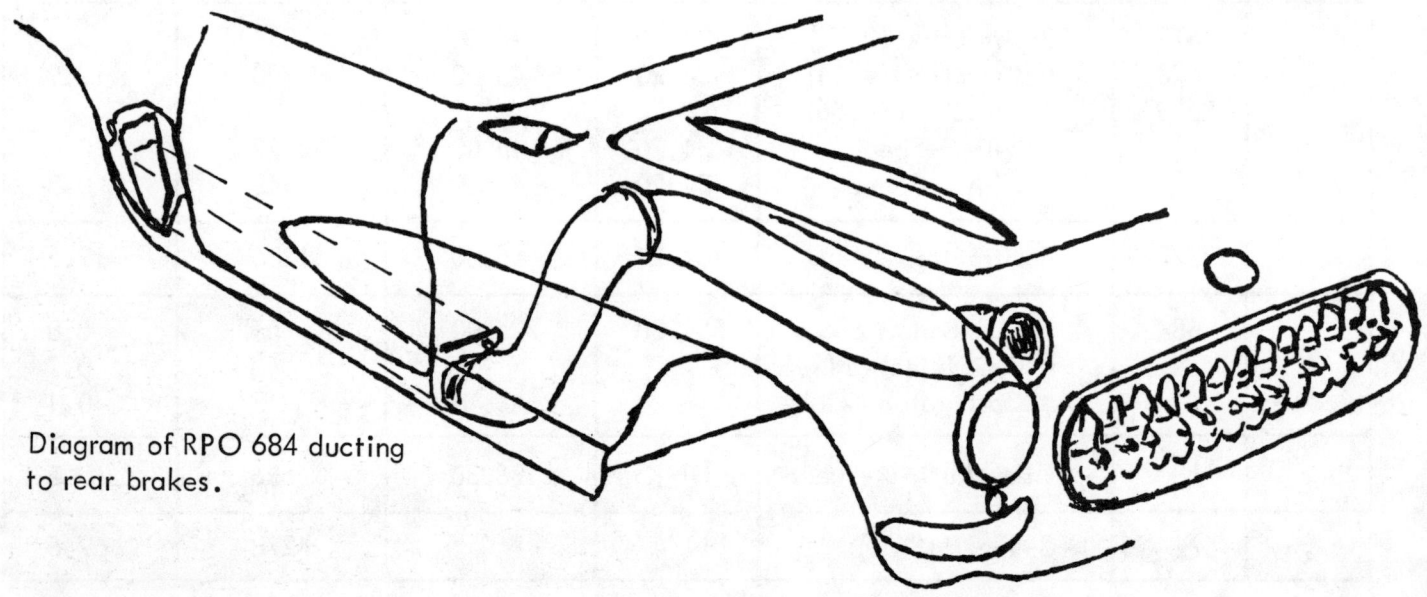

Diagram of RPO 684 ducting to rear brakes.

New, to the heavy-duty suspension package, earlier referred to as RPO 581, was an air ducting arrangement to assist in cooling the Cerametalix brakes. Utilization of air ducts and the rocker panels, as shown in the drawing, represented a practical application of knowledge gained from earlier competition.

For the dual-quad cars, the task was accomplished by trapping air on each side of the radiator and channeling its flow through heater type tubing. After the tubing passed through the engine compartment via an outlet in the inner fender panels, it was connected to a fiberglass air duct flange fastened to the front of the rocker panel. The air flow exited the rocker panel through another, larger, fiberglass duct assembly supported by a baffle and bolted to the underbody. The rear duct assembly had an esse shape design to direct the air flow into metal scoops which the owner could attach to the

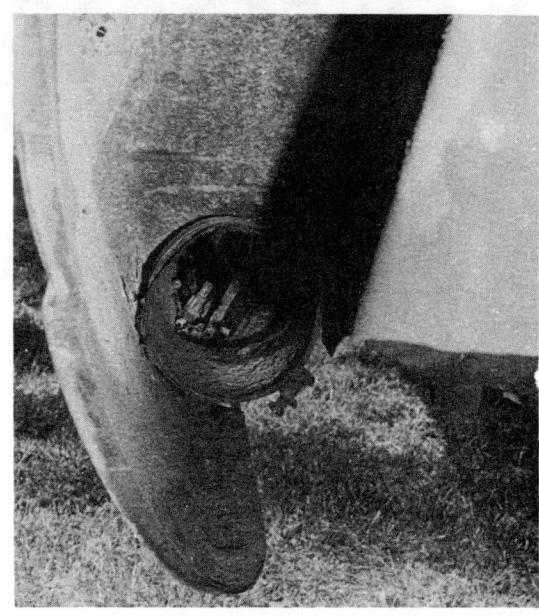

Duct opening at rocker panel.

screened brake backing plates on the rear wheel assembly.

The Corvette Service Operations Chassis Manual of 1957 contains information and several photos of the brake cooling system on a 1957 model. The RPO 684 option lasted at least partially through the 1959 model with its exotic ducting which varied from that used in 1957. During the 1959 model this ducting was eliminated but the vented brakes remained along with the added suspension items. The basic option continued through the 1962 model but was recoded in 1960 as RPO 687.

Whatever added information or insights a reader can supply regarding the RPO 684 option and its significant ducting changes, certainly will be appreciated and can be directed to my attention at: Union Bank Trust Division, P. O. Box 2193-Terminal Annex, Los Angeles, Cal. 90051.

At left is pictured rear duct outlet. Above shows fast-steering adaptor. Below shows opening in inner fender.

RESTORATION TIPS

WITH MARTIN BALL

Before we get into this issues restoration tips, I would like to include a short progress report on my project 1957 Corvette. I purchased the car in the Summer of 1969, it was a typical California car (modified). All the chrome trim had been removed, there were no front fender scoops, it had a black interior and a nice yellow ENAMEL paint job.

It was at that time that I proceeded to order everything I could to make it look like a 1957 Corvette again. By 1972 the car was 50% complete and shown for the first time at a Vintage Chevrolet Club car show. From 1972 to 1977 that yellow 1957 Corvette was getting to be a familiar sight at all the local car shows, including the NCRS California Meet last year. With help from Noland Adams and Mike Hunt on research, I started the body and paint project in July 1977.

I proceeded to strip the car of paint, reinstalling the once removed scoops, and will paint it with the original Acrylic Lacquer; Inca Silver and Imperial Ivory.

FENDER SCOOP REPLACEMENT 1956-1957

After the paint was stripped off of the front fenders, I could see the outline where the original scoops had been cut out. Using a saber saw I cut out the fiberglas patch filling the hole. Then I placed the scoop over the opening and marked it from underneath with a marking pen. To get the proper location, I took a set of measurements off of another 1957 model.

The excess fiberglas was trimmed off of the scoops with a saber saw (I had to acquire the new scoops). After sanding a groove around the scoop openings I glassed them in with a mixture of resin and chopped glass fibers, applied with a brush to the top and bottom. I finished the top with a mixture of resin and milled fibers mixed into a paste, then sanded with 80 grit paper, then 220 grit and then primed the surface.

I will include another report in the next issue. But now for this issues tips:

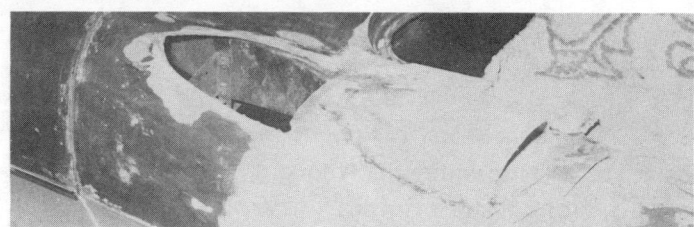
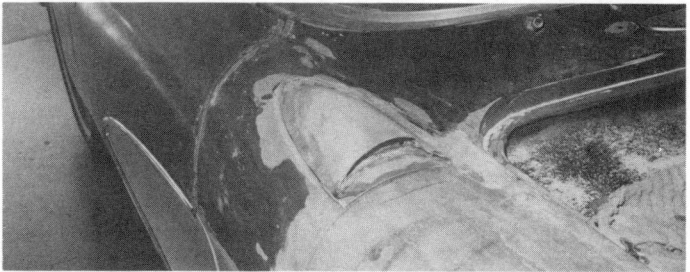

FLATTENING IMRON

Many folks have inquired about the use of Du Pont's Imron for finishing a chassis. The black available in the Imron line is a very "glossy" black, and under NCRS Judging rules, would be considered too glossy to be an acceptable finish. Al Butlin of Warren, Michigan contacted the Du Pont Factory following a chassis paint discussion at the NCRS Lancaster, Pennsylvania Meet, asking them about a recommended "flattener" to reduce the super gloss in Imron Black. The Du Pont factory people were a bit puzzled as it seems no one has ever inquired about the possibility of flattening this product. They informed Al that they would have to get back with him after they checked with their lab people. The following day, Al was informed that Du Pont 903-S Flattener mixed 10 to 20% with Jet Black Imron should give the desired finish. Al used a mix of 16% and was very happy with the resultant semi-gloss finish and he has the durability of this polyurethane enamel on his 1954 frame.

1953-1955 DOOR HINGE RESTORATION

After removing the doors and hinges, use a hydralic press to remove the pins to avoid damage to the hinge.

The parts you will need are four #9715083 hinge pins, and eight #4110660 brass bushings available from Chevrolet. The new brass bushings can be installed in the center hinge section with a vise, no reaming is necessary. You will find that the lip of the new bushing is thicker than the original nylon bushing which were prone to wear.

The other section of the hinge will probably be scored and worn from wear contact with the old bushing. Use a small file and dress the worn part of the hinge section enough so that the hinge section with the bushings installed will fit snugly when reassembled. The hinge, once properly repaired, should not pivot freely in your hand. Once on the car, the weight and leverage of the door will allow the door to swing easily but not sag.

1955-1957 ACCELERATOR PEDAL

I came across this pedal replacement at a local swap meet and thought I would pass it along. The original Chevrolet part number is #3711379 and the replacement I found is manufactured by Anchor Industries of Cleveland, Ohio under the name of Doan Replacement Parts. The Doan part number is #3310 and may be available at large auto supply houses that carry Doan Products.

I should also mention that the Doan catalog also lists a replacement accelerator pedal for the 1958-1962 Corvettes. This pedal (GM #3820328) comes under Doan number #3319.

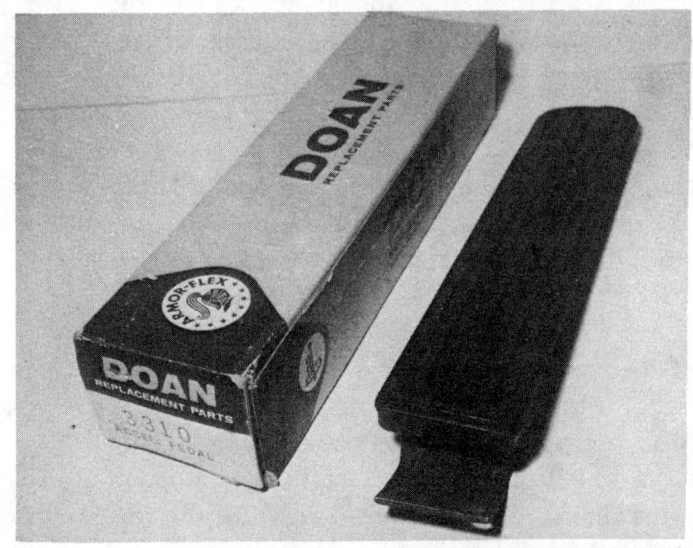

ROUNDED EDGE PARKING LAMPS FOR 1953-1957

Submitted by Kenn Carlson, Rapid City, South Dakota. He writes:

" After scouring the junk yards for '47-'50 G.M.C. pickups, '47, '48, and early '50 Cadillacs, I finally gave up and paid a premium price for some rounded edge chrome bezels for my 1955 Corvette parking lamps.

Last week I could not believe my eyes when I found the identical part on the front park light of an Old Hillman. The lens was different and the screws were not the hollow type, but the bezel was identical. I don't know what year it was, but the Hillman had single headlights and a checkered pattern grill."

As Ken points out, that early bezel must have gotten around. I should point out that the square edged bezel as pictured on the right is believed to only be correct beginning with the 1958 Corvette, however, some of the very later 1957 models also appeared with it.

1953-1955 SIX CYLINDER GAS PEDAL

While we were just on the subject of gas pedals, John Amgwert wanted to mention that the six cylinder gas pedal with bracket, Chevrolet part #3658481, was also used on 1940 through 1948 Chevrolet passenger cars.

If you have a restoration project that you would like to share with other members, or something of interest pertaining to the restoration of you Corvette (1953-1967) write it down and send it to me so that I may include it in a future issue. Send your restoration tips to:

Martin Ball
335 Aloha Drive
San Leandro, California 94578
415/352-1846

Sting Ray Fun Quiz

The NCRS wishes to thank members Paul Burrill and John E. Hamilton of Wisconsin for putting together this Sting Ray Fun Quiz. Test your knowledge of the 1963-1967 Corvettes, and we will publish the answers in the next issue.

1. What was the first year for the emergency brake lever to be located between the seats?
2. What was the first year for a telescoping steering wheel?
3. What are three differences between the early and late 1963?
4. What year coupes had vent grilles behind the side windows in the roof?
5. What years did the air cleaners use "snouts"?
6. Did all years have a passenger grab bar as part of the dash pad?
7. How many front fender side vents did the 1963-1967's have?
8. What year had the back-up lights above the rear license plate?
9. What years were the side mounted exhaust available?
10. What was the difference between the standard exhaust and the off road system offered?
11. What year were leather seats first offered and in what colors?
12. What years were knock-off wheels available?
13. What was the last year for Fuel Injection?
14. How many different types of grilles were used in the 1963-1967's?
15. Did late 1963's come without the split in the rear window?
16. What was the year for the fake grilles on the hood?
17. What was the difference between the 1963 & 1964 hoods, besides the grilles?
18. How many different types of script were used on the rear of the '63-'67s and what were the spans?
19. Were power tops available during the 1963-1967 model run?
20. How many different rocker panel mouldings were used during 1963-1967?
21. What year had a body colored gas filler door?
22. In one year, the coupe had the side windshield moulding cover the entire post, what year was it?
23. What displacement engines were available in 1963 and what horsepower?
24. What displacement engines were available in 1965 and what horsepower?
25. What displacement engines were available in 1967 and what horsepower?
26. In 1965, what was the axle ratio of code "AO"?
27. Option NO3 was available in 1965 in only one body style. What body and what option?
28. Coupes are designated by the number-_____.
29. Convertibles are designated by the number-_____.
30. What year was the teakwood wheel first available?
31. What year was the Carter carburetor last offered as standard equipment?
32. What was the first year for a molded door panel?
33. Was 1965 or 1966 the first year for a chrome door pull?
34. On air conditioned cars, was the battery on the right or left side?
35. On air conditioned cars, how does the battery come out?
36. Was the M22 Heavy-Duty 4-speed transmission available in 1965?
37. How many different types of dash knobs were used on the '63-'67s?
38. High horsepower cars had two differences in the gauges, what were they?
39. On the '63-'67s did the driver's or passenger's side wiper go on top in the resting position?
40. What year gas door had a solid silver background with crossed flags in the center?
41. A power antenna was used on what years?
42. What was the first year to use six inch wheels as standard equipment?
43. What was the first year disc brakes were offered?
44. Did all '63-'67 have a quick steering change available?
45. How was the "short throw" shifter change made to the 4-speed?
46. In 1963 the instrument dial centers were silver, what color were they in 1964?
47. What year changed the location of the inside door lock knob?
48. What year was the Muncie 4-speed transmission first used?
49. What year changed the ignition switch to not include a "lock" and "off" position?
50. In what year was the Powerglide shift pattern modified?

TECH SESSION

With SAM FOLZ

BRAKE FLUID

I would like to discuss with you a problem that has plagued me (and perhaps a lot of you) having to due with leaking and corroded brake systems. On restored cars used in carefully driven, low mileage-accumulation situations, brake shoes, and pads in the case of '65-'67 models will literally last for years.

However, the hydraulics components are not that durable and deteriorate as a function of time, even though the car is in storage.

When hydraulic brakes were introduced to the auto industry in the early thirties, alcohols or glycols were used in the systems because water which might have been used, both freezes and boils within the working temperature range, as well as being corrosive.

Petroleum-based products would have worked fine as far as the metal parts of the system were concerned, but would rot the natural rubber parts involved, as neoprene and other synthetics were yet to be developed.

The glycols that are commonly used and comply with DOT 3 and DOT 4 requirements solve the basic problems noted, except great care must be exercised in their use, as they are extremely toxic if swallowed, extremely iritating if allowed to splash in the eyes, and are very upsetting to a good paint job if spilled.

But the greatest problem to those of us restoring cars for "keeps" is the damage done to the internal metal parts of the wheel cylinders, master-cylinder, lines, and calipers on disc-brake jobs by the crud and corrosion caused when the moisture literally "sucked" from the air is absorbed by the present type brake fluids. The characteristic of alcohols and glycols occurs because they are "hygroscopic", i.e., they absorb water vapor from the air, as much as 10% of their volume, and it is this water in the system that does the damage.

You might wonder how this can happen since the brake system is "closed" when the fill-cap is on the master-cylinder. But remember, the cap must be vented, which allows movement of air and also remember that when the wheel cylinders leak-down, the fluid that leaves the master-cylinder is replaced first by air, before you replenish the fluid.

Happily, there is now a solution to the problem. On October 1, 1974, Federal specs were amended to include DOT 5 fluid which is silicone-based. Silicone has a better list of properties than any of the previously tried fluids and is non-hygroscopic and non-corrosive to all subject metals, rubbers, and paints. It is claimed that systems carrying conventional fluids can be purged and blown clear and filled with the DOT 5-type material. I guess I'm skeptical about that. I'd rather suggest that when you decide to give your pride and joy a complete brake overhaul and you start with master and wheel cylinders or calipers bright and shiny inside, with new cups and pistons, that you do the old girl a favor and try the new DOT 5 Silicone fluid. It's made by Du Pont and Dow Corning - certainly reputable suppliers, and while it sells for about $12-$13 per quart, that's not much cost to be added to the total job.

Anyway, when you tell your wife you've decided to have a silicone implant, her reaction ought to be worth twice the cost.

If you don't locate the fluid locally, you can get it, as well as further information from: John Bamberg, 8107 Dunlap, Houston, Texas 77074, or J. K. Howell, 465 N. Grace Street, Lombard, Illinois 60148.

I am most happy to try and answer your individual questions of Corvette restoration, but please include a self-addressed-stamped-envelope. Write: Sam Folz, 3824 Coventry Ave., Kalamazoo, Michigan 49007.

TECH SESSION

WITH SAM FOLZ

LEAKING CARTER YH CARBURETORS

With the onset of hot weather, the telephone and mail have brought several calls for help from owners of six-cylinder Corvettes with leaking carburetors. The problem is one familiar to enough Blue Flame Special fans to warrant further discussion.

Chevrolet, and Carter, manufacturer of the YH, specified fuel-pump pressure of three to five PSI for these cars. For reasons I cannot explain, the six-cylinder Corvette fuel pump can put out eight to ten PSI when it gets hot. You can well imagine that it takes virtually perfect needle/seat assemblies to contain that much pressure without leaking more fuel into the bowl. In the case of horizontal carburetors, the problem magnifies, as surplus fuel runs out the intakes. The result not only produces rough idle, but too rich a running mixture, and a very real fire hazard.

To control the problem, one of several procedures should be tried. First, make sure floats in all carbs are set at spec (3/8"). If carbs are on an engine with a lot of miles and have not been overhauled, it might be just as well to set floats .030 lower than spec. This will tend to lean out the running mixture, compensating for possible wear on metering rods.

Next, examine all needle/seat assemblies. Originals were metal-tipped with two springs. Newer replacements have a plastic tip called Viton, which is supposed to give a better seal, particularly under high fuel-pump pressure.

Make sure gaskets are in good shape. If you get a kit to overhaul your YH, and it happens to have been made for the YH used on the Corvair Spyder, make sure that all holes in the old bowl-cover gasket are there in the new gasket. On some you will have the pierce an extra hole.

Now, reassemble all three carburetors to the engine and fire up. Drive the car to normal operating temperature. If it still drips at one or more carbs, it's back to the bench.

Is the engine level left-to-right? Many are not. If the left side is low, as many have found, it may help to shim the left motor mount so that the engine is level when off. This procedure may also aid hard to start engines.

Then, with engine warm, insert a temporary "tee" in the fuel line ahead of #1 carburetor and measure the fuel pump pressure. If it's much above the 5 lb. PSI area, you'll probably have to make a correction here. One way to do this is to permanently add a fuel-pressure regulator in the line. These do work, but since they are not "factory", most judges will subtract a point or two, however.

Another way to solve the pressure problem is to add extra gaskets as shims at the fuel pump. This reduces the "stroke" of the pump arm and thus, its pressure. I have not had success with this method.

It was probably this problem, as well as for more efficient air-cleaners that Chevrolet changed to the second-design air-cleaner with flame arrestors and a central drain during the 1954 model.

The problem we are discussing is not unique to this car. But, because it is so over-carbureted and because the "blow-off" or flooding drains out the inlet to the ground, rather than onto the intake manifold as on a V-8, it is much more visible and much more a fire hazard. That it usually happens to three carburetors on the same engine, rather than one, makes it all the more impossible to live with.

I am most happy to try and answer you individual questions of Corvette restoration, but please include a self-addressed-stamped-envelope. Write: Sam Folz, 3824 Coventry Ave., Kalamazoo, MI 49007.

ROBERT S. MORRISON
Molded Fiber Glass Companies

The evening of October 1, 1977, we were priviledged to present Mr. Robert S. Morrison as guest speaker at the NCRS awards banquet held at the Clock Tower Inn, Rockford, Illinois.

If you have read Karl Ludvigsen's book CORVETTE, AMERICA'S STAR-SPANGLED SPORTS CAR, the name Robert S. Morrison is not the least bit unfamiliar to you. He is the founder, Chairman and Chief Executive Officer of the Molded Fiber Glass Companies in Ashtabula, Ohio. He is a pioneer in fiber glass reinforced plastics and continues to be a driving force in that industry. For his significant early contributions and continuing accomplishments of mass production techniques, and development of new products, he was named a Charter Member of the Plastics Hall of Fame.

Mr. Morrison's companies today produce a wide variety of reinforced plastic products; restaurant food trays, Sears fishing boats, concrete forms, truck and car bodies, and even an x-ray metal detector walk-through structure used in many airports, just to name a few. In addition to his business career, he is a writer and lecturer on the free enterprise system.

For those members that could not attend the Rockford meet, we are printing Mr. Morrison's very authoritative and interesting talk.

October 1, 1977

You have been meeting for three days now and probably are filled up to here with technical and business discussions, so I should tell you jokes and stories, but I am not very good at telling jokes, and I have a very serious purpose in talking to you tonight.

First, let me tell you a true story about how the Corvette came to have a fiber glass plastic body. I started in the fiber glass plastic (FRP) molding business in 1948, and since the industry was so new and very few people were in it, by late 1952 my company, the Molded Fiber Glass Co. (MFG) was the largest producer of FRP molded parts in the industry, which really didn't mean much, because none of us were very big.

Chevrolet had been the No. 1 selling passenger car year after year since the demise of the Model A in 1931. Only in 1935 did Ford outsell Chevrolet. After World War II Chevrolet's dominance continued. I was the Ford dealer in Ashtabula, Ohio, from late 1937 to early 1948 and outsold the local Chevrolet dealer, but only because he did not work as hard as I did. We used to call the Chevrolet the cast-iron six, the family car. Ford had the sporty car image, Chevrolet the conservative car.

G.M. and Chev. market analysts started looking into their crystal balls and decided the new car buyer was gradually swinging to sportier, higher performance, flashy cars. They decided to prove to the public that Chevrolet could make and market sporty cars. Ed Cole, who later became president of General Motors, was chief engineer of Chevrolet at that time. So the General Motors Technical Center and Chevrolet engineers started work on a two-door sports car. In late 1952 several engineers from Fisher Body visited me at Ashtabula and showed me drawings of a hood and rear deck, and asked me if MFG could produce them. I said yes. They went back to Detroit. I didn't hear from them, so about December 1, I phoned

So we went into Gormeson's office. He apologized for the buyer and purchasing agent not being there. He then told me the top management of both Chevrolet and GM had had a meeting on the 14th floor, the sanctum sanctorum of the top GM officials, the day before and they had decided to go ahead with a steel Corvette body. The buyer and purchasing agent had been sent out post haste to investigate sources for steel parts. I asked him why this decision was made.

He said, first, because no one, not even MFG, had large enough equipment to mold the Corvette parts. Second, MFG did not have the money or credit to finance such a plant, and third, parts this big had never been produced before by the preform — matched die molding process and the supply of people with technical know-how was too small to solve technical problems rapidly, and fourth, they wanted to place all responsibility for parts on one source, and MFG had never done any hand lay-up work.

I don't know what would have happened if I hadn't met Elmer Gormeson that morning, but I feel quite certain that if I hadn't bumped into him in front of that elevator, there would not be a fiber glass plastic body on the Corvette.

them. They said the project had been put on the back burner.

I heard nothing more from them. In mid-January of 1953 I received a wire from one of our material suppliers recommending that I go to New York City and attend the General Motors Motorama at the Waldorf Astoria. The wire did not say why I should attend, so I did not go. The Motorama opened on a Friday night. The following Monday I received a phone call from a Chevrolet engineer in Detroit asking if he and another man could come down the next day. I said certainly. The next day Carl Jakust Chevrolet chief body engineer and Jim Premo, project engineer flew down in a single-engine airplane in an almost blinding snow storm.

They had drawings of the Corvette. They surveyed the infant FRP industry and came to the conclusion that only MFG had the know-how and the smaller equipment needed to mold Corvette body parts. I assured them we could design and build the equipment needed.

For the next several weeks Chevrolet people and I met frequently discussing parts design and problems. I thought I was making progress. One day I went to Detroit to see the Chevrolet purchasing agent and the project buyer. When I got there I was told they were both gone for the day, which surprised me because I had told them I was coming. Chevrolet purchasing offices were then on the second floor of the GM Building. I went to the elevators and pushed the down button. I was standing in front of one elevator which was going up. The door opened and Elmer Gormeson, the Chevrolet director of purchases, stepped out. He said, "Bob, have you got a minute?" I sure had, because I had planned to spend the morning with the buyer and the purchasing agent.

For the next two hours I sat in his office, making phone calls, outlining plans, getting assurances of technical and financial support from material suppliers, and assuring him I would divorce myself from all other business and molding activities and devote my full attention to the Corvette. I told him about an 80,000 sq. ft. building I had heard about the day before in Meadville, Pa. I tried to cover all the objections and problems he had brought up. He said another meeting on the 14th floor was scheduled for the afternoon, and if there were any change in their plans he would get in touch with me.

I left his office about 11:30 AM feeling that the cause was lost. I had a meeting scheduled at the Kaiser plant in Ypsilanti in the afternoon. I was working with them on parts for the Kaiser Darrin, a car which some of you have seen. We molded ten of the thirteen major parts for the Darrin. Only a couple of hundred Darrins were built because Kaiser automobile ran out of money and closed down. Anyway, I had dinner with three Kaiser executives, two of them vice presidents, and left them about 8:30 PM. I then drove home to Ashtabula, about 240 miles, and got home at 1:30 AM.

My wife woke up and told me I was to call a number in Detroit, no matter how late I got in. It was Elmer Gormeson, the Chevrolet director of purchasing. He said he wanted me to go ahead and get that 80,000 sq. ft. building in Meadville because they had decided to go ahead with me and MFG on the fiber glass plastic body for the Corvette. I don't know what would have happened if I hadn't met Elmer Gormeson that morning, but I feel quite certain that if I hadn't bumped into him in front of that elevator, there would not be a fiber glass plastic body on the Corvette. I didn't sleep very well that night. The building in Meadville

MFG panels used in 1957 body assembly.

turned out to be unsatisfactory, so we built a new plant in Ashtabula and gradually got it into production. I set up a new corporation, the Molded Fiber Glass Body Co., and sold stock to outsiders, to provide the finances and working capital needed. Many of the parts for the 1953-54 Corvettes, especially the large parts, were made by the vacuum bag process, since molds for this process could be produced much more rapidly than matched metal dies. Lunn Laminate Company set up a plant in Ashtabula to mold these vacuum bag parts. As the matched metal dies came in, they would stop making that part. Such parts are not very smooth on the underside.

He finally got all the dies into production by late June, 1954. We were producing 50 sets of parts a day. On June 30, 1954 (exactly one year after the first 1953 Corvette was built) Ed Furbacker the Chevrolet purchasing agent phoned me and told me the Corvette was not selling as expected and to slow down production. We shipped 300 sets of parts in July, and 200 in August and September and then shut down completely. Why didn't the 1954 Corvette sell? It looked pretty, but it still was the old cast iron six. It was not a high performance car.

Starting in 1955 we produced 50 sets of parts a month. It took several years for volume to climb up to the 50 sets planned for 1954. In 1955 Ford brought out the Thunderbird, which at first was a two passenger sports car. It sold very well. I believe, but of course cannot prove, that Chevrolet would have dropped the Corvette in 1955-56 except for the great success of the T-Bird.

There are other details to this story but I want to skip over most of the intervening years and talk about the present-day Corvette. I have brought along with me tonight Grace Moore, who has been with MFG for many years. She is currently manager of our research and testing laboratory, but for many years was in charge of our finishing laboratory, which includes painting. Proper preparation of the surface of FRP before painting is so important that we use the term "finishing" to cover both preparation and painting. We believe she knows more about production finishing of FRP than anyone else. She has spent hundreds of hours at the Corvette plant, at Mack, at Ford truck, and at Avanti. She believes the present finishing system, which is still the same old system, used on the Corvette bodies, could be greatly improved, at a substantial labor saving. She does not consider herself an expert in shop finishing of the type you do, though she has two sons and several grandsons doing body shop work who received some training and knowledge from her. She does not plan to talk to you tonight.

Possibly some of you read the article in the Sept. '77 issue of Popular Mechanics on the Corvette. The writer surveyed several hundred owners of relatively new Corvettes, asking them what they liked and disliked about their Corvettes. Owners were very critical of the finish on present-day Corvettes. I agree the finish leaves much to be desired.

Most early Corvette parts were made by the Molded Fiber Glass Body Co. to specifications of strength, fiber glass content, surfaced characteristics that I personally set in 1953. I determined the proper thickness, .100", to go with those specifications.

As new purchasing and engineering people came into the Corvette operation, they started looking for lower prices and smoother surface finishes. Gradually other companies chiseled into the Corvette molded parts business by quoting lower prices made possible by reducing the fiber glass content of the parts and increasing the percentage of inert cheap fillers; clay and limestone. Then everyone got excited about low profile additives to the resin which result in smoother parts.

Normal polyester resin shrinks in curing. The unsaturated molecules of maleic anhydride and styrene monomer cross-link, so a cured resin takes up 6 to 8% less space than the liquid uncured resin. Inert filler helps reduce the shrink, but too much filler makes the parts weaker and more brittle. In the 1960's someone discovered that the addition of a thermoplastic polymer, such as methyl methacrylate, to a polyester resin, reduced the shrink greatly. The polymer does not cross-link with the resin, it merely swells up. It acts like an inert filler otherwise.

During the ill-conceived Federal Reserve credit crunch of 1969 when the Fed tried to stop inflation by forcing the banks to reduce commercial loans, I was forced to let Rockwell International acquire the MFG Body Company. I had other fiber glass operations, including the original MFG Co., so I dropped out of the Body Co. All during the late 1960's I had fought and argued with Chevrolet purchasing, engineering, and plastics specification people against using low-shrink resins in Corvette parts, but when Rockwell took over, they went along with whatever Chevrolet wanted, and switched over to low-shrink resins without a murmur.

Parts made with low-shrink resins are weaker, especially in reverse impact and adhesions of bonding materials and paints. Why did Chevrolet want to switch? It took less sanding, and with the ever-increasing cost of production labor in the auto plants, they were anxious to reduce labor. So the heck with the public — reduce the cost.

MFG Body Co. had developed a special isophthalic polyester resin by 1958 which was stronger, had higher strengths, particularly impact, and less crazing than other polyesters. We are now making all the parts for the Avanti body. Under the terms of the merger of the MFG Body Co. into Rockwell, my other companies and I had to agree to stay out of the automotive field for three years, but we kept our oar in by sub-contracting Avanti parts and non-current Corvette service parts for Rockwell. We are now doing most of this work, including all Avanti parts, direct. We use the best resins and highest strength fiber glass reinforcements. Those of you who have repaired both Avanti and late model Corvette parts have no doubt noticed the difference.

Going to low-profile resins was only the first step in the degradation of FRP by the auto and truck builders. High, consistent strength FRP parts are reinforced with fiber glass mat or fiber glass preforms. Another material, called fiber glass-reinforced sheet molding compound, called SMC for short, was developed in the late 1960's. Subsequently suppliers developed low-shrink resins to be used in SMC, so now the industry has low-profile SMC, which has even greater weaknesses than low-profile resin.

SMC is produced by coating a lower and an upper continuous film of polyethylene with a highly filled polyester resin to which a thickening agent has been added. Fiber glass strands are cut into 1" lengths and dropped on the resin on the lower film. The resin on the upper film is then squeezed against the fibers and the lower film through a series of rollers which drive most of the trapped air in the sandwich out. This is then rolled up into 100# rolls and put in an 85° F. maturation room for about four days. The resin thickens up so much that when several layers of it are placed in a set of dies in a high pressure press, the glass fibers and resin both are pushed into every area of the cavity. In mat or preform molding the resin flows into every area of the die cavity, but the glass fibers do not move. The flow of the glass fibers in the cavity creates orientation of the fibers, with reasonably good strength if the laminate is tested lengthwise but low strength crosswise. The mat or preform reinforced part has equal strength in all directions.

However, molders love SMC because it takes less operator skill to produce good-looking parts than it does for preform parts. Auto makers love SMC because bosses and changes in section thickness can be accomplished that cannot be done with mat or preform. SMC and its weaker sister, bulk molding compound, called BMC, are like metal die castings, except for the weakness caused by flow lines. Mat and preform are like sheet metal, which is much stronger on a psi basis than die castings.

Because of the production advantages of SMC, both auto and truck makers have commenced using SMC where it should not be used. Another case of the heck with the public.

One problem with the finish of late model Corvettes is caused by the way they assemble them. When the Corvette was first designed, it was primarily an all fiber glass plastic body. As time went on, more and more metal parts were added, primarily to help locate the fiber glass plastic parts in the assembly. Now some surface FRP panels are butted together over the metal bird cage, usually with an FRP bonding strip riveted to the metal. It is very difficult to finish off these butt joints. The bond projects beyond the surface and a worker with a grinder can dig into the butting panels. This can result in a 4" to 5" wide area which may have been repaired by putty wiping but which develops blisters when the body goes through the paint oven.

Probably the main reason for the low-grade finish on some Corvette bodies is just the lack of elbow grease. Another hour or two of finishing work per body could greatly improve the finish.

I have been a strong advocate of a four-door sedan FRP body built along the lines of a small Mercedes. Some market surveys we made years ago indicated that people will pay 12 to 15% more for a car with an FRP body than a steel body. I am talking about a body made with the right FRP materials at the right places, not a body made with china.

Now what can you and I do about it? I don't know. The MFG Companies do $10 MM or more business a year with auto and truck manufacturers, about 20% of our business volume. I am not afraid to tell a customer that he is using the wrong material or formulation, but they still make the decisions. It takes $50 to $100 MM to bring out a new car today for volume production. The auto companies hold the purse strings, and they are not likely to gamble on an FRP body, even though I tell them it is a sure thing.

Robert S. Morrison
Molded Fiber Glass Companies
P.O. Box 675
Ashtabula, Ohio 44004

Editor's note: The NCRS wishes to thank Ken Frenchak of Butler, Pennsylvania and Sam Folz for their efforts in arranging to have Mr. Morrison attend the Rockford meet.

'53 - '55 AFFAIR

WITH JOHN AMGWERT

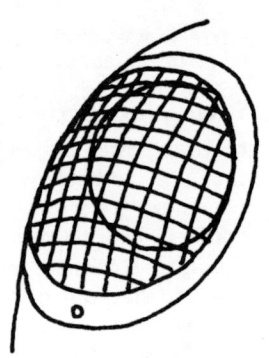

THE PULLING OF THE BODY ON E53F001076

Removing a body from the frame sounds like a monumental task, but can actually be a rather simple job. Unless you've done it before, or have assistance from someone who has, the idea is somewhat scary as it was for me. But after doing the job I am amazed at how easy it was and the short amount of time involved. For those that are contemplating body removal, I will outline the steps that I took.

In my case, most of the car was disassembled. The engine and transmission had been removed previously, as well as all the trim. My first step was to remove as many of the remaining parts as possible for the purpose of reducing weight. It is most important to mention here that you should tag all parts that are removed, making diagrams or taking photos for reference and reassembly in the future. Don't just start removing everything, throwing it in a pile, as you will never be able to correctly put them back from memory. You can devise your own system for this; I used empty coffee cans for small parts, or reassembled parts of larger units such as the bolts and hinges for the doors. Those parts removed were the doors, seats and frames, windshield assembly, top, top cover, hood, radiator, heater, radio, trunk lid, headlamps, voltage regulator, brake master cylinder, etc.

With much of the bulk weight removed, the next step was to unbolt the body mounts and additional connections, freeing the body and frame assemblies so the lift would be unobstructed. Prior to unbolting, I suggest spraying the 11 body mounts (see diagram) with a good rust penetrating oil such as WD-40 or Liquid Wrench (GM brand Exhaust Heat Valve Lubricant works excellent so I'm told!). Several applications over a period of three days should be sufficient to help prevent twisting and breaking of bolts.

I was fortunate to have assistance from Dave Nace of Omaha as he had removed the body on his 1954 serial #E54S001624 a month previous and it was most interesting to note some changes in body mounting on the two models. All mounts were identical except the four located just behind the seats. On 1953 models, these bolts come up thru the bottom securing with "caged" nuts, while '54 models have the bolts (outboard mounts secured by plates riveted in underbody) going down with nuts on the bottom. On '53 and early '54 models the outboard mounts behind the seats are enclosed between the underbody and fiberglass bulkhead and

1953 inboard mount behind seat with "caged" nut.

1954 mount bolt.

are not accessable. If you break one of these, you may be forced to cut into the panel (see photo). On later production '54 models, this panel was opened up for easy access to the mounts.

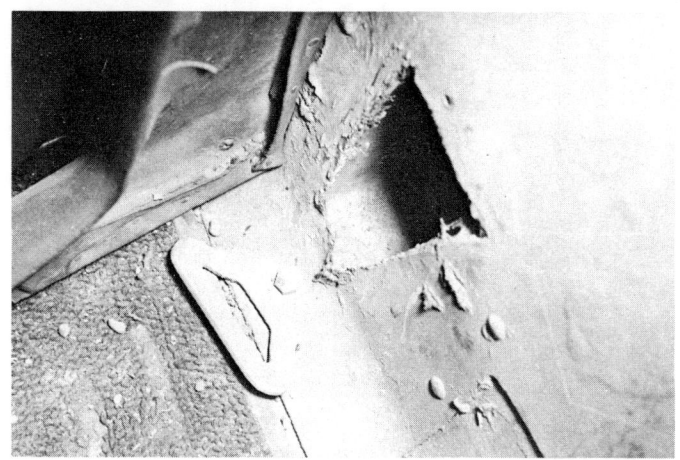

Plan on some or all of the body bolts breaking when you remove them depending on the amount of corrosion and climate the car has been subjected to. I felt fortunate that all mine came loose with relative ease.

The next step is to disassemble remaining connections. The rear bumper bar is secured to the frame with brackets that go through the body, so these will have to be removed; don't forget the exhaust extensions!

The fuel tank fitting at the bottom of the tank must be disconnected. To prevent twisting or distortion to the fuel line I suggest using flare nut wrenches for a good hold. The area of the fuel tank is where I made a big mistake which I'll discuss later.

Next, the park brake was disconnected and this can be a headache. First remove the clevis under the car that connects to the idler lever (nut held with cotter pin) so the cable will pull freely. Next, unbolt the hand lever under the dash and its retaining flange against the firewall (not the nut on the cable). Carefully pull the lever and from under the dash, slip the ball at the end of the cable out of the slot in the lever. Now, from under the hood, you can remove the spring clip and large nut retaining the cable to the brake lever. You'll also have to unbolt the cable from its routing next to the frame.

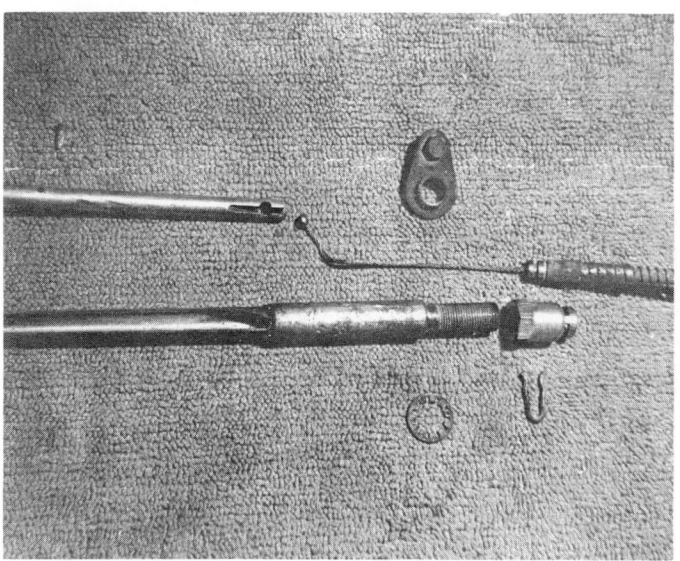

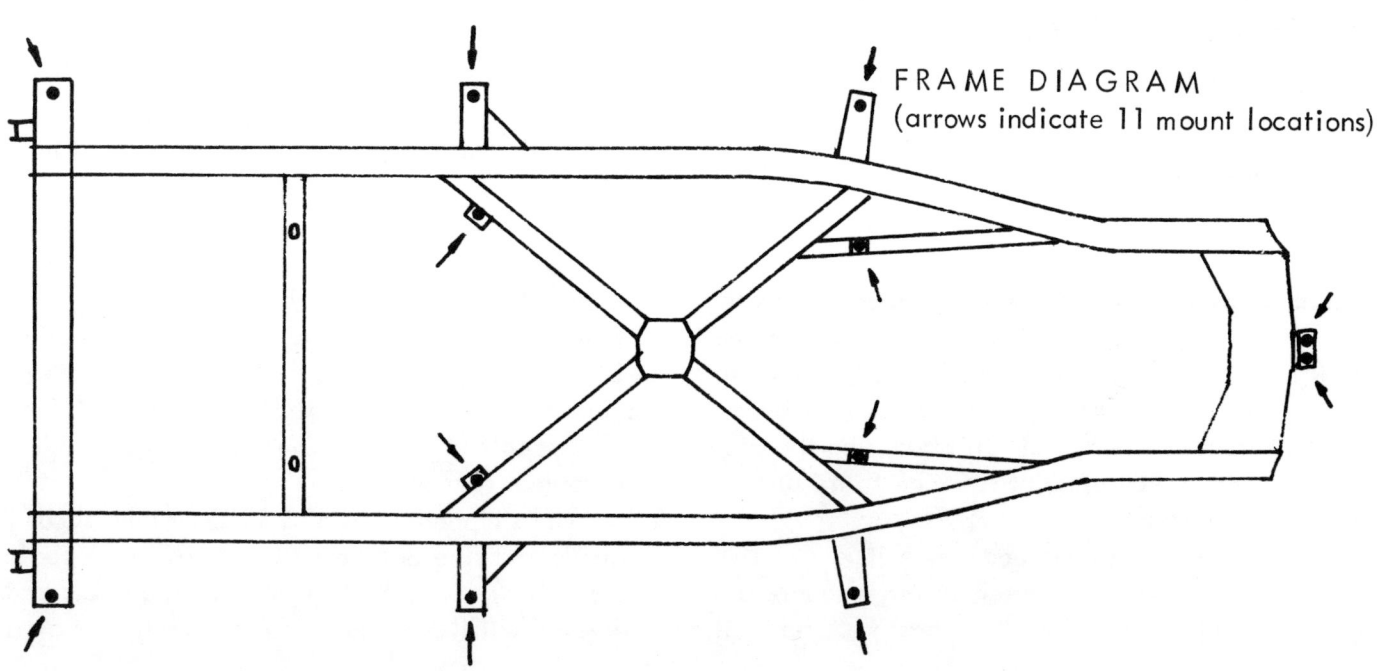

FRAME DIAGRAM
(arrows indicate 11 mount locations)

115

I suggest that you allow the steering column to remain with the body. Simply disconnect the drag link at the pitman arm (attached to the steering gear assembly) by removing the cotter pin and unscrewing the seat at the rear of the link. Then remove the three long bolts that hold the steering gear to the frame rail. At this point the steering wheel will turn freely, but don't turn it hard against the stops as the sector roller inside the steering gear may become seriously damaged! It is best to remove the steering wheel from the mast with the correct puller tool.

You are now ready to remove the body. Double check to make sure that there is no interference like wiring that may get hung-up.

Between the frame and the body at each mount there are a number of rubber cushions and metal shims. It will be very important when remounting the body that these are relocated at their right place for body and component alignment. For this I prepared a cardboard diagram of the frame and

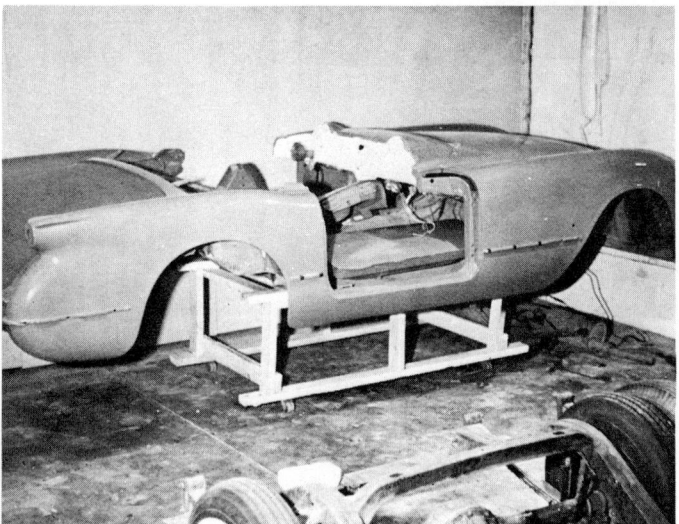

Body dolly shown here is easily made with 2 x 4's and casters.

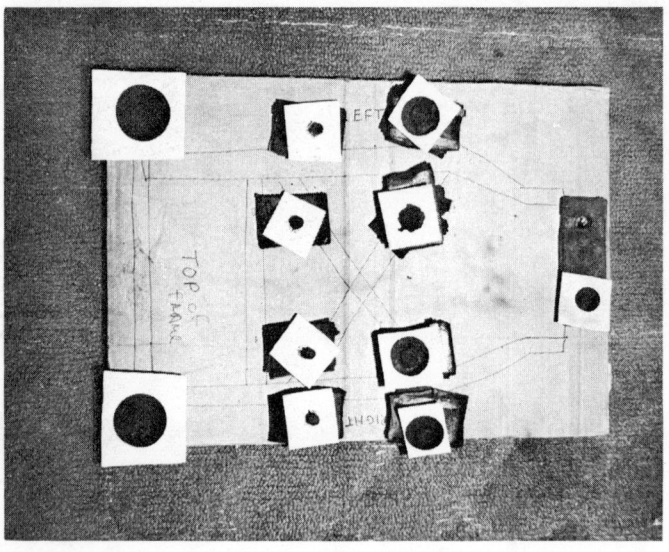

Cardboard diagram used to store bolts, cushions and shims.

mounted the body bolts at their locations, so when the body was lifted, I could transfer the shim and pads to the diagram. Since you won't have much time once the body is up, and some shims may stick to the underbody, or fall off during the process, I suggest you appoint someone to try and keep track of them.

What to do with the body once it is up? The conventional method is to set it onto a square dolly easily made with 2" x 4"s on casters. The method I chose, however, seems unconventional, but has proven to be very acceptable and one I'd recommend for several reasons. I (we) laid the body on its side, rolling it up against a wall! This saved on storage space, and allows for cleaning and refinishing of the underbody before righting later.

We were now ready for the body pull; a very tense procedure, at least for this owner! You begin to conjure visions of the body cracking and breaking in two. Let me assure you that the Corvette body is very strong, but there are some precautions. LIFT ONLY UNDER THE ROCKER PANELS; don't lift at the wheel openings, fenders, or front or rear sections!

The stripped body of a 1953 weighs about 300 pounds and five people lifted it easily. A sixth person (me), watched for any falling shims and wheeled out the frame when the body was clear.

Tire casings were laid out along the wall to cushion the side of the body as it was rolled up on its side. The bulk of the weight will be at the door area so place the tires accordingly prior to laying the body down. An old mattress would also work well here.

Up to this point everything had worked as planned, but when the body was rolled over, the mistake showed up. When I bought the car I was told the gas tank had been emptied, and the car has sat for the last two years that I've had it with the gas cap removed. When I removed the lower tank fitting, no gas came out, so I assumed it was in fact empty. It wasn't!

When gasoline evaporates it leaves a thick varnish-like sludge. Apparently this sludge clogged the lower tank fitting so nothing came out. But when the car was rolled over, on its left side, the sludge ran out the filler neck all over the floor. It reeked an awful odor that would not leave for better than a month. I suggest, and wish I had, pulled the tank out!

At any rate, it was a real feeling of satisfaction to get the body removed and it only accounted for about a tenth of the work I had envisioned. I am now in the process of restoring the frame, and in my next article, will outline the steps and some interesting features of the 1953 frames as compared to later production.

Any comments or additonal information for inclusion in this article are most welcome. Write: John Amgwert, Box 34377, Omaha, NE 68134, phone 402/493-1020.

Photo sequence shows body lift and roll-over. Note that body is handled only under rocker panel!

TECH SESSION
With SAM FOLZ

Motor Talk
Junker I.D. Plates Sought
By Fred W. Kline
Kline Communications Corp.

Insurance industry and law enforcement agencies are trying to get a movement going to require auto salvage yards to return the vehicle identification number plates off wrecked cars, according to MOTOR magazine.

Why? The easiest way of obtaining false identification for a stolen car is to buy a wreck, including the vehicle number plate, and put that plate on the stolen vehicle.

For several years now many old-car-related magazines have published ads for individuals seeking to sell, and even purchase, Vehicle Identification Number (VIN) plates and titles for vehicles that have been junked, destroyed, or "parted out". While it is assumed that these persons might be ignorant of the many state and federal laws banning such practices, they are breaking the law and the magazines may, in fact, be aiding them!

Of recent, many Corvette-related publications have also accepted and published such ads, and the frequency is increasing.

It should be mentioned here that states surveyed forbid the removal of VIN plates, period! The proper procedure, generally, when junking a vehicle is to deface by punching holes in the VIN plate so it cannot be used again, leaving it attached to the vehicle, marking the title "JUNKED" and returning it to the State Motor Vehicle Department in which it was registered.

The NCRS over the years has received such ads for VIN plates and titles offered for sale through our publication, and they have always been rejected. In all states, the sale of VIN plates and titles and their application to another vehicle is a serious crime. In cases of interstate transfer of these items, the FBI would get involved.

If your car has no VIN plate, or if you believe the plate on the car to be incorrect, it may be possible for you to correct the situation.

Using the 1968 experience Dr. John Mansell as an example, you may be able to do as he did in obtaining a new plate and a new title.

Note, here, first that the rules are not the same in all states, and John may have been lucky in dealing with the State of Ohio rather than, say, Pennsylvania, where he actually resides.

John bought a "1954" Corvette titled as a "1954 Chevrolet Convertible" from its Ohio owner. The title and serial plate gave the serial number as E54F001175. John became aware that the letter "F" was incongruous and that the body serial plate was out of spec in size and material to the original factory plate. In several long telephone calls we became convinced that the car was in reality a 1953 model, probably re-titled as a "54" to gain value in the "Blue Book".

The person who had done this merely changed the "3" to a "4" when he re-titled the car. Also, the "hidden" VIN stamping on the car's frame was proof positive of the vehicle's identity.

John solved the problem by getting the help of a Chevrolet dealer and the Zone Service Manager. They completed the necessary paper work which was forwarded with appropriate signatures to the Chevrolet Theft Bureau, then located within the Detroit Gear and Axle Plant at 1840 Holbrook Avenue, Detroit, Michigan 48212.

The Theft Bureau scans a "hot list" (NCIC) to make sure the unit is not stolen and that the description of the car is correct. They, being satisfied, asked the Chevrolet Assembly Division at Flint to prepare a replacement body serial plate. The plate was sent via certified mail back to the Chevrolet dealer involved for attachment to the vehicle.

The replacement plate is not identical to the original Corvette plate. Size is a trifle narrower, and mounting holes are on opposite corners rather than centered, one at each end. Further, the color is red on aluminum with a Chevrolet "bow tie" and space at the bottom for the numbers is reversed out.

Facsimile of mfr.'s replacement VIN plate supplied by Chevrolet to Dr. Mansell in 1968.

Once the new plate was available, it became relatively easy for John to get Ohio to issue a replacement title correcting the year and serial number.

Some states, including Pennsylvania, prefer to issue their own special replacement plates where needed. These plates in no way resemble manufacturers' plates, and numbers may bear no resemblance to original V.I.N. In fact, Pennsylvania will not allow the manufacturer to re-plate the vehicle.

I am most happy to try and answer your individual questions on Corvette restoration, but please include a self-addressed-stamped-envelope. Write: Sam Folz, 3824 Coventry Ave., Kalamazoo, MI 49007.

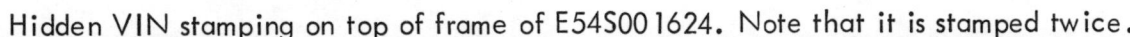

Hidden VIN stamping on top of frame of E54S001624. Note that it is stamped twice.

About ten or so years ago Sam Folz, NCRS Technical Chairman, was contacted by a young college student who had recently purchased a used 1957 Corvette. Since Sam has been known in the Kalamazoo area as very knowledgeable on older Corvettes, the student inquired on what could be done about water leaking around the front of the doors on his car. Sam was sure that he had some service data on this problem and the student said he would bring the car over.

Sam found his copy of the Corvette Body Service Operations Manual (August, 1957 and May, 1960 editions) and sure enough, pages 15 and 16 covered water leak correction. Now anyone who has ever seen copies of those manuals, knows that Figure #17 on page 16 shows the cowl drain gutter (reproduced here) and the VIN plate of E57S100001, the first 1957 Corvette assembled which was used for the photo.

When the student arrived, Sam opened the

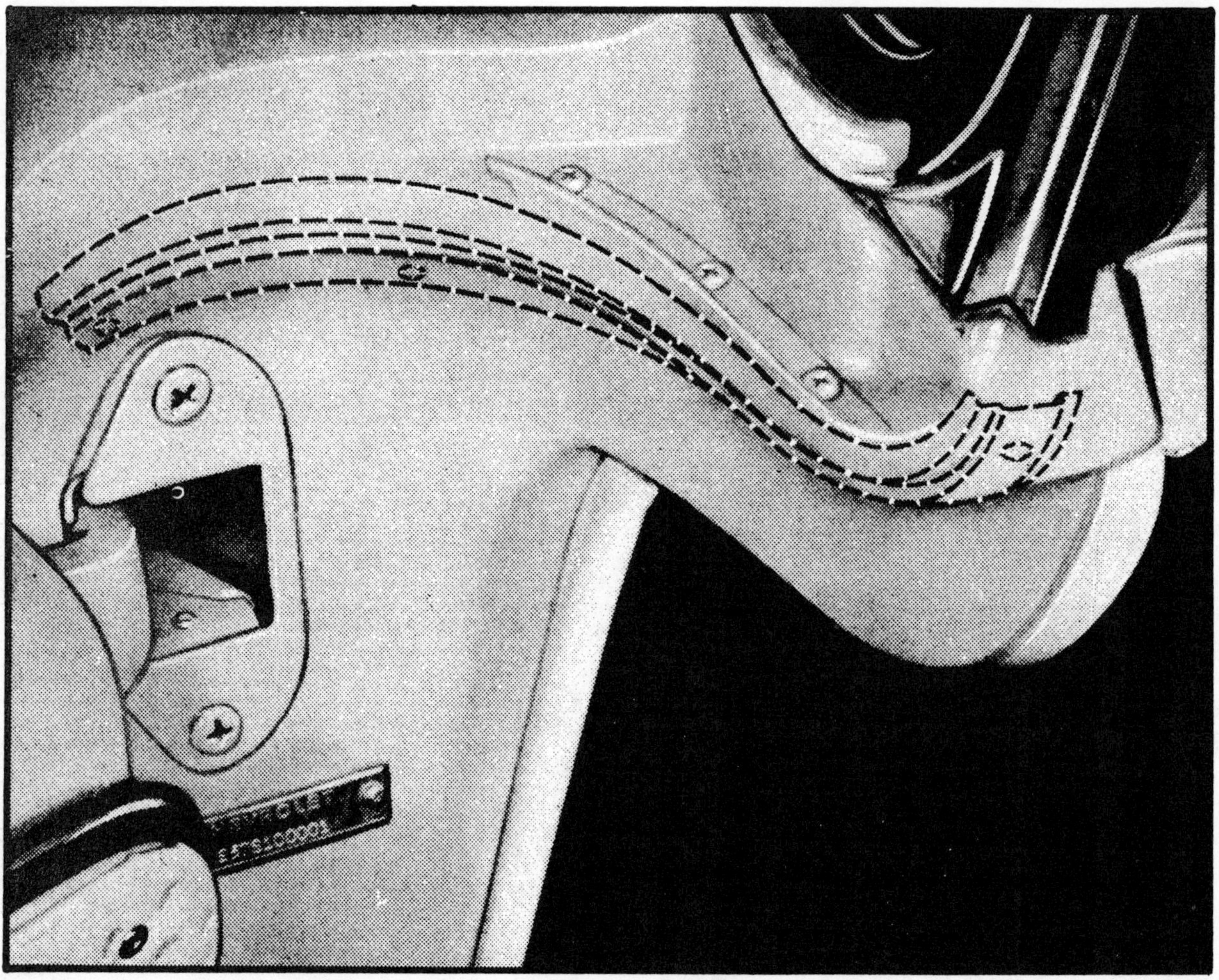

Fig. 17 Cowl Drain Gutter

door pointing out that the car did not have the longer style drain gutter as late production 1957 Corvettes used. It was at that point that Sam glanced at the VIN plate on the student's car. You can imagine Sam's amazement when he read E57S100001; he was looking at the first production 1957 Corvette, the same car pictured in the manual he held in his hand!

During the years that followed, '57 #1 changed hands again, was used as a race car, went through an engine and transmission change, but remained in the Kalamazoo area. This last October, Sam purchased the car.

While it sports fuel injection script and flags, (it was injected for awhile) the car was originally equipped with a 245 hp dual-4 bbl. engine and Powerglide transmission, power top, radio, heater and hardtop. Originally a Cascade Green model with biege trim, the car was repainted black and the interior trim dyed to match.

Sam has since sold the car to another NCRS member and surely it will appear at one of our meets in the future for all to see.

The first production 1957 Corvette as it appears today.

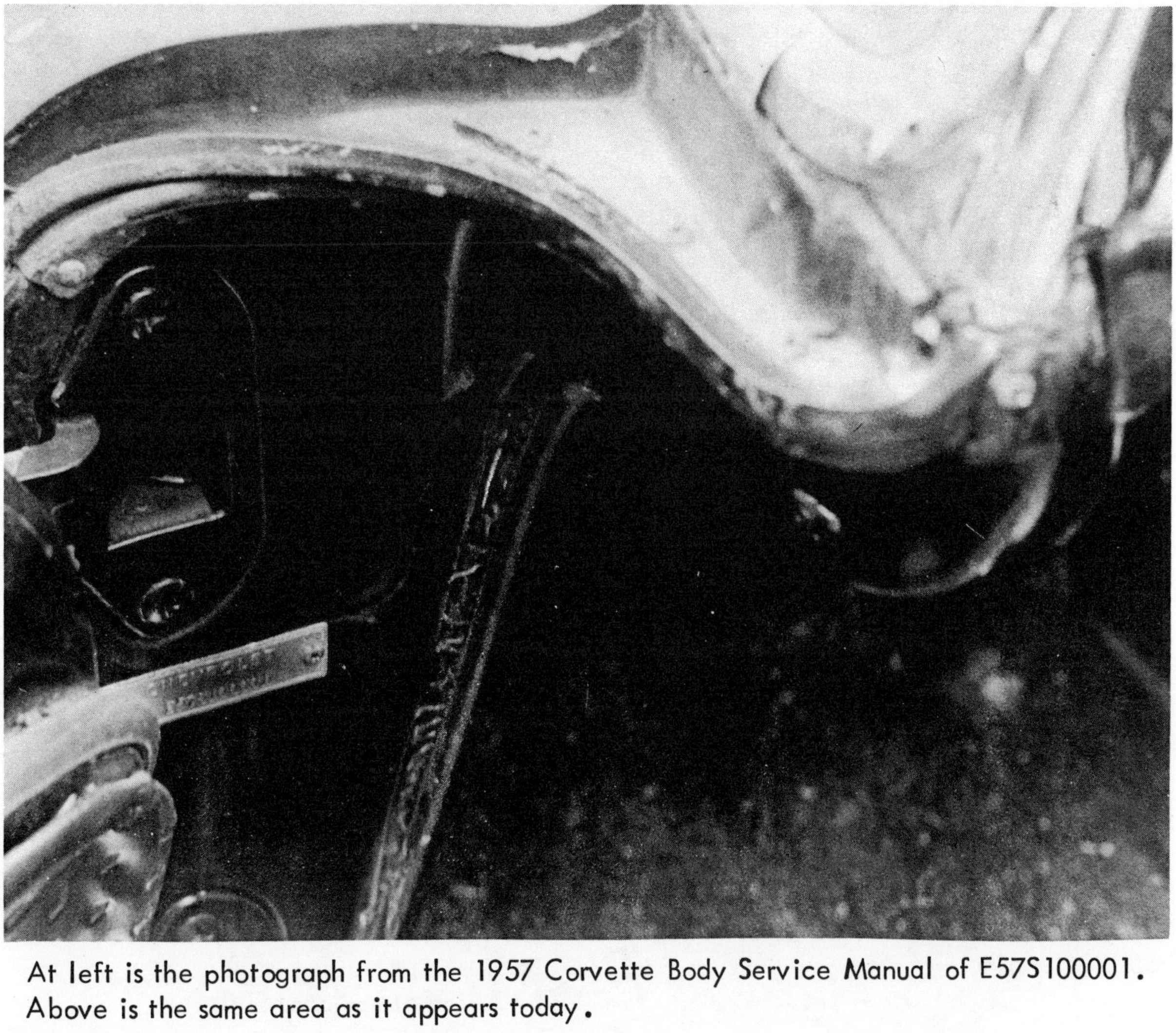

At left is the photograph from the 1957 Corvette Body Service Manual of E57S100001. Above is the same area as it appears today.

1953 - 1967 CORVETTE HOSE CLAMPS

By John Amgwert

While the topic of correct hose clamp usage on older Corvettes seems like a minor point, it is often discussed during a restoration and at NCRS judging events by serious restorers desiring use of the "correct" style. Proper clamps are one of the small finishing touches to a good restoration, while the wrong clamps can be an eyesore.

Since few cars retain their original factory clamps, determining the correct usage is nearly impossible with several different styles being used at various locations. The problem is compounded when many clamps listed in the Chevrolet parts books are "service" parts. While these "service parts will do the job, they are not necessarily the correct style used on the assembly line.

With the help of correct specified part numbers obtained from the 1956 through 1967 Corvette Factory Assembly Instruction Manuals (AIM's), Society of Automotive Engineers (SAE) Standards, existing photographs of factory-fresh engine compartments, and additional research concerning the 1953-1955 models, I will attempt to present the documentation that exists.

The chart presented here shows the various clamp locations and Corvette AIM part numbers specified, as well as quantity used in each application on '56-'67 models. I will attempt to cover the '53-'55 model clamps separately as they are harder to document.

UPPER RADIATOR INLET HOSE CLAMPS (2 used)

1956-1957 ——————— #272861 (to 11-26-56)

1957 (from 11-26-56) through 1959 —— #105479*
#111619
#443634 — All okayed for production (to 12-10-58)

*most commonly used clamp

1959 (from 12-10-58) through 1967 —— #9411656
All 283, 327, 396 & 427 engines

LOWER RADIATOR OUTLET HOSE CLAMPS (2 used)

1956 through 1960 ——————— #272863

1961 through 1967 ——————— #274765
All 283, 327 & 427 engines

1965 396 engine ——————— #274765 (1 used at water pump)
#9411668 (1 used at radiator outlet)

HEATER HOSE CLAMPS

1956-1957 — #3133537 (as required all locations)

1958 through 1960 — #272852 (2 used)
#3133537 (4 used)

1961-1962 — #272852 (2 used)
#272850 (4 used)

1963 through 1967* — #272852 (4 used from pump to res. tank to heater upper)
#272850 (2 used from manifold to heater lower)
*Note: Air conditioned slightly different.

RADIATOR RESERVE TANK

1961 through 1967 — Lower #111607 (2 used)
Upper #274337 (2 used)

HEATER AIR FLOW DUCT

1956 through 1960 — #3133386 (2 used)

1961-1962 — #9417067 (2 used) **

** Note: This part number while specified in the AIMs is believed by this author to be incorrect and should be #9417068. The 067 clamp will only open to 3.44" yet the hose is specified as 4", therefore the 068 clamp should be used.

FUEL INJECTION AIR DUCT

1957 with Air Intake — #3133386 (2 used)

1958 through 1962 — #3749810 (4 used with hi-lift cam)
#3749810 (2 used with regular cam)

1963 through 1965 — #3749810 (2 used)

RPO 684 BRAKE DUCTS

1957 through 1959 (to about 10-15-58) — #3133386 (4 used)

1962 RPO 242 CRANKCASE VENTILATION EQUIPMENT

#272848 (2 used)

With the correct specified AIM parts numbers charted, I will outline the "types" of clamp designs to which these parts can be categorized, and some specifications for each.

Clamps were supplied to GM by a number of manufacturers; major suppliers being the Corbin Screw Corporation, Wittek Mfg. Company of Chicago, and the Harrison Radiator Division, Lockport, N.Y. In most cases the supplier's identification marking and/or size number appeared on their clamps.

continued on next page...

53-'67 HOSE CLAMPS

While each manufacturer surely had performance standards for their parts, GM appears to have specified standards set by the SAE. Under SAE Standard we find four basic types of clamps used on Corvettes; Type B, Type C, Type D, and Type E. All the clamps listed on the preceding chart (with the exception of two that I will discuss separately) fall under these four SAE catagories.

TYPE B HOSE CLAMPS

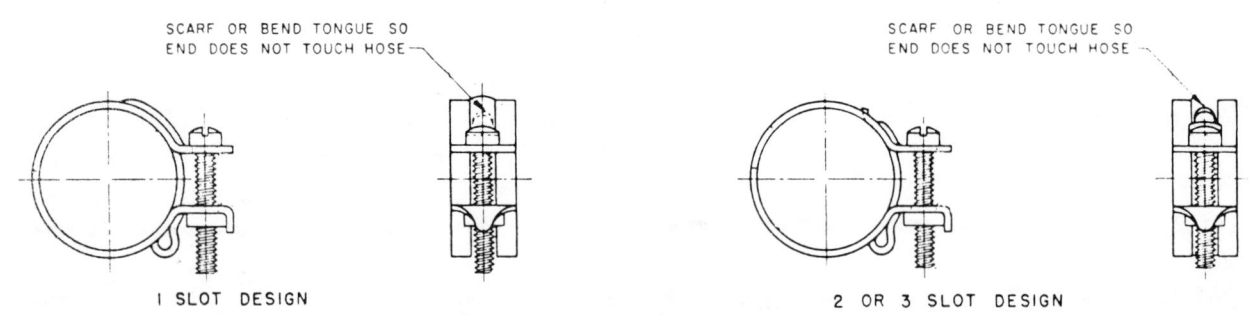

Part Number	Size	Band Width	Number of Slots in Band
#111607	1-1/32"	.50"	1 Slot Design
#111619	1-7/8"	.62"	2 Slot Design

These clamps are finished in zinc plating and use a fillister head slotted screw with 10-24 size threads.

TYPE C HOSE CLAMPS

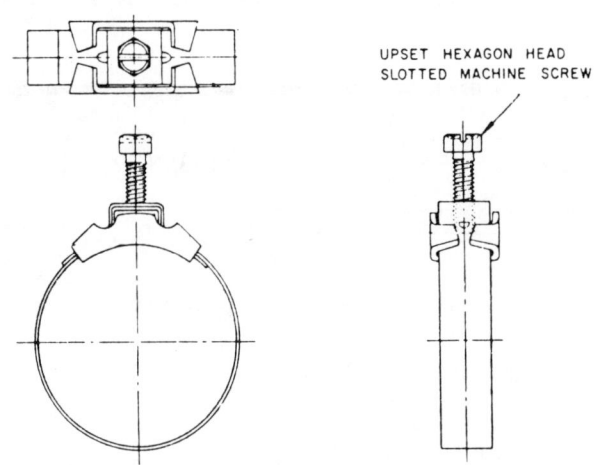

Part Number	Size Number	Diameter Open	Diameter Closed
#9411656	66	2.06"	1.69"
#274765	74	2.31"	1.94"
#9411668	80	2.50"	2.12"
#9417067*	110	3.44"	3.06"
#9417068*	138	4.31"	3.94"

*The #9417067 clamp is listed here but its application is considered incorrect due to its 3.44" opening. #9417068 is believed correct with its 4.31" opening.

Band width on all clamps is .505" and screw size and length is 12-24 x 1.00". Finish may be either zinc plating or stainless steel. This style clamp is often referred to as the "tower" design.

TYPE D HOSE CLAMPS

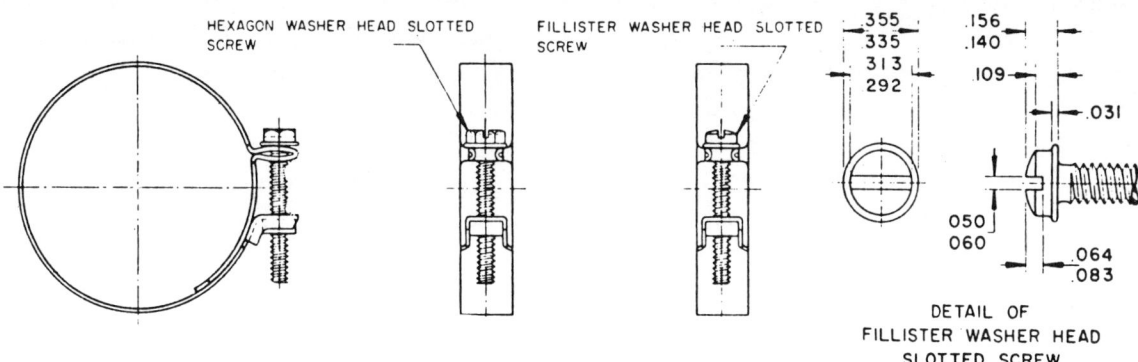

DETAIL OF FILLISTER WASHER HEAD SLOTTED SCREW

Part Number	Size Number	Diameter			Screw Type
		Open	Nominal	Closed	
#274337	23	.72"	.62"	.53"	Fillister washer head 1.12" long
#443634	63	1.97"	1.88"	1.75"	Hex washer head 1.25" long

Band width on all clamps is .505", screw threads are 10-25. Finish is zinc plating. This style clamp resembles Type B but does not appear with slotted bands.

TYPE E HOSE CLAMPS

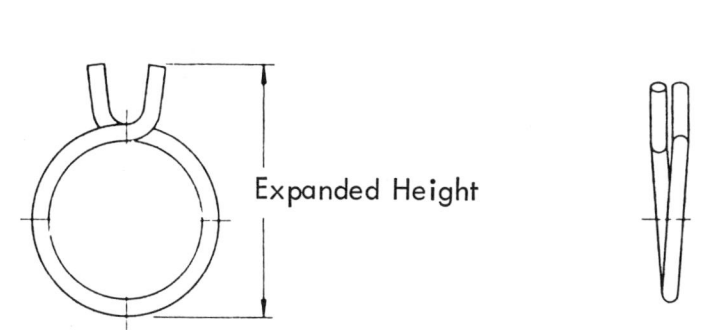
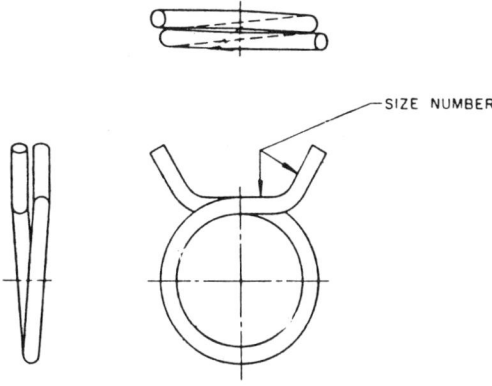

Part Number	Size Number	Diameter			Expanded Overall Height
		Max.	Nominal	Min.	
#272848*	13	.832"	.812"	.792"	1.50"
#3133537	15	----	.937"	----	----
#272850	15	.968"	.938"	.906	1.69"
#272852**	17	1.090"	1.062"	1.034"	1.88"
#272861	30	1.937"	1.875"	1.812"	2.88"
#105479	30	1.937"	1.875"	1.812"	2.88"
#272863	34	2.187"	2.125"	2.062"	3.19"

* clamp will have greenish hue
** clamp will have reddish hue

Finish is zinc chromate. These style clamps are often referred to as "wire" or "spring" clamps. More commonly, they are called Corbin clamps, referring to their patented manufacturer, the Corbin Screw Corporation. They are still used on many Chrysler Corp. cars and extensively in washing machines. A special tool is designed for their easy attachment and removal that limits the amount of expansion so as not to fracture the clamp.

continued on next page.....

'53–'67 HOSE CLAMPS

CLAMP #3133386 & #3749810

The two clamps that do not fall under the four SAE Standard categories are #3133386 and #3749810. The latter part, pictured, is still serviced by GM and my local Chevrolet dealer had several in stock at a list price of 88¢ each. These clamps were also used in the Corvair heater system. My research shows that #3133386 is very similar in design to #3749810 and can be easily modified to the #3133386 design. The #3749810 (currently serviced), manufactured by Wittek Mfg. Co. of Chicago, comes with a slotted hex head screw and a strap measuring 20".

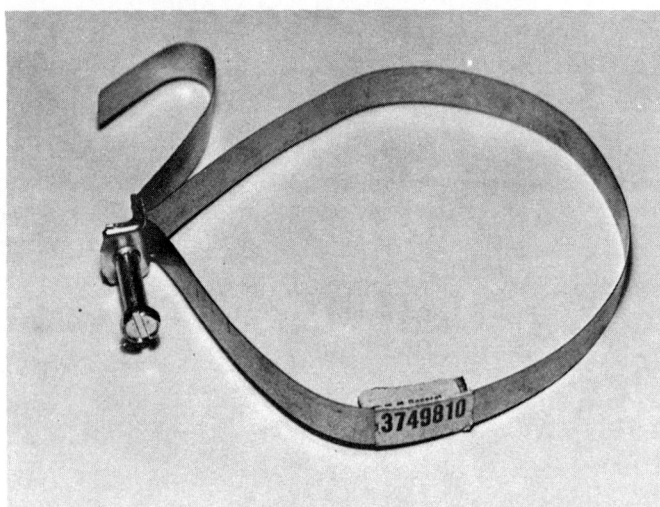

Part #3133386 was identical in design except that it used a 1/4-28 pan head screw 7/8" long and its strap was only 16" long. It should also be noted that while the modern version of #3749-810 uses the hex head screw, earlier versions used the pan head.

1953-1955 HOSE CLAMPS

The '53-'55 Corvette hose clamps are harder to document because assembly manuals did not come into use until the 1956 model. I have, however, surveyed a number of original cars and many factory photographs.

On the six-cylinder models the radiator hose clamps appear to have been of the Type B and D designs; both slotted and unslotted bands using fillister head screws. However, several late 1954 production line photos show the lower radiator hoses connected with four Type E Corbin clamps (size #26).

Photographs of new 1955 V-8 models show the use of the Corbin clamps at all locations. Also, the heater hoses on all '53-'55 models appear to have used Corbin clamps (size #15).

The 1953, 1954 and 1955 Corvette parts books show the use of #3692864 clamp. This is of the Type C "tower" design and most surely is a "service" or universal part, like those used in passenger car assembly of the era. It was not used on the '53-'55 Corvette production lines to my knowledge.

I feel that all the data presented here is documented to my satisfaction as I could not find any conflicting information. All sources agreed 100%. The only information I couldn't uncover is where to find these clamps today. The only clamp in the entire list currently serviced through Chevrolet is the #3749810 mentioned earlier. The Corbin clamps should be available in some auto parts stores. Possibly the other styles can still be located, or a supply can be scrounged at local junk yards and refinished. I did discover that Wittek Mfg. still makes at least the Type D clamps as I recently found some supplied with an after-market engine heater in a local discount store.

I should in closing mention that the often seen clamp sometimes referred to as an "aircraft" type (see photo), while currently used by GM and

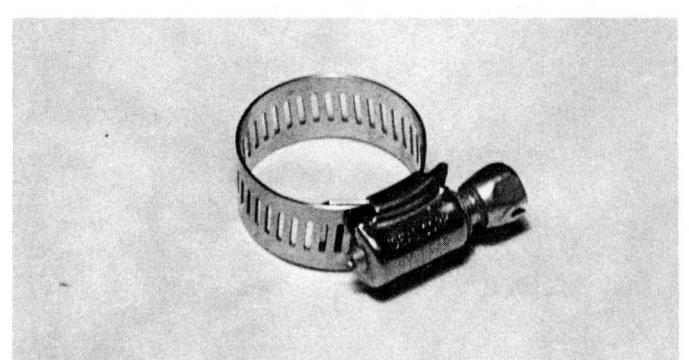

available everywhere (example: Ideal or Sure-tite) was not used on the production of 1953-1967 model Corvettes (except on air conditioning).

If you have additional data of comments, or wish information on hose clamps used at locations I did not cover like fuel tanks or smog equipment, feel free to contact me.

John Amgwert
Box 34377
Omaha, NE 68134
402/493-1020

1956/57 GAS CAPS

BY MICHAEL HUNT

Another "perishable" component of a 1956/7 Corvette is the fuel tank filler cap. Throughout the years, gas caps were frequently left behind at the gas pump, stolen, and so forth. When restoration time arrives, the need for a proper replacement is often apparent.

With "correct" caps selling for upwards of $50 nowadays, and some buyers considering themselves fortunate even to have located one, some attention is in order.

According to the relevant Chevrolet Motor Division documentation we have thus far been able to study, it appears that during the 1956 and 1957 model runs, two gas tank filler caps were available for factory use. A "domed" cap, #3708440, which is vented, is generally regarded as the 1953 through early-1957 gas cap. A "flat" cap, part #3742472, which is not vented, was used on mid-to-late 1957 Corvettes. Note in the accompanying photo that the "flat" cap is not entirely flat, and has a slightly raised circular center portion, with a square-headed rivet.

Left: #3708440 Right: #3742472

For various reasons, gas fumes and gas spillage following hard righthand turns included, a running change was made to a "vented" gas tank. The Factory Assembly Instruction Manual sketch of the vented tank was drawn 11-15-56, which would lead one to suspect that the changeover point was close to VIN# E57S100825. However, an analysis of these A.I.M. drawing dates indicates that oftentimes there was a time-lag between creation of the sketch and actual implementation out on the assembly line. Potential reasons could include a decision to deplete existing supplies of an early-style component, supply problems with a replacement part, or the typical bureaucratic inertia related to the change. At any rate, a close study of hundreds of actual existing 1957 Corvettes convinces me that the actual changeover point to the vented gas tank occurred between E57S101412 and E57S101450. The approximate calendar date for this sequence would be about 12-20-56.

Of interest here is Technical Service Bulletin #435, dated 1-18-57 (reprinted here), which instructs Chevrolet mechanics how to properly vent the earlier "unvented" fuel tanks.

Exactly how the concours judge is supposed to react when confronted with such a Chevrolet-approved dealer modification is open to debate. Personally I feel that any such dealer modification, since it falls under the heading of "factory recall", should not be demerited. If concours judging criteria is to be so "purist-oriented" that a bonafide Chevrolet-approved dealer modification is verboten, similar action would be warranted relative to repro parts, new carpeting, replating, new paint, etc. Common sense dictates a "liberal" attitude here.

A 1957 Corvette with a vented fuel tank will have a small hose and rubber grommet located adjacent to the fuel tank filler pipe.

Chevrolet Technical Service Bulletin #435
Dated 1-15-1957

CHEVROLET—CENTRAL OFFICE
DIVISION OF GENERAL MOTORS CORPORATION
DETROIT 2, MICHIGAN

TECHNICAL SERVICE BULLETIN

Service and Mechanical Department

SUBJECT: GAS TANK PRESSURE BUILD-UP
CORVETTE MODELS

BULLETIN No. TSB

SECTION

TO: ALL CHEVROLET SERVICE PERSONNEL

January 18, 1957

RECEIVED JAN 24 1957 ROCKY MOUNTAIN REGION

To prevent pressure build-up in the gasoline tank, and carburetor flooding, on Corvette Models, the gasoline tank must be vented.

The above conditions are most apt to occur when large changes in climatic temperatures take place, causing the gasoline to change in volume.

Tank may be vented by reworking as follows:

1. Remove gas tank and exhaust gasoline fumes.
2. Pierce a 3/16" diameter hole in top of tank, 7-3/4" to left of gas gauge and 1" forward of centerline of gas gauge. (See illustration)
3. Form a piece of copper tubing #1399637 (53" in length) as shown in illustration, and solder in place in pierced hole.
4. Solder two (2) clips to the gas tank (to be made locally - see illustration).
5. Drill a 1/2" diameter hole in the gas tank filler neck housing, 2-1/4" forward of centerline of gas tank filler neck opening and 2" above it (see illustration). Install #3696521 grommet in hole.
6. Install gas tank.
7. Fasten upper end of copper tube with one (1) clip (to be made up locally), and one (1) #12 - 14 x 1/2 self-tapping screw or equivalent (see illustration).
8. Install one (1) #3742472 Gasoline Filler Cap Assembly.

PARTS DATA

Quantity	Description	Part No.
3	Clip	Make up locally (see illustration
1	Grommet	3696521
1	Copper Tubing (53" length)	217276
1	Gasoline Tank Filler Cap Assy.	3742472
1	Self-tapping Screw #12-14 x 1/2 or equivalent	

HMP/lf
cc: TSB List

H. M. Page
Service and Mechanical Department

INITIAL______

G80 149-O

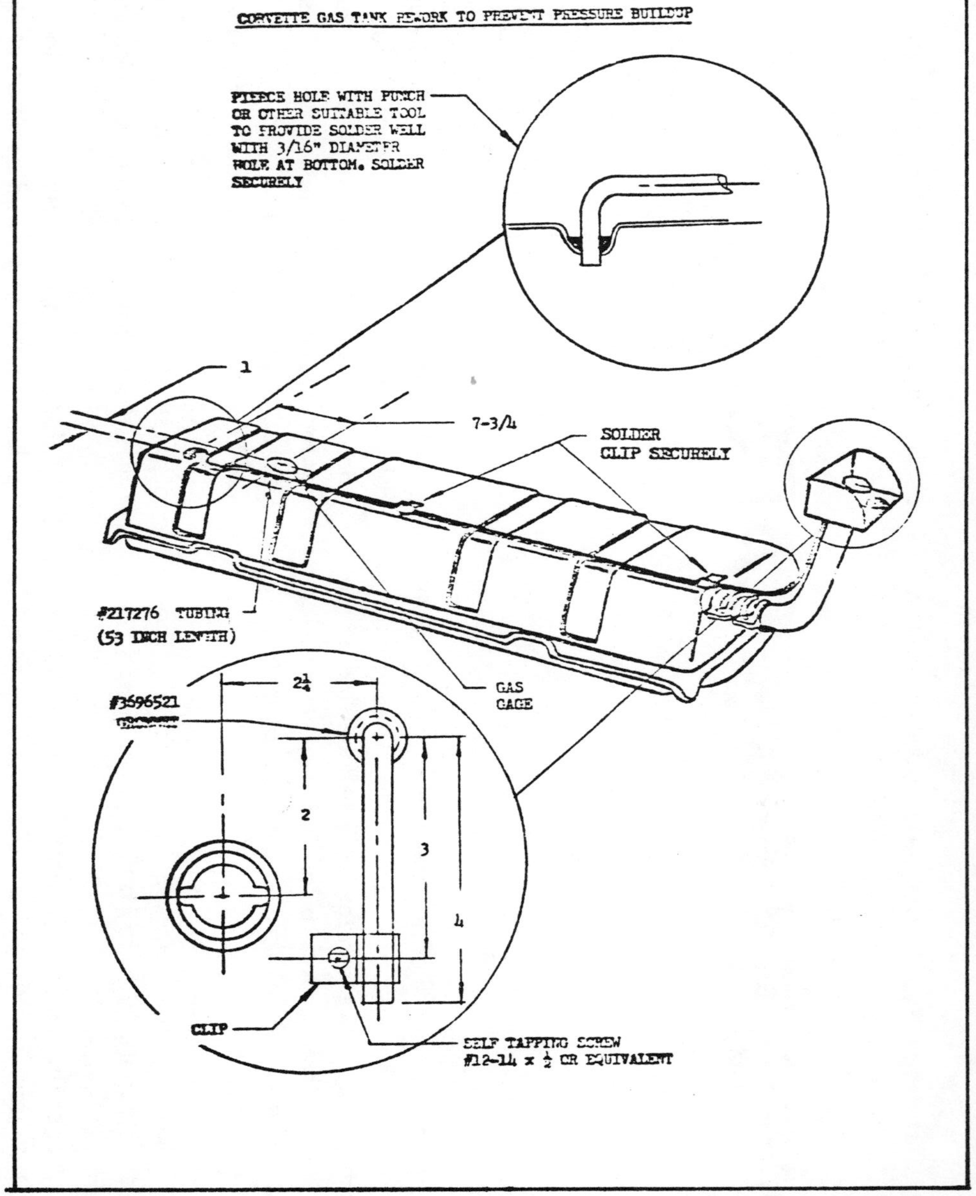

Both types of gas caps were cadmium plated. The "domed" cap carries the "Eaton" manufacturers logo on the underside as can be seen in the photo.

Underside of #3708440. Note "Eaton" logo.

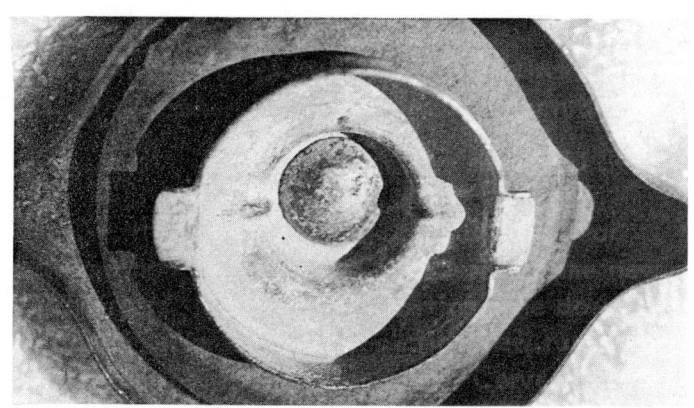

Underside of #3742472.

According to Chevrolet Motor Division specs, the "flat" cap is supposed to carry a manufacturer's identification mark. However, I was unable to locate a logo on the underside of the cap photographed, possibly due to corrosion. The flat cap shown is from an original owner late-VIN# 1957 Corvette, an exceptionally "unmolested" vehicle. The domed cap shown is from E57S101927, and has not been changed as far as the original owner can recall. E57S101927 does have the "vented" fuel tank, which supports the theory that the earliest 1957 vented-tank Corvettes were delivered also with vented caps, until factory supplies of the domed caps were depleted. Concours judges should keep this combination in mind when examining vehicles in the E57S101450 through E57S102500 range!

So much for Chevrolet documentation and the like. Enter a new problem. What is to be written about the several 1957 Corvettes, generally well-preserved vehicles, which have chromed circular gas caps as shown below?

This type of filler cap is common on vehicles having external fuel pipes, such as trucks. One of these caps shown came from a 1949 Ford pick-up truck; the other came from a 1957 Corvette, which was photographed with this particular cap on the vehicle back in 1962. Some knowledgeable 1957 Corvette owners regard the chromed circular cap as at least "possibly correct".

At this point I'd request that all you 1956/7 Corvette owners sit down and write me even a brief note regarding your beliefs on 1956/7 gas caps. Also, any information concerning the possible use of Corvette-style gas caps on other types of vehicles would be helpful, as we could pass that information along to owners who are restoring their Corvettes.

The recently-adopted NCRS 1956/7 Judging Form has been fairly well received, and already an improved version is being finalized. But continuing progress in these informational areas is difficult, at best, without regular input from knowledgeable 1956/7 enthusiasts. We're not magicians, so if you readers wish to see progress and accuracy vis-a-vis the NCRS 1956/7 Judging Form, please feel free to contact Chief Judge Bill Rhodes and/or myself:

> Bill Rhodes
> 1621 Wildwood Rd.
> Marietta, GA 30062
> 404/971-6930
>
> Michael Hunt
> 903 Swarthmore Ct.
> Madison, WI 53705
> 608/233-9226

Be sure to enclose a self-addressed-stamped-envelope (SASE) if a reply is desired.

RESTORATION TIPS

With:
Martin Ball
335 Aloha Drive
San Leandro, CA 94578
Ph. 415/352-1846

I knew that there had been some body-work done to the front end of the car when I bought it, also, the rear exhaust openings and all rear trim mounting holes were filled and painted over.

It wasn't until I removed all the paint that I could see what I had to work with. There had, in fact, been a lot of body-work done over the years!

After both front fender scoops had been replaced and primed (last issue) I proceeded to work on the rear of the car. There was two inches of solid body filler filling the exhaust ports. I drilled a large "guide" hole in the center and used a rotary file mounted in a 1/4" hand drill to ream out the ports in the fenders.

I did all the body work on the car with hand tools. A "long board" was used to straighten out the fenders; it looks like a long sanding block with handles. They are available at most paint stores selling automotive paint and body supplies.

I will have another progress report in the next issue.

53-55 DOOR HINGE RESTORATION

To follow-up on information presented in the last issue, I received a note from George Wright of Northridge, California. George mentions that the bushings (#4110660) listed in the last issue have changed in part number to #9721917. You will need eight of them for both doors.

63-67 LOWER RADIATOR CUSHIONS

Dan Hennigan, South Charleston, Ohio wrote: "I had to replace the radiator and support on my 1964 Corvette and the lower cushions #3786786 were not to be found anywhere. I tried and successfully used two grommets from a Vega cam cover #3977197 at about 20¢ each and they did just fine."

REPAIRING STRIPPED SCREWS IN FIBERGLASS

Submitted by James Kalivoda, San Diego, California. "In past issues of the CORVETTE RESTORER, several methods of repairing pulled through screw holes in door panels, etc., have been discussed. I use a method that seems as effective & a lot easier. Enclosed is a photo of a Ford headlamp rim nut, Ford #376309-S. They come in a package of 30. Using them is simple, just file out the enlarged hole until slightly square and push the plastic nut into place. I have used them everywhere on my Corvette that the standard self-threading upholstery screw is used."

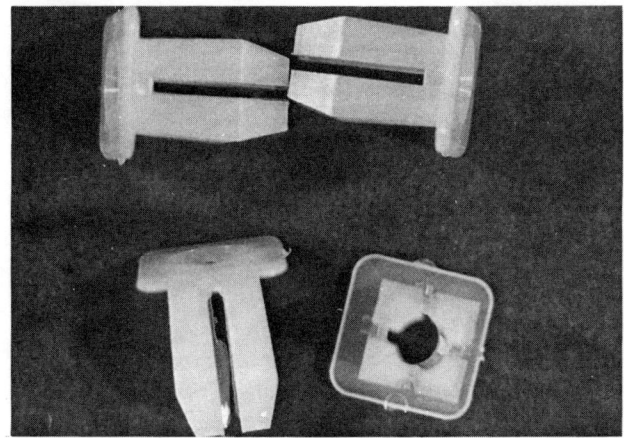

ONE METHOD OF EXHAUST MANIFOLD RESTORATION

Submitted by Bill St. Clair, Warren, Michigan. He writes: One of the hardest vehicle components to restore and keep in concours condition is the exhaust manifold. Rust or oxidation always comes back and most coatings that will withstand heat have some sort of color that would not meet the standards of the discriminating restorer.

I have successfully tried a technique that involves baking on a copper coating to a point where it turns gray and looks like a freshly sandblasted cast iron part. Here are the details:

1. Remove and sandblast all rust from the parts.
2. Spray with a copper paint, use a whole can per engine. That means many coats to prevent drips and sags. The higher the copper pigment content, the better. Rustoleum brand has the highest I've found at 7.1%.
3. Bake in your oven above 450° for about two hours or until it turns gray. A normal outside exhaust fan is adequate, of course an open window wouldn't hurt.
4. Let cool before handling to avoid marking the coating. After it is completely cool, you can handle it normally.

I am told that rust will not form unless you drive in the salt air at the ocean or on salted roads in the winter.

58-60 REAR REFLEX BUTTON INTERCHANGE

Submitted by Ron Mikielski, Wildes-Barre, Pennsylvania. Ron writes: "I noticed one day while ravaging through a local junk yard that the taillights on a 1956 Chevrolet have reflex buttons with the "Guide X42" marking, like the 58-60 Corvettes use. After taking one off and examinimg it more closely, I found that it is exactly the same (including the metal back which is crimped around the sides of the plastic). The only difference is the stud on the back as it is about half as long as the Corvette reflector. This however is easily remedied and at the junkyard price of $1 each you can't go wrong."

LATE 54-55 WHEEL WRENCH HOLD-DOWN CLIPS

Al Butlin of Warren, Michigan recently found the exact replacement clips that hold the lug wrench in place at the back of the trunk on late '54 and '55 Corvettes. They are called "Gripper Clips" made by the Gibson Good Tool Co. and are the small size (they make several) to hold 3/8" and 5/8" diameters.

The original Chevrolet number is 3713871, however these Gripper Clips are the same part as the original right down to the patent number stamping; Gibson Tool being the Original Equipment Manufacturer (OEM).

The clips sell for around $1 for a package of five, available at most hardware stores.

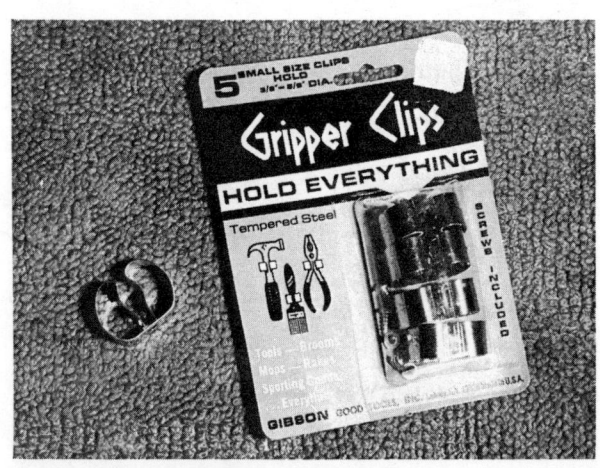

Sting Ray Fun Quiz — ANSWERS

Here are the answers to the Sting Ray Fun Quiz, prepared by Paul Burrill and John E. Hamilton of Wisconsin, that appeared in the last issue on page 31.

1. 1967
2. 1965
3. Outside mirror; bins under seats; fiberglass headlamp housings; wheelcover finish; gas filler cover....
4. 1964-1965
5. 1963-1964-1965
6. No, 1967 did not
7. '63 & '64 – 2 (non-functional)
   '65 & '66 – 2 (functional)
   '67 – 5 (functional)
8. 1967
9. 1965-1967 (late '64 possible according to Factory A. I. M.)
10. Less restriction in off-road system
11. 1963 – Tan only
12. 1963-1966 ('67 wheels were bolt-on)
13. 1965
14. 3 grilles
15. No
16. 1963
17. 1964 hood did not have recesses
18. 2 – 1963-1965, 1966-1967
19. No
20. Five (different each year)
21. 1967
22. 1963
23. 327 c.i.; 250, 300, 340 & 360 HP
24. 327 c.i.; 250, 300, 350, 365 & 375 HP
    396 c.i.; 425 HP
25. 327 c.i.; 300 & 350 HP
    427 c.i.; 390, 400, 430 & 435 HP
26. 3.70:1 ratio
27. Coupe – 36 gallon fuel tank
28. 19437
29. 19467
30. 1965
31. 1965
32. 1965
33. 1966
34. Left
35. Through left wheel well access panel
36. Yes – with 365, 375 & 425 HP only according to 1965 Factory A. I. M.
37. Four – '63-'64 same, '65-'66-'67 each were different
38. Higher tachometer red-line and higher oil pressure gauge
39. Passenger side
40. 1963
41. 1965-1967
42. 1967
43. 1965
44. Yes (extra holes in steering arms)
45. By changing shifting rods to other holes in brackets on transmission
46. Black
47. 1967
48. 1963
49. 1965
50. 1965

TECH SESSION

With SAM FOLZ

DON'T JUNK IT - SIT ON IT!!

One of the most common mistakes a restorer can make if he's new at the game is to throw out broken, worn or corroded parts from his project after he has secured replacements. Don't do it! I'm as guilty as the next person, but I hope that I've learned my lesson.

Ten years ago, when rebuilding the engine in my 1953, Magnaflux showed a cracked cylinder-head. The quick, economical fix was to replace the head with a good, used one for $15 from a salvage yard. Fortunately, I had not scrapped out this very rare part and was recently able to take advantage of greatly improved technology in welding. While expensive, the cost of restoring the head to usable condition was far less than what you'd expect to pay for a super-rare part at a swap meet, and the car now has the original head with the rare casting number (3836066).

Further, and along this line, a well written article in a current hobby publication describes the use of modern, industrial-grade epoxy adhesives applied externally to both cylinder heads and to block castings to seal water-leaking cracks in those parts. When smoothed over and feathered-in, and painted, the repair is quick, inexpensive, durable, and is not visible.

Another sometimes overlooked technique applicable to the eight cylinder heads, which do not use replaceable valve guides, is to have a shop "KNURLIZE" the valve holes. This technique "upsets" the metal in the hole and reduces the net inside-diameter. Granted, this isn't exactly "blueprinting" the engine, and no case is to be made for being "just as good" as a new head, but if your car is to travel only the "Show and Display and Occasional Personal Use" road that so many restorations see when completed, the procedure solves the problem of valve-guide wear very successfully. I've used it on two engines and speak from experience.

Parts of less durable nature than heads and blocks are equally worth saving. I can't tell you how many times I've examined a ragged old factory-original Corvette soft top for construction and dimension details. I've traced at least a dozen pieces from a worn, tattered original paperboard trunk divider panel. The same is true with even small remains of original carpet and seating materials.

This isn't intended to be a case against "Cleanliness is next to Godliness," but catalog, file, or otherwise save those replaced parts that have an "original" story to tell later!

I am most happy to try and answer your individual questions on Corvette restoration, but please include a self-addressed-stamped-envelope. Write: Sam Folz, 3824 Coventry Ave., Kalamazoo, MI 49007.

1956-1962 HARDTOP IDENTIFICATION

By Michael Ernst

There is nothing more prominent or in plainer view on a Corvette of any year than the top. Nothing is more obvious, then, than an incorrect hardtop. Altough tops made any year from 1956 through 1960 will fit any car made '56-'60, that doesn't mean they are correct. All '56 thru '60 hardtop headliners corresponded in color and vinyl pattern to the car's interior, so that rules out most interchanges. Also, all hardtops with original windows have date stampings in each window, which clearly identify them as a top

manufactured in a certain month and year for a certain model year.

1956 was the first year the hardtops were offered for production by Chevrolet, and the '56 top is characterized by a thin aluminum strip on the header portion of the hardtop, above the windshield. Sometime during the 1956 model run, it is believed, and running through the '62 model, a three-piece stainless steel moulding was added to the front header for assembly and appearance purposes. Both '56 and '57 tops featured a waffle-pattern headliner.

Those two tops, as well as '58, '59, and '60 fastened to the car in a similar manner. Each had two latches fastening it to the windshield, and had three brackets along the rear bow, through which bolts passed to fasten it to the rear deck soft top cover of the car.

The 1958 Corvette hardtop is in a class by itself. It was the only model to use the pebble-grain, or "Chatham" grain vinyl, on all the upholstery material including the hardtop headliner.

The exterior appearance of the '58 top was a carry-over from the '56-'57, as those three tops featured a three-piece molding around the rear bow. One piece extended on each side from the front to the rear of the side window, where they were joined by a single "long" molding extending all the way around the back. Over each joint was fastened an inverted "T" shaped molding to bridge the gaps.

The '59 and '60 hardtops then featured a one-piece molding, extending around the entire rear bow. Those two tops use a headliner vinyl which matches that of the interior in grain and color.

The 1961 Corvette hardtop shows numerous changes. The body received a rear "windsplit" running down the car's centerline, so the hardtop

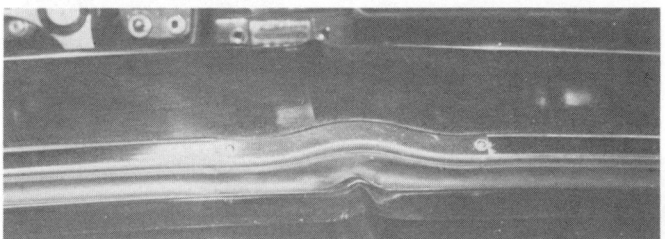

for '61 and '62 was redesigned to fit. Even disregarding that change, the '61-'62 tops will not interchange with earlier tops because the rear deck was designed with a flatter contour, less rounded than the earlier cars.

Mounting was also changed in '61-'62, with brackets on the rear bow located right next to each door, the center bracket removed, and the two rear brackets moved several inches toward the rear centerline. All '61 and '62 hardtops used only a white headliner, and are interchangable except for the date stampings in the plexiglas windows.

If you are considering the purchase of a hardtop, there are certain items to be aware of. Hardtops have a tendency to lose the center clip front molding. Many '56-'60 tops, because of the rear center clip, often have a cracked back window in the small area around that center mount. And the '61-'62 tops are often missing the two brackets adjacent to the doors.

Replacement rear windows are still available from GMPD, as are front latches, and rear hold-down bolts. Side windows and headliners are available from reproduction sources. But, rear brackets and interior and exterior stainless moldings are nearly impossible to find, and are priced accordingly if available.

1961-1962 MATURED MACHINE

WITH REV. MICHAEL ERNST

Photos by John Marquardt

THE DATING GAME!

Many date codes are stamped or cast on various parts and sections of the 1953 through 1967 Corvettes. That dating information is useful to the enthusiast: 1) to determine more about the "personality" of a car, 2) to authenticate whether or not a car is truly "original" or "stock", or 3) to help assemble the correct components for a NCRS Concours.

In this article I will trace 1962 Corvette 20867S112231, a base-engine, four-speed, very original car, assembled about the 5th of June, 1962. (Chevrolet figures show the last '62 built in May, 1962, was number 12,035. Given a production rate of approximately 93 per day, it was likely assembled the third working day of June. Allowing for Saturday and Sunday, the 2nd and 3rd, Tuesday June 5th, was the third working day.)

Castings in parts were done by the supplier as well as some of the stamping codes. Other stamping codes were done by Chevrolet at St. Louis (or Flint in the case of a '53) during Corvette assembly. It is important to note that neither suppliers nor Chevrolet necessarily use a "first-in, first-out" system on parts, so a given part may sit in the back corner of a holding room or warehouse some time before it is needed, or accessable.

A note on casting and stamping dating systems - most use an alphabetical letter to designate the month of manufacture: "A" is for January, "B" for February, and so on through "M" for December, skipping the letter "I" to avoid confusion with the numeral "1".

All the following castings and stamped numbers are correct for a 1962 base-engine 250 HP, four-speed Corvette. Starting with essentials, the engine block casting date was E292 - E for May, 29 for the 29th, 2 for '62. (For location of engine casting dates consult CR Vol. Three, #3, page 12.) That block, cast on May 29th, was assembled at the Flint engine plant on May 31, as read from the engine stamping on the front right side. That stamping reads F0531RC - F (Flint), 05 (May) 31 (the thirty-first) RC (base 250 HP engine with manual transmission). That sequence alone is interesting - cast May 29, assembled May 31, and installed in the car

continued on next page...

June 5th in St. Louis. Other '62's have been observed with as long as six weeks between the engine assembly and installation.

A note on engine stamping - the assembly date and suffix were stamped at the time the engine was manufactured, the serial number as stamped on the same pad (2112231) was stamped at St. Louis when the engine and the chassis were mated. There is a difference in the size of numeral dies used.

The cylinder heads were cast E112 (May 11, '62), casting number 3795896. The intake

manifold casting date is A222 (Jan. 22, '62), casting number 3783244.

The electrical generator is stamped 1102174 2E3 (May 3, '62).

The radiator coolant expansion tank/reservoir is stamped 62E (May, '62).

The foil tag on the Carter WCFB carburetor is stamped H 9 1 (apparently August 9, '61) as well as having the carb model number 3191-S and the part number 3788246.

The ignition distributor has a foil tag with 1110984 2D 13 (April 13, '62).

Car number 12,231 is obviously a late production car, as only 14,531 1962's were made, yet the radiator has the metal tag that is associated with the earlier 1962's produced, and has a date stamping of 61K (October '61).

Obviously, the radiator, like the carburetor, was not first-in, first-out. Later radiators with the non-metal tags have the dating code stamp on the top of the radiator.

The transmission case and tailshaft housing are both cast with the date 5 9 62, and the side cover has 5 9 62A on it. Other 1962's have shown less uniformity - some have components cast as much as 10 months apart.

On the transmission case, next to the side cover, the following is stamped:

WE 2823

2112231

It is obviously two separate stampings: the 2112231 was stamped as the transmission was mated to the engine and chassis, the WE 2823 was stamped when the transmission was assembled. Translated, the WE 2823 means: W (Warner), E (May), 28 (the 28th) 2 ('62), and the 3 (3rd shift). Thanks to Loren Lundberg of Glendale, Arizona, for the information on decoding that one!

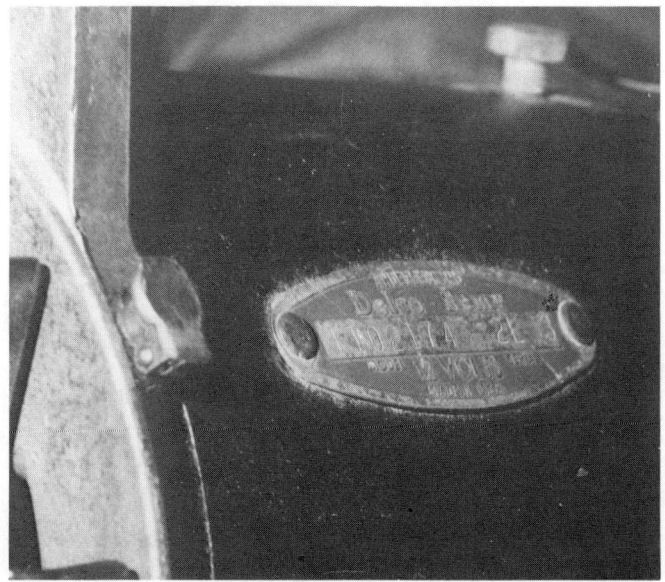

Other items with dates: The left-hand door post was stamped in blue ink "Jun 1 1962" on the portion of the post assembled inside the door. The clock was stamped in black letters on the back "May 62". All three hardtop windows are original, and are stamped "3 62", indicating a March date.

Other 1962's have been observed with date stampings on the windshield frame under the weatherstripping, on the back of the tachometer, speedometer, radio, gauges, on the back of the door panels, on the inside of the doors, and on the trunk lid under the hinge mount.

1962 number 12,231 was not sporting the original water pump which would have had a date code, and was missing the original starter which also would have a date code on the identification tag.

Locations from car to car are not uniform, and may have been left to the whim of the foreman or assembler.

There are likely other locations I haven't covered or discovered -- owners help me out!

The dating game is enjoyable, as it tells you the personality of a car. Using the above as a guide, can help you determine the originality of components on your car or others.

UPDATE - In reference to the 220° or 240° temperature gauge on 1962's that I discussed in the last article, there seems to be evidence that this change did not occur overnight! It probably took place for quite a while. I have received correspondence form '61 owners who have the 240° gauges in original cars, and have later '62's with 220° gauges, earlier with 240° gauges, etc., and there seems to be no correlation with performance options, either. What have you got??

I would also like to hear from 1961 owners with the flat aluminum expansion tank above the radiator!!!

Rev. Michael Ernst
P. O. Box 36
Bowler, WI 54416
Phone: 715/793-4608

RESTORATION TIPS

The '53-'67 hose clamp article in the last issue was apparently well received from the number of comments that were received.

Don Mullendorf of Livermore, Cal., wrote to say that his black 1954 model used the Corbin (type E) style clamps extensively.

Dennis Kremer of Dubuque, Iowa, also wrote that the 2" diameter style type "B" slotted clamps are available from Ford under part #8287, as well the Corbin style 1" diameter clamps for the heater hoses (Ford #18473) and that sets are priced under $2 !

Bill Mock of Bartlesville, Oklahoma, contacted me saying that he sells many of the clamps listed in the last issue. However, Bill claims that the #30 and #34 Corbin clamps will not fit their early Corvette applications as listed in the article, as they are too small! He says that #32 and #36 must be used respectively.

I checked into this and the following information comes from Jon Blanchetter, an engineer at Rochester Products:

"On the Corbin clamp subject, my upper and lower hoses are 1 7/8" O.D. and 2 1/8" respectively. I used those clamps recommended in the article, and by Corbin for those diameters, namely the #30 and #34, and had no problem. I believe the problem the other member had was installing the hose, then trying to expand the clamp from position "A" over the bump to position "B". You should install on the hose first, position "C", then push the hose on, and move the clamp to position "B". In fact, this is a must as you cannot expand enough to get over the bump. Don't attempt to expand the clamp over the bump, and you'll be OK!"

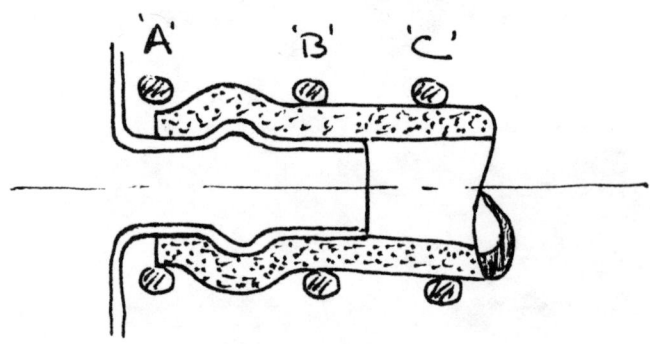

Jon also mentioned that the people at Corbin are very nice and the address is: Corbin Hose Clamp, Division of Emhart Corp., 225 Episcopal Rd., Berlin, CT 06037, (203) 225-7411.

Recently at a "swap-meet" in Lincoln, Nebraska, your editor spied a vendor who was selling an air cleaner that looked very similar to the later six-cylinder style used on the Corvette. Since I was not certain of the aircleaner's application, I paid the man $3 and took my chances!

Pictured here is one of the Corvette "pot" cleaners at right, and the "mystery" aircleaner on the left. The mounting base for both cleaners is identical. However, while the Corvette's top cover is generally smooth and in chrome finish, this other cleaner has stamped ribs forming a six-pointed "star" and is painted black.

I have heard of this mystery cleaner before, alledged to have an application on some early Chevrolet or maybe Ford.

In looking over some photos that I have, I noticed that this type of air-cleaner was used on the Motorama Corvette prototype EX-122. This car used three of these cleaners, all chrome, mounted vertically directly to the carburetors, rather than two cleaners being mounted to the duct system as on later production 1954's.

If any member knows of the original application of this type air-cleaner, let me know!

Sam Folz recently found an original style glass bowl type fuel filter as used on some early Corvettes. The part currently serviced by Chevrolet uses a slightly different filter element and metal head, so when Sam got an original style unit, he searched for the correct filter. He found that Fram still services a CG-3 filter, which replaces the GM 854347 part, costing $2.85 list.

I recently received an ad from a member selling "NOS late 1954 windshield washer pumps" for $24, and have seen recent ads in other publications for that part as high as $75!

A quik call to Trico Products in Buffalo brought some welcome information. It seems that Trico still services that part #AWS-2 without the glass jar for $8.70 including handling. If you need the jar, you may find one in an old GM car at a wrecking yard, or Trico services their #82895-1. The Trico jar is slightly smaller in height so you will have to cut off a small piece of the plastic "pick-up" end.

I also found out that Trico has a rebuilding service for their vacuum style wiper motors. They suggest you send them the motor, including description, marking the parcel "MOTOR FOR REPAIR" to:

Trico Products Corp. Plant #2
2495 Main St. Dock #3
Buffalo, NY 14214

Trico still has some of the parts, and the rebuilding cost is around $6 plus parts. They will rebuild the unit if they can, and send "COD". Remember that Trico only rebuilds "their" vacuum wiper motors, as used on the six-cylinder Corvette.

For availability and ordering the pumps, Trico suggests that you contact your local part's store selling Trico Products.

NCRS member Billy Buckner of Hueytown, Alabama, recently sent some photos of his 1957 Corvette serial number 6148, in hopes that someone can answer questions about some unusual features on the car.

It's originally a fuel injected model, with hardtop only, four speed transmission, and the color appears to have been black.

It has the 1110908 distributor, and apparently a column mounted tach, as well as holes in the left side for the 579E option air-intake.

On the frame behind the battery tray the fuel line is protected by a heavy gauge steel pipe about two feet long. Just in front of the battery tray where the brake lines ,"junction", a metal air scoop/heat shield is attached.

A photo of the rear of the frame shows an additional bracket on both sides used to mount a rubber rebound cushion, immediately behind the front, rear spring, perch.

He would like to locate a previous owner named David Jess McQueen, who lived in Torrence, California, and Clovis, New Mexico. If anyone knows anything about the car's features, or the previous owner, contact: Billy Buckner, 3317 Crescent Dr., Hueytown, Alabama 35020, phone 205/491-5463.

1956-1962 OIL FILLER CAPS

by EDWIN S. GURDJIAN

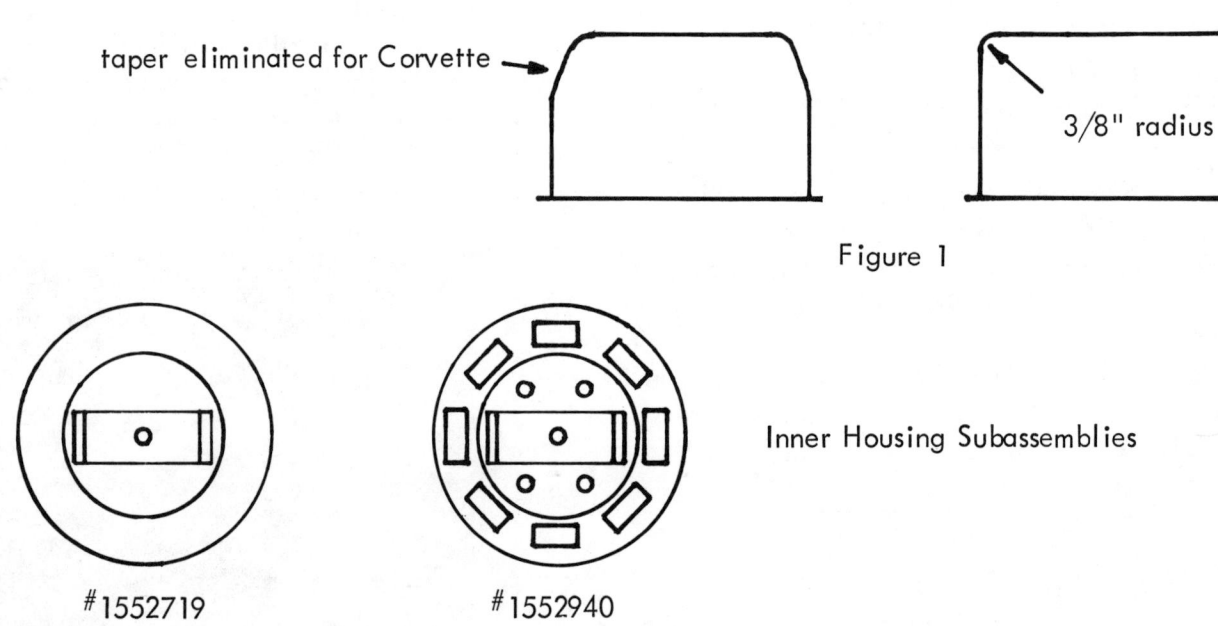

Figure 1

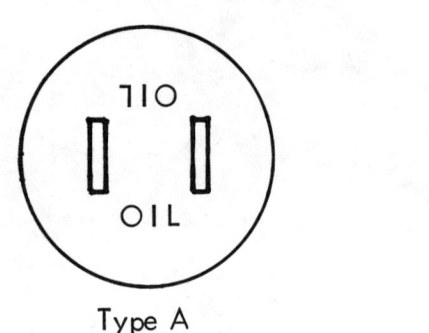

#1552719
Non-breathing (closed)

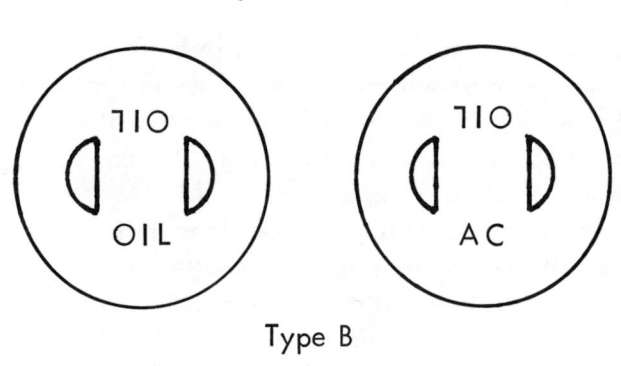

#1552940
Breathing (open)

Inner Housing Subassemblies

Type A

Type B

Figure 2

Only two oil caps, #1552719 & #1552940, were used on Corvette engines from 1956 through the 1962 model year. With the assistance of AC engineers, the Corvette Assembly Manuals for those years, and a Chevrolet Technical Service Bulletin #263 from 1956 (see CR Winter-1975, Vol. One, #3), I have been able to document the histories of these caps and their applications. It must be noted that specific dates found in this article will refer to "AC" manufacturing changes, and not directly to Corvette assembly. However, the dates given will generally reflect the era that the changes found their way to the Corvette line.

The #1552719 cap originally was a "breathing" type, but was modified to "non-breathing" status in February, 1956.

The #1552940, first made in April, 1956 when the need for a breathing type cap for "street" engines became apparent, was almost identical to the original "breathing" #1552719.

Note the similarity of dates for AC production changes between the two caps.

OIL CAP #1552719

In 1956 Chevrolet Engineers involved in a racing program requested that AC make a non-breathing oil cap. Accordingly, on February 2, 1956, AC made four changes on a previously breathing type cap #1552719 which was first produced on November 29, 1955. The copper mesh filter element was removed, eight rectangular openings and one 7/32" hole were removed from the inner housing, and the taper of the outer housing was eliminated (see figure 1). The resulting cap was cadmium plated and top cover read "OIL/OIL", the two words being inverted.

No further changes in design occurred until January 21, 1960. At that time, the inner housing subassembly consisting of the inner housing, a clip and a rivet, which were combined into a single subassembly #5646619 (all part of #1552719 cap!). This resulted in no visual change.

On April 21, 1961 the markings on the outer housing were changed from Oil/Oil, to "AC/Oil", the two words being inverted. The finish plating continued to be cadmium until November 8, 1961 when it was changed to chromium.

Later that month, November 27, 1961, the part's name was changed from "crankcase breathing assembly" to "oil filler assembly". No further changes occurred until 1965. On March 2, 1965 the inner cap diameter tolerance was increased, a very minor point. On May 31, 1966 the inner housing subassembly #5646619 was replaced by #6424406. The difference between the two was that the clip on the former protruded $\frac{1}{2}$", while the latter protruded 9/64", another minor point!

OIL CAP #1552940

Several months after all early 1956 Corvettes were supplied with the non-breathing #1552719 caps, difficulties with oil control, secondary to inadequate crankcase ventilation in non-racing conditions, became apparent. Oil cap #1552940 was designed to solve this problem. The outer housing of this unit was cadmium plated and was essentially the same as the outer housing of #1552719. The dates of any changes, dye indents, plating and markings (Oil/Oil etc.) are the same for both caps.

The inner housing contained eight rectangular openings, four 7/32" holes and a copper filter element.

A decal outlining the cleaning instructions, was used until December 28, 1960.

This cap was used on all hydraulic lifter engines from about May, 1956 through 1962. The date of initial AC production was April 25, 1956.

As with cap #1552719, on January 21, 1960 the inner housing subassembly was combined. Changes from Oil/Oil to AC/Oil and from cadmium plating to chromium occurred on April 20, 1961 and November 9, 1961 respectively. On November 27, 1961 the part name was changed from "crankcase breather" to "oil filler and breather cap assembly". The final change occurred on January 23 & 24, 1967 when the copper ribbon filter element was replaced by aluminum.

APPLICATIONS

Oil cap #1552719 was used on all Corvettes from the beginning of 1956 until May, 1956, and on all solid-lifter engines thereafter. This cap was a non-breather, so never used a cleaning decal!

Oil cap #1552940 was used on all hydraulic-lifter engines after May, 1956.

Until at least mid 1961 the caps were cadmium plated and read Oil/Oil.

All caps had dye indentations in the outer housing - none were smooth (see figure 2). Two types of indentations have been noted. The date of change at AC from type "A" to type "B" was October 16, 1957. Type "B" persisted through the 1962 model year.

In mid 1961 the outer housing markings were changed from Oil/Oil to AC/Oil. Some of these caps were produced in cadmium plate. It is not certain whether they were used on 1961 Corvettes. Chromium caps were not available until November, 1961. It is not certain whether they appeared initially on the 1962 model or were a running change.

The author wishes to acknowledge the assistance of several AC engineers who wish to remain anonymous without whose help this article could not have been written.

Edwin S. Gurdjian
161 Canterbury Rd.
Bloomfield Hills, MI 48013

Photos and Story By GENE DRESSEN

FUEL INJECTION UNIT #7017380

The 7017380 model fuel injection unit was used on the 375 HP Corvette engine in 1964 and 1965. The first few 1964 Corvette models used a re-calibrated 7017375 unit, stamped "R" on the plenum chamber identification tag. The re-calibration was necessary to meet the demands of the new engine which carried larger heads and a new camshaft.

The cranking signal valve, which was first used on the 7014900, was dropped from the starting circuit of the 7017380. In its place was incorporated an electric fuel valve, which allowed fuel to bypass the fuel meter pump, providing fuel pump pressure directly to the nozzles. This circuit was rendered inoperative once the engine was started. This same starting procedure was used on the first 1957 units up through the 7014800 units.

There were a number of changes that were made to the 7380. The first was cosmetic. The St. Louis assembly plant started stamping the car's serial number on the plenum chamber. This was possibly done in an attempt to identify the origin of stolen units. It is believed by many people who are familiar with this procedure, that it was started in 1965, but, in fact, it was used on the 1964 Corvette as early as vehicle number 14,848. The accompanying chart shows that vehicle (1964) 16,068 was also stamped in this manner. Unlike the 1965 units which carry the stamping on the right rear side of the plenum chamber, the 1964 was stamped on the front of the plenum, on the heavy boss to which the chrome vent tube clamp is attached.

All 1965 Corvettes and all 1964's produced at least after vehicle 14,848 should carry the car serial number on the plenum chamber.

The next modification the 7380 received was to incorporate a screen on the waste side of the spill valve through which the excess fuel could flow, thus reducing the unstable condition of the fuel returning to the fuel bowl. There was also a baffle installed on the lower side of the fuel meter cover directly over the fuel float. This was installed to control the slopping fuel from leaving the fuel bowl vent. The baffle was secured with a threaded stud which protruded up through the lower right bolt hole in the main control diaphram cover. The cover was secured in this location with a washer and nut. The earliest evidence I have of this was on 1964 car #16,068.

At some unknown time there were also modifications made to the choke assembly. These were to increase cold starting performance.

Upon looking at the table, you will note that

Plenum chamber ID tag. At front of the unit is the boss (where chrome vent tube attaches) where the 1964 vehicle number is stamped on later cars.

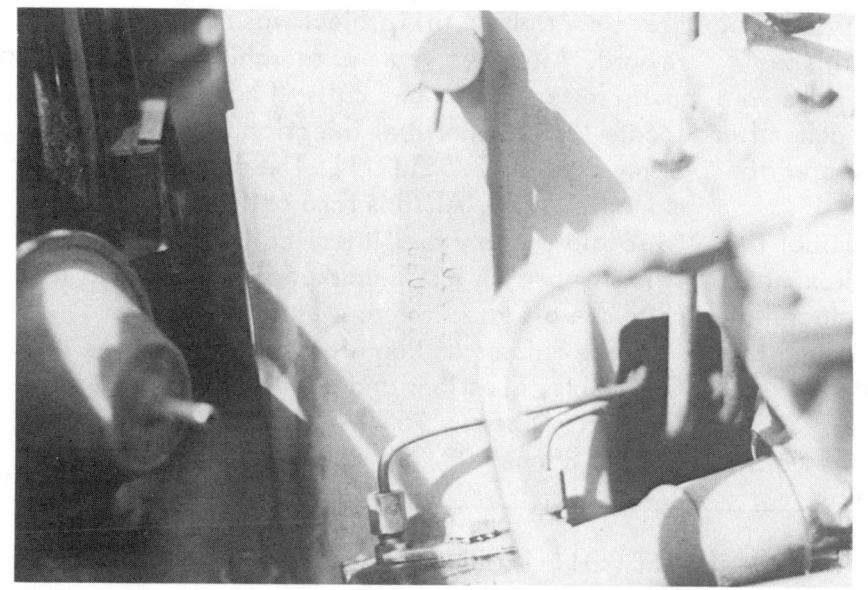

Car serial number stamped on 1965 Corvette injection unit on right rear rear side of plenum (hose disconnected).

Nut & stud securing fuel baffle in fuel bowl. Foil tag shows coded date of fuel meter production.

continued on next page....

the plenum chambers are listed in sequence. You will notice that there is quite a bit of confusion in vehicle serial numbers in the first eight units listed. I do not know the reason for the car serial numbers being so far out of sequence at this particular time. There was possibly an attempt to use up all the remaining "out of sequence" parts before they got too far into the 1965 model year.

You will note that from plenum number 2523 that there was near perfect order maintained. Those slight inconsistencies can be attributed to the random selection of fuel units by the engine plant and by engine selection from stock at St. Louis assembly. Whatever the problem, it appears that it was corrected.

You will also note that there are a few units that don't have car serial numbers stamped on them. These units apparently were not originally installed at the factory. It may have been units in this sequence which were sent to the warehouse to be sold as "service" parts. This could have been done after an adequate supply of units had been delivered to the engine plant.

If the table can be used to indicate actual figures, it would appear that there were approximately 2,150 #7017380 fuel injection units manufactured, about 1,200 going for the 1964 model year and the the other 950 going for the 1965's. (Editor's Note: As published by NCRS in 1975, Vol. One, #3, Rochester records show that there were 2,114 of the #7017380 units shipped for vehicle assembly, and 67 units for "service".)

The documented figure for the factory fuel injected 1965's is 771. That left less than 200 units that were not originally installed on the 1965.

I undertook the project of documenting the 1965 factory fuel injected Corvette with the idea of accumulating and dissimulating as much data as possible. I have talked with many people who are very knowledgeable on the subject. I have learned many things, and have much still to learn. The only way we are able to eventually come to a knowledge of some things is to make assumptions at first. The assumptions that I have made here, are based on a great amount of research. Until we can open the door at GM, we'll have to be content with our assumptions!

Undertaking this project was not without some reward. After two years of searching, which include many letters and phone calls, I have been able to locate the original fuel injection unit that came off of my car, 194375S102111. The unit had been removed in 1970. All this time and money spent just to locate a crazy fuel injection unit with some numbers stamped on it. I'm asked if it was worth it. I think we all know the answer.

The figures and opinions are those of the author Comments, questions and additions can be sent to: Gene H. Dressen, 753 Wayne, Pocatello, Idaho 83201, phone 208/233-2527.

MODEL 7017380 FUEL INJECTION IDENTIFICATION

Plenum Serial	Car Serial	Nut?	Stamped?	Plenum Serial	Car Serial	Nut?	Stamped?
1549	4107889	no	no	2597	5105168	yes	yes
1591	5110692	yes	yes	2629	5106210	yes	yes
1745	4114848	no	yes	2692	5107446	yes	yes
1778	on '64	no	no	2694	5107218	yes	yes
2027	from '64	no	no	2730	5108178	yes	yes
2158	5102111	yes	yes	2737	5107798	yes	yes
2234	4116068	yes	yes	2832	5109858	no	yes
2245	5100943	yes	yes	2893	5110006	yes	yes
2255	-	yes	no	2901	5110588	yes	yes
2261	-	yes	no	2975	5112692	yes	yes
2338	-	yes	no	2976	5112030	yes	yes
2355	-	yes	no	3011	5113618	yes	yes
2523	5105094	yes	yes	3051	-	yes	no
2538	5104696	yes	yes	3062	5115129	yes	yes
2539	5105248	yes	yes	3138	5123074	yes	yes

1965 CORVETTE GAS DOOR LID

Photo and Story By James Howlett

Today, more people are noting small differences in their Corvettes that until now have gone unnoticed. One of these differences is the original factory gas door on the 1965 models. Some one-owner cars with the factory gas door lids have a definite silver center ring, while other '65's have a gold center ring.

Several contacts with people at Chevrolet have brought differences of opinion on the subject. One source states that as the gas door lid is exposed to the elements of the sun, temperature variations, and age, the silver takes on a yellow-gold tint. I have noticed this phenomena in a number of silver gas door lids. The yellow-gold tint is not uniform and has a "washed-out" look. Conversely, these mysterious gold lids have a definite uniform color. The gold inner ring reflects on the silver outer ring and makes it appear to be gold.

Another source poses the running substitution theory. The thought here is that perhaps a shortage occurred during peak production and another supplier filled the need with gas door lids having this difference in the color of the center ring.

Still another suggests the possibility of an unnoticed slip-up in plating a number of lids at the OEM (Original Equipment Manufacturer) plant. Just last Summer I saw a 1977 Corvette come into the local Chevrolet dealership with a standard chrome plated mirror on the driver's side, and a painted sport mirror on the passenger side. If this situation could occur, then a quantity of gold lids could occur, going unnoticed.

If the reader wishes to identify the gas door lid on his car, he should carefully check the flag poles and the outer ring at several different angles. This will help determine if the outer ring has faded into yellow-gold or if it retains the silver color. The center ring will be a uniform color about the shade of 14 karat gold.

From the 1965 Corvettes I have examined, I find a pattern beginning to surface. Some cars produced from the mid to late model run have a gold center ring on the gas door lid. Silver seems to be the predominate color, and all early 1965 Corvettes I have examined have silver center rings.

No pattern has shown up yet on any definite time span such as gold lids on all Corvettes produced an any given week or month.

I am presently conducting a survey on '63 through '67 Corvettes, much the same as others have done on the earlier solid axle cars. I hope to offer more on the color differences in the 1965 gas door lid as the survey helps glean information. If you have a 1965 Corvette and would like to help the effort, I would like to hear from you. I am especially interested in unmolested, original cars. Be sure to enclose a self-addressed-stamped-envelope if a reply is desired. Contact: Jim Howlett, 1205 West Waldo, Independence, Missouri 64050, phone 816/461-6242 before 9:30 PM CST.

TECH SESSION
With Sam Folz

10-7 FOR THE WINTER

Even though good driving weather for most of us in the Northern part of the country has just arrived, by the time you read this it won't be too soon to make plans for winter storage of your collector Corvette, and the return to the old "beater."

There are probably as many ways to store a car for the cold months as there are people with opinions, so I'll pass a few ideas along for what they're worth and you can decide what's right for you.

For purposes of discussion, we'll assume you do not have a heated garage, and that it gets cold and damp where you live.

The system I have used for the past ten years or so is a simple one:

1. Top-off the gas tank with fresh gas. This forces moisture-laden air out of the tank to minimize corrosion.

2. Change oil and lubricate chassis.

3. Over-inflate tires to about 35 PSI to minimize "flat-spotting" and sidewall bulge.

4. Polish all painted and chrome surfaces with a good wax or glaze.

5. Cover car with a car cover that breathes, such as cotton or cotton-polyester blend so that there's no trap of condensation.

6. "Fire up" every three to four weeks. Run engine at 1,000-1,500 RPM for 30-45 minutes so that every component comes up to operating temperature and the exhaust system dries out. During this time turn on radio and heater for a few minutes so all components, both electronic and mechanical stay dry and in operating condition.

7. Reduce engine speed to idle and drive the car backward and forward in garage to work transmission seals, axle seals, pinion seal, and both master brake cylinder and wheel cylinders.

8. Occasional operation of air conditioning on vehicles so-equipped will keep the system free of moisture and provides lubrication of seals and compressor bearings. Bear in mind that GM compressors are designed to *not* operate when the outside air temperature approaches "freezing."

When Spring arrives at last, you're ready to roll out and go, as the vehicle has really never been out of service.

If you find it inconvenient to get to the car and move it through the winter, you may want to take it out of service more thoroughly. I'd suggest you consider:

1. Block it up off the ground so the tires are relieved.

2. Stall the engine out by flooding it with a light oil fed through the carburetor(s). You might consider a mixture of 50% kerosene and 50% Casite. This is commonly used in our area for storage of gasoline-engined boats and performs well. The Casite makes the kerosene cling to walls, valves, and rings and gives good internal corrosion protection. Spring startup is easy with little or no plug fouling.

If you choose to remove the battery from the vehicle you'll be farther ahead if you make sure that it is fully charged and stored in a cool-to-cold place. Warm storage increases the leak-down rate and increases the likelihood of plate sulphation.

Should you be planning to store for a period longer than the normal Winter season, I'd suggest you consider draining the tank, replacing fuel with a small amount of white gas if you can get it, and running that fuel through the induction system prior to shutdown. White gas will be more stable in the event of evaporation and would leave no varnish.

Also, give a thought to protection against rodents and bugs. De-Con for rats or mice placed in the storage area is a good idea, and moth crystals are a good precaution.

Your thoughts, ideas, and results that have worked for you would be welcomed and shared with members.

Sam Folz,
Technical Director
3824 Coventry Ave.
Kalamazoo, MI 49007

RESEARCH PROJECT 1956/7
With Michael Hunt

1957 CORVETTE IGNITION DISTRIBUTORS: F.I. OPTION

The purpose of this essay is twofold: 1) to explain which ignition distributors were used with which 1957 Corvette F.I. engine/transmission/VIN# combinations; and 2) to introduce the "time-lag" phenomenon sometimes characteristic to existing early documentation on the topic.

Regarding the "time-lag," the student of early Corvette F.I. applications should bear in mind the facts that from late-1956 until almost mid-1957, fuel injection was very new, was developmental by nature, and it was scarce. Numerous changes were made during this period, to the Rochester Ramjet unit itself, and to certain corresponding equipment, such as the Delco-Remy ignition distributors.

Now, some 20-plus years later, enthusiasts attempt to pin down the various changes and configurations by studying available documentation. Such documentation, however, can be misleading, even when bearing one of the prestigious Chevrolet Motor Division logos. One reason for this is a "time-lag" which sometimes existed between the actual assembly date of the early F.I. cars and the eventual publication and dissemination of mechanical/technical information on the early F.I. configurations. On occasion, and examples can even be found in the generally reliable *Corvette News* publication (for instance, ref. Vol. 1 Nr. 2 p. 17), the information which did reach print was either: 1) generalized; 2) "theoretical" in nature; or 3) reflected certain "late-date" realities which were simply not correct or accurate for "early-date" F.I. cars. Therefore a too-literal reliance upon some nominally authoritative "official" documentation can produce unsatisfactory results.

This brings us to the ignition distributors actually used on the early 1957 F.I. cars. Now almost without exception, available documentation lists ignition distributors for the 1957 F.I. Corvettes as shown in the following table:

Distributor Part Number	Horsepower Rating	Transmission Type
1110889	250/283	Manual
1110905	250/283	Manual
1110906	250	Automatic
1110908	283	Manual

With this thinking in mind, restorers of 1957 Corvettes with the RPO579C option (fuel injected 250hp engine and Powerglide transmission) have searched high and low for 1110906 distributors when restoring such vehicles. And concours judges, ever mindful of the distributor arrangement in the preceding table, have accordingly demerited vehicles

(continued on next page)

FUEL INJECTION

FI-Page 9
SERVICE AND MECHANICAL DEPARTMENT
PRODUCT ENGINEERING
PRODUCT DATA BOOK
SECTION VIm GROUP 2

TECHNICAL INFORMATION

SUBJECT	INFORMATION
Ignition Distributor - Oil Leaks.	In cases where difficulty is experienced due to engine oil entering the Ignition Distributor Bowl on F.I. equipped engines a 3/16" drain hole may be drilled in the circular groove in the lower part of the distributor body. Ignition Distributor 1110905 has an "O" ring seal at the shaft bearing location. 3-13-57

Fuel Injection Spark Advance Settings

Engine	Distributor	Camshaft	Trans.	Spark Setting at Idle	Spark Setting at 1000 RPM
283-V8	1110905	Std. High Lift (#3733431)	Auto.	12° BTDC (Do not exceed 14° BTDC)	18° BTDC (Do not exceed 20° BTDC)
283-V8 Corv.	1110905	Same	Same	Same	Same
283-V8	1110905	Duntov (High Performance #3736097)	Manual	4° BTDC (Do not exceed 8° BTDC)	10° BTDC (Do not exceed 14° BTDC)
283-V8 Corv.	1110905	Same	Same	Same	Same

3-13-57

not thus equipped. Similarly, even the first version of the NCRS 1956/7 concours judging sheet reflected thinking that *all* 250/PG cars must be equipped with 1110906 distributors. That oversight has been corrected in the second version of the NCRS 1956/7 concours judging sheet.

During recent years, I occasionally encountered evidence that a 1110906 distributor was not necessarily correct for a 250/PG 1957 Corvette. Also the 1110905 is obviously a replacement (running change) for the lower-numbered 1110889, and since part #1110906 follows part #1110905, it is almost a certainty that the 1110906 did not even exist until *after* the 1110905 had been introduced. With this in mind, I recently had the good fortune to compare notes with a very perceptive enthusiast named Steve Ames, who owns and operates Ames Performance Engineering, Bonney Rd., Marlboro, NH. 03455 (603-532-7331 days, 603-876-4514 evenings). As a part of his business, Steve rebuilds many distributors, and he keeps track of what he learns in the process. It was Steve's contention that like the manual transmission cars, the Powerglide-equipped 1957 250hp F.I. cars would also have used 1110889 (early) or 1110905 (mid-late) distributors, with the 1110906 being used *only* very late in the 1957 model run, and through the early *1958* F.I. production.

Steve's theory was soon substantiated by the following Technical Information bulletin, from Chevrolet's Service and Mechanical Dept. to the Division's field personnel. This Tech Info bulletin was graciously supplied by a fellow NCRS member, who also happens to be a GM employee, and who shall remain anonymous.

The bulletin substantiates the change *from* the 1110889 distributor *to* the 1110905 distributor, which occurred shortly before 3-13-57, and which is valid for *all* 1957 F.I. Chevrolets and Corvettes, regardless of horsepower rating or transmission combination. As the bulletin explains, the 1110905 distributor is basically a 1110889, which has been improved (O-ring added) to eliminate an oil vapor leakage problem. In addition, Steve Ames notes that: 1) the basic casting for the 1110905 distributor was made slightly heftier, so that additional material could be cut away for the O-ring; and 2) late 1110905 distributors also have a bearing retainer, apparently added to reduce bearing wobble.

Based upon a study of the preceding bulletin and upon the date codes appearing on distributors from 1957 Corvettes which I've surveyed, I have constructed the following table. The VIN#'s listed are *approximate*, and are as accurate as possible with the documentation at hand.

1957 FUEL INJECTED CORVETTE IGNITION DISTRIBUTORS

Distributor Part Number	Horsepower Rating	Transmission Type	Centrifugal or Vacuum Advance	Single or Dual Points	*Approximate* Vehicle Ident. Numbers Range
1110889	250	Manual/Auto	Centrifugal	Dual	E57S100001 — 102750
	283	Manual	Centrifugal	Dual	E57S100001 — 102750
1110905	250	Manual	Centrifugal	Dual	E57S102751 — 106339
	250	Automatic	Centrifugal	Dual	E57S102751 — 104750
	283	Manual	Centrifugal	Dual	E57S102751 — 106339
1110906	250	Automatic	Vacuum	Single	E57S104751 — 106339
*1110908	283	Manual	Centrifugal	Dual	E57S103750 — 106339

*Note: Generally speaking, the 1110908 distributor is part of the RPO579E package, and is used to drive the #1548680 8000rpm AC column-mount tachometer. However, some 1110908 distributors apparently were delivered on *late* 1957 F.I. cars intended for street use. In such instances, a threaded cap covers the tachometer-drive outlet.

Interestingly, Steve also reports seeing 1110906 distributors dated 7L18 and 7L19, which translate to December 18, 1957 and December 19, 1957, respectively. These dates fall well into the 1958 Corvette model run — something for 1958 F.I. enthusiasts to think about. Of course, it is *possible* that such "late" 1110906 distributors were originally installed on 1958 F.I. Chevrolets, instead of 1958 F.I. Corvettes. The F.I. option, incidentally, was available on Chevrolet passenger cars through the 1959 model year.

On a final note: we are now seriously collecting and studying the date codes found on distributors. A study of these date codes is essential to refining our understanding of exactly how and when these various distributors were actually used. For instance, the original 1110889 distributor from 1957 Corvette E57S101927 is dated 6L13, which equates to December 13, 1956. This particular vehicle was assembled approximately January 15, 1957, and was delivered to Humphrey Chevrolet in Milwaukee, Wis., during the final week of January 1957. Thus the time-lag between the distributor assembly date and the vehicle assembly date was approximately one month. This is a fairly typical time span between a component sub-assembly and the vehicle final assembly.

At this point I would request that those of you who own 1957 F.I. ignition distributors send me a brief note, containing the entire distributor number, including the date code. And if the VIN#, engine #, F.I. unit type and serial #'s from the vehicle which supplied the distributor are known, please also include them. Such information should be sent (enclose SASE if reply desired) to: Michael Hunt, 903 Swarthmore Ct., Madison, Wis. 53705.

POSTSCRIPT:

In my recent gas cap essay (Vol. 4 Nr. 3 pp. 22-24) and in a follow-up comment (Vol. 4 Nr. 4 p. 15), I expressed some uncertainties as to whether the gas caps should be cadmium- or zinc-plated. NCRS member Rick Kilmer has supplied additional information on the #3708440 "domed" cap, insofar as it applies to these caps as used on 1953-5 Corvettes. Rick obtained this information from a GM print dated 7-8-53, revised 12-11-54. Notations on the plating, which may also be valid for the 1956-7 gas caps, are as follows:

1. Must withstand 32 hour salt spray test without rusting.
2. Pressure valve must start to open between 1.50 PSI to 2.50 PSI. Vacuum valve to open from 0 — .50 PSI.
3. All steel parts must be zinc plated (GM 4252M) or cadmium plated. Finish to be as taken from the plating bath.

Thanks Rick . . .

1961-1962 MATURED MACHINE

With Rev. Michael Ernst

Photos by JOHN MARQUARDT

FUELER OR FOOLER?

How many times has someone told you "I have a '62 fuel car," or "this car was originally a fuel car but the unit was taken off."? Many individuals may even have original "fuel" cars and don't realize it, and others have "fuelers" which really never were.

There are a number of ways, some quite reliable, others less, to determine if a 1961 or 1962 Corvette was originally equipped with the fuel injection option. Many of the criteria will also apply to earlier model Corvettes. Not any one single determining feature is totally reliable, but when evaluated along with others, they may give a fairly accurate picture.

The first and least reliable, is the presence or absence of the "Fuel Injection" emblems. Anyone can drill holes and hang-on a new set of emblems, but if they are *not* present, don't discount the car as being a candidate for fuel injected status. Check the inside of the fender to see if the location holes have been filled. The 1961 models had a three-stud emblem located high on each front fender, while the 1962's

1958-1961 Corvette fuel injection emblem.

1962 Corvette fuel injection emblem.

had a two-stud emblem located under the crossed-flags emblems.

It takes only a few minutes to remove or bolt-on an injection unit, but if one is present, check the identification tag. The 1961's should have a 7017200 or 310 unit with hydraulic-lifter engines, or 7017250 or 320 with the high-lift cam, solid-lifter engines. The 1962 units are 7017355, 360, 365 or 370. Beware though, as number plates are being reproduced so an incorrect unit sporting a seemingly correct number is possible.

Is the correct engine block there? This is much harder to fabricate, but counterfeits are showing up. All 1961 engine casting numbers should be 3756519 and all 1962 engine casting numbers are 3782870, located at the right rear, top of the block. The stamped engine identification code (located on the pad at the right front of the cylinder block next to the cylinder head) should have the sequence number of the car (proceeded by a digit indicating year: "1" for 1961, or "2" for 1962), plus a date code for engine assembly, ending in a two-letter suffix. That suffix should be "CR" for the hydraulic-lifter 1961 F.I., "CS" for the solid-lifter 1961 F.I., or "RF" for the 1962 F.I. engine.

The right-hand exhaust manifold on the F.I. car should not have a hole drilled on top (used for a heat tube to the carburetor's choke). There should be a crossover pipe in the exhaust (though some carbureted engines also used this item) and the right-hand exhaust manifold used a spacer in lieu of a heat-riser valve used on carbureted engines. Obviously, the exhaust items may have been changed over the years.

A rather reliable guide is to look at the location of the windshield washer system (standard equipment beginning in 1961) if it is still there, or signs of its original location. All 1961 and 1962 F.I. cars had a right-hand mounting of the system's main components while the carbureted versions mounted on the left. Even if the parts are missing, there should be holes in the inner fender indicating original placement. Above the battery will be two holes drilled three inches apart for the vacuum tank assembly. There will be three holes drilled vertically 1 3/4" apart on the inner fender about in line with the front-right valve cover bolts for the washer reservoir heat shield. Between those two mountings will be four holes drilled in a rectangular pattern for the reservoir bracket. On both 1961 and 1962 F.I. models there should be a 7/8" hole drilled on the firewall behind the right side female hood latch through which the large windshield washer hoses pass to the passenger compartment. Note that 1961 Cor-

Hole through firewall and remains of grommet used to locate hoses for windshield washer system.

Right side mounting of windshield washer components.

Clip mounted next to wiper motor used to retain washer hose.

(continued on next page)

vette 275 horsepower models which used a generator driven tachometer will have an additional large hole adjacent, for the tach drive cable. On non-F.I. 1962 cars there is a small 1/4" depression (dimple) to indicate where the hole should be drilled for the windshield washer hoses. There should also be a small clip (or hole drilled for same) on the horizontal surface outside of the female latch for hose retention (see photo).

Now we should take a look at the left inner fender area. The F.I. air cleaner was fastened with two bolts to a bracket riveted to the fender's backside, just below the fender lip. This part is very difficult to forge. On the backside is a metal plate with two square-head nuts and is center-riveted to the panel. Likewise, the front bracket for retention of the F.I. fresh-air intake hose (as specified for 1961 315 horsepower and 1962 360 horsepower models only) is attached to a metal reinforcement plate retained to the panel by two rivets. This piece is about three inches above and slightly towards the firewall from the stabilizer bar. On the left inner fender there should also be evidence of holes for mounting two other hose retaining brackets (on cars so-equipped) as well as one or two holes for lower mounting of the F.I. air cleaner.

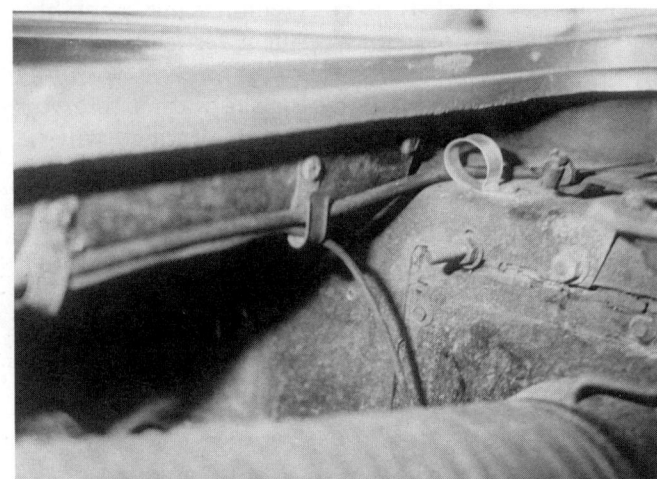

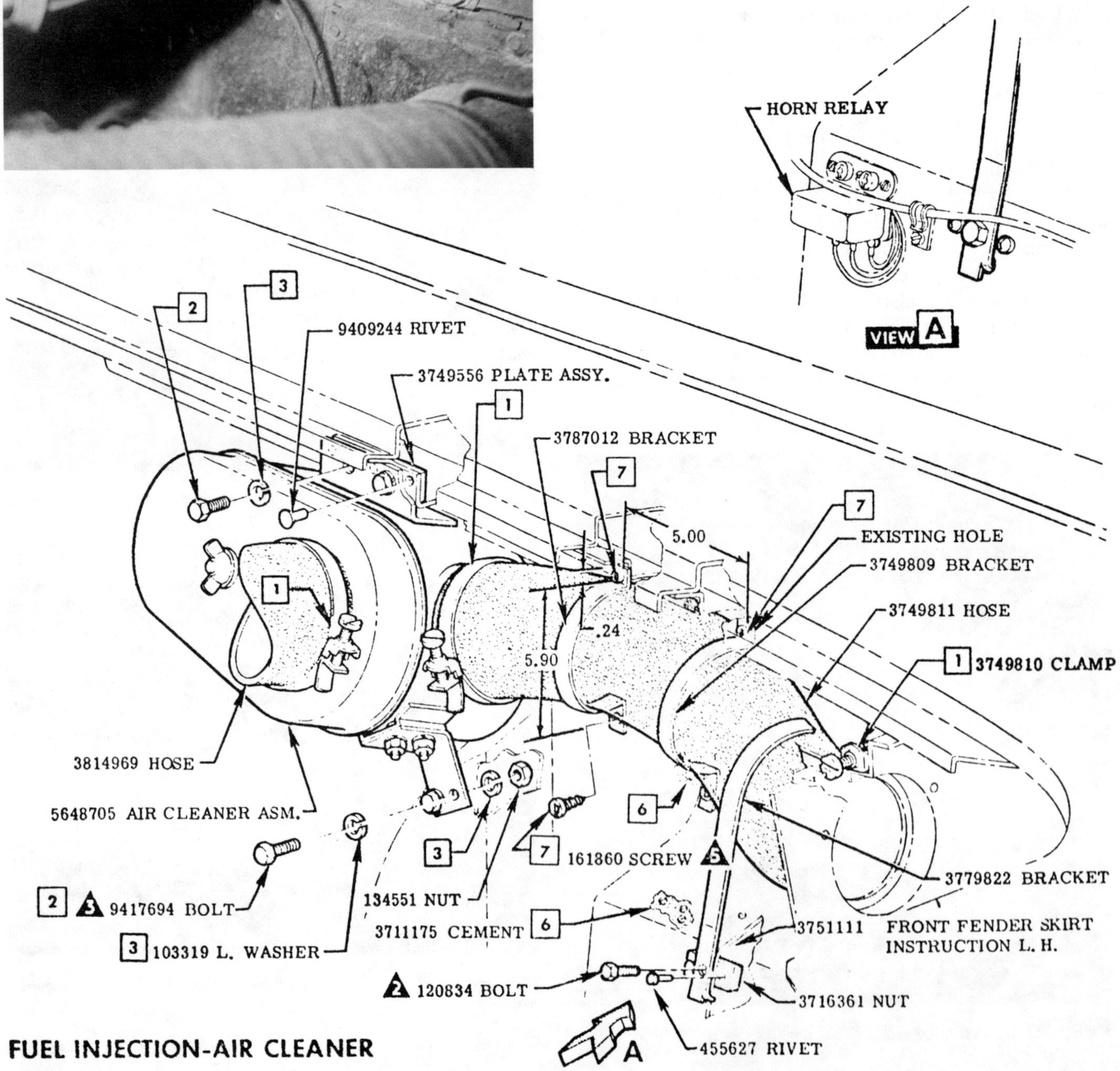

FUEL INJECTION-AIR CLEANER

Air cleaner mount.

Coil bulge in distributor shield.

Another extremely reliable indicator is the location of the tachometer cable hole in the firewall. The 315 horsepower 1961 F.I.'s had a large hole drilled for cable and grommet in the center of the firewall, above the transmission tunnel. No other 1961's were drilled there. All 1962 models, both F.I. and carbureted, had a distributor driven tach, however the F.I. car will have a hole drilled to the left of the wiper motor centerline, while the carbureted models had a hole drilled slightly to the right. The F.I. 1962 has a 3/8" depression (dimple) to the passenger side of the cable hole where the carbureted model's cable hole would have been drilled. Underneath the dash, in the passenger compartment, the insulation mat against the firewall has a 4" long hole for the tach cable on the F.I. car: considerably longer than for a carbureted model.

So much for the most reliable data — now some other odds and ends. Fuel injected 1961's and 1962's should have the 7-rib cast aluminum value covers, but these are not unique only to the F.I.'s. On the tach face, solid-lifter F.I. cars (in fact all solid-lifter 1961's and 1962's) should have a black background of 0-1000 RPM; tan for 1000-4000; green for 4000-6300; orange for 6300-6500; and red for 6500-7000. Again, this is not unique to F.I. cars. The F.I. distributor cover should have a coil bulge on the right-hand side and will fit the carbureted car, but not vice-versa.

The horn relay, according to the Corvette Factory Assembly Instruction Manuals, should be mounted lower on the inner fender for F.I.'s equipped with the high-lift cam (315 HP and 360 HP), apparently for clearance of the air intake hose used on those cars. While the manual specifics that the horn relay will be mounted higher on the inner fender on the carbureted and regular cam F.I. (275 HP 1961), it has shown up in either location on many F.I. cars regardless of horsepower rating.

One added note of interest: Beginning with 1962 F.I. models, rubber seals on each side of the radiator were attached to the front of the support with rectangular retainers. (See 1962 Assembly Instruction Manual section 582, sheet 8.00.)

Hopefully the preceding will enable the observer to decide if that 1961 or 1962 Corvette is a real "fueler" or not. Good Luck ! ! !

UPDATE!

1. It appears that 1962's were built at a rate of 75 per day, not 93 as mentioned in my previous dating article.
2. Bill Clupper of Cortland, Ohio, advises that 1962 owners looking for the discontinued tach cable boot #3784992 might check with Corvair NOS parts suppliers. The identical part was used as a Corvair throttle shaft boot.
3. Dating codes have been found on frames, stenciled below the driver's door area; rubber stamped on the wiper motor; and on the fiberglass portion of the of the heater intake, against the gasket which seals it to the firewall.
4. Ed Gurdjian indicates that exhaust manifold bolt locks now serviced by GMPD are a different part number and are more rounded in design than the original 1955-1962 part. Originals should be plentiful on junk yard V-8's.

Rev. Michael Ernst
P. O. Box 36
Bowler, Wisconsin 54416
Phone: 715/793-4608

The Flint Corvette Plant

By John Amgwert

On the Corvette's 25th anniversary I feel it is most appropriate that we take a close look at the original assembly plant in Flint, Michigan, where the initial three hundred 1953 models were built.

Preliminary production began in mid-June, with the first unit (E53F001001) completed on June 30, 1953 (a Wednesday). The rate of assembly was generally slow at first and probably averaged one car per day due to a general lack of assembly know-how and techniques generally associated with new models, especially when one considers the Corvette's fiberglass reinforced plastic body. This one car per day rate can be evidenced through the fact that car serial number E53F001076 (the 76th 1953 built) shows a rear axle date code of September 19th: an indication that that vehicle had to reach final assembly some time later that month. The assembly rate was then increased to about three cars per day and production finally reached six cars per day toward the end of the 1953 model run. Just exactly when the last car (E53F001300) was assembled is not known for sure. However, we do know that car number 289 was completed on Friday, December 18th (or possibly Monday, December 21st, the next working day) so it is safe to assume that 1953 Corvette production ceased by Christmas.

The site chosen and converted for the 1953 Corvette assembly operations was the old Chevrolet Customer Delivery Garage located at Van Slyke and Atherton Road in Flint. The building still stands (a new front addition and overhead parking area were added several years ago) and is now the General Motors Assembly Research Center, operated by the Chevrolet Division. As it was for the 1953 Corvette operation, Assembly Research is the "pilot-line" of all future GM models: most recently for the 1979 front-wheel drive Buick Riviera, Oldsmobile Toronado, and Cadillac Eldorado, as well as the 1980 X-bodied Chevrolet Nova, also to be front-wheel drive. This pilot-line center is used to develop assembly methods and techniques, as well as providing extensive training for the various plant personnel from around the country that will eventually be producing the new models. One of the individuals directly involved with assembly of the first Corvettes, Mr. Thomas R. Le Gault, is now the Administrator of Pilot Operations at the GM Assembly Research Center.

Reliable sources indicate that there were between 50 and 75 persons actively working on the Corvette project, both assembly and engineering/management personnel, at any one time, with as many as 150 individuals involved during the entire project. Mr. Gordan Tanner, who worked on the Flint Corvette line, said recently that he had to be replaced as he couldn't take breathing the airborne dust from working around the fiberglass bodies.

Staffing the production line were personnel "borrowed" from other Chevrolet manufacturing and assembly plants, whose knowledge and skills would be helpful for assembly of the first Corvettes. It has been alledged by some that quality-control on the 1953 Corvettes was poor, but it is quite apparent from speaking with persons involved with the project that Chevrolet chose assemblers possessing extreme skill and craftsmanship to build these early cars.

What follows on the next several pages are a few photographs, many never before published, which depict assembly at the original Flint Corvette Plant. Most important among these are about a dozen photos taken of the first production unit (E53F001001) as it neared completion. Actual shots of Job Number One are all identified, and were taken during the week that preceded June 30th at the request of Mr. Myron Scott, the Chevrolet public relations man who is credited with naming the Corvette.

Photos courtesy Chevrolet Division

These 1953 Corvette fiberglass body panels (supplied from outside sources) are "nested" in stacks at the beginning of the body assembly line. The nesting feature was not designed into the panels, but was advantageous for shipping and storage.

Body subassemblies were prepared first. Here the assembler is bonding and riveting the under-panel which will cover the fuel tank, and house the convertible top directly behind the seats.

This body subassembly requires a "jig" fixture, used to insure proper positioning and fitting of all panels. Here the front "skirt" panel is being positioned on the jig, where it will be fitted with bolts and rivets to the metal radiator support and inner fender panels which are already in place.

Top: *The Flint plant paint-booth handled one body at a time. Here, 1953 Corvette Serial Number One (mounted on a body "dolly") receives its Polo White paint as well as red trim paint and engine compartment "black-out" paint before moving to the polishing area.* **Middle:** *Serial Number One moves from paint area to the trim line where windshield and bumpers are installed.* **Lower left:** *Body subassemblies are mated, bonded and riveted.* **Lower right:** *Serial Number One moves down the body trim line, being fitted here with a parking lamp.*

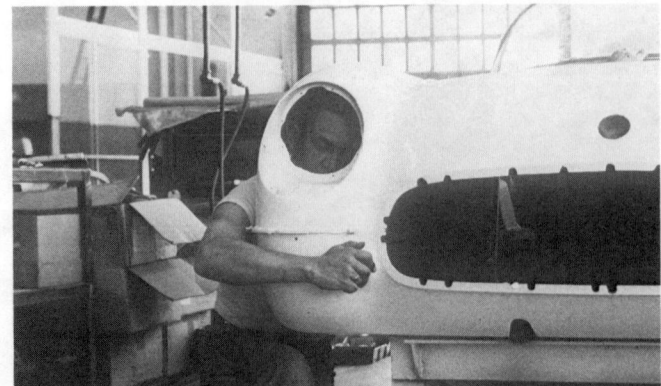

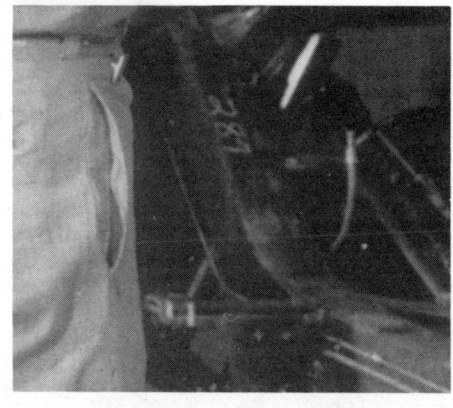

Top and right: *The body and chassis of 1953 Corvette number 289 are mated on Friday, December 18, 1953. Visible on the right frame-rail "kick-up" over the rear axle is the number "289" written in chalk (see photo enlargement at right). Other photos taken during the session show that the next chassis is numbered "290".* **Lower left:** *The body of Serial Number One has now been mated to the chassis. Note chassis in foreground is car number two.* **Lower right:** *Serial Number One is near the end of assembly with final trim and wiring being connected. Two assemblers are fitting stainless trim and aligning side-window to door while another worker is attaching turn indicator switch housing to steering column.* **Following page:** *Photo of chassis line during early 1953 assembly. Note the inverted frame with rear axle being lowered, engine being installed just ahead, and body farther down the line. Also note the parts bins, engine test stand in center, crated engines, and body assembly area in background.*

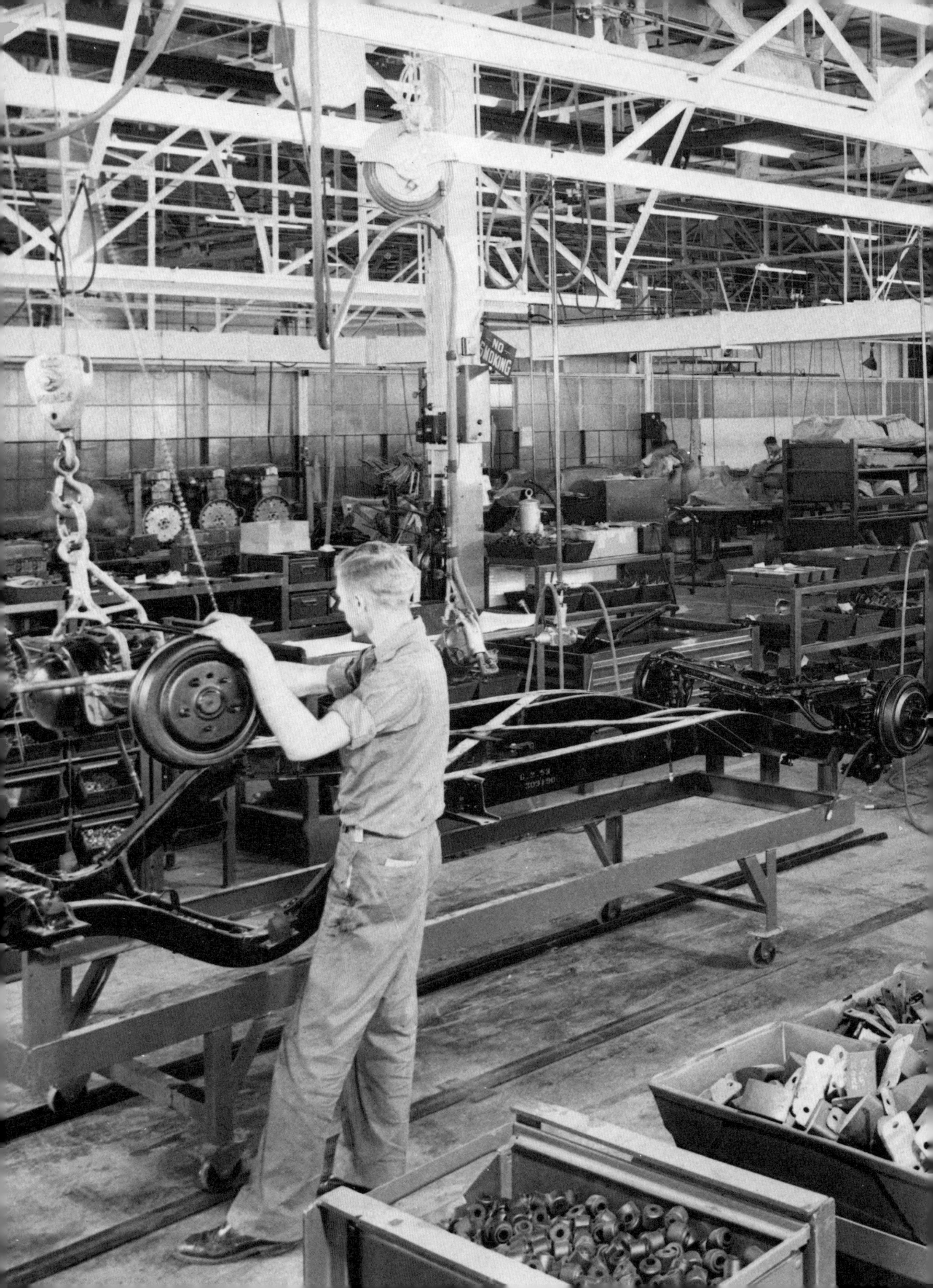

Serial Number One is a hub of activity. Steering wheel is being installed and most major trim is in place.

Serial Number One is being fitted with hoses for windshield washer system and cable to tachometer. Door closure with side vent window is being checked and note on the extreme left the front bumper grille guards which are not yet installed.

The front grille guards are in place now, and Serial Number One's hood is being adjusted for correct alignment and hinge operation.

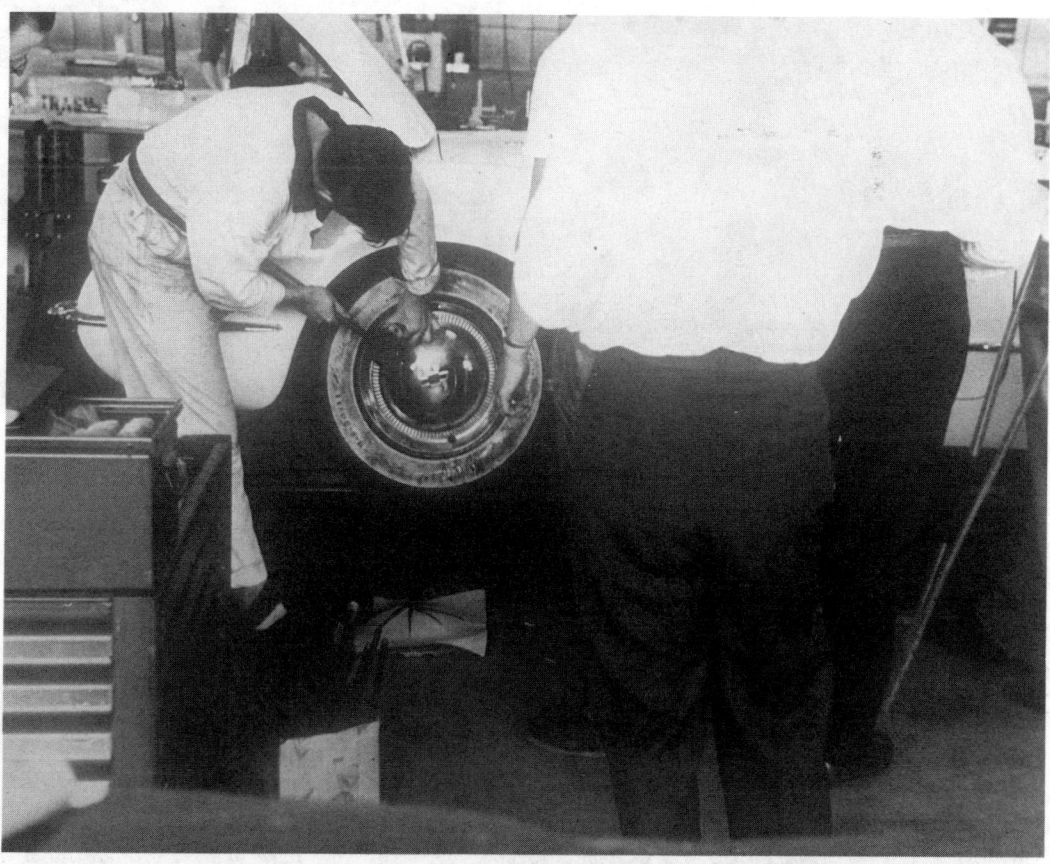

Serial Number One receives its wheelcovers. Note the use of the 1953 Chevrolet Bel Air "domed" covers which were supplied with approximately the first 25 Corvettes that year.

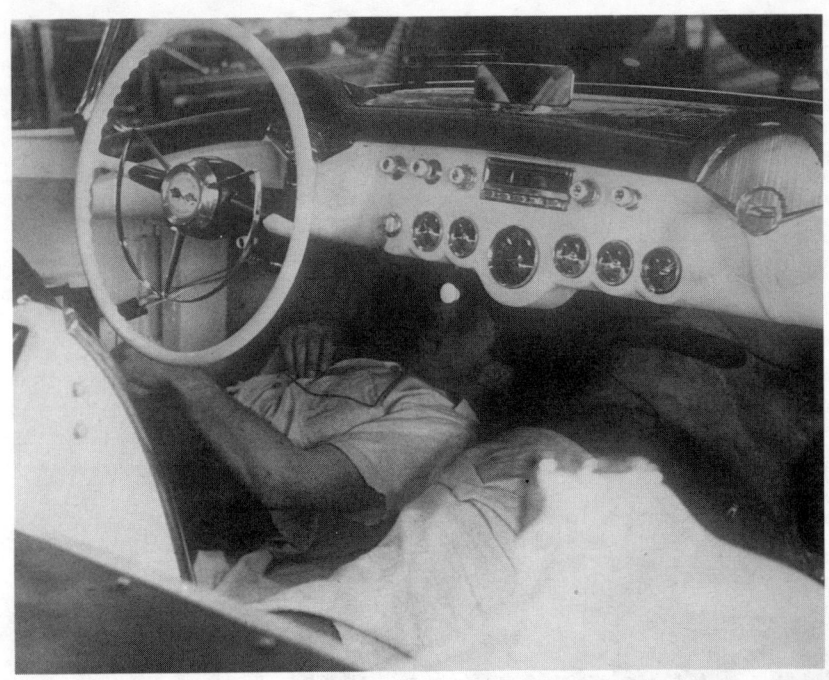

Serial Number One will soon be operational as the final dash board wiring is connected. Note the chrome speaker grille used, which was changed to black finish on later production 1953's to better match the speedometer.

Horn operation is checked in this photo and note that the two courtesy lights under the dash are glowing.

The old story that the electrical system in Serial Number One would not work due to grounding of the wires to the fiberglass body should be laid to rest once and for all with this photo as the park lights are operational. Following the electrical check, the upholstery trim and rugs were installed and Job Number One was washed for the famous photo session as it was driven off the line.

Chevrolet Motor Division
General Motors Building
Detroit 2, Michigan

CORVETTE IN PRODUCTION

(8695)

RELEASE 11:00 A.M. June 30, 1953

Automotive Research Library
★ PETERSEN PUBLISHING CO. ★

FLINT, June 30 — The American automobile industry's first production sports car with a plastic laminated fiber glass body was completed here today as the first Chevrolet Corvette came off the line of the Chevrolet Flint Assembly Plant.

T. H. Keating, Chevrolet general manager, announced that the factory list price of the Corvette would be $3,250.00 including a 1953 Powerglide automatic transmission as standard equipment.

Thus, in one day, Chevrolet answered the two top questions most often asked by some four million persons who have seen two experimental models of the Corvette at the GM Motoramas and other special events at which it has been shown since January. They wanted most of all to know when Chevrolet would start production and how much the Corvette would cost.

"This occasion is historic in the industry," Keating said. "The Corvette has been brought into production on schedule in less than 12 months from designer's dream to tested reality.

"The engineers want to keep on testing these first cars for a few thousand more miles, but it may be most important to Chevrolet's future plans to learn the amazing flexibility that is demonstrated here in working out new design ideas in plastics."

The Corvette assembly line, its bins filled with all the nuts and washers and fasteners and trim pieces necessary for continuing production, has been set up in a separate building at the Flint Assembly plant.

(more)

Corvette in Production ————2.

It is a miniature assembly line, only six chassis' long, but with every place on the line filled with the additional chassis and component parts of the subsequent bodies needed to keep assembly rolling. However, the line is big enough for the initial rate of production which Chevrolet has established for pioneering in a new field of plastic bodies.

The Corvette's 50-a-month schedule compares with more than 7,700 a day, which Chevrolet builds in steel in all its 27 manufacturing and assembly plants in 20 cities, in 10 states strategically scattered for most efficient car and truck distribution throughout the country.

Keating revealed that production will build up from this small beginning to the 50-a-month rate, and added:

"We expect to complete our original schedule of 300 Corvettes in this model year, and start getting 1,000 plastic bodies a month for the 1954 production of the Corvette."

This new type American sports car is only 33 inches high. It is powered with a stepped-up Chevrolet 1953 "Blue Flame" engine, and 1953 Powerglide automatic transmission. The production Corvette, like the show cars that have been on tour, is a two-seater painted white, with a red cockpit, and other trim in red and chrome. It is 70 inches wide, 167 inches long on a 102 inch wheelbase, and has a curb weight of approximately 2900 pounds.

—ge—

This is a copy of the original Corvette press release dated June 30, 1953, which announced production of the first vehicle. (Press release courtesy of Mr. Spence Murray and Petersen Publishing Library.)

Mr. Tony Kleiber, a body assembler, prepares to drive Serial Number One off the assembly line on the morning of June 30, 1953. Next to Tony is Mr. R. G. Ford, General Manager of Chevrolet Assembly Plants, and Mr. F. J. Fessenden, Flint Plant Manager.

Before the car was actually driven away, the occasion was celebrated with this photo of some of the project staff gathered around the vehicle with an appropriate plaque, which is being held by Tony Kleiber.

BODY PANEL ALIGNMENT 1963-1967

By Joe Clark

In any Corvette restoration, one of the more important aspects making up a really fine job has to do with proper fitting and alignment of the fiberglass panels that move. On the cars produced between 1963-1967, this alignment involves not only the hood, convertible deck lid, and doors, but also the unique rotating headlight assembly.

One of the easiest ways to spot a Corvette that has been collision damaged is to check the alignment and spacing of doors, hood and lights.

Because of the shape and bumper arrangement of the Sting Ray front end, the swing-out headlights are particularly susceptible to even minor jolts inflicted by other cars of varying bumper heights. Therefore, caution should be used in analyzing this area because a repair here does not necessarily indicate a violent crash (Merely parking lot rash).

Let's suppose you own a car that has been damaged in the front, or that you are contemplating the purchase of one that you suspect has had damage. How do you determine seriousness of damage and steps necessary for correction?

To get the answers we visited the shop of Bill Denny in Havre de Grace, Maryland. Bill, who is a member of N.C.R.S., has a long-standing interest in and knowledge of Corvettes. What follows are his suggestions on alignment of the critical areas in question.

There are several major dimensions with which to be concerned:
1. Overall contour when viewed from the top (belt line).
2. Evenness of belt line when viewed from the side.
3. Proper operation and alignment of headlight doors, when open and closed.
   A. Gap.
   B. Fit of door to overall contour (closed).
   C. Spacing during operation.
4. General fit of doors and convertible deck lid.

The 1963 Corvette Shop Manual ST-21 in the "Body" section gives factory recommended specifications for spacing gaps by inches as follows:
1. Headlights 1/16" to 3/16" with even gap all around. At no time in any position should the revolving units contact the surrounding nose panel.

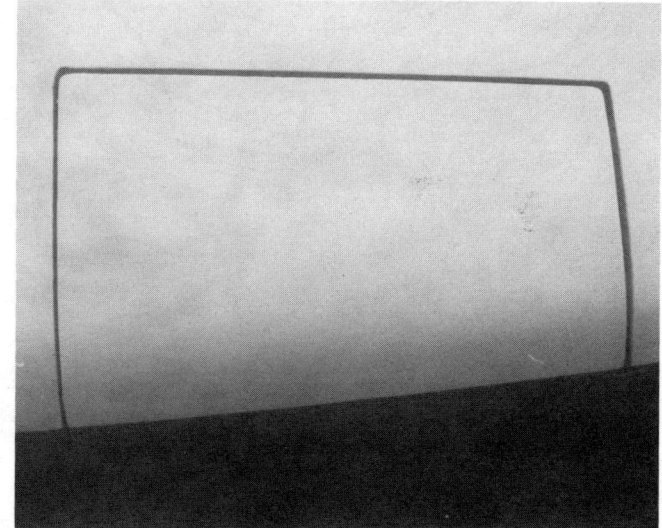

Example of good headlamp fit.

2. Hood 1/8" to 1/4" on the front edge, 1/16" to 1/4" on each side. The fit should be made not only keeping gaps in mind but also the alignment of the sculpted center windsplit and the ideal of a smooth, horizontal contour.
   Note: The overall hood position should be adjusted first. Catch Adjustments are done last. Do not slam the hood if it is in a new position!
3. Doors should have a 1/8" to 1/4" gap all around and match general body contour and shape.

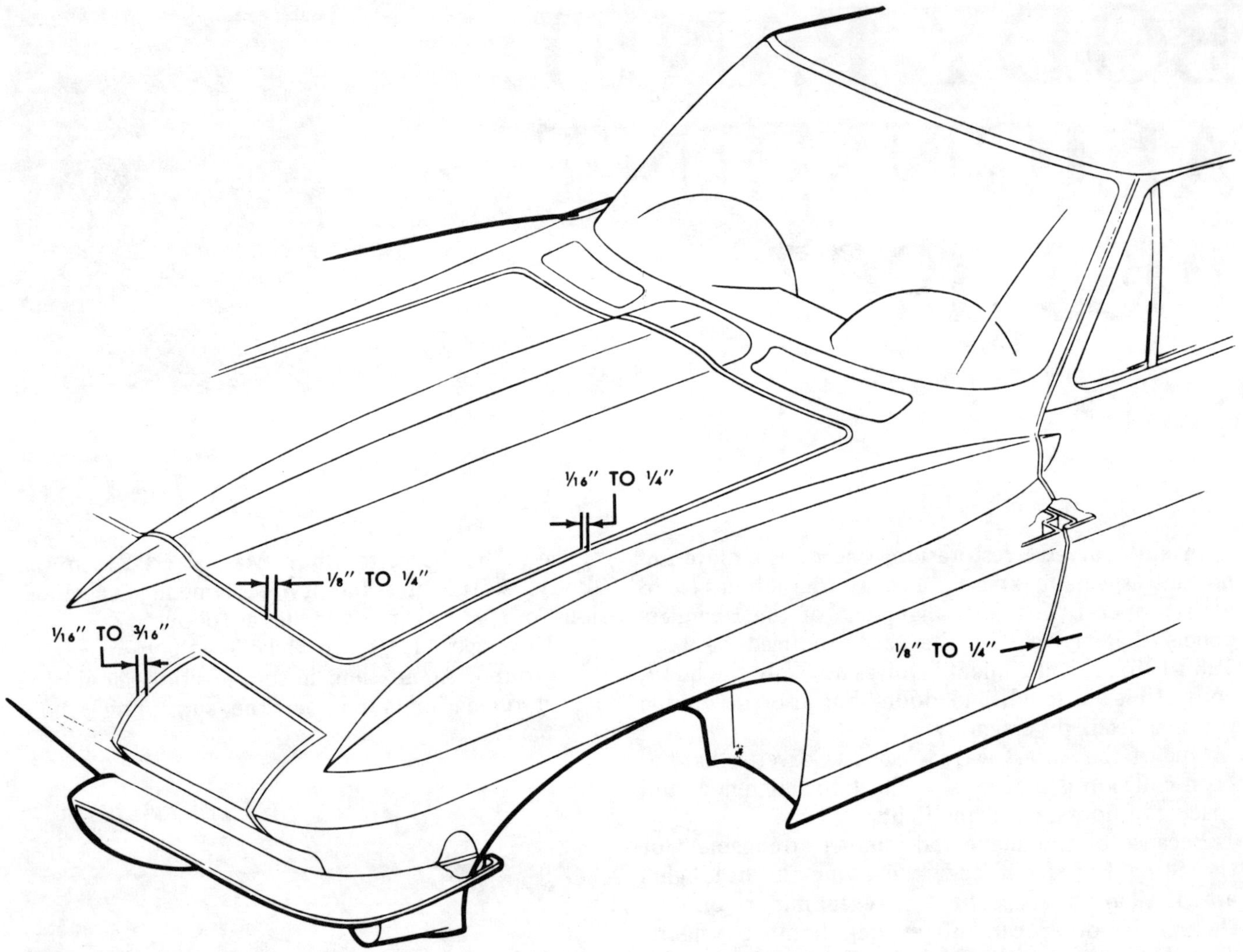

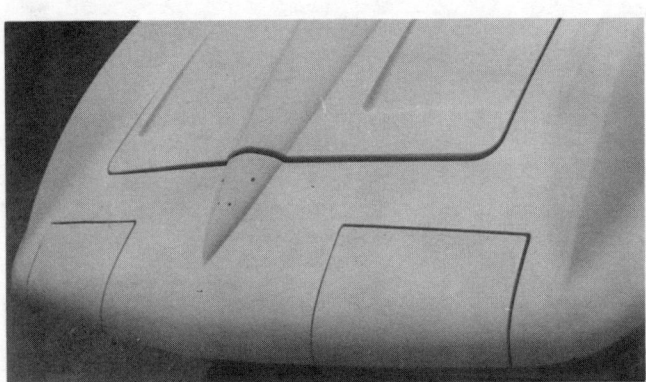

Examples of poor hood panel fit.

4. On the convertible, the deck lid over the folding top should be positioned so as to best match the rest of the upper rear area. The factory specs call for 1/16" to 3/16" on the sides, 3/16" to 1/4" on the rear edge.

This area is perhaps the most difficult to correct for a variety of reasons. First, the factory fit and shape here is, or was, on many cars very poor. In addition, it is a spot where two moving panels (door and deck lid) come together. Both move in different directions and so compromises must be made. Couple the above to the fact that there is maximum flexing of the body at this point and one can see why problems arise.

Before removing any body panel, scribe around the hinge to make re-installation easier. An easy way to scribe the hood is to use a black spray bomb. This marks clearly hinge and bolt head positions. Scribing also helps to ascertain the amount of movement made to assure proper fit. This in turn will help determine the size of catch adjustments to the new position. Any shims found should be taped to the hinge where they were used to assure proper re-installation. All hinges and catches or strikers are adjustable. Slotted

(continued on next page)

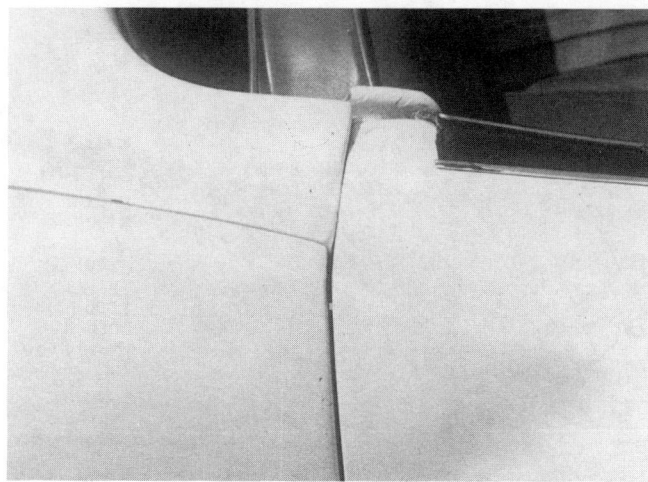
Example of poor door and top-lid fit.

Poor panel contour alignment and fit.

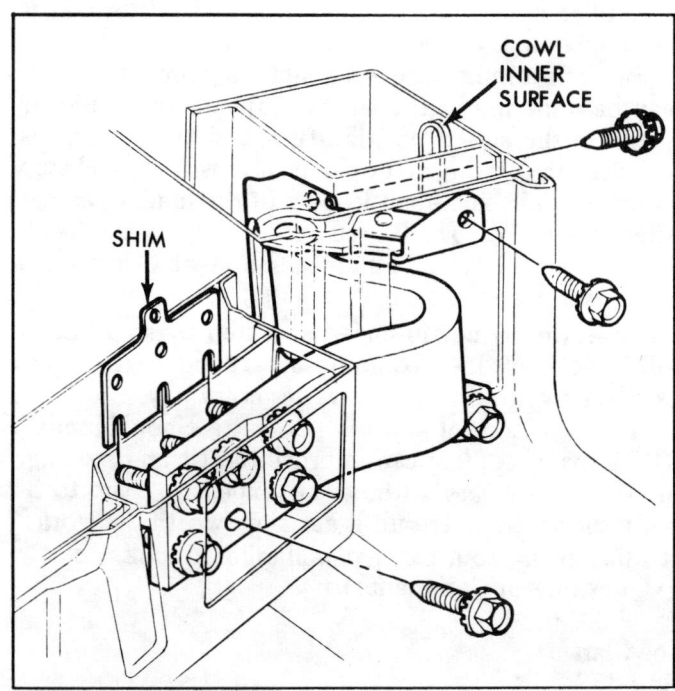
Typical door hinge.

holes allow fore and aft or left and right movement. Care should be taken to adjust the catch or striker to match the new hinge position. *DO NOT SLAM UNTIL SURE!* In every case, adjust hinge first, catch to match.

Special mention should be made regarding window fit being thrown off by door adjustments. This will happen on the convertible in the window up position if the door has been moved any great distance.

There are 5 adjusting points on each door to control window axis and bumping points. (It is suggested that a shop manual be consulted for more accurate detail regarding these adjustments, should they become necessary).

Lastly on doors, Bill recommends if new weatherstripping is to be installed, that this be done before fitting any panels. (On a repaint, tape in temporarily). The new rubber can have a drastic influence on gaps — especially on those huge Aerocoupe doors in the roof area.

The headlights on the Sting Ray present a host of unique problems. According to many, the factory fit was not all that good. Before trying to align the headlight area, be sure that both your light units are complete. They consist of a large number of component parts and even the smallest shim or bushing is important.

Once you are sure that you have two complete units, look your car's front over carefully. How does the whole area look? How much filler has been accumulated? Are there cracks? Are they deep? How does the front edge of the hood match contour? Would a total resection be sensible using all new panels? Are any parts of the rotating headlights bent?

Poor refinish on lamp opening.

In most cases, a resection will not be necessary and if the light units are complete, adjustment and fitting can proceed. Further, in repairing the front,

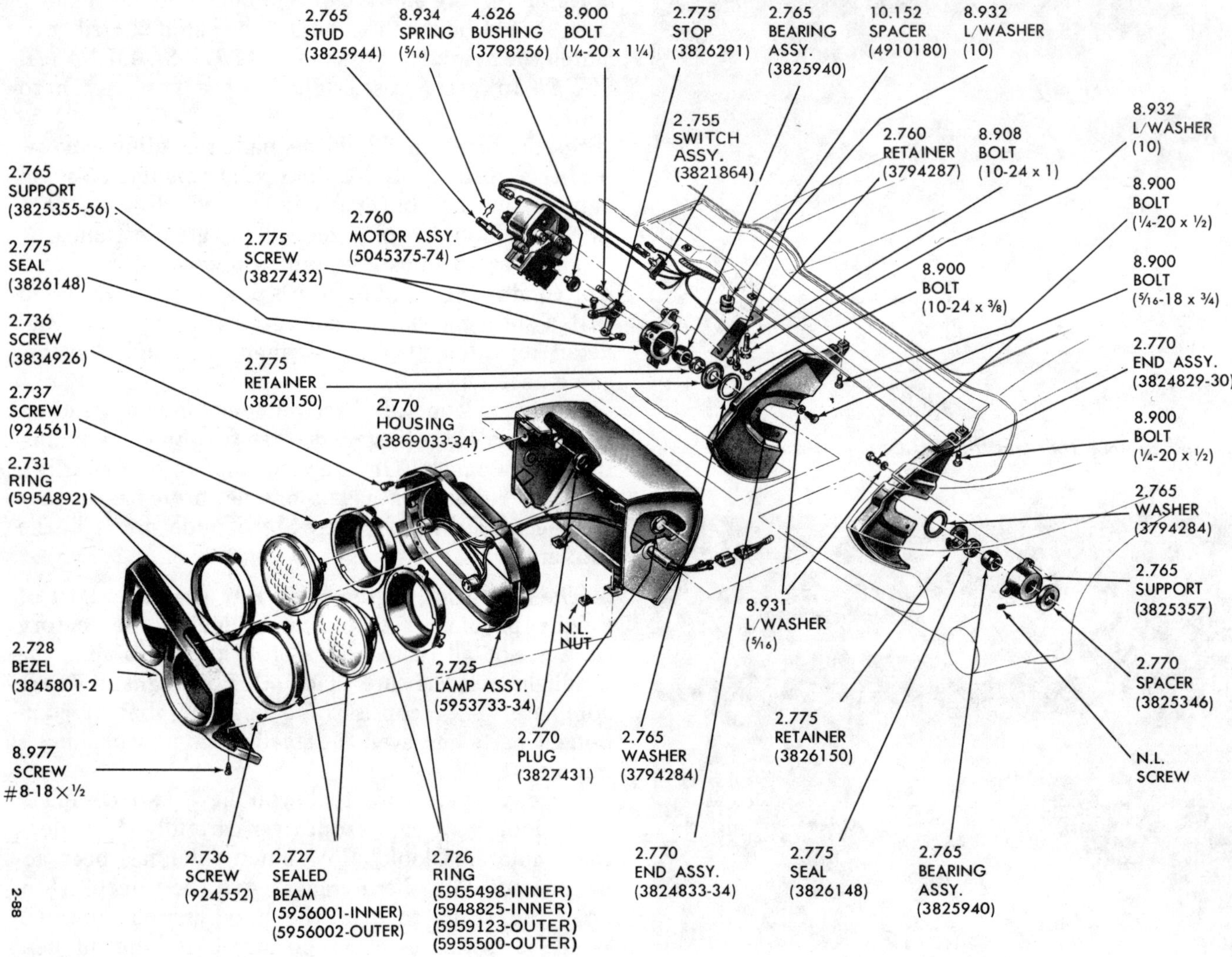

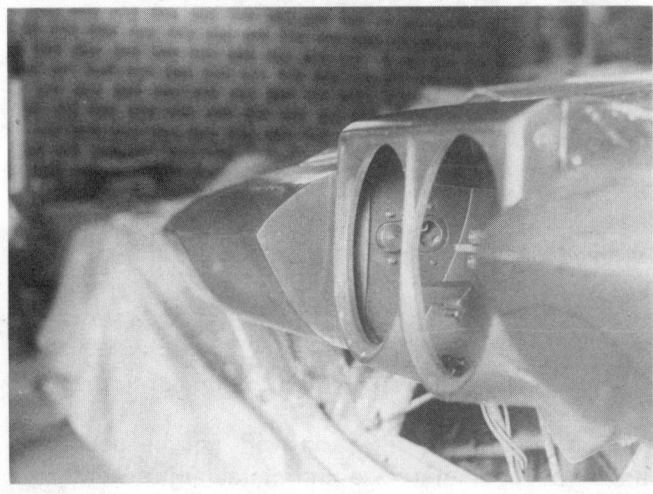

Bill says there is nothing wrong with using filler on cracks or breaks if it is done properly. Using mat and resin first on any break and finishing with a proper type of filler will be almost as good as a whole new panel. Cracks or crazing marks should be ground to the glass layer and filled. Use of a chemically compatible filler is most important. (Don Bailey's or GM is recommended) to avoid reappearance later on.

In reassembling the headlights, alignment and fit can be done minus the lamps. Adjustment should be made in the closed position first, and then clearance checked in rotating and open positions. The final step is proper finishing and clean-up of the inner openings themselves. This small area shows only in the headlights open position, but means a great deal to the car's overall appearance.

While this is not intended as a step by step "how to" article, it does contain some good suggestions from men who work on Corvettes every day.

With the aid of a 1963 Corvette Shop Manual ST-21 many readers can improve the fit and spacing on their own cars without an expensive visit to a body shop. The end result is certainly worth the work. It's like giving your car that well tailored look.

Questions or Comments to:

Joe Clark
Box 353
Havre de Grace, Maryland 21078
301-939-2467

Proper finish on head lamp opening.

BASIC ELECTRONICS
By Charlie Elman

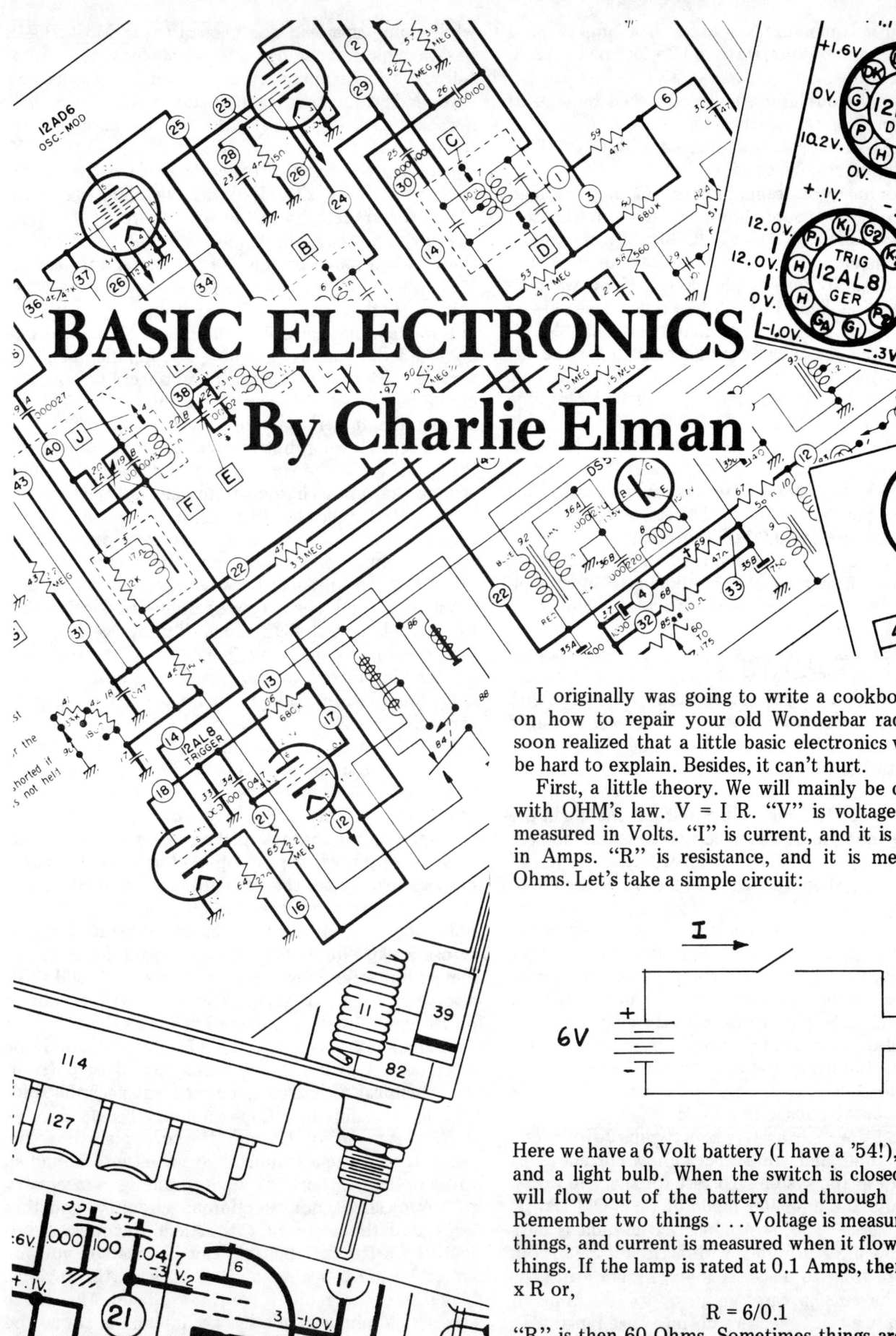

I originally was going to write a cookbook article on how to repair your old Wonderbar radio, but I soon realized that a little basic electronics would not be hard to explain. Besides, it can't hurt.

First, a little theory. We will mainly be concerned with OHM's law. V = I R. "V" is voltage, and it is measured in Volts. "I" is current, and it is measured in Amps. "R" is resistance, and it is measured in Ohms. Let's take a simple circuit:

Here we have a 6 Volt battery (I have a '54!), a switch, and a light bulb. When the switch is closed, current will flow out of the battery and through the lamp. Remember two things... Voltage is measured across things, and current is measured when it flows through things. If the lamp is rated at 0.1 Amps, then: 6 = 0.1 x R or,

R = 6/0.1

"R" is then 60 Ohms. Sometimes things are rated in Watts. The relationship for Watts is P = I V. "P" is power and it is measured in Watts. If a lamp is rated at 12 Watts, and 6 Volts, we have $12 = I \times 6$ or $I = 12/6$, which is 2 Amps.

To do any troubleshooting, you would be wise to acquire a multimeter which can measure Volts, Ohms, and Amps. Unfortunately multimeters which do these sort of things usually do not have Amp ranges high enough for many currents in cars, but they are high enough for radio troubleshooting. These multimeters are usually called VOM's (Volt-Ohm-Milliammeter), and are available at any electronics distributor.

Going back to our simple circuit, if we want to know why the light doesn't work we have several options. We could put the meter on the "Volt" scale with the range switch high enough for the expected results (If the meter has a 1, 3, 10, or 30 Volt range selection we should set it to the 10 Volt range if the system is 6 Volts, and 30 Volts for a 12 volt system). The meter is then placed across the lamp to see if any voltage is getting there. If the meter measures 6 Volts, then the lamp is probably bad. But, the socket may be corroded. If there is 0 Volts measured across the lamp, then the circuit is probably open. This can mean an open fuse, or bad switch, or broken wire. The next step would be to trace back and measure across the switch to see if voltage is getting that far.

Let's say that voltage was getting to the lamp's socket and we suspected the bulb was open. The next step would be to measure the bulb's resistance with the VOM. As we saw above, the bulb will probably be in the range of 1 to 100 Ohms. The VOM should be put into the resistance mode and the range switch set into a low range. Then the meter can be placed across the bulb OUT OF THE SOCKET. Meters in the resistance mode must never be placed into a hot circuit. If the bulb is open, the meter will read "infinity" (the same as when the leads are not connected to anything).

A word of caution about ignition systems is called for. The ignition system "steps up" the battery's voltage when the engine is turning — the engine does not have to be running for there to be high voltage on the coil and spark-plug wires. With the engine off, the coil can also be checked for open windings. The same is true for the generator and starter. Unfortunately there is no sure fire way to verify shorted turns in any of the above coils with a VOM.

Let's say your car battery slowly runs down over a period of time, and you suspect a low current short somewhere in the system. To test for this, we would want to use the ammeter mode of the VOM. To review the basics again, remember that current is measured through, or in series, with a circuit. So for our test, we are going to place the meter in series with the battery. Currents in cars can go up to 100 Amps or more. But we can't measure up into that range with an ordinary VOM. Currents of that range are usually found when starting or charging the car battery. So while doing this test, don't start the car. Most VOM's have a high current position — usually for 10 Amps full range (10 Amps maximum). Disconnect the positive end from the battery and touch the VOM's negative (usually black) lead to the bare positive terminal of the battery. Next, VERY QUICKLY, lightly tap the positive (disconnected) battery cable with the VOM's positive lead while watching the meter. If the meter deflects in the wrong direction, reverse the leads and try again. If the meter deflects off scale, there is too much current for the meter to measure. Make sure that the interior lights are off, and other things of that nature. There should be very little current flowing, usually to the clock. My car showed about 150 milliamps (1 Amp = 1000 milliamps). Currents greater than this might be a concern to you, and could be traced by opening up the circuit and observing the meter's reading. Ideally there should be no current flowing, but in practice there usually is a little. This may be due to dirt and grease mixtures around the various harness terminals.

Next, let's talk about capacitors. The caps of concern to us are made by taking two very long strips of metal (aluminum) and placing them next to each other with an insulator between them. A connection is made to each sheet (plate) of metal. Notice that the two plates DO NOT touch. Without getting deep into the theory, let it suffice to say that caps allow alternating current to pass across the insulator, and stop direct current (like from a battery) from passing through. This is what they are SUPPOSED to do, but if they are bad, they do allow DC to pass through. Think about it for a minute, there is a lot of noise generated by the spark system and by the brushes of the generator. This noise can and does get transmitted through the air and gets picked up by the car radio. That is why these caps are placed around the wiring harness usually at the regulator and generator, and through the ignition shielding.

If you placed a VOM, in the resistance mode, across a cap you might notice an initial jump of the meter, but after a few seconds the meter should show a very very high resistance. This is done with the meter on its highest scale. If the meter shows a deflection of 10 percent or more, the cap is leaky and should be discarded. Also if the cap looks dented or puffy or if a chemical discharge is coming out near the leads it is also probably bad. Caps cannot be fixed.

Now for radios. I won't try to explain how the radio converts electromagnetic waves into sound in this article. A thorough understanding is necessary to troubleshoot non-functioning circuitry, and that is beyond the scope of this article. But most radios (and TV's for that matter) can be fixed if you are armed with a few hints and tricks. First the obvious. Make sure the radio is getting voltage. Also make sure the antenna is good. The antenna is connected to the radio through a length of coaxial cable (coax). Coax is merely a shield (copper braid) wrapped around a center conductor. The shield is connected to the radio's case. The case of the radio is connected to the battery's negative terminal and is referred to as GROUND. A simple test to make is to unplug the antenna from the radio, and measure across the plug with the VOM in the resistance mode. It should look like a open circuit. If not then the center lead, which is the antenna's active lead, is shorting some or all of the signal to ground. Temporarily use a short length of wire for a bench antenna. Next check all the tubes and the vibrator on a reputable tube checker. Shorted or gassy tubes should be replaced. Some weak tubes may work for awhile, but if your time is worth anything, you might as well replace them also. If all this doesn't fix it, then settle down for some fun.

It is really unnecessary to have a schematic to fix anything internal. They are available through many sources such as John Amgwert (he has schematic's for '53 — '55 and '62) or a publication called Sams Photofact. These are available through TV supply houses or sometimes public libraries. If the exact schematic isn't available, you can sometimes get by with a similar model's. You might also try the repair shops in the area — good luck.

The approach we are going to use is one of looking for bad parts, and not trying to follow the signal path. There are three main types of parts which we are going after. Capacitors, resistors, and electrolytics (these are special power supply capacitors).

First capacitors. These guys look like cylinders with a lead coming out of each end. They vary in length from .5" to 2.5", and .25" to 1" in diameter. The worst offenders are beige colored and coated with wax. Others are black plastic with color bands around them. Their values are marked on their case (both voltage and capacitance). The black ones use a standard color code which the parts distributor will know (it is also in the schematic both in the circuit drawing and in a table). More about these later.

Second are resistors. There are several types, but one type is known in the trade as "bread-and-butter" because that is what it puts on the repairman's dinner table. The resistor is also cylindrical, but usually .5" in length and .125" in diameter. The particular ones I referred to do not have a smooth body — they look slightly wrinkled. A resistor's size also varies with its power rating. Power supply resistors are generally larger because they have to dissipate more power. When a section of the circuit pulls excessive current, these resistors can overheat and crack or break. If you see anything radically wrong or discolored, it should be replaced. All resistors are marked with at least three color bands which tell their value. Pamphlets or charts are available which interpret these bands. Once you know the value, and their tolerance, you can attach one lead in the middle and measure the resistance with the VOM in the resistance mode.

Electrolytics are polarized (marked with a + sign at one end) and either loose in the circuit or mounted to the chassis (radio's) usually in the area around the power transformer (the big black thing with the steel core). To dispense with electrolytics now, look for damage or leaking chemicals. Their value is marked on their case (both their capacitance and voltage rating).

Now for some tricks. To test a capacitor for leakage we need to apply a large voltage to one side, and see if the VOM, in the voltage mode, can measure any voltage on the other side. To do this we need to look at the schematic to find the capacitors, and whether they have one of their terminals connected to a high voltage point. About 80% of them will be. We next want to cut the OTHER lead in the middle so that we can use the remaining section to solder the old (if good) or new capacitor in with a minimum of disturbance to the rest of the components. You should turn off the power to cut or solder components. Now turn on the set and measure the side of the capacitor which is still soldered in. The voltage should be close to that stated in the schematic. Now place the probe to the cut end of the capacitor under test. There might be a jump of the meter, but after a few seconds, there should be NO voltage on the loose end. If there is, replace the culprit. Repeat the procedure for the others. To test the capacitors who don't have a high voltage side, you need to cut both sides, and temporarily solder one side to a high voltage point and do the same test. If you don't like to work around high voltage, you can buy a high voltage low current battery and do the same test. The battery should be around 90 volts. Hook it up like shown below.

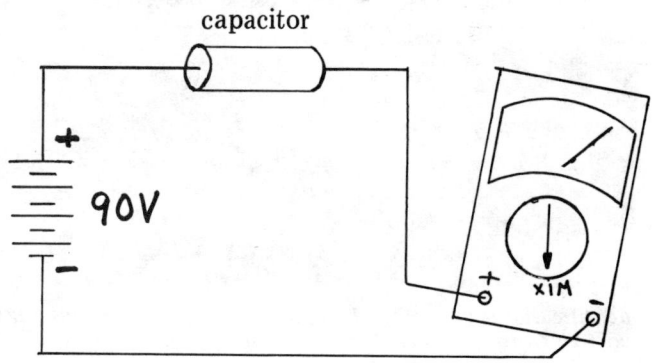

I replaced about 15 capacitors in my '54 by this method. Another hint — replace the large capacitor in the vicinity of the vibrator if it is original. It is usually rated at 1600 volts, costs about $1.25 and sometimes doesn't fail the above test. This guy can adversely affect the operation of the vibrator.

I will answer any questions if supplied with a *SASE*.

Charlie Elman
1494 Marlbarough Ave.
Los Altos, CA 94022
415/967-7650

1953-1967 CORVETTE RADIO IDENTIFICATION

by John Amgwert

This 1958-1960 radio #987730 was recently found in a wrecking yard, having been installed by someone in a 1956 Chevrolet. The radio was operational and the wrecking yard price was only $10.

Corvette radio identification can be a simple matter when the restorer is armed with some basic information. The accompanying chart identifies the radio receiver numbers as indicated in the 1973 edition of the Chevrolet Radio Parts Catalog P & A 5B. All Corvette radios are manufactured by GM's Delco Division.

The part number of each radio set is printed on a paper tag glued to the inside of the receiver's cover. This identification tag is easily found (assuming that it hasn't been removed during prior service) by removing the cover facilitating access to the radio's tubes. The tag also serves as a diagram for tube location on sets so-equipped.

All Corvette radios, factory-installed, from 1953 through mid-1963 were the signal-seeking type *only*. The terms "signal-seeking" and "Wonder Bar" are interchangeable, however the trade-name "Wonder Bar", while appearing in some earlier literature, did not see usage on the set itself until the 1957 Corvette radio (and possibly late-1956). It should be noted that *no* push-button-only AM radios were ever factory-installed in a Corvette. From 1958 through 1960, Chevrolet did service dealer-installed push-button-only radio kits for the Corvette, complete with ignition shielding for both the carbureted and F.I. models. This push-button-only receiver (the same one used in the passenger car) would fit the Corvette dash perfectly, and this explains the sightings of these radios in Corvettes of the 1958-1962 era. Manual-tuning-only radios are also seen as they too, will fit the dash.

The 1953-1967 Corvette radios, with the exception of the 1958-1960 set #987730, do not interchange with any other Delco radio used in any Chevrolet (or GM car for that matter). Some internal radio component parts such as the signal-seeking mechanisms will interchange as all GM Divisions (Buick, Cadillac, etc.) also offered Delco signal-seekers. This is worth remembering if you should need small repair parts.

Identification tag and tube location diagram for #987730 radio glued to the receiver access cover.

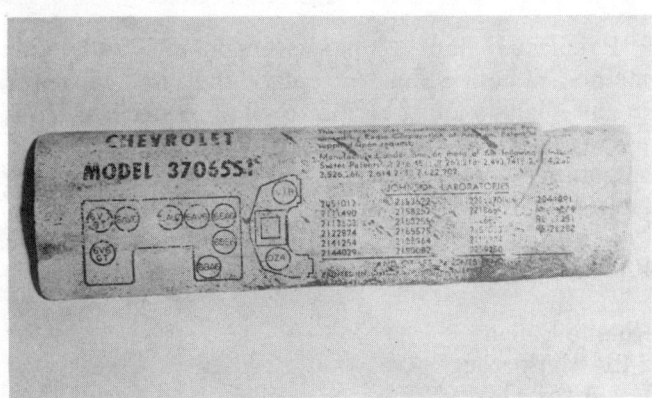

Identification tag for a 1954 #3706551 Corvette radio.

1953-1967 CORVETTE RADIO IDENTIFICATION CHART

Year	Radio Set Number	Radio Type
1953-1955 (6-volt)	3706551*	Signal Seeking
1955 (12-volt)	3711897*	Signal Seeking
1956-1957	3725156**	Wonder Bar
1958-1960	987730***	Wonder Bar
1961	985003****	Wonder Bar
1962	985383****	Wonder Bar
1963	985396	Wonder Bar
1963	985686	AM-FM Push Button
1964	985921	AM-FM Push Button
1965-1967	986281	AM-FM Push Button

* *During the 1954 model run, this radio received Conelrad Civil Defense markings at 640KC and 1240KC on the dial face, 1953 and early 1954 radios had no markings. 6-volt and 12-volt radios are identical in appearance.*

** *The 1956 radio will have a plain touch-bar while the 1957 radio will be engraved "Wonder Bar."*

*** *The 987730 radio set interchanges with the 1958-1960 Chevrolet passenger car. The push-buttons are flat.*

**** *Some early 1962 Corvettes may have been equipped with the 985003 radio. Both radios used in 1961 and 1962 used push-buttons with curved finger-indentations.*

Restorers of the 1953-1957 model Corvettes should be aware that the radio's separate speaker/power supply unit is identical, or at least similar, to those used by some of the other divisions, and even some other auto makes using Delco radios (the Nash is a purported example and I'm sure there are others).

Radio control knobs are worth mentioning in the area of interchange. While the 1953-1954 Chevrolet passenger car's radio volume and tuning knobs are the same design as those used in 1953-1955 Corvettes, the Bel-Airs, etc. got black knobs as opposed to white ones in the Corvettes. Excellent reproduction white knobs are available however. The inner "tone" and "more-stations" sensitivity knobs were also used on at least the 1953 era Buicks (maybe others!). The inner tone knob will be the same on all applicable Buick radios, but the more-stations knob will only be found on the signal-seeking models, naturally.

1956 and 1957 Corvette radio knobs (volume and tuning) will be the same as the 1956 Chevrolet's and the chrome inner "winged" controls can be found in Chevrolet pick-up trucks of the era. The 1958 through 1960 Corvette knobs were the same as used in the 1957 Chevrolet passenger car, and the 1961 through 1964 Corvette knobs come from the 1961-1963 Chevrolet.

There are some external identifying characteristics worth noting. During the 1954 Corvette model run, the tuning face received a small white dot at both 640KC and 1240KC to indicate Civil Defense Conelrad stations. The earlier radios had no such markings. As mentioned earlier, the 1957 Corvette radio reads "Wonder Bar" on the signal-seeking activator control, while the 1956 bar was plain.

The push-buttons on the 1958-1960 radio were flat while the radios for 1961 and 1962 had curved finger-identifications. There were also some changes in the numbers on the tuning face of some of the 1963-1967 AM-FM push-button Corvette radios: 1964 radios, as an example, will appear with either two or three megacycle characters on the FM scale.

Lastly, radio speakers are available, but beware when ordering these from *some* Corvette part's suppliers as a few restorers have been getting replacement speakers of an incorrect ohm rating which does not match that required by the radio receiver. Your best bet here, if you have a bad speaker, is to get it re-coned, an inexpensive job.

STRANGE 1953 CORVETTE ENCOUNTERS— OF THE THIRD KIND!

By John Amgwert

In presenting the strangest 1953 Corvette story that I have ever encountered, I must first discuss some background. As you know, Corvette restorers have long been serial-number-conscious, especially with regard to the 1953 model. Generally, when someone says they own a 1953 Corvette, the question that follows is "What's the serial number?" For some reason there is more prestige in owning, for example, number 99 rather than number 100, or vice versa. When you get to the real low numbers, such as one of the first ten, a 1953's serial number seems to mean more than its condition, at least in the area of its value. Regardless of whether this is true or not, the very low numbers always tend to draw excitement.

This serial number consciousness got a boost around the beginning of this decade when the December/January, 1970 issue of CORVETTE NEWS (Chevrolet's "buff" magazine sent to owners) ran an article about the remaining 1953 models known to exist. During the year preceding that issue, the CN staff conducted a search (through its readers) for the remaining cars by offering as incentive to the owners an engraved silver fascia plate (dash plaque) containing the owner's name and Vehicle Identification Number (VIN). Owners merely needed to send CN a pencil tracing of the cars VIN plate as proof of existence, to be eligible. CORVETTE NEWS also had a duplicate fascia plate made for themselves, which would be affixed to a display containing all the 1953 Corvettes uncovered. (Of interest here is the whereabouts of that display today, as rumor has it that the plates were melted down for their silver.)

It goes without saying that the lowest serial numbered car found through the CN search would ultimately be declared a "winner" of sorts, and to the owner would go a special "gold" fascia plate (rather than silver). This distinction went to Mr. and Mrs. Ed Thiebaud, Southern California turkey farmers, who sent in a tracing for E53F001003; that of the third production Corvette.

This widely published photo shows Ed and Jean Thiebaud with their car. The picture has appeared in several Petersen publications, as well as the March 9, 1970 issue of AUTOMOTIVE NEWS and many newspapers nationwide.

N.C.R.S. Director Noland Adams saw Thiebaud's VIN plate, E53F001003, and the car many years ago remembering it as "a very complete, original-condition 1953 model, in need of restoration."

In the several years following the CN search, Mr. Thiebaud and his car received much notority in various auto magazines such as MOTOR TREND. To my knowledge, only three exterior photos of that car have ever been published (there may have been others) and very few details (such as the car's history), if any, are known, other than what the owner may know.

Serial Number One and Two have never officially been verified as existing, other than the reported rumors that Number One was/is in South Euclid, Ohio, and Number Two had turned-up first in Sacramento, California, and more recently in the Minnesota/Iowa/Wisconsin area. These rumors are considered a hoax rather than fact as a verification inspection by an "authority" is somehow always thwarted, never materializing. You can, however, imagine the excitement that initially surrounds these rumors when such a reported "find" is made. The following "find", though, is not based on rumor, but rather fact, and you will find it both interesting and strange.

Mr. Phil Havens (an attorney with the office of the Attorney General in Lansing, Michigan) joined N.C.R.S. in July, 1977. He purchased a 1955 Corvette (VE55S001312) within the last year from an individual in his state. Phil contacted me last August seeking engine codes relative to that model, and wanted to know who he could get in touch with in his area for information on 1955 models. I sent Phil the engine data and mentioned that he should contact Sam Folz in nearby Kalamazoo.

A month went by and Sam was contacted by Phil. He had just removed the body from the chassis and, upon locating the frame's two "hidden" VIN stampings, was surprised to find that they didn't match the body serial plate. Phil admitted to Sam that he was not sure he understood what the letters and numbers stood for, feeling there was a possibility that he didn't even have a Corvette frame.

Sam inquired as to the frame's VIN stamping and Phil read it . . . . "E53F001003" . . . . Sam was momentarily silent!

After regaining his thoughts, Sam said that it was indeed a Corvette frame; from 1953 Serial Number Three.

Sam asked if he could get tracings, not mentioning to Havens that E53F001003 is, or was, reportedly owned by another individual. Two days later the tracings arrived, and Sam (who is not easily excitable about such things) became *most* interested!

That night I received a call from Sam and was filled-in on the events of the past several days. What a story!

Havens was informed that E53F001003 was owned by Mr. Thiebaud (which he did not previously know) and immediately contacted the Michigan State Police for the purpose of checking his frame. The frame stampings were inspected and found to be in order, with no evidence of an "overstamp." California officials were contacted, but no record of E53F001003 was shown in their files.

Continued on next page

Frame stamping "E53F001003" located on left frame rail.

A number of questions were running through our minds relative to the 1955 body removed from the frame. It is, in fact, a 1955 Corvette V-8 body. What then, is going on here?

Frame stamping "E53F001003" located on top side of X-member.

Sam decided it was time to go to Lansing and see for himself.

The accompanying photos and captions illustrate the deviations from normal production parts in the areas of side body mounting frame-brackets and the unusual V-8 motor mounts used on this frame. These modifications, according to Sam, appear professionally done, especially the body brackets which required excessive pressure stamping. At this point, any logical reason for these body mount modifications can only be estimated. Further, inspection of the 1955 body leaves many questions to be answered.

Above: *Phil Havens removes one of the special-made V-8 engine mounts on 1953 frame Number Three. There appears to be little, if any, evidence of the original six-cylinder engine mounts (located just to the rear of these V-8 mounts), and the area shows evidence of yellow zinc-chromate primer (light area around motor mount in photo).*

It was later realized that California, in 1953, registered some cars by engine serial number rather than by VIN. How then, could the engine number of Mr. Thiebaud's car be determined? It couldn't. But several days later, while going through the original issue of CORVETTE NEWS, I noticed the picture of E53F001003 contained the California license plate "FIH 657." The next day I was told that the tag was registered to Edward August Thiebaud of Creston, California, on April 16, 1976 as a 1953 Corvette serial "LAY 303666." Further, the only previous owner assigned was Sharon L. Crockett, 7367 Walnut, Hollydale, California, up through December 31, 1963. (The vehicle was not registered in California from 1963 to April 16, 1976.) The car is indeed registered by its engine, and it is important to note here that "LAY 303666" is the earliest recorded 1953 Corvette engine number known by us to exist.

In the meantime, Sam had put Havens in touch with a 1955 frame, which he purchased to continue the restoration. Upon examining the two frames, Havens noted several oddities in the 1953 unit.

Below: *Photo shows rear view of motor mounts used for V-8 installation, as well as a 12-volt battery tray's ingenious mounting to the frame's existing 6-volt tray fitments, locating the larger battery more to the outside for clearance of the V-8 engine. Note also the use of a fast-steering adaptor on the central "third-arm" (as was available on Corvettes beginning in 1957) and fuel and brake lines run to the outside of the right frame rail as on all 1953 frames.*

Above: *Close-up of left-rear side body mount. Note the good weld quality and severe form in stamping. Developed-length of part prior to 90° bend-down is same as production part. Note: The rear axle used with the frame is a post-1955 unit.* **Above left and left:** *After Havens purchased a correct 1955 frame, he set it on the 1953 chassis and these photos illustrate the front and rear side body mount bracket modifications. Note that, as on all 1953's and a few very early 1954's, the fuel and brake lines are mounted against the outside of the frame rail (very early in 1954 production the lines were moved to the opposite side of the same frame rail).*

Left and right below: *Shows VE55S001312 body cowl (firewall) panel produced from metal molds. Underlying paint indicates the steering column was white and presumably used red-rimmed wheel. Note that lower left of one photo shows remains of 1953 six-cylinder style washer jar bracket on right inner fender while the left inner fender shows holes for 1955 style jar/bag installation (no evidence of washer pump remain).*

Very little history is known on VE55S001312: Havens was told that it came to Michigan from California, and an old T. Michaelis Corvette Supply Christmas part's tabloid shows "E555001312" (sic) was for sale (if it is the same car) by that firm back in 1975.

Many questions remain unanswered: How did the frame become mated to a 1955 body? . . . . What significance do the frame modifications indicate? . . . . And most importantly, what is the frame VIN stamping of Mr. Thiebaud's car?

1956-1962 CORVETTE IGNITION SHIELDING

By Edwin S. Gurdjian
161 Canterbury Road
Bloomfield Hills, MI 48013
313/647-2990

Drawings by Barbara Streble and John Amgwert

Most N.C.R.S. members are aware of the basic components of ignition shielding — the top distributor cover shield, vertical and horizontal shields, support brackets, wing bolts, and hex bolts. (see figure #1) Many members however, are not aware of the variations between the model years and fewer yet are aware of the discrepancies between the originals and the reproductions. In fact, much of the impetus for this article resulted when this writer discovered he had been sold a "bogus" reproduction fuel injection, top distributor shield by T. Michaelis Corvette Supplies. This shield did not resemble even closely (other than in function) any such shield made by General Motors for any model year Corvette.

FIGURE #1

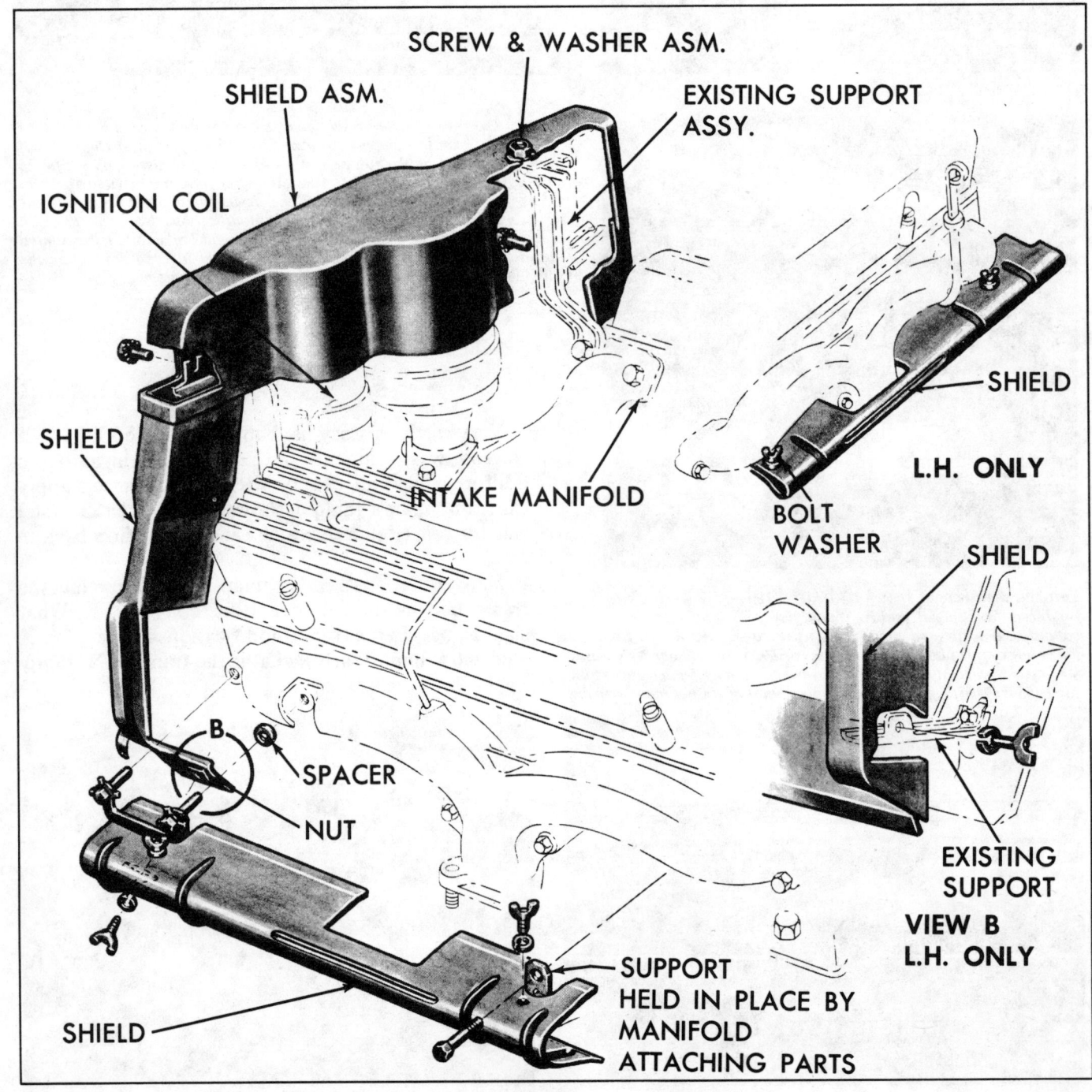

TOP DISTRIBUTOR SHIELDS

Top shield #3730328 was used on all carbureted (radio equipped!) Corvettes from model year 1956 through 1961. It, however, was revised several times during this period. (see Figure #1 & #2)

The first change occurred (according to the blueprint) on March 27, 1956 when the 9/32" top hole (used for bolt attachment to the support bracket) was revised from a round hole to a 9/32" x 15/32" slot.

Until April, 1956 the top shield had front and rear skirts made of chromed steel (see figure #2). Notice in the photo how the top portion is continued over the entire lateral edge ("A"). After April, 1956 the sides of the top shield were formed by the front and rear skirts, and the entire shield was made of stainless steel, rather than chromed steel.

In May, 1956 the notch for the accelerator linkage was modified. No further changes occurred until late March, 1960. At this time the rear depression ("B") was removed, front and rear skirts were revised with front skirt being made longer ("C"), a hole was added (production jig), rear attaching holes were changed to slots, and a front skirt depression was added. It is not certain when this new modified top shield appeared in production - it may not have appeared until some time during 1961 model production. Bear in mind that this shield was used on carbureted 1961's, and remains available from Chevrolet at this writing although the quality of the "service" part leaves much to be desired.

FIGURE #2

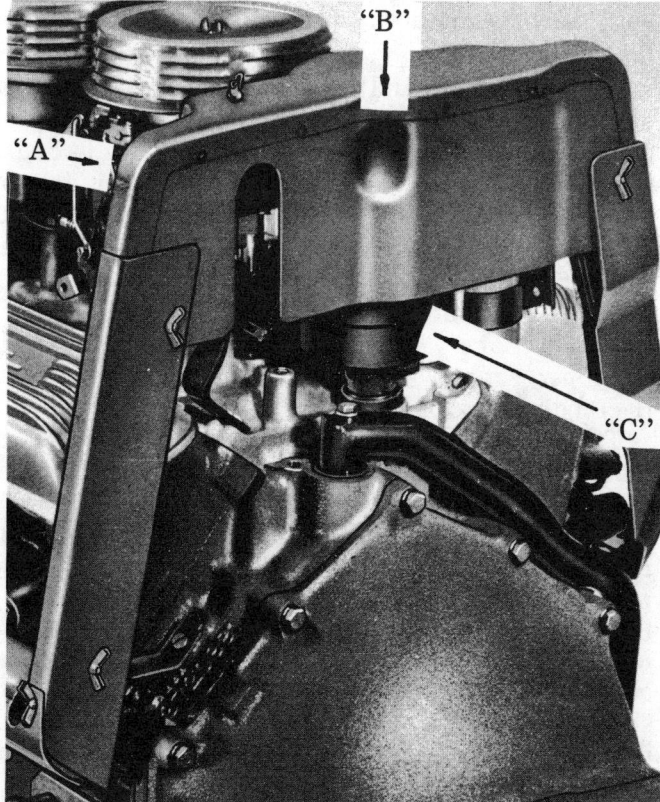

The 1962 Corvette Assembly Instruction Manual (AIM) specifies top shield #3798636. This cover was identical to the previously used #3730328 cover (post 3/60 version) except for a revision in the right slot.

Top shield #3741865 was used on 1957-1961 fuel injected Corvettes. Production of this shield began around August, 1956 and the initial version had a short front skirt. This front skirt had *no* cut-outs, except for the accelerator linkage.

Around May, 1957 the front and rear skirts were revised (see figure #3), in the area of the notches front and rear for the accelerator linkage, and the addition of two notches on the lower edge of the front skirt at the distributor.

FIGURE #3

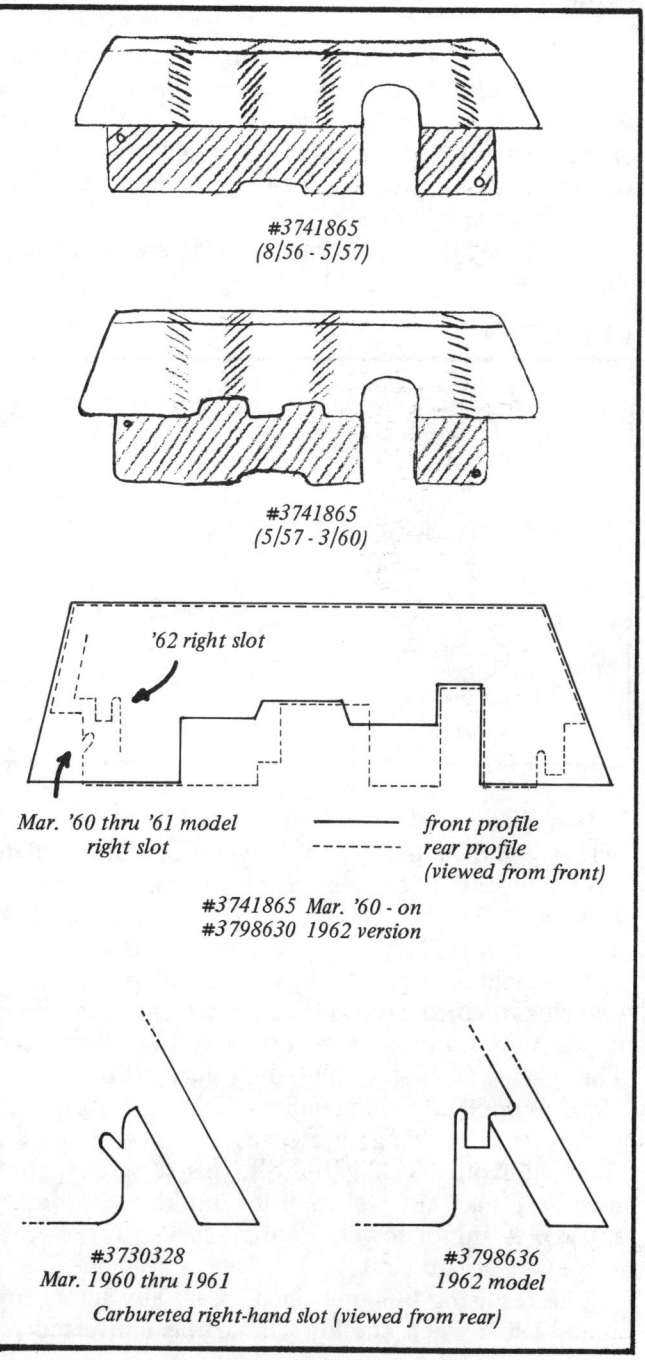

Continued on next page

In March, 1960 the front and rear skirts were again revised, being made longer on the front (see figure #3). A hole (production jig) was added, and the rear holes were replaced by slots, as had also been done to the carbureted version of this top shield.

The 1962 fuel injection model's top shield #3798630 was identical to the late version of #3741865 except for revision of the right slot.

Excellent reproductions of all three F.I. top shields are available from Jerry Kohn in Sawyer, Michigan. These are distinguishable from originals because of their better quality stainless steel (won't hold a magnet — originals will) and deeper spot welds.

VERTICAL SHIELDS

The left vertical shield #3728949 was first produced in July, 1955 (for the 1956 model). In September, 1955 the upper end was revised, being shortened. This allowed the top cover shield to fit over the vertical shield. The attachment bolt holes were enlarged from 9/32" to 3/8".

In May of 1957 the lower end of this vertical shield was revised (see figure #4).

FIGURE #4

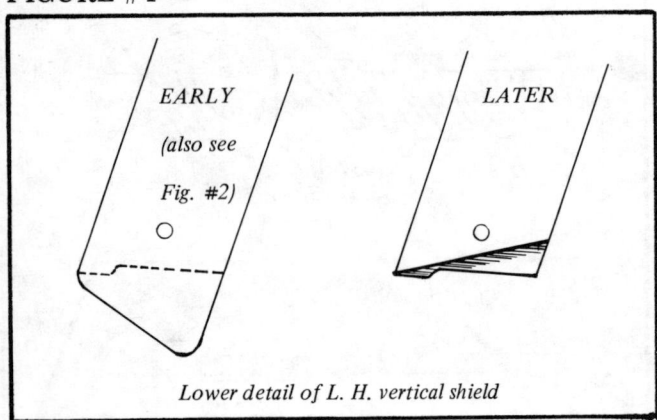

Lower detail of L. H. vertical shield

It appears that all left-hand vertical shields made before mid-January, 1961 were chrome plated steel and the later ones made of stainless steel. In July of 1961 the thickness of the material used was increased from .021" to approximately .035".

The right vertical shield #3728950 is one of the two shields currently available from Chevrolet, though it bears only a vague resemblance to the original part. This part was first produced in July, 1955 (for the 1956 model). In September, 1955 the upper end was revised — being shortened. The bolt holes were enlarged from 9/32" to 3/8" (this same change, remember, had also taken place on the left vertical shield). A minor lower end dimensional revision was also made at this time.

The resulting unit remained essentially intact until June, 1961 when the lower hole was converted to a slot (see figure #5), and the material thickness went from .021" to about .035". The dementional changes that exist between the 1961 unit and those available today appear to be secondary to poor quality control rather than a change in specifications.

FIGURE #5

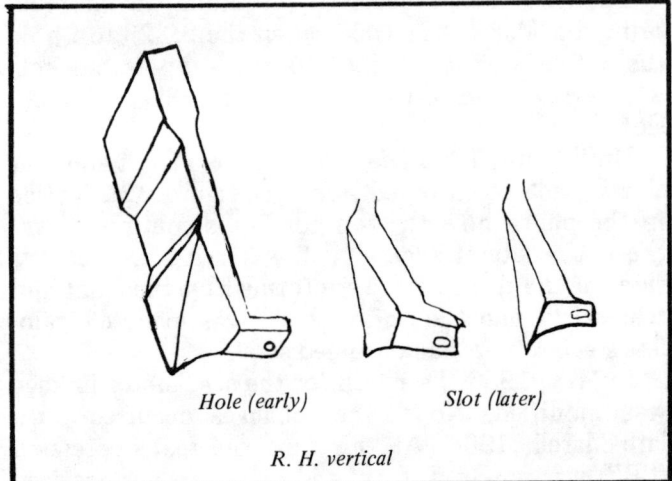

Hole (early)   Slot (later)

R. H. vertical

Note that drawing on left and center attempt to illustrate the change in the production shield from a hole to a slot. The drawing on the right illustrates the GM "service" part in the area of the slot which is much narrower than the original production part used in Corvette assembly.

HORIZONTAL SHIELDS — 1957 THROUGH 1962

The Corvette factory AIM calls for horizontal shields #3736235 (left-hand), and #3736236 (right-hand) for model years 1957 through 1961.

In 1962, introduction of the 327 cubic inch engine with larger exhaust manifolds required the use of horizontal shields #3796647 (left-hand), and #3796648 (right-hand). These 1962 model shields have significant differences from the earlier shields. On the right side the upper manifold cut-out is identical in length at 3.53", but the 1962 version is deeper — 2.31" versus 2.50". The lower manifold cut-out on the #3736236 is 5" x 3.09", while on the #3796648 shield it is 5.16" x 3.25". In addition, the lower cut-out on the #3736236 has a notch for the auto choke valve spring. After September, 1961 an upper cut-out and lower notch were added for the oil dipstick, for the 1962 shield.

The larger exhaust manifold cut-outs on the 1962 model shields required the addition of inner metal reinforcement to prevent warpage.

With the following facts in mind, the deficiences of the reproduction horizontal shields are readily apparent. The cut-outs are of the 1962 size and shape, but there is no reinforcement bar and no "dye-in-indent" at the attachment bolt hole. On extremely close inspection of a reproduction, one will note a slight lack of clarity in the ribs. Thus the reproductions do not accurately represent either the earlier or later model shields.

Photograph shows a 1962 horizontal shield in the foreground with reinforcement bar.

The differences between earlier and later model left-side shields are, as with the right-side, confined to the manifold center cut-out size and the addition of the reinforcement strip. The cut-out dimensions of shield #3736235 are, for the top, 3.80" length by 2.31" depth. The bottom cut-out is irregular, being 3.75" in length but, because of a taper, varying in depth (see figure #6).

FIGURE #6

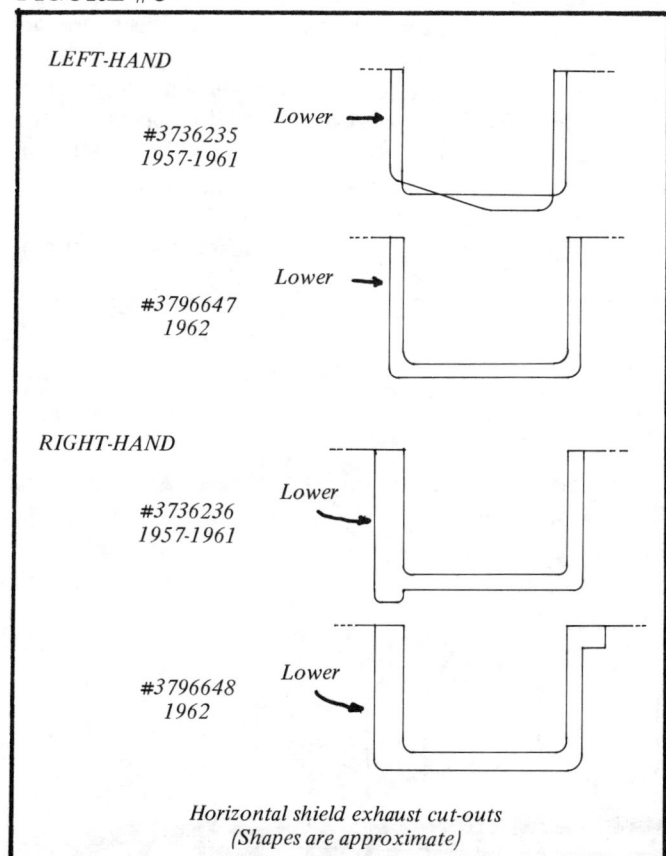

Horizontal shield exhaust cut-outs (Shapes are approximate)

It is interesting to note that the blue-print for #3736235 calls for rectangular cut-outs at top and bottom, but every #3736235 that I've inspected (over 100) had the non-rectangular bottom cut-out. It was several months before I was able to answer the question as to how such a discrepancy could exist. Prior to the introduction of the #3736235 shield (May 7, 1956) Chevrolet had produced a left-hand shield #3736165 (March 12, 1956). This latter part was never used on any model. The blue-print indicates it was to have no rear bottom cut-out (#3736235 had no rear bottom cut-out until July 2, 1957). After July 2, 1957 many shields were produced that were, strictly speaking, neither #3736165 or #3736235. It seems clear that the vendor saw fit to ignore, and Chevrolet Engineering did not notice, the discrepancy between the print and product.

As with the right-hand shield, the reproduction resembles the 1962 shield but does not have the reinforcement strip.

HORIZONTAL SHIELD HISTORICAL DATA

Right-hand

#3736236	4/2/57 printed completed — no revisions
#3796648	11/16/60 print completed
	6/30/61 change from chromed steel to stainless steel
	9/19/61 notch and cut-out added (for oil dipstick)
	2/13/62 change from stainless steel to chromed steel

Left-hand

#3736235	5/7/56 print completed
	7/2/57 rear cut-out added
#3796647	11/21/60 print completed
	6/30/61 change from chromed steel to stainless steel
	2/13/62 change from stainless steel to chromed steel

Notice that according to the blue-print specifications the 1962 shields were made stainless steel from 6/30/61 to 2/13/62. Exactly how many were produced is not known.

SHIELDING ATTACHMENT BOLTS & WASHERS

	1957	1958-61	1962
Top Shield	3728415 Wing-bolts	121798 Hex-bolts 120380 Washers	423554 Hex-screw & washer Asm.
Horizontal Shields	120380 Washer At all locations	3728415 Wing-bolts 120380 Washers	3728415 Wing-bolts 120380 Washers
Vertical Shields			

NOTE: Blue prints indicate top shield attachment bolts changed from "Wing-type" to "Hex-head" with 1958 model due to hood clearance.

FIGURE #7

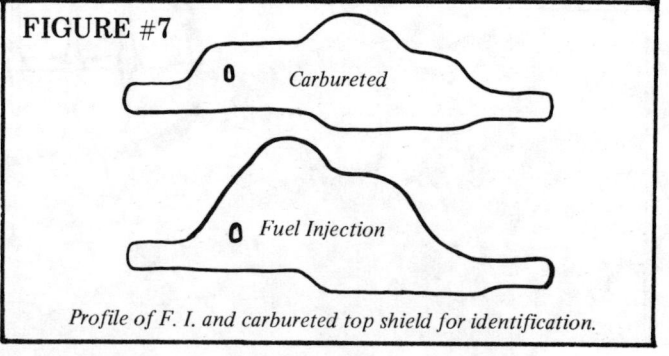

Profile of F. I. and carbureted top shield for identification.

1953-1960 GRILLE TEETH PLACEMENT

By John Amgwert

A restorer faced with extracted teeth (on his or her car) need not seek-out the services of an orthodontist to straighten out the situation. Trying to identify a bicuspid or molar when it comes to the 1953-1960 grille teeth can be quite a job when one refers to the old Dental Journal (in this case the earlier Chevrolet Part's Catalogs of that era), in an effort to restore a Corvette's "toothie" smile.

Seriously though, for purposes of identification and correct location of the commonly referred to "grille teeth" (or "vertical bars" as Chevrolet called them) I have constructed the accompanying diagrams. These are based on past part's books, and my own experience acquired while disassembling the grilles on Dave Nace's 1954 and Dr. Bruce Rauscher's (yes, he's my dentist) 1960: both fine original examples.

The 1953 through 1957's 13 grille teeth are arranged beginning in the center (the largest in size) with six teeth to each side which either get progressively smaller in size, or show a slight variation for mounting to the horizontal grille bar. The teeth on each side of center are symmetrical, being inverted from those on the opposite side.

The hollow inside area of these cast pot-metal

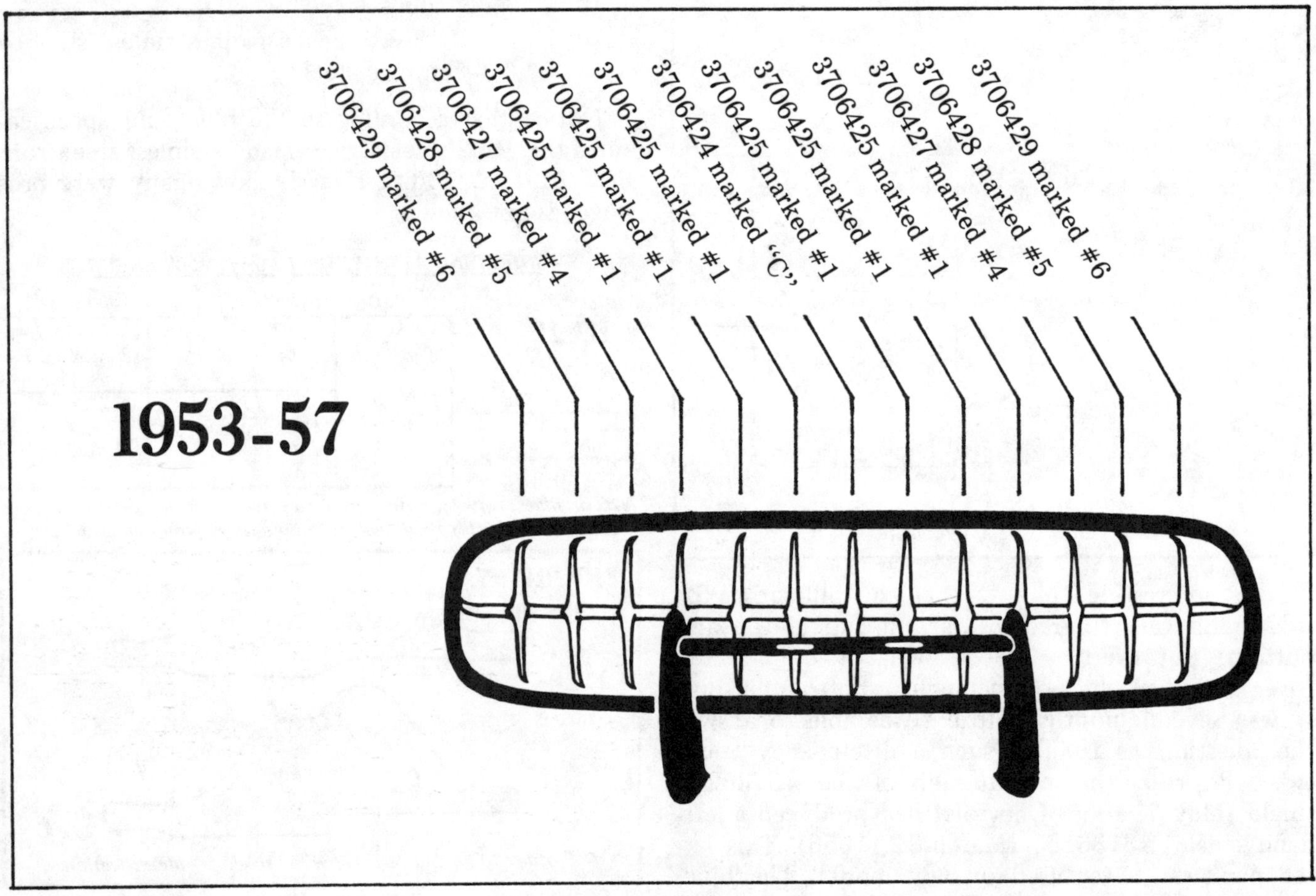

```
3706429 marked #6
3706428 marked #5
3706427 marked #4
3706425 marked #1
3706425 marked #1
3706425 marked #1
3706424 marked "C"
3706425 marked #1
3706425 marked #1
3706425 marked #1
3706427 marked #4
3706428 marked #5
3706429 marked #6
```

1953-57

teeth will show the part number needed for identification (see photo), as well as a code number (or letter

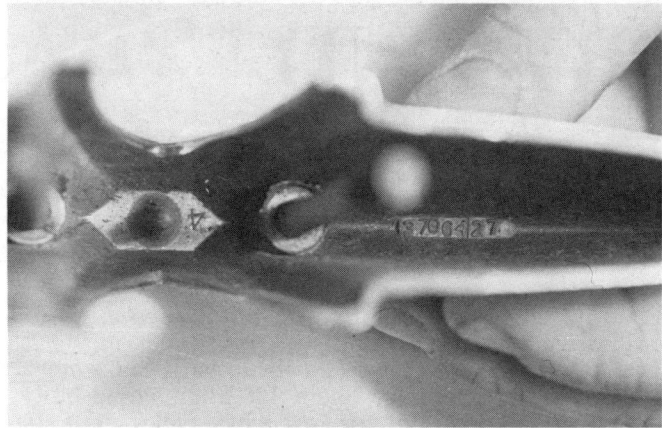

"C" for *center*) referring to its location installation sequence. The center position is "C", followed by #1 through #6 positions moving outboard of center. As you can see from the 1953-1957 diagram, positions #1, #2 and #3 used the same tooth #3706425 (coded #1), followed by #3706427, 428 and 429 (coded #4, #5 and #6 respectively). The confusion exists, apparently, because the #1 coded tooth holds three positions on the grille bar.

Restorers of the 1953-1957 models should take note that the #3706429 (coded #6) tooth, which is the smallest in size, on each end, was discontinued from service by the General Motors Parts Division (GMPD) shortly after the 1957 model-year. The early 1960's and later parts books instructed that the #3706428 (coded #5) tooth would have to be substituted *in pairs* at the #6 location to maintain symmetrical appearance if replacement of one end tooth became necessary.

Beginning with the 1958 Corvette (and continuing through 1960) the grille was redesigned and the number of teeth was reduced to nine. I have long thought that the positioning of the teeth on the 1958-1960 models was exactly the same as 1953-1957, the two earlier end teeth merely being eliminated, but this is not so. These later models are confusing relative to tooth number and positioning on the grille bar. The center tooth (coded "C") is the same, as is the next tooth (coded #1). However, the #2, #3 and #4 positions use a #3706427 (coded #4), another #427, and a #428 (coded #5) respectively.

Interestingly, the teeth #3706428 that I examined on the 1960 model show a part number of #3706428-9, the "-9" not appearing on the earlier #428 tooth, and no code "5" was present. Obviously, as mentioned earlier, by 1960 this part became the replacement for, and assumed the identity of, the discontinued #3706429 (coded #6) tooth used through 1957.

These 1953-1960 grilles are quite pleasing appearance-wise, but are a toothache to clean and polish. In closing, I will pass-on a tip I heard concerning a good chrome polish . . . . you guessed it . . . toothpaste!

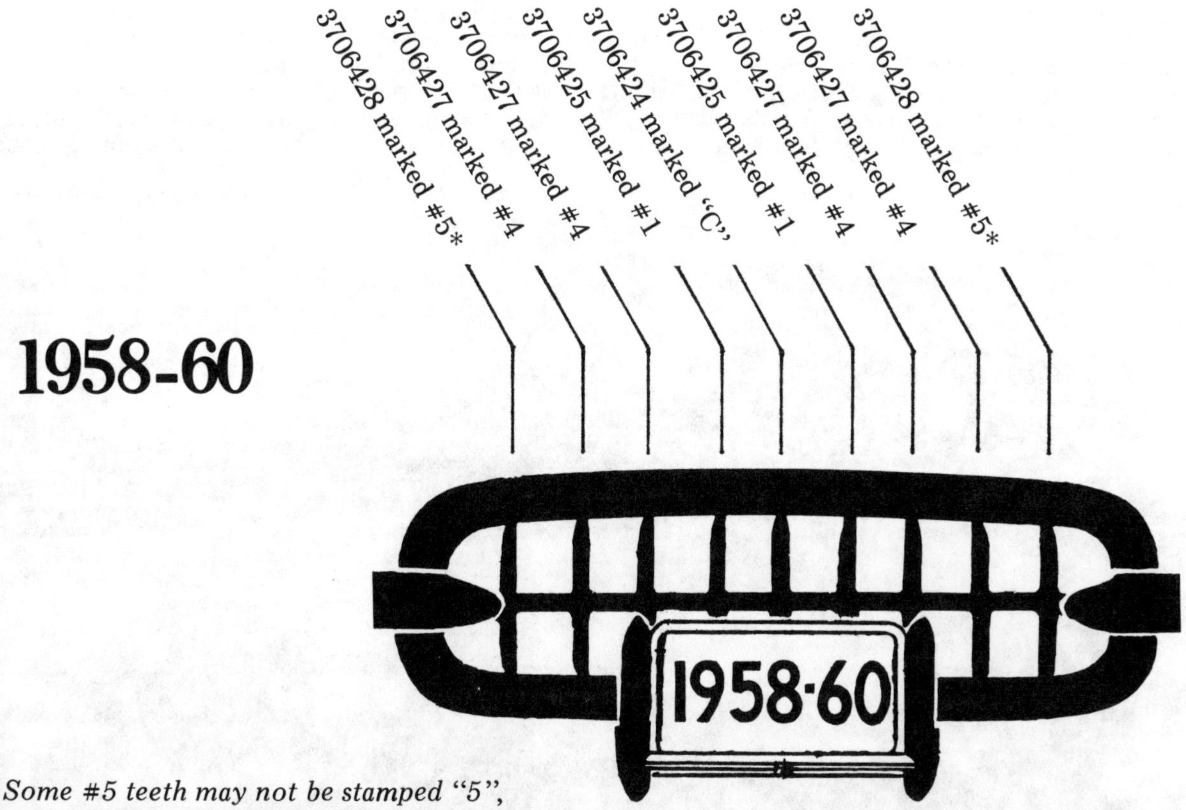

1958-60

Teeth (left to right):
- 3706428 marked #5*
- 3706427 marked #4
- 3706427 marked #4
- 3706425 marked #1
- 3706424 marked "C"
- 3706425 marked #1
- 3706427 marked #4
- 3706427 marked #4
- 3706428 marked #5*

*NOTE: Some #5 teeth may not be stamped "5", however the part number 3706428-9 will appear.

Part One:
THE HISTORY AND RESTORATION OF EX-122

By John Amgwert

In presenting the history and restoration of the 1953 Motorama Corvette show car (EX-122), I have chosen to divide the story into two parts. First we will look at some of the history behind the car from its beginning, up to the time the present owner contacted Mr. Jon Blanchette of New York for the purpose of restoring the vehicle. The second part of the story will deal with Jon's restoration.

Playing an important part in this story is Mr. Russell F. Sanders, a retired General Motors Executive, who owned EX-122 from April, 1956, until October, 1959, at which time it was sold to its present owner. Mr. Sanders has first-hand knowledge of the Corvette project from the beginning, working for Chevrolet Engineering starting in 1934, and becoming Assistant Chief Engineer at Chevrolet in the mid-fifties. During World War Two, he was involved with the 4 x 4 (four-wheel-drive) truck building program and was later responsible in the early 1950's for much of the development of the new Chevrolet V-8 engine introduced for the 1955 model year. Mr. Sanders authored *"The New Chevrolet V-8 Engine"* (Society of Automotive Engineers Paper Number 441), presented to the SAE 50th Anniversary Meeting at Detroit in January 1955.

In correspondence concerning the early Corvette project and EX-122 Mr. Sanders wrote: "In the early part of 1952, the Styling Section of G.M. built a proposed model of the Corvette for Executive Approval. It was made of wood, clay, plastics and metal. It had no engine or running gear but looked like you could drive it away.

"After it was decided to go ahead with the project as a production vehicle, Chevrolet Engineering built an experimental model for test and development. It had the mechanical components to develop ride, handling, performance and durability, but did not look like the styling model because the body was just something to ride in. After being tested to death, it was scrapped. It was a machine to test components; it was an ugly work-horse. Several more were built and tested.

"Concurrently, the fore-runner of EX-122 was built in Chevrolet Engineering. It was to represent, in all details, the Corvette to be made in production later."

This "fore-runner to EX-122" as Mr. Sanders described was the Corvette displayed at the 1953 G.M. Motorama show held at the Waldorf-Astoria Hotel in New York City. The show was open to the public January 17-22, 1953 following a press preview on the 16th. The car was the first running Corvette built for show.

The Motorama Corvette was constructed by the Experimental Department of Chevrolet Engineering during the latter part of 1952, the car representing the intent of production drawings then being released for the 1953 production model. Plaster molds taken directly from the clay styling model were used to make the fiberglass body (plus a couple other bodies

Chevrolet Chief Engineer Ed Cole (left) and General Manager Thomas H. Keating inspect the 1953 Motorama Corvette at the Waldorf show.

that were used on test cars). The cost of construction was estimated by Mr. Sanders to be $55,000/60,000 and he says, "Workmanship and quality were the best possible at Chevrolet Engineering because it was to be used in the Motorama." At this time the car was white, had red interior and trim, six-cylinder Chevrolet high-performance "Blue Flame" engine and a special high-capacity Powerglide transmission.

While the Corvette project had been code-named "Opel" during most of the early development, the name "Corvette" (defined as a small warship) is credited to Mr. Myron Scott the Chevrolet public relations executive who originated the yearly Soap Box Derby. It is interesting to note that a G.M.-New York press release, sent out just prior to the 1953 Motorama, called Chevrolet's entry the "Courvette" (sic) throughout the news story. At any rate, the 1953 Motorama Corvette debuted at the Waldorf show with "Corvette" in gold script on the front and rear, as well as in the plastic emblems used at the front and for the center of the steering wheel.

Following the Waldorf show, the car was carried, babied and handled very carefully through the other G.M. Motorama presentations in Miami, Houston, Los Angeles, San Francisco and Kansas City, as well as other shows and fairs in the United States. Following this tour, which ended during the Summer of 1953, it was displayed in the lobby of the G.M. Building in Detroit for a considerable period.

The "Old" and the "New" – The 1953 Motorama Corvette poses with its counterpart of 40 years earlier.

In addition to the show car's body, several other bodies for testing were molded from the initial clay model. These three photos are of one of those test cars. Note that the left-front fender differs significantly from the right, moving the headlamp forward, and also the changes in right and left rear trim – thus allowing stylists to visualize both concepts. This vehicle was apparently a working car, as evidenced by the engine vacuum gauge mounted in the radio speaker cove.

PART ONE: THE HISTORY AND RESTORATION OF EX-122

Continued

At this point in the story I want to briefly touch on the possibility of *two* Motorama Corvette show cars. The Chevrolet press release dated June 30th, 1953 (see pg. 33 of Summer '78 *RESTORER*) mentions "show cars" and several publications at the time specifically mention "two show cars". This question was asked of Mr. Sanders and he comments: "Regarding the showing of two Corvettes in the original Motorama shows — one was the Styling Mock Up Model and the other was the fore-runner of EX-122. There were no other cars to show that had the Corvette styling -- only some of the 'work-horses' and I know they were not exhibited." It should be noted that the running prototype (EX-122) was the actual New York' Motorama Corvette.

Numerous factory photographs exist, however, showing many, many detail changes giving credence to the theory that more than one show car existed. It is known that while the car was on tour, crazing of the body occurred, necessitating refinishing, and several deletions were made (or another car built) in the area of the top-fender air scoops, exterior door opening buttons, and dash vent controls to more closely resemble the soon-to-be-released production model. A thorough discussion and the evidence supporting the two car theory warrants another story in a future issue.

By late 1953 the production model Corvette became more common and the original Waldorf Corvette

1953 Waldorf show — **Above:** *car is readied for display.* **Above right:** *press photography session.* **Below:** *movie star Joe E. Brown is seen in the crowd.* **Right:** *hood opened and closed during show by hydraulic cylinders – tag at lower right says "Show Car – Hands off Please".*

was retired from shows to the Engineering Department and used for testing. At that time the new Chevrolet 265 cubic inch V-8 engine was being developed and one was fitted in the car for performance demonstrations. As a result, it was decided to go with the V-8 in Corvette production for 1955.

With the added V-8 power the engineers were concerned with vehicle durability, so the car was taken to G.M.'s Milford, Michigan Proving Grounds and underwent a 25,000 mile durability test, then completely torn down and each part examined and reported-on for production evaluation. Following this test and inspection the car was reassembled and updated with prototype production components.

Actually, during the period from late 1953 through April, 1956, the car was constantly being fitted with prototype parts as well as being updated. The original Motorama body had to be scrapped, and was replaced by a production 1955 V-8 body. Some of the prototype components added were: rear deck latches, heater system, cowl vent mechanism, windshield wiper system, radio, wheel-covers (1956 variety), rear chrome pieces, and a 1956 style rear axle and housing.

Concerning Chevrolet's last rebuild of the car, Mr. Sanders has written: "I was in charge of the Experimental Department at the time and saw to it that the car was rebuilt in the very best of condition. A new (or rebuilt) 265 V-8 engine was installed. This was the second V-8, the first was used up on test work and durability. To my knowledge, both engines were 265's. It was repainted red, a new top and new white seats installed, new speedometer installed, transmission was completely overhauled, safety items were replaced and a new set of tires put on.

"It became an 'Engineering Demonstrator' (and show car) and I think it was at that time that the number 'EX-122' was assigned to the car. It was used as a courtesy car for about 5,000 miles and then put up for sale. I purchased the car from Chevrolet on April 11, 1956."

Russ Sanders' snapshot of EX-122 taken in 1956.

EX-122 then went to Rochester, New York, when Mr. Sanders became Director of Sales and Engineering at Rochester Products Division of G.M. He and his family used the car on a daily basis until October, 1959, at which time it was sold to the present owner, Mr. Jack Ingle.

Jon Blanchette, a Senior Engineer at Rochester Products, became involved with the car in August, 1973, and he writes: "The present owner drove it daily until 1968. By that time the frame was rusted out, it had been involved in several accidents, and was mechanically 'tired'. At this time, the owner decided the car was definitely worth saving, and took it to a shop for restoration. Unfortunately the shop indiscriminately ripped the car apart with no regard to reassembly. Trim was pried off and bent, screws and nuts sheared off, parts thrown in the corner and lost, fiberglas filler put into the frame holes, sandblast sand was in every moving part, and to sum it up, reduced the car to a 'total disaster'.

Photos taken by Jack Ingle when body first removed in 1969.

"I entered the picture in August, 1973, when the owner contacted me and asked if I could salvage the 'remains', and properly restore it. I took the job on, with the restoration intent to be as the car was when Chevrolet sold it, in April, 1956. To restore it back to the 1953 Motorama configuration was impractical, if not impossible, as its first original components had long been scrapped."

At this point I will conclude Part One of the EX-122 story. Part Two will cover Jon's five-year restoration of the vehicle, and it'll be presented in the next issue of *The CORVETTE RESTORER*.

1963-1967 INDEPENDENT REAR SUSPENSION

By Joe Clark

One of the major design changes in the Sting Ray series Corvettes was the completely new undercarriage built into both the front and rear of the new car. This new system can really be thought of as Zora Arkus Duntov's genius at its finest.

In a movie shown at the recent N.C.R.S. convention in Flint, Zora is shown asking test drivers specifically about the ride and handling of the then-new 1963 cars. Their reactions was most enthusiastic — especially Dr. Dick Thompson's, who had much race experience in early Corvettes.

As I stated in my first article, the overall considerations in any redesign at Corvette have always been cost, utility and serviceability. These limits therefore dictate simplicity even in unique applications such as the independent rear suspension for 1963.

For the new Sting Ray, the front received a ball joint suspension of shared components with its passenger car brothers. The old king pin design was now dead — after a very long run indeed.

But for 1963 the real excitement was to be found in back. There, much to the credit of G.M. design and management, the Corvette was allowed to have its own completely unique suspension design — and what a design it was. Just try and imagine the extent of original thinking and decision-making that produced this radical independent rear suspension as a production reality.

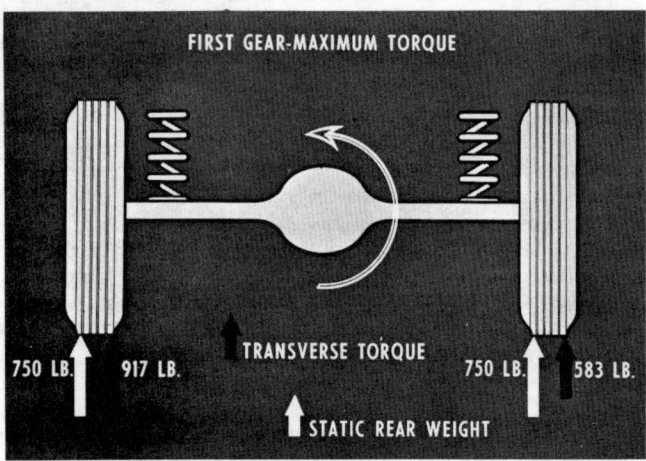

Why was the new system so much better than the conventional straight axle? Lets look at a few numbers and pictures to illustrate. Refer to Figure 1. As shown, one can easily see the effects of transverse torque as well as the tendency towards axle dipping upon application of power. The axle is not only whipped by the movement of the drive shaft torque, but also the tractive motion of the tires to the road causes the dipping or waving along the springs. Obviously our old straight axle is subject to a great deal of stress — all sprung — that is — all mounted to the chassis by flexible springs.

The resulting movements of the conventional axle can and do influence handling and ride in many ways. On a dry road, pointed in a straight line, these forces may not be noticeable. Conversely, on a wet or twisting road, in either the accelerating or decelerating mode, fish tailing and axle hopping can be a very real and pronounced concern to any driver.

Further, in a left hand turn, using the axle shown in Figure 1 the traction breaking skid would be even more pronounced as more weight is shifted off of the wheel having the most drive torque pressure. As in any design, the less torque load transfer the better the traction and stability of the vehicle.

In the illustration of the new suspension, it is not hard to see how the new independent concept solved many of the old handling problems.

With the differential now frame mounted, the transverse torque force is virtually eliminated. This in turn leads to a far higher and more even rate of tire to road adhesion because the entire axle no longer moves — nor is subject to drive torque, or road bumps. Now, only one wheel at a time is stressed with no live transfer of effects as in a solid axle connection. Axle dipping is also controlled by the use of torque control arms as illustrated in Figure 2.

The independent configuration has the additional advantage of increasing the sprung to unsprung weight ration resulting in a greatly improved ride. Not only is the weight of the differential a help but the live axles can be isolated from the chassis with greater ease than the conventional solid unit. Finally, the direct transfer of bumps,

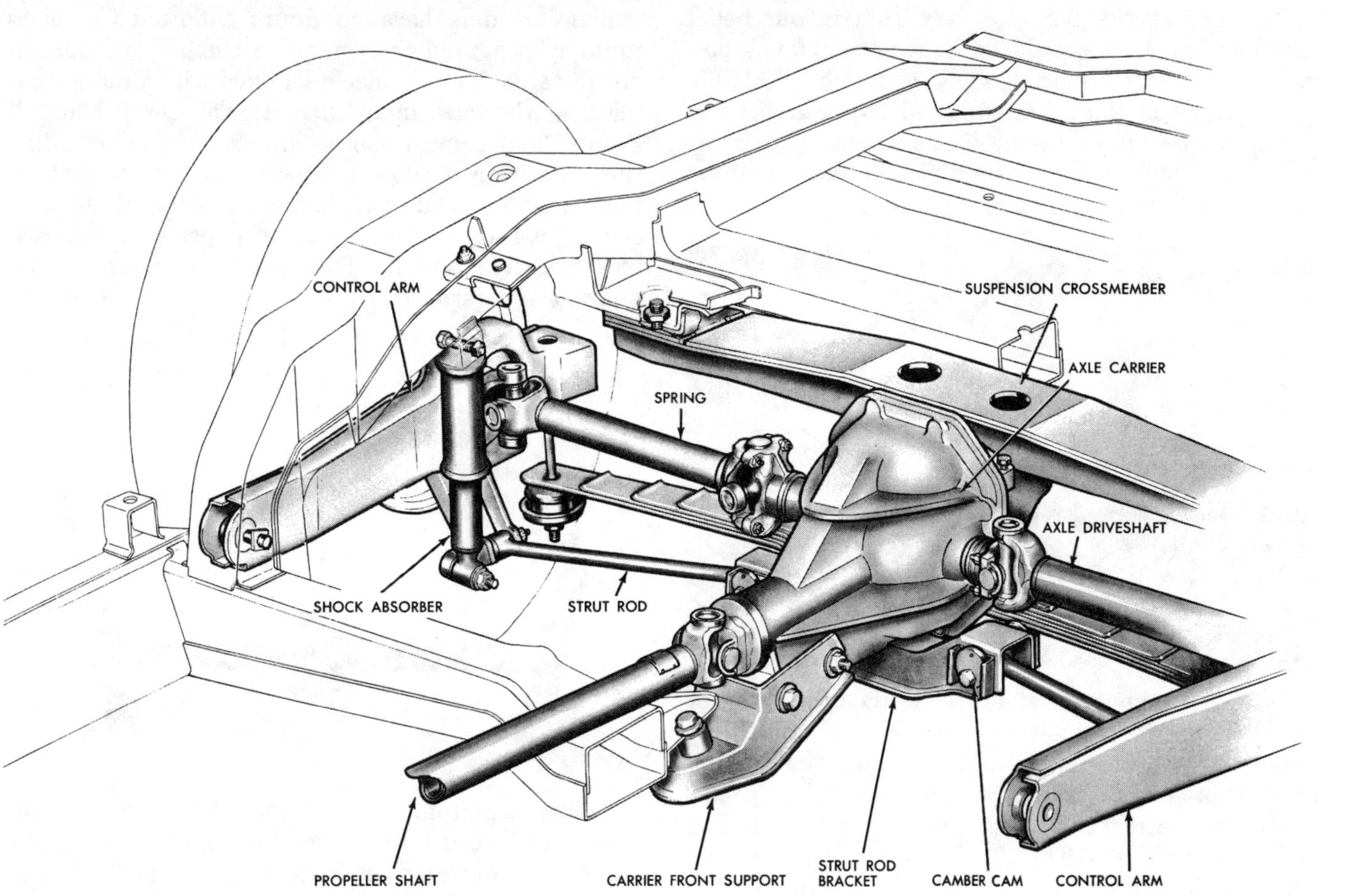

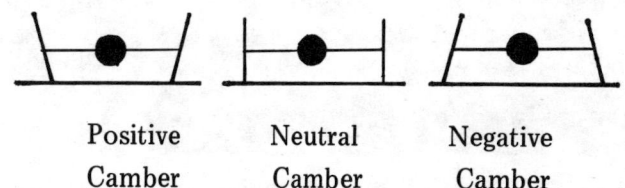

Figure 2 — Rear suspension and driveline components.

jolts and jounces is far less noticeable because the two sides of the car function independently of one another.

Every improvement has its price and this system is no exception. While the ride and handling are greatly improved, this new undercarriage requires maintenance of a complex nature.

Those readers who have been to their dealer or alignment shop and observed a Corvette *backed on* to a front end machine have a hint of some of the required attention that the newer cars demand. For unlike the 1953-1962 cars, the Sting Ray has adjustments for both camber and toe in/out at the *rear* wheels.

Toe-in is defined as the amount of difference, in fractions of an inch, that wheels are closer together in front than at the rear when measured at hub height.

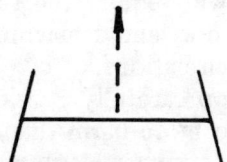

1963 specifications call for a toe-in angle of 0" to 1/8". That is, the front to rear difference between wheels should be 0" to 1/8" at hub height. The toe adjustment on 1963-1967 cars is made by inserting shims of varying thickness inside the frame side member on both sides of the torque control arm pivot bushing. (Consult your shop manual for specifics).

Remember that when aligning the Sting Ray's rear suspension the car is *backed on* a machine normally used for front suspension alignment and toe-in will read as toe-out, and toe-out will read as toe-in.

Camber is the outward tilt of the wheels, from top to bottom:

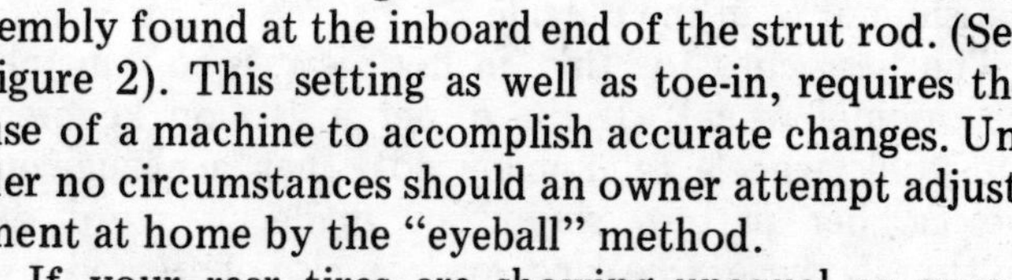

| Positive Camber | Neutral Camber | Negative Camber |

Wheel camber adjustment on this series Corvette is obtained by moving the eccentric cam and bolt assembly found at the inboard end of the strut rod. (See figure 2). This setting as well as toe-in, requires the use of a machine to accomplish accurate changes. Under no circumstances should an owner attempt adjustment at home by the "eyeball" method.

If your rear tires are showing unequal or excessive wear, it is possible that some adjustment should be made in the rear suspension. If the settings are incorrect it is easy to see why tires can slip, skid or scuff along the road.

Continued on next page

We here at N.C.R.S. are very firm in our belief that any Corvette should be kept as original as possible. However, recognizing the large number of 1963-1967 models running around with flared fenders prompts mention of the problems wrought by changing wheel type and tire sizes. These have a direct bearing on both front and rear geometry.

When an owner varies tire location by the use of reversed wheels, non-stock mags, etc., several things happen that upset rear suspension adjustment. Many of these non-stock wheels require adapters or spacers to fit lug patterns or clear brake calipers, on cars with disc brakes. When either is used, camber is influenced because the wheel has moved the weight bearing surface of the tire outward — away from car centerline. This change gives less leverage to the

spring end, increases spring loading and results in a sagging negative camber attitude. Obvious effects are poor tire wear as the inside tread bears more punishment than the outside.

The best cure for this, in my view, is to reinstall the original wheels. If the owner insists on keeping non-stock wheels (and many do), then a change in the camber pattern should be made. A word of caution however; bearing load is also increased by various wheel types and the results can be quickly worn out wheel bearings as well as excessive wear on other suspension parts such as bushings, spring ends and other moving components.

Many readers have no doubt followed Corvettes running in a squatting, negative camber attitude. In my research for this piece, I talked with a number of talented Corvette men (in particular our friend Bill Denny) and came upon an interesting fact regarding this condition. Often, a negative camber attitude is not caused by camber adjustment or excessive loading at all. Instead, in the opinion of experts, it is caused by excessive toe-out. That is, the rear wheels are pointed outward in front. This, if the reader can

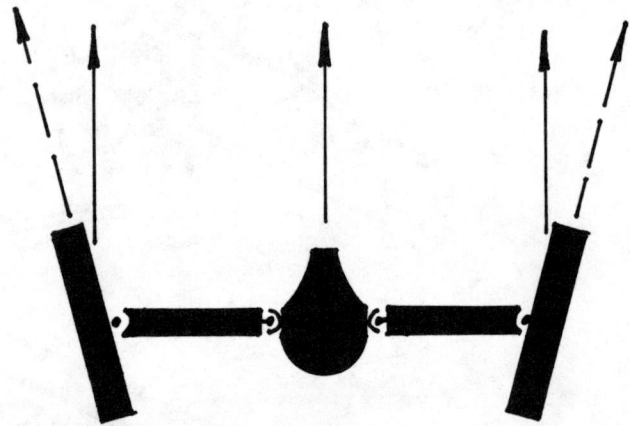

visualize, will tend to pull the wheels apart as the tires are dragged into a semi-plowing situation. Something has to give and it is the camber that is thrown negatively as the tires scrub along pulling the suspension outward into an improper configuration.

These same experts pointed out that toe-in adjustment is not only critical but extremely difficult to do and that many shops will go to great lengths to avoid having to make changes in these settings. Here again, if toe adjustment is your problem, no amount of camber change is going to help. For even if the negative camber is adjusted out, the forces of poor toe-in adjustment are still working on the tires — they are just not as evident.

Many owners I talked with a recent events had no idea that there were any sort of adjustments on the Sting Ray rear suspension. For many owners the existance of these settings is very important because they drive their cars. Those who trailer their cars should also be aware of proper maintenance and adjustments.

As with any front suspension adjustment, the rear of your car will require the services of an expert with proper tools and a machine for conformation to factory specifications.

Choose your shop carefully — ask around. An untrained man can do more harm than good if he does not understand this truly fine system.

Joe Clark
Box 353
Havre de Grace, MD 21078
301/939-2467

CORVETTE MODELS
With Dr. Michael Zimmerman

Corvette Models: 1/24th "Metal Master" '53-54

This issue's column deals with a paradoxical model, Monogram's '53-54 Corvette 1/24th scale "Metal Master." The concept of building a metal model of a plastic car is of course paradoxical to begin with, although it does have certain advantages. The body can be primed and painted in an original color, using spray paints available from most of the Corvette parts shops. As my daughter Jill and I already have a nice '53 in our collection, we chose to build this model as a Pennant Blue/Shoreline Beige '54, the necessary engine parts for this conversion being supplied in the kit.

There are some problems with the metal body, which is generally very nicely cast. A few moulding lines have to be filed flat and the entire body must be rubbed down with fine steel wool to prepare it for painting. The spray paint gives a very rough finish, which must be allowed to dry for a week and then compounded and polished to bring out the gloss. In the course of compounding it is inevitable that paint will be removed from high points, requiring brush touch-up. Fortunately, the brushed paint dries with a high gloss and, if done carefully, can be polished so as to be almost unnoticeable. The side chrome is moulded in and can be painted with care, or you can use an aluminum foil called "Bare-Metal" which simulates chrome.

The major paradox of the kit is that the best parts are the frame and engine, which are all plastic. They fit together well and look very realistic. The snap-in white walls are excellent. It is particularly easy to do the wheels correctly, as they are chrome over red plastic. Scrape the chrome off the ribs and rims, spray with Glosscote, and you have a perfect wheel.

This red plastic creates difficulties elsewhere, however. If you are using plastic glue, the chrome has to be scraped to glue in the lights and covers, windshield, license plate cover, etc. The red shows through, giving a very unrealistic effect. Five-minute epoxy (Devcon) would be a much better choice for these areas.

The headlight covers are clear plastic, and I can't believe anyone could paint the grillwork in silver. The license plate cover traps the glue vapors inside. The resulting fogging of the cover is just like the real thing, but this design flaw in the original car would be better not duplicated in the model. I even tried drilling two small holes in the cover for drainage, but, again like on the real car, it didn't help.

Two other problem areas are the hood hinge, which simply doesn't work, not allowing the hood to set all the way down, and the front emblem and gauges, which are in very shallow relief. It is almost impossible to paint these items realistically. AMT'S '53 Corvette model is much better in this respect.

The Monogram model is a lot like a good college quarterback — a lot of potential but adjustments should be made to make it in the pros. Unfortunately for the modeler, these changes should be made by the manufacturer — better detail moulding and white or clear plastic under the chrome.

In spite of these deficiencies, careful assembly and

painting can still result in a very attractive model. My thanks to the owners of the Pennant Blue '54's at the N.C.R.S. Flint meet for letting me crawl all over their cars to get the details for this model.

The remainder of this column will be devoted to some general techniques and hints for modelers.

Chassis and engine: I always use glossy paints, except for fan belts. While instructions usually suggest flat black, on this scale pieces in flat black are virtually invisible. Certainly all detail is lost.

White walls are a problem. Airplane dope does not adhere well to vinyl, and enamels such as the Humbrol I previously advised simply never dry, always remaining tacky to the touch. If you can avoid touching the tires, the enamels are probably better.

Most instructions tell you to remove pieces from the "tree" and paint them as they are used. I have found it best to remove all the pieces (following the order of the instructions), cement together as many as possible, and paint all pieces of the same color at the same time. This approach gives more uniform color, better adhesion between non-painted surfaces, and saves paint. Details and chrome trim can be brush painted, using a good artist's brush (clean carefully after use).

The best glue to use is liquid with a brush in the cap. Chrome or paint must be scraped off and glue applied sparingly. The best way to glue in windows is by scraping any paint or chrome off the frame, putting the window in place, and flowing a small amount of cement into the junction with the brush tip. Allow to dry thoroughly before moving (a good general rule).

Interiors: Light colors, such as tan, white, or light blue are best, dark colors obscuring detail. You can get away with black in a convertible, but not in a coupe. A light cover of Dullcote (or spraying flat and using a little Glosscote) gives a realistic semi-gloss appearance. The seats should be glued in before painting, as it is impossible to scrape paint off the "carpeting" and get the seats to adhere. Dashboards should be painted separately, as you can't get the detail in once they are in place.

Exterior: The tricks to painting the exterior are in washing the body with liquid dishwashing detergent, doing the inside first, and using two or three light coats. Metallics should be gloss coated, as it makes them shinier and prevents tarnishing. Window mouldings must be chrome painted before inserting the windows.

Assembly: Care must be taken in inserting the interior and chassis into the body. The body should be placed on a soft cloth, as it is all too easy to scratch the roof while working the chassis in. Cement should be flowed into junction points to hold the chassis in the body.

Display: I build clear plastic cases for my models. Most cities have plastic shops that will cut 1/8" sheets to your specifications. The same plastic glue can be used, with masking tape to hold the edges together till the glue dries. Two cautions: (1) don't let the glue contact the tape, as it will flow under the tape and over the surface of the case, and (2) make the case big enough — building models is addictive!

Next column — the SR-2.

Michael R. Zimmerman, M.D., Ph.D.
1390 Esch Ct.
Ann Arbor, MI 48104

1958-1962 CORVETTE WINDSHIELD WASHER VACUUM TANKS
By Ed Gurdjian

Occasionally, having a Factory Assembly Instruction Manual (A. I. M.) creates more problems than it solves. Many owners of 1958-1962 Corvettes have wondered about differences that may exist between the various windshield washer system vacuum reserve tanks used.

The 1958, 1959 and 1960 Corvette A. I. M.'s show #3741901 tank for single four barrel carbureted cars, and #3752343 tank for dual four barrel and fuel injected models. The tanks are identical, the difference in part numbers indicates only the direction of the vacuum valve fitting (diagram shown).

In the 1961 A. I. M., tank #3741901 was changed to #3814232 on 4/25/61. This tank, after the first four months of production, had its seams copper brazed rather than welded. It used weld bolts (round flat head with no slot or recess). The valve was directed as shown. The F. I. and dual four barrel equipped cars (through 1961) continued to use the #3752343 tank, according to the A. I. M.

Those in possession of a 1962 A. I. M. will note that it specifies a #3814232 tank for both carbureted and F. I. models and that it also indicates a change-notation in Section 582, Sheet 7.00, from a #3752341 tank to #3814232. The part #3752341 is not a reserve tank at all, but is rather the part number for the system's fluid-container bracket. Perhaps this change-notation should have read #3752343, but at any rate it is in error and is most confusing. Actually the #3752343 tank was used on very early F. I. '62's and used the anchor nut on the inner fender for securing the tank. The later '62 F. I. cars used the #3814232 tank and this required deletion of the anchor nut, being replaced with standard lock washers and nuts.

The 1958 through 1961 Corvette A. I. M.'s specify that only the single four barrel models use the left-hand mounted vacuum tank and washer fluid container, while both dual four barrel and F. I. models use a right-hand mounted system. There is some controversy however, in that many dual four barrel cars appear with the left-hand mounted components —does anyone have a non-F.I. car with a right-hand system?

Edwin S. Gurdjian
161 Canterbury Road
Bloomfield Hills, MI 48013
313/647-2990

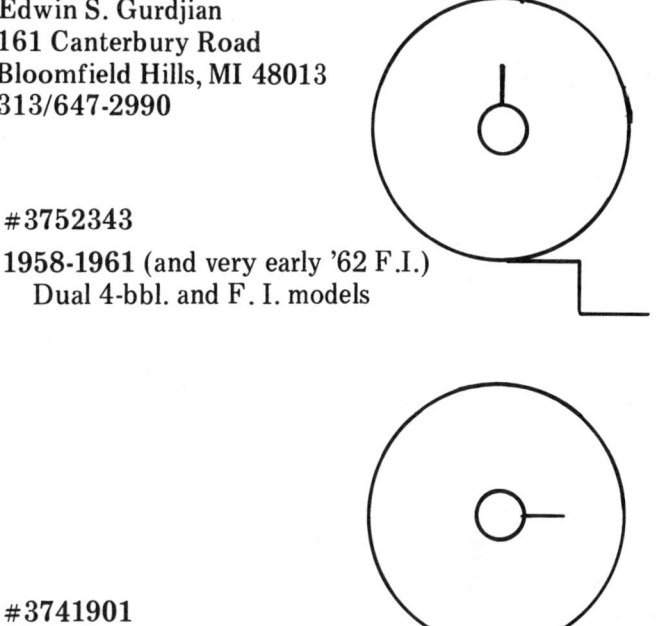

#3752343
1958-1961 (and very early '62 F.I.)
Dual 4-bbl. and F. I. models

#3741901
1958-1961 (to 4/25/61)
Single 4-bbl. model

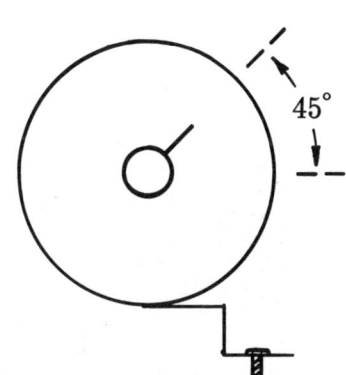

#3814232 (uses weld-bolt)
1961 (from 4/25/61)
Single 4-bbl. model
1962 — All except early F.I.

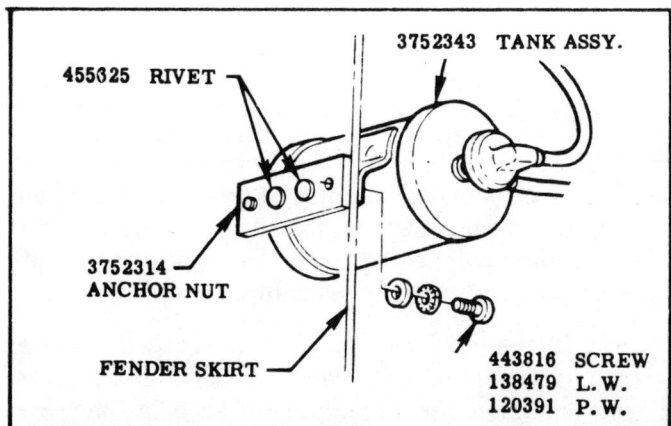

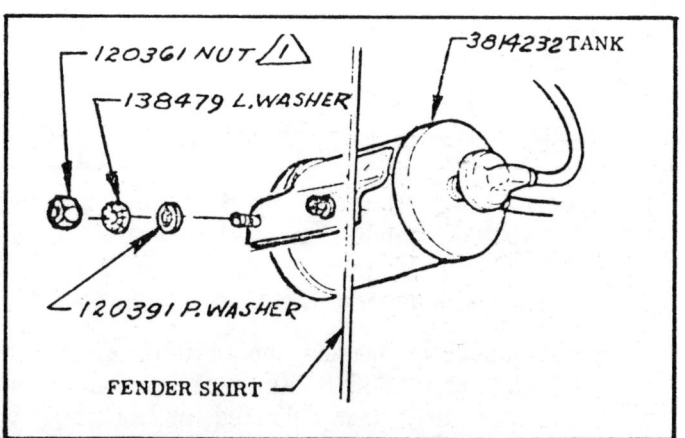

Left illustration shows F. I. model tank with anchor plate, right shows tank mounting with weld-bolt.

RESEARCH PROJECT 1956/7
With Michael Hunt

UPDATE: 1957 FUEL INJECTED CORVETTE IGNITION DISTRIBUTORS

Thanks primarily to strong reader response following the recent distributor essay (*CR* Vol. 5 Nr. 1 pp. 5-7), I am now able to present a slightly refined version of the applications table featured in that essay. And a note of caution: information of this nature is still in the "developmental" stage. It should be studied closely, it may be regarded as fairly reliable for restoration or judging purposes, but it is not intended to be the final word.

And a minor correction for the distributor essay: *all* post-1110889 distributors had the bearing retainer, not solely the late-1110905 models.

Any additional information on 1957 f. i. ignition distributors would be appreciated, especially information which might tend to substantiate unusual or unexpected applications. Letters should be addressed to Michael Hunt, 903 Swarthmore Ct., Madison, Wis. 53705 (Ph: 608-233-9226). Be sure to enclose a SASE if a reply is desired.

UPDATED TABLE — 1957 FUEL INJECTED CORVETTE IGNITION DISTRIBUTORS

Distributor Part Number	Horsepower Rating	Transmission Type	Centrifugal or Vacuum Advance	Single or Dual Points	*Approximate* Vehicle Indent Numbers Range
1110889	250	Manual/Auto	Centrifugal	Dual	E57S100001 – 102500
	283	Manual	Centrifugal	Dual	E57S100001 – 102500
1110905	250	Manual	Centrifugal	Dual	E57S102501 – 106339
	250	Automatic	Centrifugal	Dual	E57S102501 – 104300
	283	Manual	Centrifugal	Dual	E57S102501 – 106339
1110906	* 250	Manual	Vacuum	Single	E57S104301 – 106339
	250	Automatic	Vacuum	Single	E57S104301 – 106339
1110908	** 283	Manual	Centrifugal	Dual	E57S103750 – 106339

*Note: Although the 1110906 distributor is generally found on late VIN# 250hp Powerglide-equipped vehicles, solid information now available indicates that in some instances the 1110906 distributor was also used on late VIN# 250 hp *manual* transmission-equipped vehicles. This appears to be another example of the factory using available parts, in order to keep the assembly line rolling.

**Note: Generally speaking, the 1110908 distributor is part of the RPO579E package, and is used to drive the #1548680 8000rpm AC column-mount tachometer. However, some 1110908 distributors apparently were delivered on *late* 1957 F. I. cars intended for street use. In such instances, a threaded cap covers the tachometer-drive outlet.

1965

1965 CORVETTE OPTION PRODUCTION

R.P.O. Code	Description	Options	% Usage	Available on*
A01	Tinted Glass – All Windows	8,752	37	1
A02	Tinted Glass – Windshields	7,624	32	1
A31	Windows – Electric Control	3,809	16	1
C07	Auxiliary Top	7,787	51	2
C48	Less Heater	39	.1	1
C60	Air Conditioning	2,423	10	1
F40	Special Front/Rear Suspension	975	4	1
G81	Differential Carrier – Positraction	19,965	85	1
G91	Rear Axle – 3.08:1	1,886	8	1
J50	Power Brakes	4,044	17	1
J61	Drum Brakes	316	1	1
K66	Transistor Ignition	3,686	16	1
L75	Engine – 327/300 H.P.	8,358	35	1
L76	Engine – 327/365 H.P.	5,011	21	1
L78	Engine – 396/425 H.P.	2,157	9	1
L79	Engine – 327/350 H.P.	4,716	20	1
L84	Engine – 327/375 H.P. – F.I.	771	3	1
M20	4-Speed Transmission	21,107	90	1
M22	4-Speed Transmission – Heavy Duty	30	.1	1
M35	Powerglide Transmission	2,021	9	1
N03	Gas Tank – 36½ Gallon	41	.5	3
N11	Off Road Service Exhaust	2,468	10	1
N14	Side Mounted Dual Exhaust	759	3	1
N32	Teakwood Steering Wheel	2,259	10	1
N36	Telescopic Steering Shaft	3,917	17	1
N40	Power Steering	3,236	14	1
P48	Aluminum Wheels – Quik Take-off	1,116	5	1
P92	Whitewall Tires	19,300	82	1
T01	Gold Stripe Tires	989	4	1
U69	Radio – AM/FM – Push Button	22,113	94	1
Z01	Comfort & Convenience Group	15,397	65	1
–	Leather Trim Combination	1,793	8	1
–	Two-tone Leather Trim	335	1	1
Std.	3-Speed Transmission	404	2	1

* 1 – *both Coupe & Convertible* – 23,562 Total Units 100%

2 – *Convertible only* – 15,276 Units 65%

3 – *Coupe only* – 8,186 Units 35%

Source: Chevrolet Motor Division

1966

1966 CORVETTE OPTION PRODUCTION

R.P.O. Code	Description	Options	% Usage	Available on*
A01	Tinted Glass — All Windows	11,859	43	1
A02	Tinted Glass — Windshield	9,270	33	1
A31	Windows — Electric Control	4,562	16	1
A82	Head Restraint	1,033	4	1
A85	Shoulder Harness	37	.1	1
C07	Auxiliary Top	8,463	48	2
C48	Less Heater	54	.2	1
C60	Air Conditioning	3,520	13	1
F41	Special Front/Rear Suspension	2,705	10	1
G81	Differential Carrier — Positraction	24,056	87	1
J50	Power Brakes	5,464	20	1
J56	Heavy Duty Brakes	382	1	1
K19	Air Injection Reactor	2,380	9	1
K66	Transistor Ignition	7,146	26	1
L36	Engine — 427/390 H.P.	5,116	18	1
L72	Engine — 427/425 H.P.	5,258	19	1
L79	Engine — 327/350 H.P.	7,591	27	1
M20	4-Speed Transmission	10,837	39	1
M21	4-Speed Transmission — Close Ratio	13,903	50	1
M22	4-Speed Transmission — Heavy Duty	15	.05	1
M35	Powerglide Transmission	2,401	9	1
N03	Gas Tank — 36½ Gallon	66	.7	3
N11	Off Road Service Exhaust	2,795	10	1
N14	Side Mounted Dual Exhaust	3,617	13	1
N32	Teakwood Steering Wheel	3,941	14	1
N36	Telescopic Steering Shaft	3,670	13	1
N40	Power Steering	5,611	20	1
P48	Aluminum Wheels — Quik Take-off	1,194	4	1
P92	Whitewall Tires	17,969	65	1
T01	Gold Stripe Tires	5,557	20	1
U69	Radio — AM/FM — Push Button	26,363	95	1
V74	Hazard Warning Switch	5,764	21	1
—	Road Hazard Package	16	.05	1
—	Leather Trim Combination	2,002	7	1
Std.	3-Speed Transmission	564	2	1

*1 — *both Coupe & Convertible* — 27,720 Total Units 100%

2 — *Convertible only* — 17,762 Units 64%

3 — *Coupe only* — 9,958 Units 36%

Source: Chevrolet Motor Division

1967

1967 CORVETTE OPTION PRODUCTION

R.P.O. Code	Description	Options	% Usage	Available on*
A01	Tinted Glass — All Windows	11,331	49	1
A02	Tinted Glass — Windshield	6,558	29	1
A31	Windows — Electric Control	4,036	18	1
A82	Head Restraint	1,762	8	1
A85	Shoulder Harness	1,426	6	1
C07	Auxiliary Top	6,880	48	2
C08	Exterior Soft Trim Roof Cover	1,966	14	2
C48	Less Heater	35	.2	1
C60	Air Conditioning	3,788	17	1
F41	Special Front/Rear Suspension	2,198	10	1
G81	Differential Carrier — Positraction	20,308	89	1
J50	Power Brakes	4,766	21	1
J56	Heavy Duty Brakes	267	1	1
K19	Air Injection Reactor	2,573	11	1
K66	Transistor Ignition	5,759	25	1
L36	Engine — 427/390 H.P.	5,933	26	1
L68	Engine — 427/400 H.P.	2,101	9	1
L71	Engine — 427/435 H.P.	3,754	16	1
L79	Engine — 327/350 H.P.	6,375	28	1
L88**	Engine — 427/430 H.P. — Heavy Duty	20	.09	1
L89**	Aluminum Cylinder Heads w/L71	16	.07	1
M20	4-Speed Transmission	9,157	40	1
M21	4-Speed Transmission — Close Ratio	11,015	48	1
M22	4-Speed Transmission — Heavy Duty	20	.09	1
M35	Powerglide Transmission	2,324	10	1
N03	Gas Tank — 36½ Gallon	2	.02	3
N11	Off Road Service Exhaust	2,326	10	1
N14	Side Mounted Dual Exhaust	4,209	18	1
N36	Telescopic Steering Shaft	2,415	11	1
N40	Power Steering	5,747	25	1
N89	Aluminum Wheels — 15 x 6L	720	3	1
P92	Whitewall Tires	13,445	59	1
QB1	Red Stripe Tires	4,230	18	1
U15	Speed Warning Indicator	2,108	9	1
U69	Radio — AM/FM — Push Button	22,193	97	1
—	Leather Trim Combination	1,601	7	1
Std.	3-Speed Transmission	424	2	1

    * 1 — *both Coupe & Convertible* — 22,940 Total Units

      2 — *Convertible only* — 14,436 Units 63%

        3 — *Coupe only* — 8,504 Units 37%

    **Entered production February, 1967   Source: Chevrolet Motor Division.

1963-1967

FINDING YOUR CORVETTE ORDER COPY
J. M. CLARK

By Joe Clark

Most of us remember as children the excitement of a treasure hunt, or the fun of digging in the bottom of the Cracker Jack box for the hidden prize.

A similar delight is available to owners of 1967 and later Corvettes. The prize takes the form of a 6½" x 8½" sheet of paper with the words "Corvette Order Copy" printed in the upper right corner.

This small sheet, if located, can be the owners key to an accurate evaluation of what his or her car was when it emerged from the St. Louis plant. Obviously it is invaluable in determining authenticity and as an aid to an accurate restoration — especially if the car has been altered drastically over the years.

The order copy was glued to the top of the gas tank of each car before the body was lowered onto the chassis. It is most often found to the left of the filler neck — but they have also appeared to the right.

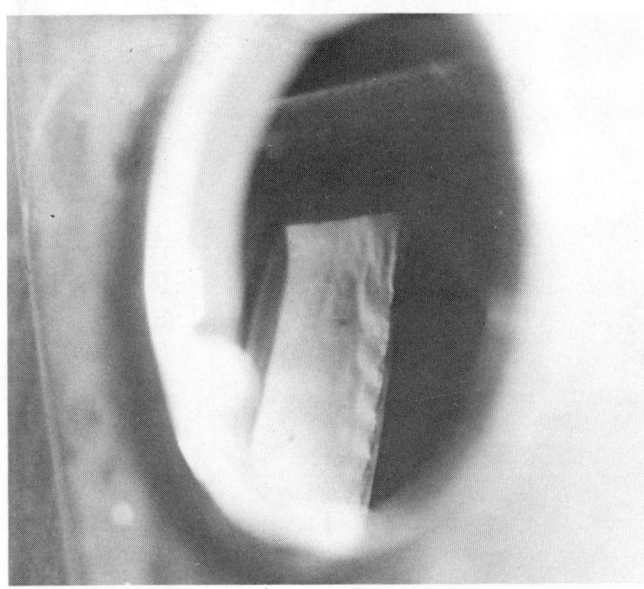

The 1967 Corvette Order Sheet glued to the top of the fuel tank, as seen through the fuel filler opening on the rear deck.

As the reader can see from the sheet printed herein, the data listed includes: 1. Identification number (not VIN however) 2. Date order was received. 3. Expected date of production. 4. Order number 5. Zone number 6. Dealer number 7. Model number and name 8. Paint name and number.

The rest of the sheet details trim and options on the car by name and number.

In preparing this article, the author used three Corvettes — all 1967.

Car number I — 1967 convertible, serial #194677S-117736. This is an Elkart Blue, 1 top, 427, 390 hp, 4 speed with factory air. It originally had, according to the order form, a blue convertible top. The car turned out to be completely original with the exception of the convertible top as detailed by its order form. The condition of its order form is very poor.

Car number II was a coupe, serial #194377S113718 and its form is in relatively good condition. This car, when purchased by its present owner, had been highly modified (fender flares, flames, engine with race cam, etc.). However, the price was right and the owner, an N.C.R.S. member, decided to go ahead with a restoration as nearly original as possible.

Before proceeding, it was decided to retrieve the order form from the tank to verify exactly what the car had been. In this case, unlike the convertible, the order copy held one large surprise — someone in the past had changed the car over to an automatic. The car was originally a 4 speed. Close examination of the under dash area confirmed this change, revealing the sawed off stub of the clutch pedal arm.

It was further suspected that the car might have been changed over to an air conditioned car by the use of parts from a wreck. Happily, the sheet verified the original factory installation.

The third car was another convertible, serial #194677S122849. This is a very high serial number — 91 cars from the end of the 1967 run. The order copy was not retrieved from this car, but by removing the rubber boot seal from around the filler neck, we were able to see that it was in place to the left of the filler neck. The car is an original Ermine White, small engine, automatic with black interior, radio and power brakes.

By comparing the two sheets some interesting light is shed on Corvette production in 1967.

The order for the coupe #113718 was received on February 14, 1967; the expected date of production was March 24th, but the actual build date was March 6th.

The convertible #117736 order came in on March 20, 1967; the expected production was April 28th

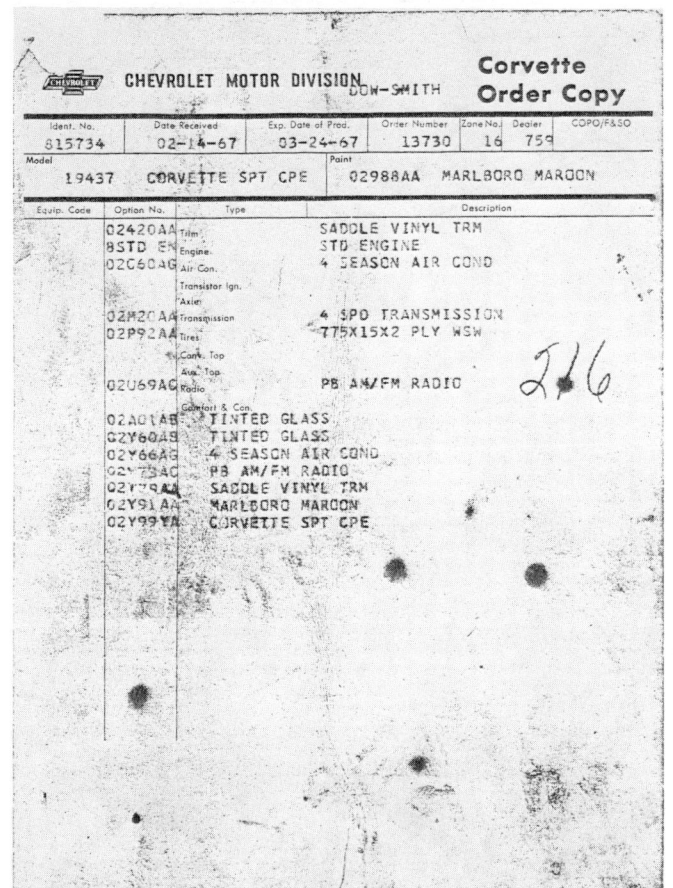

Chevrolet Motor Division
H06
Style 67437 A-1092 Body
Trim 420 988 Paint
Body by Chevrolet

Coupe #194377S113718

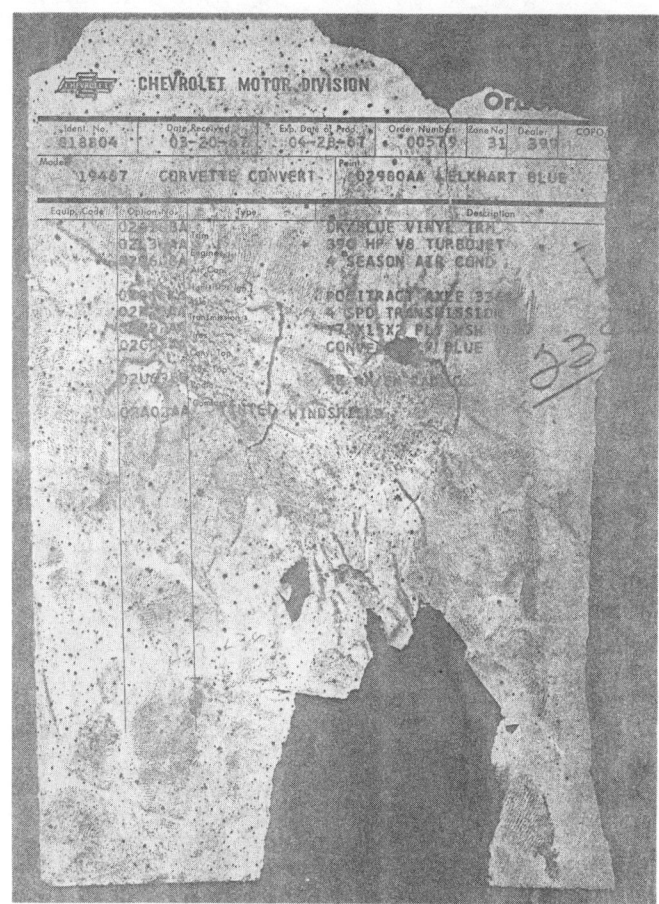

Chevrolet Motor Division
J3
Style 67-467 S-7753 Body
Trim 418 BA 980 AA Paint
Body by Chevrolet

Convertible #194677S117736

and the actual build date, according to the under dash data plate was May 3rd. Apparently production was running close to demand in February but had fallen behind by April. The production lag from "order received" for the coupe was only about 3 weeks. The convertible's lag was a little over 6 weeks.

These cars are 4018 units apart and were built, according to the letter and number code, about 8 weeks from each other. Roughly, this puts production at 95 cars per day (based on 42 working days divided into 4018).

Comparison of "Identification numbers" (not the VIN number) yields a mystery. Common sense would indicate that the numerical difference would correspond to the serial number difference. However, the result is a seemingly unrelated 3070. Does any reader have information on this?

Facsimile data plates are included for both of our sample cars and next issue we will do an article on the information contained on these plates.

To the best of our knowledge, 1967 was the first year of the gas tank mounted order copy. A 1966 with the build sheet located behind the right kick panel under the dash was shown in the last issue. Can anyone else supply information?

If you wish to go after your own order form — Read On: (Start with a near empty tank).

1. Place car on ramp or a rack. If you jack the car, be sure to block it.
2. Remove spare tire carrier lid and take out spare. (Fig. 4)
3. Remove lid, bolted attachments and the carrier itself. (Fig. 4)
4. Remove the "U" bolt attachments at both rear tail pipe shields. (Fig. 5)
5. Separate the exhaust system at the crossmember tube by loosening "U" bolt. (Fig. 6)
6. Remove both rear muffler brackets from the frame and slide muffler system rearward. (Fig. 5)

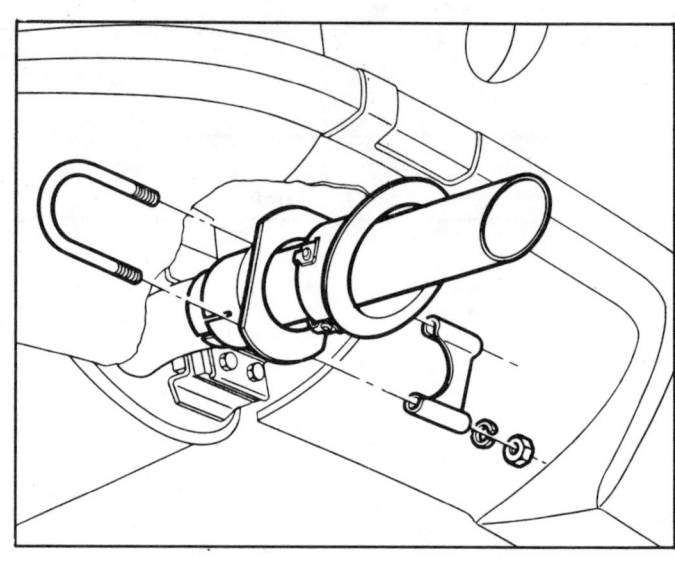

Fig. 5—Exhaust System Tail Pipe Shield Attachment

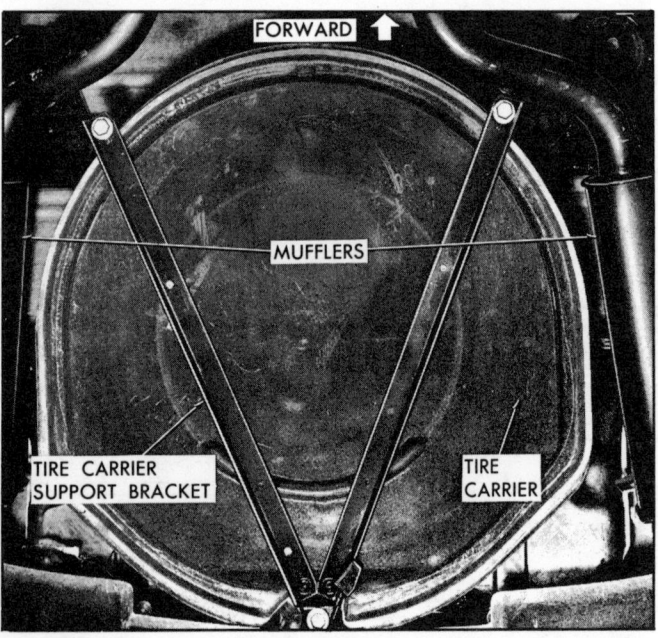

Fig. 4—Spare Tire Carrier Installed

Fig. 6—Exhaust System Crossmember Tube Attachment

Fig. 7—Fuel Tank with Spare Tire Carrier and Mufflers Removed

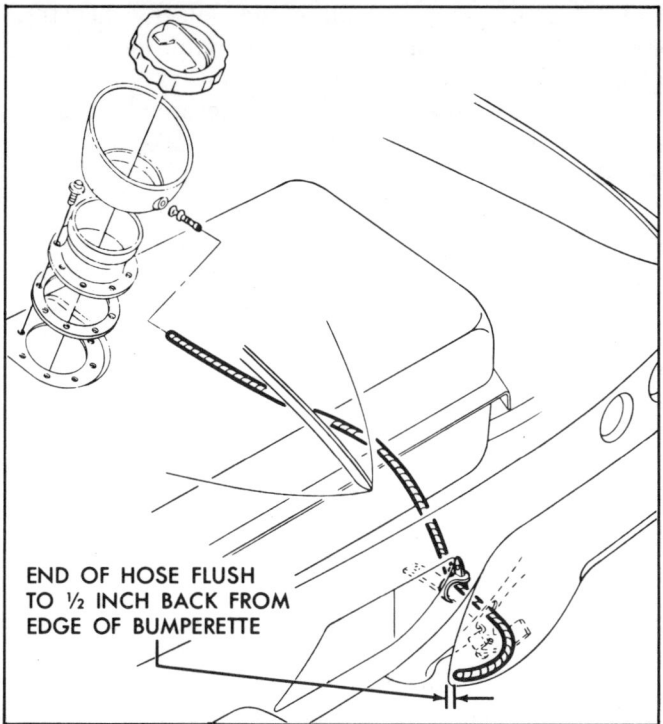

Fig. 8—Gas Tank Filler Neck Vent Hose

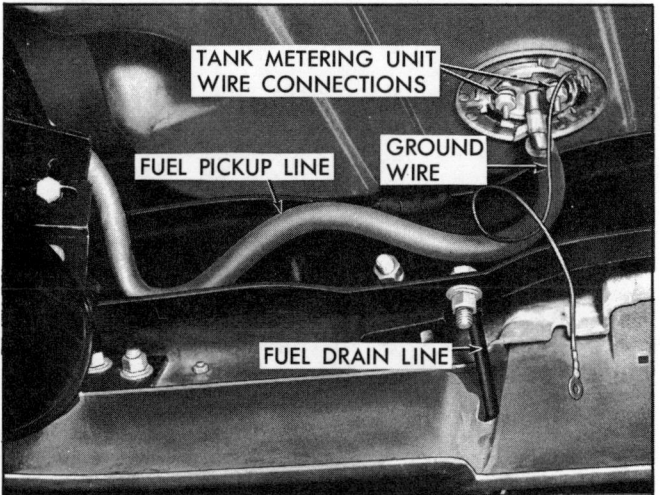

Fig. 9—Fuel Tank Metering Unit, Wires and Lines

7. Remove two fuel tank metal strap reinforcements and retaining bolts located at front side of the tank. (Fig. 7)

8. Disconnect fuel tank metering wires. (Fig. 9)

9. Remove fuel pickup line. (Fig. 9)

10. Remove gas cap, filler neck boot and disconnect drain line from the boot. (Fig. 8)

11. Remove fuel tank support frame attachment bolts and support. (Fig. 7)

12. Gently lower tank, rotating toward front of vehicle. At this point, get a flashlight and check to see if the order sheet is in place. If so, continue to lower the tank and then, with the aid of a razor, gently cut through the glue.

NOTE: If total removal of the tank is carried out on the Aero Coupe, the filler neck must be removed.

In some cases the paper is folded; others were glued flat. You may want only to clean, read and copy your sheet, leaving it in place. If no sheet is found, check the back, front and sides of the tank.

Reinstallation Instructions: (From shop manual)

Note: Place hoses and wires to one side and position anti-squeak pads to the crossmember, cemented to the support and attached to the tank. Replace with new pads as required.

1. Hook reinforcement straps at the rear frame crossmember. (Crimp strap ends at rear frame attachment.)

Note: Make certain strap ends (pins) are hooked and anti-squeak pads are properly positioned.

2. Slowly rotate fuel tank into position.

CAUTION: Aero-Coupe — Install filler neck after tank is installed.

3. Attach fuel tank support at the frame side rails.

4. Attach the reinforcement straps at the front of the tank to the fuel tank support, attach the strap guide, bolt and nut and secure with the nut and lockerwasher assembly.

5. Connect the filler neck boot to the drain hose of the tank and install boot around filler neck.

6. Connect the fuel pickup line, ground wire and make certain that the fuel drain line is flush to ½" inboard of the rear bumper opening.

7. Attach tank metering unit wires (Fig. 9).

8. Replace fuel in tank. Replace gas cap.

9. Check for possible leaks.

10. Reconnect the exhaust system by reversing the above removal procedures.

11. Install spare tire carrier by securing the bolt attachment.

12. Install the spare tire in the tire carrier.

Well, thats about it. We know that order forms were glued to tanks of 1967 and later cars. If any reader has found these sheets anywhere else we would like to know about it. Please include year, model, and location, and we'll publish any date we get. Happy Hunting!

Write to: J. M. Clark
P. O. Box 353
Havre de Grace, MD 21078

FUEL INJECTION DISTRIBUTOR RECONDITIONING

By Gene H. Dressen

In May of 1977 I finished a very extensive restoration on our factory fuel injected 1965 coupe. With only 50 miles on a new engine we left to attend the Big Sky Corvette Meet in Billings, Montana. We had nothing but problems in getting there, and they were all with the fuel unit and distributor. I didn't need any problems on our planned trip to the 1978 Corvette Corral in Bloomington, so I removed the engine to replace the timing chain and gears and the pressure plate. I also detailed the engine again. It was a mess after the overheating problems on the way to Billings. Just 3 days before leaving I pulled the faulty pressure plate just installed, and the night before I replaced the universal joints in the driveline. Although I had done all the restoration myself, and was now quite confident in the mechanical condition of the car, I was still somewhat apprehensive when we finally pointed our Corvette east on what was to become the most tiring 5 day, 3400 mile trip my 5 month pregnant wife and I will ever make.

You may wonder what preparing for the trip to Bloomington has to do with a distributor. Well, it just so happens that the only trouble we had on the trip was with the distributor. At Billings I had fixed one problem, but had no warning of this one. If I would have done like I should have, I would have disassembled the distributor and replaced all worn parts, but like most of us, the extent of my restoration here was a clean up and a paint job. I felt that if it worked, that was enough. Well it wasn't. After 19 straight hours of running 3000 plus rpm, 4.11 gears and all, the engine started to act up. I pulled into the first town we came to, to locate and correct the problem. There aren't too many fuel injection services in central Nebraska, so I knew I was on my own to find and fix the problem. When I opened the hood I immediately noticed oil leaking from the distributor cap! I also knew what the problem was, and what I would have to do to fix it.

My first fix was to replace the points, since the ones I was running on were very badly burned. Hopefully this would let us run for another 19 hours. Well, we barely made it to Omaha before the engine started to falter again. Now I had to make a permanent fix.

What had happened was that the combination of 30 weight oil, high oil pressure, high rpm, and a used distributor had caused two of the three oil seals in the distributor to rupture. The oil was being forced from the cross shaft chamber up the mainshaft onto the points, and the points were having difficulty firing in the oil. I made a repair that allowed us to finish the trip with only having to adjust the points once. I purchased two sets of points (one as a spare) and an 8 inch piece of three-sixteenths inch steel brake line, with fittings.

What I was going to do was decrease, but not shut off completely, the supply of oil to the distributor cross shaft gears. I removed the original steel line from the distributor and bent the new line to fit. I couldn't bring myself to destroy the original! I then crimped the center of the new line so I could just barely blow air thru it. This would allow adequate oil to pass thru the line, and would hopefully relieve some of the pressure. Under normal conditions the normal supply of oil to the distributor doesn't cause leakage problems, but when the seals are bad, you will know it. After installing the new line and a new set of points. we continued on to Bloomington.

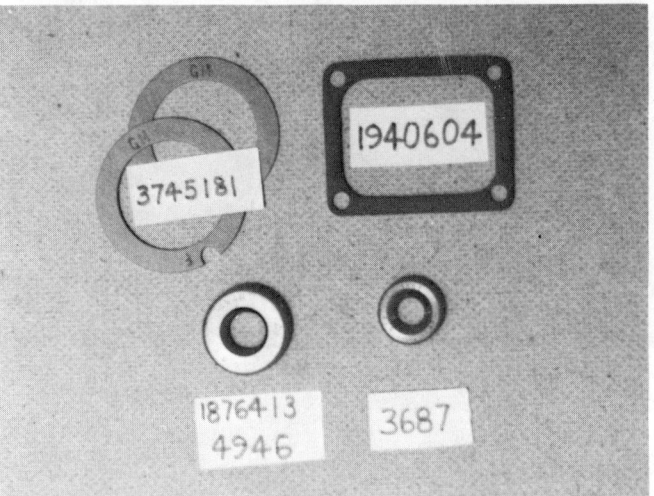

When I returned home I purchased the seals and gaskets I would need to repair the distributor. They are shown in the photo. I purchased the large mainshaft seal, p.n. 1876413, from GM. List price of $1.66. This seal carried a Chicago Rawhide number of 4946, list price at a local supplier of $2.09. I was unable to locate the cross shaft seal in the GM parts book, so I took the number from the seals in the distributor. This seal was also from CR, number 3687. This single lip seal also interchanges with 3680, a double lip seal. They both listed for $1.87. Two of either of these seals are required.

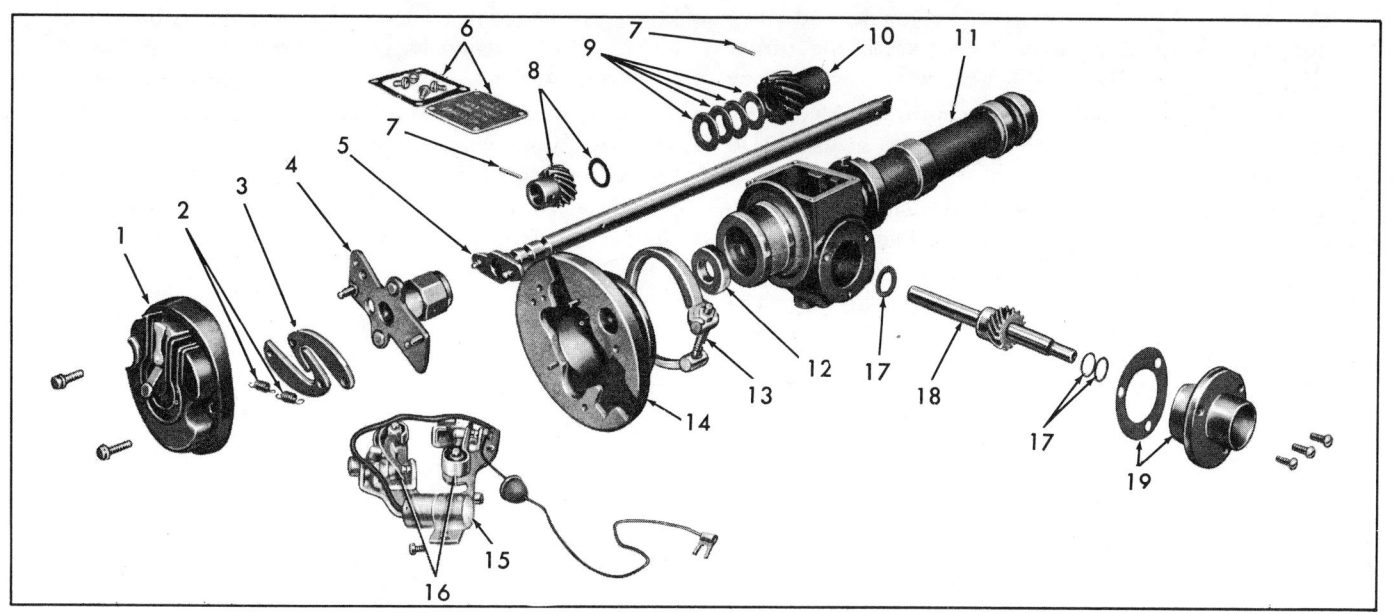

Fig. 2—Dual Point Distributor—Exploded View

1. Rotor
2. Weight Springs
3. Advance Weights
4. Weight Cam
5. Mainshaft
6. Cover Plate and Gasket
7. Roll Pins
8. Cross-Shaft Drive Gear and Washer
9. Distributor Drive Gear Shims
10. Distributor Drive Gear
11. Distributor Housing
12. Seal
13. Clamp
14. Breaker Plate
15. Condenser
16. Ignition Points
17. Cross-Shaft Gear Washer
18. Cross-Shaft and Gear
19. Cross-Shaft Retainer Cover and Gasket

With a few improvised tools and a few hours, I was able to repair my 1111070 distributor. The procedure I will explain can be used on all fuel injection distributors, although the mainshaft seal removal and installation may be somewhat different. This is how I did it.

Remove the cover plate, the cross shaft cap and coupler, and the cross shaft from the lower distributor housing, being careful to retain the shims and washer on the shaft. Drive the pin from the lower drive gear. Retain all shims. You should note that there is a one-half tooth difference in the pin hole location between the two sides of the gear. Mark the gear and mainshaft so you can reassemble them as they were. This one-half tooth difference sometimes makes it difficult to get proper advancement on the distributor because of the closeness of the coil, plenum chamber, and vacuum advance diaphram. This was the problem I fixed in Billings. Carefully drive the pin from the upper drive gear located in the cross shaft chamber. After the pin has been driven thru the mainshaft, the mainshaft can be removed from the housing. Again locate and retain the gear, pin and washer just removed.

At this point the distributor is stripped down enough to allow the replacement of the oil seals, but since we are this far, I would recommend a complete disassembly for cleaning and inspection purposes.

The point plate can now be removed by the first removing the retainer clip from the top of the upper mainshaft bushing and removal of the ground strap

Housing separated, showing upper mainshaft bushing and clamp.

retainer screw. If present, remove the vacuum advance diaphram. The next thing is to separate the upper housing from the lower. To do this you must be very careful not to bend or break the clamp. Loosen completely the clamp screw securing the two housing. Do not attempt to remove the clamp, it will bend, but very carefully separate the two housings while expanding the clamp enough to allow one edge of the end of the clamp to slip into the gap forming between the two housings. Work at it, but be careful. Once the two housings are separated you can remove the clamp. You should find a thin paper washer between the two housings, also a felt and plastic cap from around the upper bushing tower. Remove the grease from the pocket under the plastic cap.

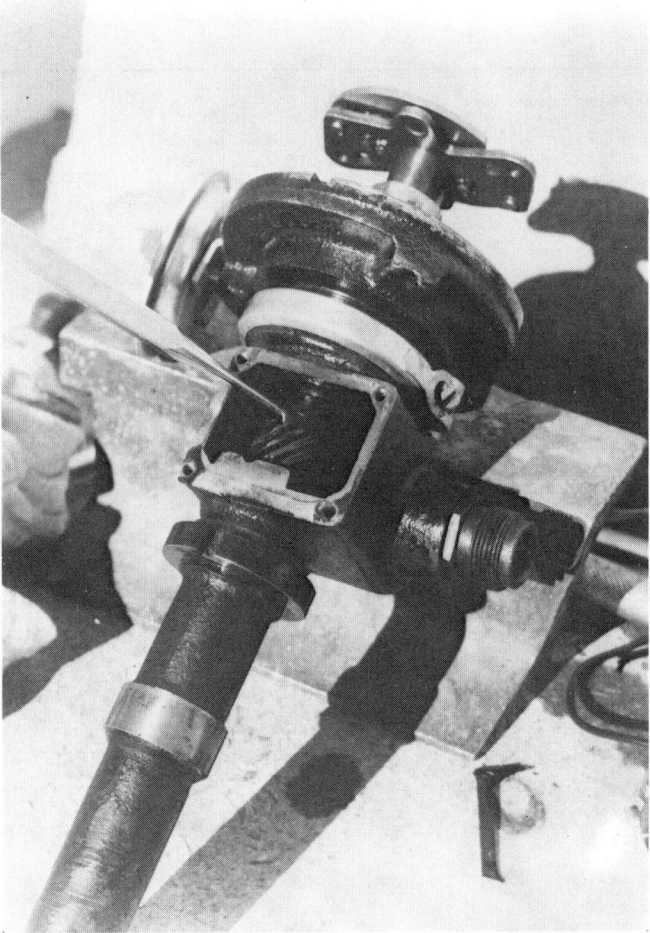

Carefully drive pin from cross shaft drive gear.

The large mainshaft seal, located in the top of the cross shaft chamber, can be removed by prying it out with a screwdriver, using another driver as a fulcrum. While working with the lower housing extreme care must be taken not to damage the exposed upper brass bushing.

I attempted to remove the cross shaft seals by inserting a fine thread nine-sixteenths tap into them, and then driving the two from the housing, but the seals turned. To remove the seals, I took an old, cheap three-sixteenths blade screwdriver and with a torch, heated and bent the tip to approximately 45 degrees. I carefully inserted the tip from the inside thru the bushings and into the inside of the seal, then tapped on the end of the screwdriver to remove the seal. I was now able to thoroughly clean the distributor parts before assembly.

Mainshaft seal located inside cross shaft chamber.

On the 1111070 distributor the large mainshaft seal cannot be installed by driving it into location. It must be pulled into place. Again I did not have the proper tools, but I was able to locate things in my "junk" drawer that worked perfectly. I took a three-eighths inch bolt about four inches long, a couple one inch flat washers, and a solid alternator pulley from a Sting Ray. The pulley slips around and extends above the upper brass mainshaft bushing to protect it. With a flat washer on the bolt, insert the bolt down thru the pulley, the brass sleeve, and into the new seal that has been coated with a sealer, then another washer and finally the nut. While holding the nut with a wrench, and after making sure that the new seal is square with the housing, carefully tighten the bolt to pull the seal into place. Be sure that the upper part of the seal is installed first. Setting the seal to a

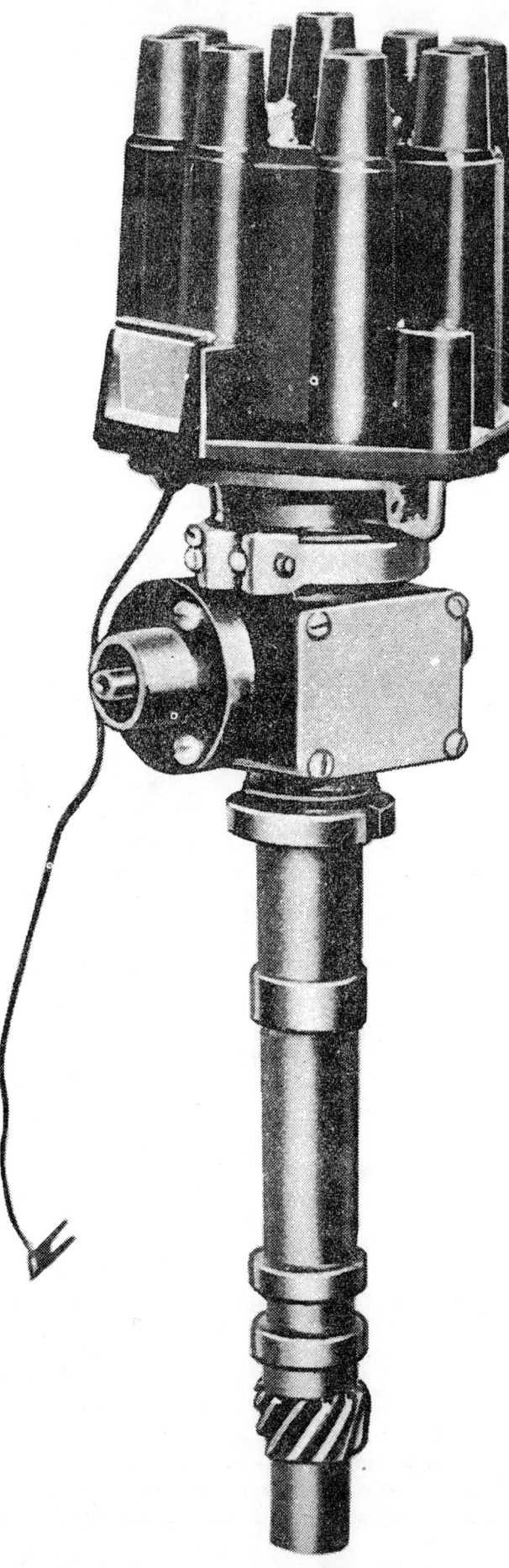

different depth will allow the new seal to miss the wear groove in the mainshaft that was formed by the old seal.

The cross shaft seals can be driven into place with one of the best poor-mans drivers, an inverted socket. Make sure the socket won't get wedged in the housing while driving the new seal, and be sure not to drive the seal too deep. If you use a socket too small in diameter, you will ruin the seal. I know.

You can now start to reassemble the distributor. Pack the grease well in the upper part of the lower housing with a good quality grease. Now grease and reinstall all parts in the reverse order of disassembly. Be sure to reinstall the tachometer drive gear on the mainshaft when you slide the mainshaft into the housing. Replace all shims in their original locations. Be careful when driving the pins into location. Use a punch to avoid hitting the gear with the hammer.

This completes the seal replacement. As I mentioned, all fuel injection distributors can be rebuilt in the same manner. The outly for parts was less than $5.

You may encounter parts in your distributor that should be replaced. As of December 1978 the 1111070 distributor is still available from GM. List price is $237.00. Hopefully you won't need to buy a new one. But if you do need parts, some of them are still available from GM. I got the following numbers from a December 1978 Delco-Remy distributor breakdown listing. Many of these parts have been dropped from the GM parts books for a number of years, but are currently still available. The part number and a description of these parts follows: 1956078, mainshaft; 1963774, shaft; 1935632, cam; 1938656, gear; 1941237, gear; 1937986, seal; 1961252, upper housing, $113 list, $67.80 wholesale; 1961254, lower housing, $250 list, $150 wholesale; 1940639, clamp; 1940657, plate; 1941323, gasket; 1939939, coupling. When you consider the price of a new lower housing, you can now see why I warned you to be careful with it. All of these parts are currently available from factory thru any Delco-Remy parts house.

May I make one suggestion in closing. Don't go out and order all the parts that are still available for the distributor. If you need a part, and it is available, buy just what you can use. Hopefully then the remaining parts will be around for all of us to purchase.

There are companies that advertise in some of the Corvette publications who rebuilt, repair, and provide some repro parts for the distributor. If you encounter problems with your distributor, these people may help you. This would be particularly true of the 1957 fuel injection distributors. Remember, take your time while working on your distributor, and use a small hammer! Good luck.

Gene Dressen
753 Wayne
Pocatello, ID 83201

Part Two
THE HISTORY AND RESTORATION OF EX-122

by John Amgwert

The first running prototype Chevrolet Corvette built for show and display purposes was the hand-built car that debuted at the 1953 GM Motorama held at New York City's famed Waldorf-Astoria Hotel in January of that year. Following its initial showing at the Waldorf, this car traveled the country delighting crowds at the other cities hosting the 1953 Motorama: Miami, Houston, Los Angeles, San Francisco, and Kansas City. This Corvette played to more than 1.4 million people. Those that missed the Motorama also got a glimpse of the new car as it starred in its own movie, "Hall of Wonders," a Chevrolet publicity film narrated by none other than everybody's favorite TV personality of the day, Dave Garroway.

This single little plastic bodied white Corvette created an instant sensation, beginning a love affair that has lasted some 26 years, and nobody is ready to stop counting. But what happened to that first hand-built prototype that started all the fuss? Years later, as Corvette production rolled along, that show car became just a memory, all but forgotten.

Back in the 1960's, Jon Blanchette, a senior engineer for Rochester Products Division of General Motors in Rochester, New York, heard tell of a fellow in town that supposedly owned the first Corvette ever built. While that statement today would probably make blood pressure rise in most Corvette buffs, at the time, Jon was inclined to respond with a "Well, that's nice," not giving it much thought. As he saw it, the first Corvette ever built was a 1953 model, and the car in question must surely be one of those first 300 production Corvettes built in Flint, Michigan.

No one would ever suspect the original prototype.

Jon is not your typical Corvette buff. With an interest in early model Corvettes (at the time he owned and restored a 1954), and his career as a crack engineer at Rochester, he has a mastery of carburetion and fuel injection. It so happens that automobile restoration has always been his leisure-time activity. It was common to see Jon and his 1954 Corvette attending old car gatherings in the Great Lakes area.

One day in 1968, Jon got a call from Mr. Jack

Ingle of Rochester. Ingle had heard about Jon's interest and expertise in old Corvettes, and called to inquire about the possibility of restoring one that he had owned for many years. He happened to mention that it was the first one ever built. Jon thought that that was nice and discussed the car's condition, but was in no position to help with a restoration of someone else's Corvette. Subsequently, Jack Ingle took his Corvette to a local shop for restoration. The two men would have no further contact, at least for several years.

Some five years later, 1953 Corvette owner and historian Sam Folz, a Kalamazoo, Michigan, packaging salesman who spends his free-time as Technical Director for the National Corvette Restorers Society, sat down at home to read the latest copy of Sports Illustrated Magazine. In that particular issue (Decem-

ber 4, 1972 edition) there just happened to be an interesting article entitled "The Marque of Zora," telling the life story and Corvette' involvement of Zora Arkus-Duntov. Sam was astonished to read that the original 1953 Motorama Corvette (code-named EX-122), referenced in the article, was *still* in existence. It even stated that the car was owned by a New York textile machinery manufacturer named Jack Ingle. After a fast call to Sports Illustrated, Sam learned that the car was in Rochester.

The only Corvette person that Sam knew in Rochester was Jon Blanchette. In fact, they'd been friends for many years through a mutual interest in early Corvettes. Sam immediately called with this newly discovered information about EX-122, and asked Jon to check into the story.

Jon vaguely remembered talking to this fellow Ingle back in 1968, but until Sam's call, he had had no idea that Ingle owned *that* car. With this, Jon thought it best to re-introduce himself.

He called Ingle, and learned that EX-122 was still in the body shop after five years. Ingle said that the car was supposedly nearing completion, and was just about ready to contact Jon to see if he would be interested in finishing the job. Ingle was not completely satisfied with the progress, or lack of it, of the car's restoration. Jon agreed to take a look.

Ironically, when Blanchette first laid eyes on the original EX-122 Corvette, he determined immediately that the car was *already finished* — the shop had literally destroyed it!

The Ingle family has owned the car since October of 1959, during which time it had been driven daily until 1968. Mrs. Ingle nearly totalled it in the early 1960's, and it was suffering the usual problems of a rusting frame and tired mechanical components.

When the shop people got hold of EX-122, they indiscriminately tore it apart without regard to reassembly. As Jon recalls, "The trim was pried off and bent, screws and nuts sheared off, parts thrown in the corner and swept up with the floor to be discarded and lost, fiberglass filler had been put into the rusted frame holes, everything had been sandblasted (all together), sand was in every moving part, and to sum it up, they reduced the car to a 'total disaster'."

It must be understood at this point that EX-122, the original Motorama Corvette, had undergone numerous changes and modifications by Chevrolet engineers after it was retired from the 1953 show circuit. The original hand-built Motorama body was scrapped, and replaced in 1955 with a production Corvette body. The entire drivetrain was updated with production and prototype V-8 parts, and production and engineering sample components and accessories were used extensively. From 1954 through 1956, the car was used for test purposes.

The code-number "EX-122" was assigned to the car around 1956, when Chevrolet rebuilt it, and sold it to Russ Sanders, an assistant chief engineer with the division. Sanders later came to the Rochester Division and eventually sold EX-122 to Jack Ingle.

Just how the car became known as EX-122 is an interesting story, as Jon relates, "There is a department at Chevrolet that handles all the company' cars: obtaining, selling, scrapping, and assigning them to individuals and groups, etc. When an EX number is needed for some project, an individual in the department assigns a number from a record book.

(continued)

"Sometimes an EX number is assigned to a production vehicle (the production number being removed and the EX number substituted). Generally they are assigned to only prototype or modified vehicles that will not be sold. Up until 1960, they did sell EX vehicles, but Company' policy since then has forbid this: The car either has to be converted back to a production vehicle and number, or scrapped.

"The actual assigning book is a stenographic spiral bound notepad, and shows EX number, date assigned, vehicle description, and disposition. The numbers are assigned consecutively from one through 999, and then start over again. It takes anywhere from four to nine years before the numbers repeat. The number EX-122 was assigned in 1956 to the Motorama Corvette prototype at the time the car was last rebuilt. Also, the entry shows it sold to Russ Sanders in 1956.

"EX-122 was also assigned to one, maybe two, other vehicles, before the last time, in 1972, to a 1974 "X" body Nova. The entry shows this last EX-122 was barrier crashed in September, 1974, and then scrapped."

Jon Blanchette agreed to salvage the "remains" of EX-122 in August of 1973. To properly restore the car, he had to completely start over, from scratch. While Ingle had intended in 1968 to have it restored back to the original Motorama condition, Jon states, "I took the job on, with the restoration intent to be as the car was when Chevrolet sold it, in April, 1956. To restore back to the 1953 Motorama configuration was impractical, if not impossible, as its first original components had long been scrapped."

The restoration began with complete disassembly and cataloging of all parts that remained. Fortunately, the drive-train components last installed by Chevrolet were still intact.

The engine was a correct 1955 Corvette 265 cubic inch block with serial number 0215185F55FG (as indicated on the original Michigan registration slip that had been kept), mated to a 1955 Corvette Powerglide automatic transmission. The rear axle in the car was of the 1956 style, using a welded-on inspection cover as opposed to the bolt-on cover used on 1955 and earlier models.

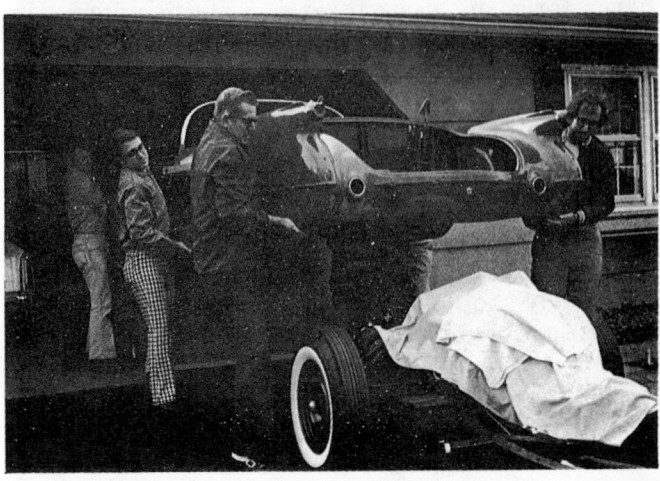

Mr. Jack Ingle (left) and Jon Blanchette.

The frame on EX-122 was a real mess! The restoration shop had used fiberglass filler to cover all the rust deterioration in the metal. This had to all be "knocked-out" and properly repaired via welding.

Jon believes that the frame on EX-122 *is* the original Motorama car frame, as inspection indicates much hand-work. Further, the area notched in the right hand side rail girder for clearance of the V-8's fuel pump was made by hand. Jon noticed much evidence of unexplained holes drilled in the frame, but could not find any indication of a serial identification number stamping. Another frame modification concerned the use of a 1956 style intermediate crossmember, over the axle; the crossmember being notched in the center for clearance of the larger 1956 style rear axle housing used.

Prior to reassembly of the chassis, the frame rails were sprayed internally with a zinc-chromate primer to prevent further deterioration. The rear axle and all suspension parts were inspected and rebuilt.

The body was again completely stripped (the restoration shop had painted it Polo White) due to very poor fiberglass repairs. Meticulous preparation went into the body prior to painting. Every nook and cranny had to be cleaned, as sandblast sand was everywhere.

While Jon had the car at the paint shop, near-disaster struck as the doors of EX-122 were stolen. Luckily, the police were able to close in on the culprit, who dumped them and ran. The doors were missing for about a month.

Again, many body components and accessories of EX-122 were non-production in nature. The cowl vent mechanism, for example, looked like standard Corvette, but when the old paint was removed, it was obvious that this was model-shop made. It contains file marks and scribe lines where centerlines were laid out for the drilling of holes in the arms and linkage brackets. Also, the Delco signal-seeking radio used in EX-122 contains an "engineering sample" identification tag stamped with an "XP-595-1" model number (XP indicating experimental).

The car's heater system is the 1956 and later fresh-air type, and under the hood it appears as though it was released for production. However, under the dash, the fiberglass ducting is unique to this car.

Instrument gauges are standard production Corvette parts, containing 1954 and 1955 test dates on their rear housings. The cloth date tags attached to each seat back and cushion frame indicate that they were made in 1954. The car showed the remains of both types of windshield washer systems as used during 1955 Corvette production; both the suspended "squash" pedal pump, and the coordinated push pedal through the floor (Jon chose to restore the car using the suspended pedal type, with the blue vinyl washer fluid bag).

The chrome bumpers and bright trim on the car were all production parts, except that EX-122 sports the addition of a short upper vertical bumper bar at both rear corners, above the rear "bullet" pieces.

(continued)

EX-122 on display at the Sloan Museum in Flint.

Jon's restoration of EX-122 took five years of steady pugging away to complete. During this period, he figures that an average of 20 hours per week was put in on actual work, not including the amount of time spent on researching and locating needed parts.

Contacts within the National Corvette Restorers Society proved to be a tremendous help. NCRS member Jay Kellogg, an employee at GM's Inland Division plant in Dayton, Ohio, found the original tooling mold for making the windshield gasket. It just so happened that the chief engineer at Inland was a Corvette buff, and Jay was allowed to clean up the mold and run a new glass gasket seal for EX-122.

The finished restoration of EX-122 was completed in June of 1978. Just three days after the car was completed, Jon trailered it to Flint, Michigan, for showing at an NCRS event, being displayed inside the Alfred P. Sloan Museum of Transportation.

The restoration of EX-122 is magnificent! Every detail of the car is perfect! Jon Blanchette did his homework extremely well, with the car being absolutely as correct and authentic as he could make it — the way it was in 1956.

The color combination is Gypsy Red exterior lacquer and Ivory interior vinyl upholstery with contrasting red stitching, beige rugs, and white painted lower dash. The luggage compartment is red with a black rubber trunk mat and Ivory side-window storage bag. EX-122 appears, correctly, with a soft top frame modified to incorporate the 1956 style rear bow latches, as well as 1956 full wheelcovers.

The engine compartment is superb. It properly sports engine accessories from both the 1955 and 1956 model. Ignition shielding is strictly 1955, while the valve rocker covers and carburetor air cleaner are later style. No expense was spared in renewing any part of this car.

How does the owner, Jack Ingle, feel about his car? Jack is afraid to drive it, leaving that task to Blanchette. He's inclined to think it's too good (if that's possible). But words and pictures just cannot describe EX-122 as it appears today: You'd have to see it for yourself.

POWER TOP RESTORATION

By Rick Nagy

One area that in the past has been foreign to many Corvette enthusiasts is the restoration of the hydraulic assisted folding top, commonly known as the power top. This is due mainly to the rarity of the option on production cars and the lack of parts available to repair and restore the unit. I wasn't aware of the lack of knowledge on this subject until just recently, having sold my '65 convertible for an original '62 with power windows and top.

Probably the best single source of information is the 1953 to 1962 *Corvette Servicing Guide*, ST-12 (Available from Helm, Inc.). The manual goes into detail on servicing the unit, but says nothing concerning rebuilding it.

Once it is understood what the components of the power top are, and how they operate, it will be much easier to pinpoint the actual problem or problems and correct them. The system consists of: one manually operated control switch, located on the lower left end of the dash on 1956 and '57s, and just above the radio in the center of the dash on 1958 through '62s; one 12 volt electric motor coupled to a hydraulic pump; two solenoid valves, which regulate the flow of hydraulic fluid; one folding top cover hydraulic cylinder; two folding top hydraulic cylinders, located just to the outside of each seat in the top well; two folding top cover limit switches, which control the travel distance of the top cover; two folding top limit switches; two safety switches, which prevent the system from operating when either a) the deck lid is open, or b) the top cover is in the latched position; two 30 amp fuses, which were used on '58 through '62 units (14 amp fuses were used on '56s and '57s); and one circuit breaker.

Upon purchasing the car, I found all of the components intact, but not operating. The unit had never been tampered with, so that made it easier for me.

The power top option consists of 3 systems: mechanical, electrical, and hydraulic. The mechanical system is the same as with a manually operated top. Operating the top by hand, I noticed that none of the bows or the top itself were binding anywhere, so I discounted that as one of my problems.

Next I dove into the electrical system. I discovered that I was getting current from the dash switch to the motor, but it refused to operate. This is the heart of the entire system as the motor operates the pump, which in turn propels hydraulic fluid to the solenoid valves. I then sent the motor out to be rebuilt, as the brushes were broken. It was also decided at this time that the motor shaft seal should be replaced. This seal is found on the motor shaft itself and prevents the hydraulic fluid in the pump from leaking into the motor. Although this part is not available from G. M., it was easily replaced with an O-ring, having an inside diameter of ¼ of an inch. A word of caution is needed here: Be extra careful disassembling and reassembling the unit as the larger seals on both ends of the pump are not available either and aren't easily replaced. I then proceeded to examine the rest of the electrical system for shorts and faulty wiring, and luckily, found no further problems.

Having remedied the electrical problems, I began to trouble-shoot the hydraulic system. The first thing I did was to visually check for leaks or kinked lines. This is important as it would tend to restrict the flow, thus drastically reducing the amount of pressure in the system. Knowing that the unit had been unoperational for several years, I figured that the valves were frozen shut. This is possible because brake fluid used in the system tends to solidify when found in a system that hasn't been operated for a period of time.

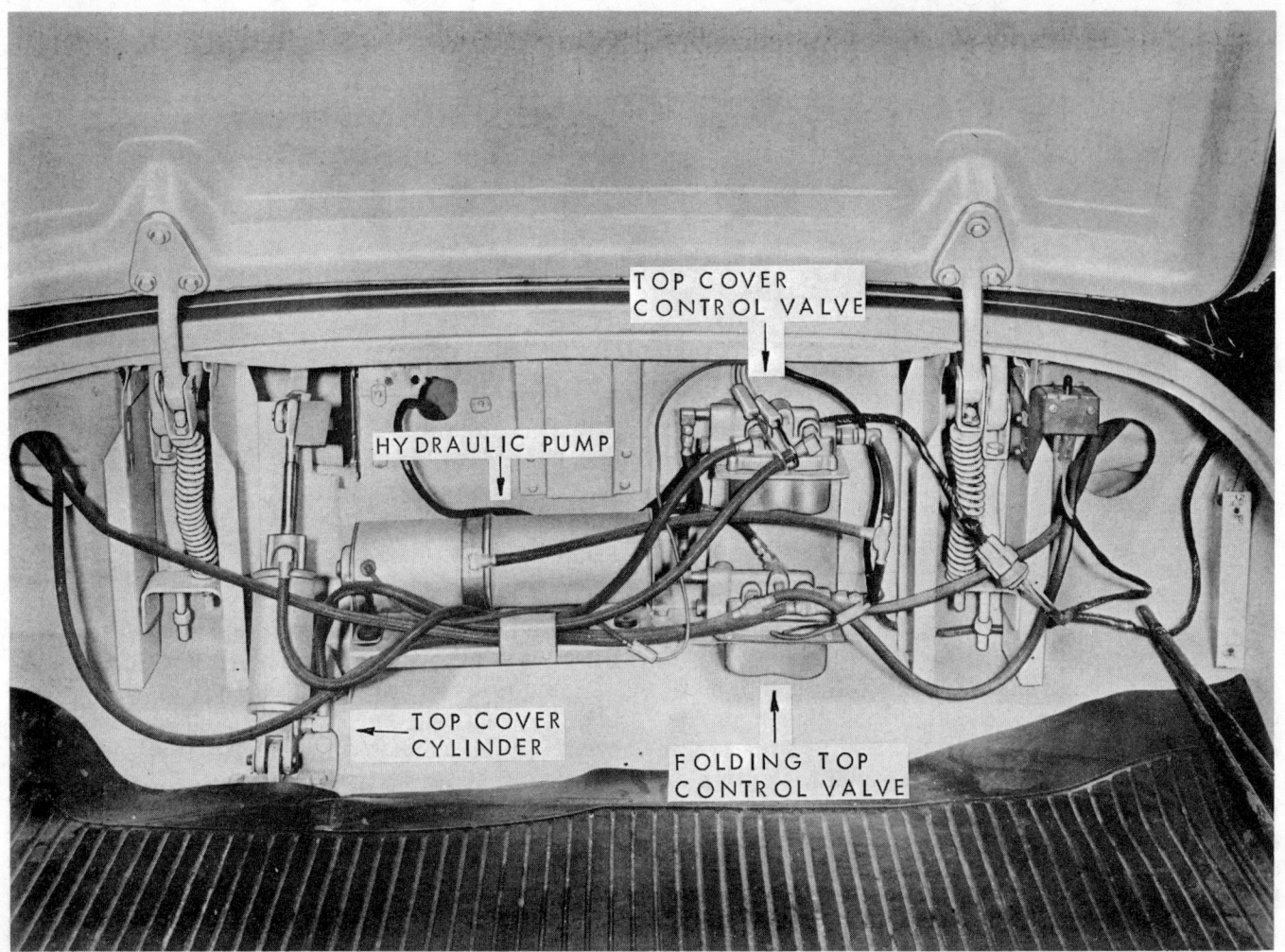

The valves were then hot-tanked, which removed both old brake fluid and corrosion.

After reassembling the entire system, I filled the pump with Delco Supreme #11 brake fluid, with the convertible top in the raised position. One point to remember about brake fluid: Try not to spill any, as it works as an instant paint remover. The pump took approximately 36 fluid ounces till the level of the fluid reached the bottom of the filler plug. Because the system is self-bleeding, I had to fill the pump 6 times, lowering and raising the top in between each refill. At this point the level remained stable and the pump was full.

The end result was well worth the effort. Can you imagine the looks you get while putting your top down at a stoplight? It's an incredible sight!

I would like to especially thank Ron and Al of Speedometer Electric in Hayward, California, who devoted much of their personal time and attention to the project. Thanks are also extended to Noland Adams of Albany, California, who supplied additional technical information for this article.

I heartily welcome all questions and comments.

Rick Nagy
18636 E. Cavendish Dr.
Castro Valley, CA 94546

(wiring diagrams on next page)

Supplemental Information

In the past, members have commented on having trouble locating a source for the rebuilding of Corvette motor pumps, and especially the three lift-cylinders used in the system.

Mr. Paul B. Wiesman of Hydro-E-Lectric, 48-B Appleton, Auburn, MA 01501, Phone 617/832-3081, informed me that his firm is now making replacement cylinders for the 1956-1962 Corvettes. He also has suitable replacement motor pumps available (they are *not* Corvette but are compatible), or can rebuild your original.

As for the hoses used in the Corvette, Mr. Wiesman cannot make up new ones, but mentioned that if there is enough demand he might be able to persuade the original manufacturer to run new ones.

Normal charges by Hydro-E-Lectric are: $57 to rebuild motor pumps; $25 to rebuild lift-cylinders (add $12 if new rod-shaft is needed); $99 for new replacement motor pump; and $75 each for new replacement lift-cylinders. All new items are guaranteed for one year.

Further, based on his experience, Mr. Wiesman recommends that, as opposed to using brake fluid, a better alternative is to use General Motors automatic transmission fluid in the power top hydraulic system.

Mr. Wiesman will be most happy to help if you have problems or questions.

John Amgwert, editor

Power Top Wiring Diagrams

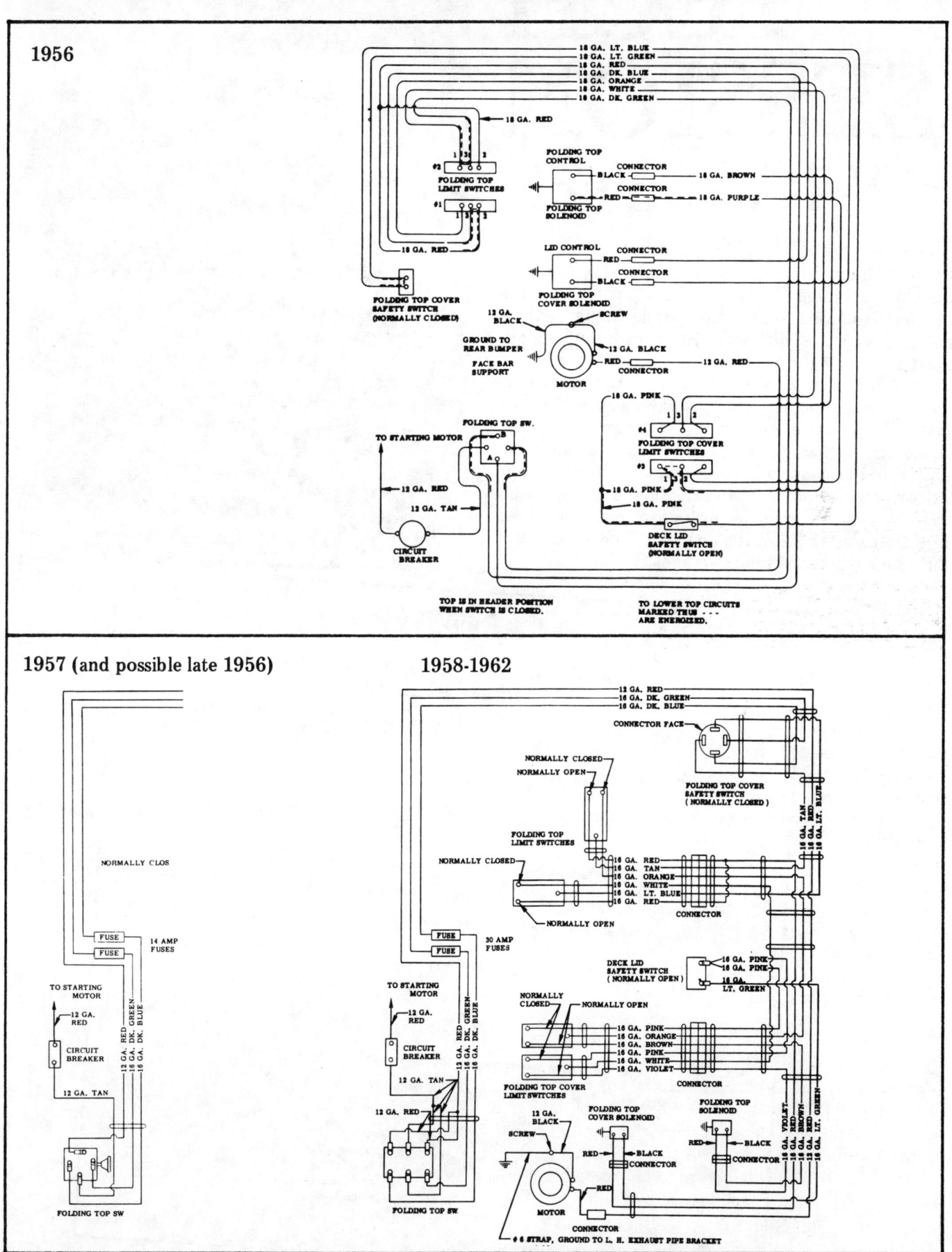

TECH SESSION
With Sam Folz

One of my favorite Sidney Harris columns is entitled, "Things I Learned While on the Way to Looking Up Something Else." This seems to often fit some of the situations I encounter while preparing this column, and this little exercise in carburetor alignment is no exception.

I recently purchased a "Uni-Syn" multiple carburetor synchronizer so that I could balance the two "funny" SU carbs on my MG. In case you're not tuned in to that game, the SU carb is a side-draft and is used in pairs on the four-cylinder MG and other British engines. Both carbs are alike, and are to be exactly synchronized in operation like the three side-draft Carter YH carbs on a six-cylinder Corvette. But that's where the similarity ends.

CARBURETER
TRADE MARK REG. U. S. PAT OFF
MARCA REGISTRADA

CARTER CARBURETOR CORPORATION, ST. LOUIS, MO., U. S. A.
GENERAL BULLETIN

ALL ACCOUNTS

BULLETIN NO. 40 - CHEVROLET
DATE March 17, 1954

SUBJECT: CHEVROLET CORVETTE
(YH-2066SA - CHEVROLET 3706151)

The 1954 Carter equipped Chevrolet Corvette is now on the street. The parts and service specification page (Form 5039), plus detailed throttle linkage adjustment information is in the mail. The three (3) carbureters are identical.

The throttle valve synchronization cannot be over-emphasized. Approximately 2° of throttle valve opening (above idle) on all three carbureters will give 40 MPH under road load conditions.

Your usual good cooperation, in supplying service material and service information where needed, will help insure the success of this installation.

V. F. Thompson,
Service Manager

VFT/rm

cc - Extra copies and Personnel

The "Uni-Syn" is a simple, low cost manometer with an adustable air-flow control which, when held over the air inlet of a running engine and regulated, causes a "float" to rise or fall on a column of air in a sight gauge. When throttle plates of a two-carb or a three-carb engine are synchronized, the float will take a stationary position in the center of the gauge when held at each carburetor. Very simple and efficient!

Now, neither Carter nor Chevrolet recommended this procedure for carburetor synchronization in the 1953-1955 period, or later, so far as I know. Rather, they described a mechanical procedure to align the three throttle plates with the engine at rest by backing off the three idle speed adjustment screws (one on each carb) and then adjusting linkage so that the front and rear carbs are closed — and therefore opened — with the center carburetor which is the only one of the three to retain a working idle-adjust screw. A procedure is described where an eagle eye is required to detect shaft motion (rotation) at one end of each carb when pressure is applied with the fingers at the opposite end. This procedure gets tougher as you change corrective lenses to bi-focals and then to tri-focals. The "Uni-Syn" accurately puts all three throttle plates in a position to let the CFM through each carb be identical regardless of engine speed, and after all, that's what carburetor synchronization is all about.

Now, for the "new" discoveries. The April 1954 edition of "Chevrolet Service News," Volume 26, No. 4, on Page 3, clearly refers to the change from the Carter carburetor #2066S to the "SA" version as "Late 1954" and refers to the "S" version as "1953" and early 1954." "National Service Data" book sheet on 1953-1955 Six-Cylinder gives the same information. This conflicts with data on the latest NCRS judging form, which suggests that a later 1953 engine might have "SA" carburetors. Further, on Page 4, same issue, a description of the synchronization procedure suggests that the change to the 1954 type linkage corresponds with the change to the "SA" carburetor. The earliest 1954 engines might have had 1953 style, one-piece links.

For those of you who might wonder just what the difference is between the "S" and the "SA" carb, the answer is: "Very little."

The January, 1954 copy of Carter's Form 5039C (presented in this issue), which is a complete parts list, shows these differences:

1. Vacuum spark advance port is made smaller on later "SA" production. Note: Early "SA" production same as "S."
2. Throttle-shaft lever assembly altered. "SA" is a little longer.
3. Throttle-shaft arm assembly. Changed from iron casting to sheet metal.
4. Pump diaphragm assembly. Change features unclear, but "SA" pump is the correct replacement in an "S" carb.

So much for what I was looking for. Here's some other stuff I ran into. The photos in the April and May, 1954 "Service News" also show some other details clearly on the 1953 engine and compartment on which appears to be a production car:

1. "Scratch" on air cleaner to align cleaner to carb is clearly seen in pix and referenced in text. Proper position of scratch at air horn boss (top) puts inlet screens *DOWN*. Airflow pattern through venturi is then correct. Cleaners to be attached when adjusting idle air bleed and idle speed.

2. Female hood catches, front hinges, and front "pop-up" spring bolts and cups have *NO* paint on them.
3. Two dis-similar styles of 90° brass vacuum fittings are installed on the intake manifold on this engine.

SAM FOLZ

Form 5039B
CARTER CARBURETOR CORPORATION, ST. LOUIS, MO., U.S.A.
CHEVROLET 2066S-2066SA
January, 1954
Revised November, 1955

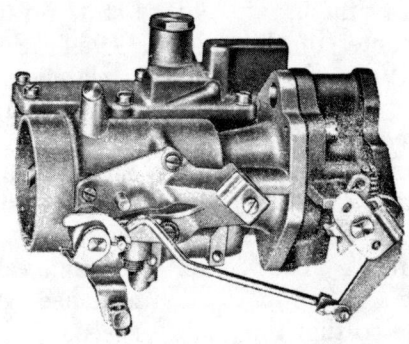

Three Carbureters Per Engine

CHEVROLET CORVETTE 1953-1955

Casting Number 1082 on Face of Flange

YH Horizontal Carbureters Nos. 2066S-2066SA

CARBURETER SPECIFICATIONS

For Chevrolet 6 Cylinder Engine: 3-9/16 Inch Bore, 3-15/16 Inch Stroke

Dimensions: Flange size, 1¼ inch 3 bolt. Primary venturi, 11/32 inch I. D. Secondary venturi, 11/16 inch I. D. Main venturi, 1-5/16 inch I. D.
Float Level: See adjustments.
Vents: Outside, none. Inside, balance vent tube to air horn ahead of choke valve.
Gasoline Intake: Spring loaded needle. Size No. 46 (.081 inch) drill in needle seat.
Low Speed Jet Tube: Jet, size No. 70 (.028 inch) drill. By-pass in body, size .0492 inch diameter. Economizer, in bowl cover, size No. 54 (.055 inch) drill. Idle bleed, in bowl cover, size No. 58 (.042 inch) drill.
Idle Port: Upper port, slot type, length .162 inch; width .030 inch.
Idle Port Opening: Top of port to be .124 to .128 inch above top edge of valve with valve tightly closed.
Set Idle Adjustment Screw: ½ to 1½ turns open. For richer mixture turn screw out. Idle engine at 450 r.p.m. gear shift lever in Drive position.

Main Nozzle: Nozzle is installed permanently. Do not remove.
Metering Rod: Economy step, .061 inch diameter. Power step, .058 inch diameter.
Metering Rod Jet: Size No. 45 (.082 inch) drill.
Metering Rod Setting: See adjustments.
Accelerating Pump: Diaphragm type, vacuum and mechanically operated. Pump discharges into nozzle passage. Intake check ball seat, size .115-.120 inch diameter. Discharge check ball seat, in body, size .115-.120 inch diameter. Pump bleed, in diaphragm housing, size No. 73 (.024 inch) drill. Vacuum passage restriction, in body, size No. 46 (.081 inch) drill. Vacuum bleed, to throttle bore, size No. 65 (.035 inch) drill. **Pump jet is permanently installed, do not remove.**
Pump Adjustment: None.
Choke: Manual, interconnected with throttle.
Vacuum Spark Port: Slot type, size .125 x .041 inch. (2066S-2066SA early prod.) Bottom of port to be .026 to .036; (2066SA late prod.). Top of port to be .016 to .026 inch above top edge of valve with valve tightly closed.

Motor Tune-Up—Be Accurate! Always Use Feeler Gauges!

CAUTION: Change worn or leaky flange gaskets. Tighten manifold bolts and test compression before adjusting carbureter.

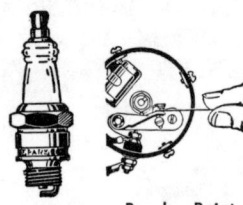
Spark Plug Gap .035"

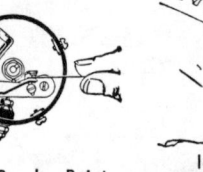
Breaker Point Setting .018"

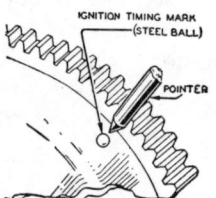
Ignition Timing Breaker Points to Open: T.D.C. (When Steel Ball on Flywheel is in Line with Pointer)

Valve Setting (Hot) Intake .010" Exhaust .020"

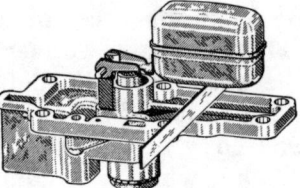
Float Setting ⅜ Inch (Use gauge T109-80)

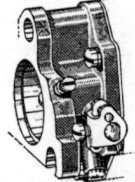
Idle Adjustment Screw Setting ½ to 1½ Turns Open

CARBURETER ADJUSTMENTS

Float Adjustment: With gasket removed, bowl cover assembly inverted and float resting on pin in seated needle, the distance from the bowl cover to the top of float should be ⅜ inch (gauge T109-80). Do not depress float lip against spring loaded pin in needle, but let float rest of its own weight. Adjust by bending float lever. Float setting must be checked with bowl cover held at eye height in a level position.
Float Drop: With bowl cover assembly held in upright position, the distance between float seam (at free end) and bowl cover should be 2". Adjust by bending stop tab on float arm.

Metering Rod Adjustment: This adjustment is important and should be checked each time the carburetor is reassembled. Insert gauge (Tool T109-104) in place of metering rod, seating tapered end of gauge in metering rod jet. Hold gauge vertical to insure seating in jet. With throttle valve tightly closed, press down on diaphragm shaft until metering rod arm contacts lifter link at diaphragm stem. With diaphragm shaft held in this position, metering rod pin must rest lightly on metering rod gauge. To adjust, bend metering rod arm. Use bending tool T109-22.

Fast Idle Adjustment: With choke valve held tightly closed, there should be .020 inch (gauge T109-29) clearance between throttle valve and bore of carburetor (side opposite idle port). Adjust by bending offset portion of choke connector link (use bending tool T109-213).

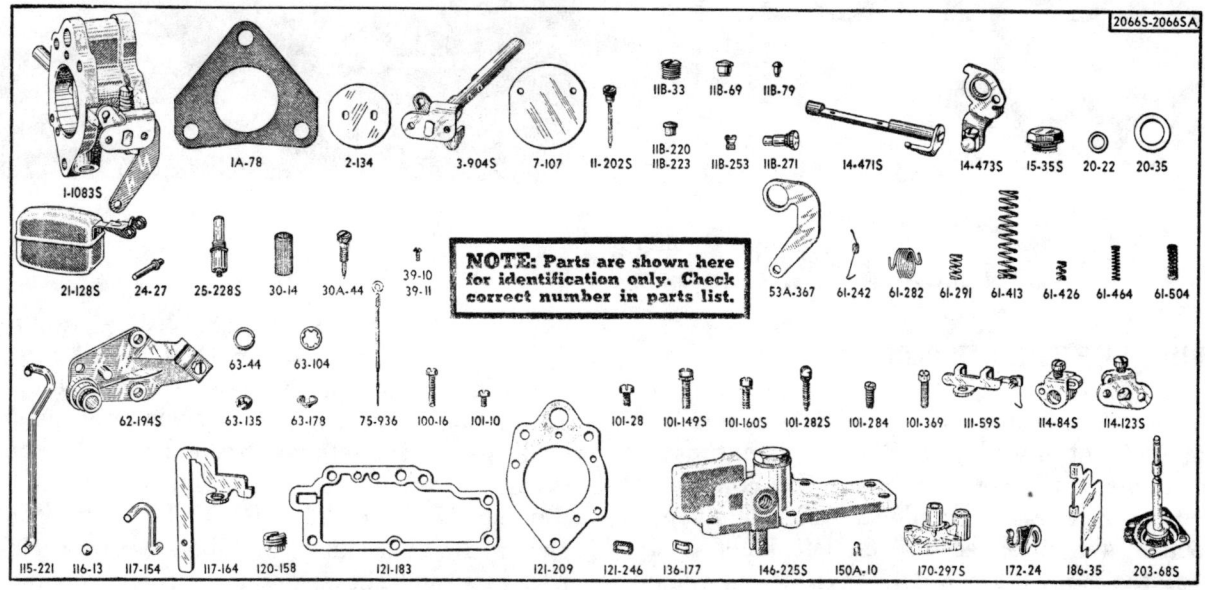

Chevrolet 1953-1955—Carbureters Nos. 2066S-2066SA

WHEN SERVICING, USE GASKET ASSORTMENT No. 248; REPAIR PACKAGE No. 1771

PART NAMES IN CAPITAL LETTERS, LISTED BELOW, INDICATE CONTENTS OF REPAIR PACKAGE

Part No.	PART NAME
1-1083S	Body flange assembly
1A-78	FLANGE GASKET
2-134	Throttle valve
3-858S	Throttle shaft and lever assy. (2066S) (Sup. by 3-904S)
3-904S	Throttle shaft and lever assembly
7-107	Choke valve
11-202S	LOW SPEED JET ASSEMBLY
11B-33	Pipe plug
11B-69	Rivet plug
11B-79	Rivet plug .... (3)
11B-220	DIAPHRAGM HOUSING RIVET PLUG
11B-223	Nozzle passage rivet plug
11B-253	Pump discharge check plug
11B-271	Idle port rivet plug
14-471S	Choke shaft and lever assembly
14-473S	Choke lever assembly
15-35S	Strainer nut assembly
20-22	Needle seat gasket
20-35	BOWL STRAINER GASKET
21-128S	Float and lever assembly
24-27	Float lever pin
25-228S	NEEDLE, PIN, SPRING AND SEAT ASS'Y
30-14	BOWL
30A-44	Idle adjustment screw
39-10	Choke valve attaching screw .... (2)
39-11	Throttle valve attaching screw .... (2)
53A-367	Fast idle arm
61-242	Metering rod spring
61-282	Choke spring
61-291	Throttle lever adjusting screw spring
61-413	PUMP DIAPHRAGM SPRING
61-426	Idle adjustment screw spring
61-464	PUMP DISCHARGE CHECK SPRING
61-504	UPPER PUMP SPRING
62-194S	Choke tube bracket assembly
63-44	Choke lever retainer ring
63-104	Throttle shaft retaining ring

Part No.	PART NAME
63-135	Upper pump spring retainer
63-178	Diaphragm spring retainer
75-936	METERING ROD—STANDARD
100-16	Throttle lever adjusting screw
101-10	Wire clamp screw
101-28	Throttle shaft arm attaching screw
101-149S	Body flange attaching screw and washer assembly .... (3)
101-160S	Bowl cover attaching screw and washer assembly .... (6)
101-282S	Diaphragm housing attaching screw and washer assembly .... (4)
101-284	Choke tube bracket attaching screw .... (3)
101-361	Choke tube clamp attaching screw (2066S) (Sup. by 101-369)
101-369	Choke tube clamp attaching screw
111-59S	Metering rod arm assembly
114-84S	THROTTLE SHAFT ARM ASSEMBLY
114-123S	Throttle shaft arm assembly (For throttle linkage) (2066SA)
115-221	Choke connector rod
116-13	PUMP INTAKE AND DISCHARGE CHECK BALL .... (2)
117-154	THROTTLE SHAFT ARM CONNECTOR LINK
117-164	PUMP LIFTER LINK
120-158	METERING ROD JET
121-183	BOWL COVER GASKET
121-209	BODY FLANGE GASKET
121-246	PUMP LIFTER LINK GASKET
136-177	Pump lifter link washer
146-225S	Bowl cover and strainer assembly
150A-10	Pin spring .... (2)
170-297S	Pump diaphragm housing assembly
172-24	Choke connector rod retainer
186-35	Fuel bowl baffle plate
203-53S	Pump diaphragm assembly (2066S) (Sup. by 203-68S)
203-68S	PUMP DIAPHRAGM ASSEMBLY

NOTE: Figures in parentheses indicate number of pieces used in one carburetor. Where no figure is shown, only one is used.

RESEARCH PROJECT 1956/7

With Michael Hunt

THE BIRTH OF THE AIR BOX:

The Chevrolet Motor Division (CMD) named it an "air intake," but nowadays 1957 Corvette enthusiasts prefer to use the term "air box." The component referred to is a rather crude rectangular fiberglas box which was attached to the left inner fender panel of the forty-three RPO579E/RPO684 Corvettes assembled during the 1957 model run. Prior to the introduction of the air box, Corvettes being run in competition were often limited by their inadequate braking systems. The air box was but one part within the RPO579E/684 heavy-duty package, offered in response to competition needs. For a related look at the RPO684 brake/suspension package, see Fred Thompson's essay (*CR* Vol. 4 Nr. 2 pp. 6-7).

For the fuel injected cars (RPO579E) only, the air box functioned as an integral part of the rear brake air ducting system, as it channeled cool incoming air back toward the left rear brake drum. A second function involved forcing a supply of cool air into the Ramjet f.i. unit. The RPO579E cars lacked the chromed circular air cleaner base seen on RPO579A/B/C cars; and the essential air filter element was instead mounted in the rear portion of the air box. The eight carbureted (270 hp) RPO684 cars built in 1957 had 4" diameter corrugated air hose in lieu of the air box.

In recent years, 1957 enthusiasts have debated the question of precisely when the air box made its debut. The introduction date is important, since it can be

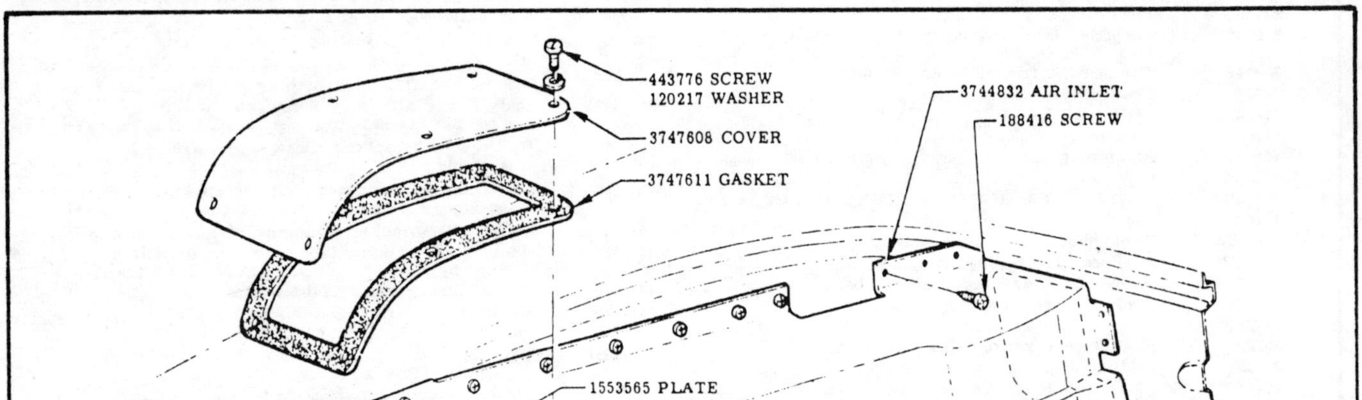

218

related to the VIN# of any 1957 Corvette being restored or judged — or being considered for investment purposes. A too-low VIN#, on what appears to be an air box car, could suggest a "built" (i.e., bogus) vehicle.

Engineering sketches of the heavy-duty components generally bear April-July 1957 drawing dates. This would suggest an introductory VIN# of perhaps E57S103750 for this running change, IF the paperwork preceded the creation of the actual parts. Interestingly, this is post-Sebring (3-23-57), but more about that later.

Over a period of time some seventeen air box cars were located and surveyed. And true to expectations, VIN#'s for surviving vehicles began at E57S103963, and ranged upward to approximately E57S105700. Then came an unexpected development, with an appearance at a 1977 Illinois NCRS meet of E57S100-834. This low-VIN# vehicle sported an air box, full rear brake air ducting, and even the round accelerator rod common to f.i. cars. The car also had a non-vented gas tank, indicating that it was definitely a pre-E57S101450 vehicle, and not merely the recipient of a VIN# tag transplant. Color was white, which is true for more than half of the surviving air box cars.

Although there were skeptics, I have remained convinced that the #834 car is legitimate. The answer to why #834 precedes the H.D. equipment paperwork sketch dates can probably be found in Karl Ludvigsen's fine Star-Spangled book (pp. 61-65). Mr. Ludvigsen writes that two "racing prototypes" were build during November 1956 (E57S100834 was assembled approximately 11-15-56). These two full-RPO cars were then tested and evaluated, with an eye on the planned CMD team appearance at Sebring (3-23-57). While at Sebring, the two November prototypes were used as "mules," while two fresh 1957's and one tailfinned S-R Corvette (a 1956 model, with a more-rounded version of the air box) were run in the actual race. (see photo in Model section)

The two 1957 Sebring team cars (VIN#'s probably around E57S102600) must also be regarded as "early" air box cars. In order to legitimately use the RPO579E/684 package at Sebring, CMD had to "homologate" these competition components, thereby making them available to the buying public. Thus CMD began regular production of the competition-tried-and-tested package following the Sebring event. The paperwork, which has at times confused us, was drawn at about the time the competition package was turned over to the St. Louis assembly plant.

Sooner or later some of the RPO cars will start showing up on the NCRS circuit, and the question arises as to how such vehicles should be judged. The existing concours sheet does not make specific provision for RPO cars. Two choices would be: 1) the creation of a judging form solely for RPO cars; 2) a "flexible" use of the existing judging forms. Personally I would opt for the latter. Considering the difficulty in obtaining accurate RPO car data, and considering the rough life the surviving cars have invariably lead, it may never be possible to devise a suitable RPO car judging form. But in many respects the cars aren't that much different from their "street" counterparts. The condition of paint, chrome/stainless, interior, and body can all be gauged on a comparative basis. The air box is, in effect, an elongated air filter element holder, and as such its condition may be judged as is the normal f.i. car air cleaner base. Similarly the rear brake ducting may be treated as just another part of the body, and up-front "elephant ears," finned brake drums, and vented backing plates may be treated as additional braking system parts. What will be required is sufficient maturity and understanding from the judges themselves. The judging sheets are as correct and complete as is possible at the present time, and a judicial use of them is essential.

1956-1965 CORVETTE RADIATOR CAPS

By Edwin S. Gurdjian
161 Canterbury Road
Bloomfield Hills, MI 48013
313/647-2990

At the NCRS Flint Meet several members asked me to do a research article on radiator and gasoline caps. This article will present documented information on the radiator caps, and I'll present the gas caps in a future issue.

For the most part there is little controversy concerning radiator caps. The accompanying chart summerizes specified radiator caps from the Corvette Factory Assembly Manuals (1956 through 1965 editions) as well as illustrations representing blueprint details for the various caps.

Several points require clarification. The three approved caps for 1956-1960 copper radiators were rated at seven p.s.i. and were made by the AC Spark Plug Division of General Motors (#850549), Standt (#3708174) and Eaton (#3708173). Of interest here, while researching this article I obtained information through General Motors Purchasing that suggests that from 1957 through 1960 the Eaton cap #3708173 was used exclusively and a *"do not purchase"* order was applied to AC cap #850549 and Stant cap #3708174. I would be interested in hearing from anyone who believes they have an original #850549 or #3708174 cap on their 1957-1960 Corvette. The AC #850549 was available in at least two, and possibly three, designs, the most recent designs identified as "RC-1" types. The latest design RC-1 remains available today as a service part.

Caps #861362 and #861306, rated at 13 p.s.i., were both made of aluminum and were used with aluminum radiators. Service manuals cautioned the use of a cap containing brass parts with an aluminum radiator as serious damage would result — also the use of a brass or cast-iron drain plug (rather than aluminum) would also lead to eventual serious radiator damage, resulting in replacement.

Cap #861306 deserves special mention in that it does not actually appear in the currently available 1961 Corvette Factory Assembly Manual. Sheet Number 5.00, Section 11-13, which only shows later cap usage, had been superceded during the 1961 model-year and the earlier used Sheet 5.00 had to be retrived from micro-film records. The micro-film shows the use of #361306 on early 1961 Corvettes. This small instance brings up many implications regarding just how much reliance can be placed in these manuals. Cap #861306 was replaced in late February, 1961 by #861307. This cap was almost identical to #861306 except that it was zinc plated. If any owners of 1961 models have the #861306 cap, I would like a picture or drawing of specific markings and the serial number of the car.

Of side interest, cap #861362 was apparently the first "coolant-recovery-type" cap produced. This cap was used by G. M. in litigation regarding patents of such caps several years ago. While the 1973 model Corvette is thought to be the first to use a coolant-recovery system, the early design 1960-1961 aluminum radiator with the built-in expansion tank utilized this principle.

1956-1965 CORVETTE RADIATOR PRESSURE CAPS
(As specified by the respective Factory Assembly Manuals)

Model Years	Radiator Type	Cap Part Number	Pressure
1956 through 1960	Copper	850549 3708173 Optional* 3708174	7 Pounds
1960-1961	Aluminum w/built-in expansion tank	861362	13 Pounds
1961	Aluminum w/separate supply tank	861306 861307 After Feb. '61	13 Pounds
1962 through 1965	Aluminum w/separate supply tank	861307	13 Pounds

*All three designs approved for use in production.

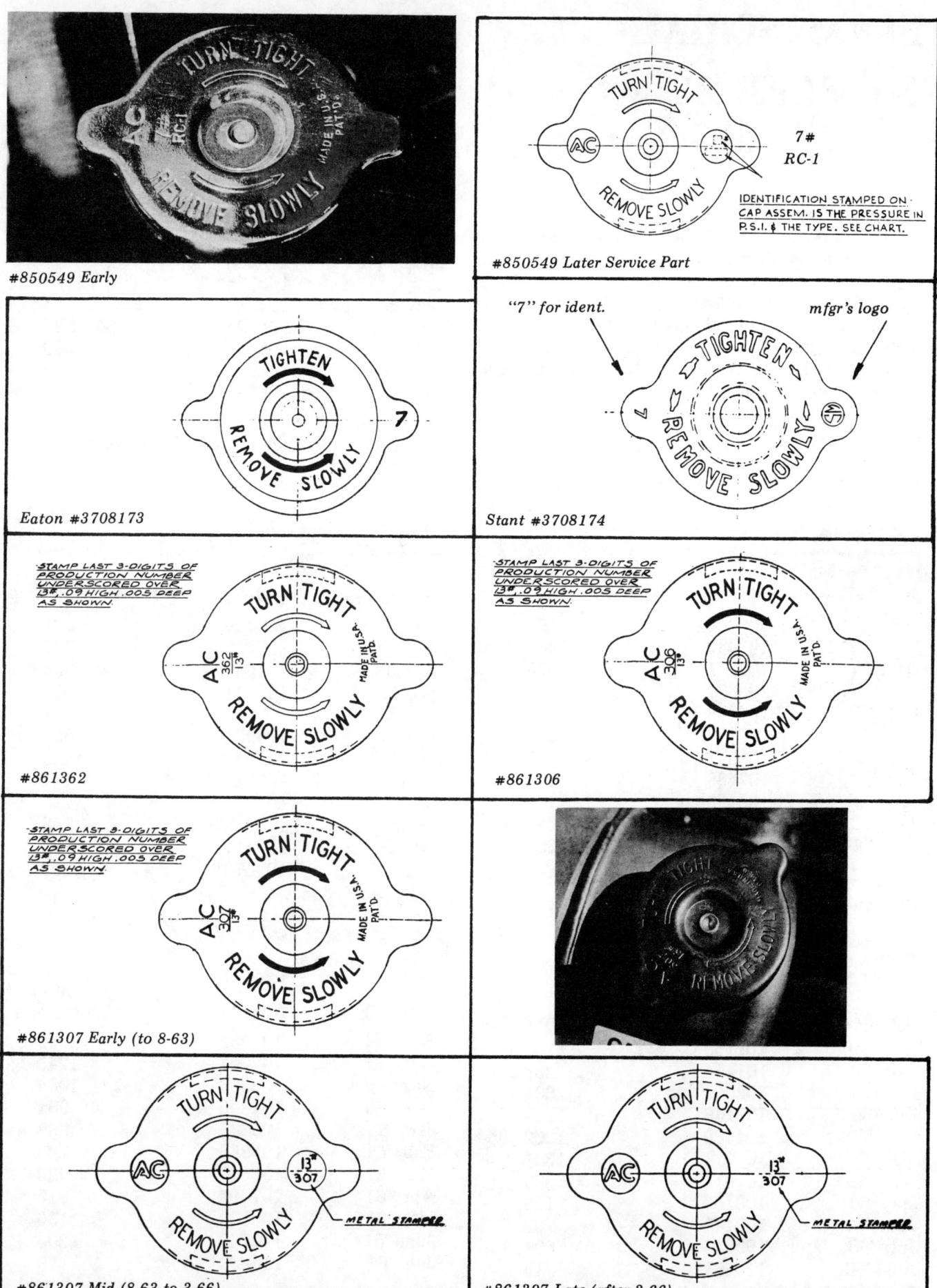

FINAL SERIAL NUMBER BY MONTH

The charts presented here have been constructed from Chevrolet data, and indicate the final serial number produced at the end of each month listed. Note that the 1957 listing is partially estimated, as the data is incomplete; all data for 1958-1967 is complete and correct according to documents. The 1965 listing is of interest as here it indicates 23,564 units were produced, while other Chevrolet documents show a 23,562 final figure.

1957 Model Year

Month/Year	Serial #	Monthly Production
Oct. '56	100580	580
Nov. '56	101070	490
Dec. '56	101650*	
Jan. '57	102150*	
Feb. '57	102600*	
Mar. 29, '57	103089**	
Mar. '57	103135*	
April 9, '57	103268**	
April '57	103725*	
May '57	104331	
June '57	104924	593
July '57	105584	660
Aug. '57	106229	645
Sept. '57	106339***	110

*estimated
**According to Technical Service Bulletin #295
***End of Model-run

1958 Model Year

Month/Year	Serial #	Monthly Production
Oct. '57	100486	486
Nov. '57	101443	957
Dec. '57	102511	1068
Jan. '58	103677	1166
Feb. '58	104789	1112
Mar. '58	105779	990
Apr. '58	106544	765
May '58	107489	945
June '58	108192	703
July '58	108840	648
Aug. '58	109168*	328

*End of Model-run

1959 Model Year

Month/Year	Serial #	Monthly Production
Sept. '58	100409	409
Oct. '58	100632	223
Nov. '58	101587	955
Dec. '58	102641	1054
Jan. '59	103962	1321
Feb. '59	104921	959
Mar. '59	106033	1112
Apr. '59	107144	1111
May '59	107934	790
June '59	108702	768
July '59	109437	735
Aug. '59	109670*	233

*End of model-run

1960 Model Year

Month/Year	Serial #	Monthly Production
Oct. '59	101168	1168
Nov. '59	101454	286
Dec. '59	102059	605
Jan. '60	103158	1099
Feb. '60	104360	1202
Mar. '60	105711	1351
Apr. '60	107011	1300
May '60	108167	1156
June '60	109149	982
July '60	109846	697
Aug. '60	110261*	415

*End of model-run

1961 Model Year

Month/Year	Serial #	Monthly Production
Sept. '60	101052	1052
Oct. '60	102301	1249
Nov. '60	103355	1054
Dec. '60	104306	951
Jan. '61	105203	897
Feb. '61	105966	763
Mar. '61	106889	923
Apr. '61	107804	915
May '61	108960	1156
June '61	110160	1200
July '61	110939*	779

*End of model-run

1962 Model Year

Month/Year	Serial #	Monthly Production
Aug. '61	100443	443
Sept. '61	100827	384
Oct. '61	102065	1238
Nov. '61	103465	1400
Dec. '61	104766	1301
Jan. '62	106234	1468
Feb. '62	107585	1351
Mar. '62	109116	1531
Apr. '62	110519	1403
May '62	112035	1516
June '62	113459	1424
July '62	114520	1061
Aug. '62	114531*	11

*End of model-run

1963 Model Run

Month/Year	Serial #	Monthly Production
Sept. '62	100675	675
Oct. '62	102756	2081
Nov. '62	104047	1291
Dec. '62	105972	1925
Jan. '63	107976	2004
Feb. '63	109814	1838
Mar. '63	111833	2019
Apr. '63	114128	2295
May '63	116409	2281
June '63	118524	2115
July '63	120990	2466
Aug. '63	121513*	523

*End of model-run

1964 Model Year

Month/Year	Serial #	Monthly Production
Sept. '63	101741	1741
Oct. '63	104045	2304
Nov. '63	106063	2018
Dec. '63	108091	2028
Jan. '64	110297	2206
Feb. '64	112322	2025
Mar. '64	114570	2248
Apr. '64	116865	2295
May '64	118805	1940
June '64	120920	2115
July '64	122229*	1309

*End of model-run

1965 Model Year

Month/Year	Serial #	Monthly Production
Aug. '64	100227	227
Sept. '64	101425	1198
Oct. '64	STRIKE	—0—
Nov. '64	103347	1922
Dec. '64	105754	2407
Jan. '65	108442	2688
Feb. '65	111059	2617
Mar. '65	113936	2877
Apr. '65	116516	2580
May '65	118753	2237
June '65	121216	2463
July '65	123562	2346
August '65	123564*	2

*End of model-run

1966 Model Run

Month/Year	Serial #	Monthly Production
Sept. '65	102031	2031
Oct. '65	104384	2353
Nov. '65	107186	2802
Dec. '65	109892	2706
Jan. '66	112587	2695
Feb. '66	115283	2696
Mar. '66	118091	2808
Apr. '66	120664	2573
May '66	123016	2352
June '66	125469	2453
July '66	127720*	2251

*End of model-run

1967 Model Year

Month/Year	Serial #	Monthly Production
Sept. '66	102110	2110
Oct. '66	102685	575
Nov. '66	104981	2296
Dec. '66	107110	2129
Jan. '67	109465	2355
Feb. '67	112264	2799
Mar. '67	115316	3052
Apr. '67	117395	2079
May '67	119747	2352
June '67	122214	2467
July '67	122940*	726

*End of model-run

"BRINGING UP THE REAR"
By Rev. Mike Ernst

1961-1962 MATURED MACHINE

The opportunity to check out a correct cylinder block or generator on a Corvette is much easier than checking for a correct rear axle, with regard to casting number, casting date, and the assembly date and axle code stampings.

Yet what is correct? Where are the numbers amidst all the accumulated dirt and oil? It is actually possible to determine what is correct and what is not.

Initially it should be mentioned that the car serial number was never stamped on the axle housing (or "carrier" as GM called it). Therefore, unlike engines beginning in 1960 and transmissions from around 1961 on, you cannot unequivocally determine whether or not the axle is the original factory unit.

There are a number of identifying elements. First — what is the casting date of the carrier? The casting date code is identical to that used for casting the engines, in that the coding system is the same. It begins with a single alphabetical letter to designate the month, starting with "A" for January, "B" for February and so on, a one or two digit number indicating day of the month, followed by a single digit signifying the year. Thus, E142 is May 14, 1962.

Obviously the date casting must be earlier than the manufactured date of the car. A proper date however, can also be found on a passenger car of the same vintage.

The casting number (not to be confused with the date casting) identifies the casting mold, and those used for the Corvette axle housings interchange with passenger car units. Correct casting numbers used for 1957 through 1962 Corvettes and passenger cars are:

    3725899 for non-positraction
    3789812 with positraction

Note: Positraction axle housings also carry a large cast-in "P" next to the casting number.

That much is identical with passenger car units. The assembly axle code stamping data however, signifies the difference between the Corvette and other model units. See chart, page 24.

Opposite the casting number and date (refer to sketch) is a shallow stamping made up of two letters and a two or three digit number code. On the illustrated differential, the casting date is E142 (May 14, 1962), and the stamp code is CA 5 17: the "CA" indicates the axle ratio and vehicle equipment, while the "5 17" indicates the axle was assembled on May 17th. The accompanying chart contains the best possible listing for all axle codes for 1961 and 1962, and you will note that "CA" signifies a 1962 standard 3:36 ratio non-positraction axle mated to a manual transmission, or Powerglide.

A reasonably correct chart of rear axle codes is contained in the front section of any Chevrolet Corvette or passenger car and truck parts catalog, and includes most model years. However, printed here is a most complete, revised list for the 1961 and 1962 Corvette models.

One additional note of interest — beginning with the 1959 model year, there were no longer separate

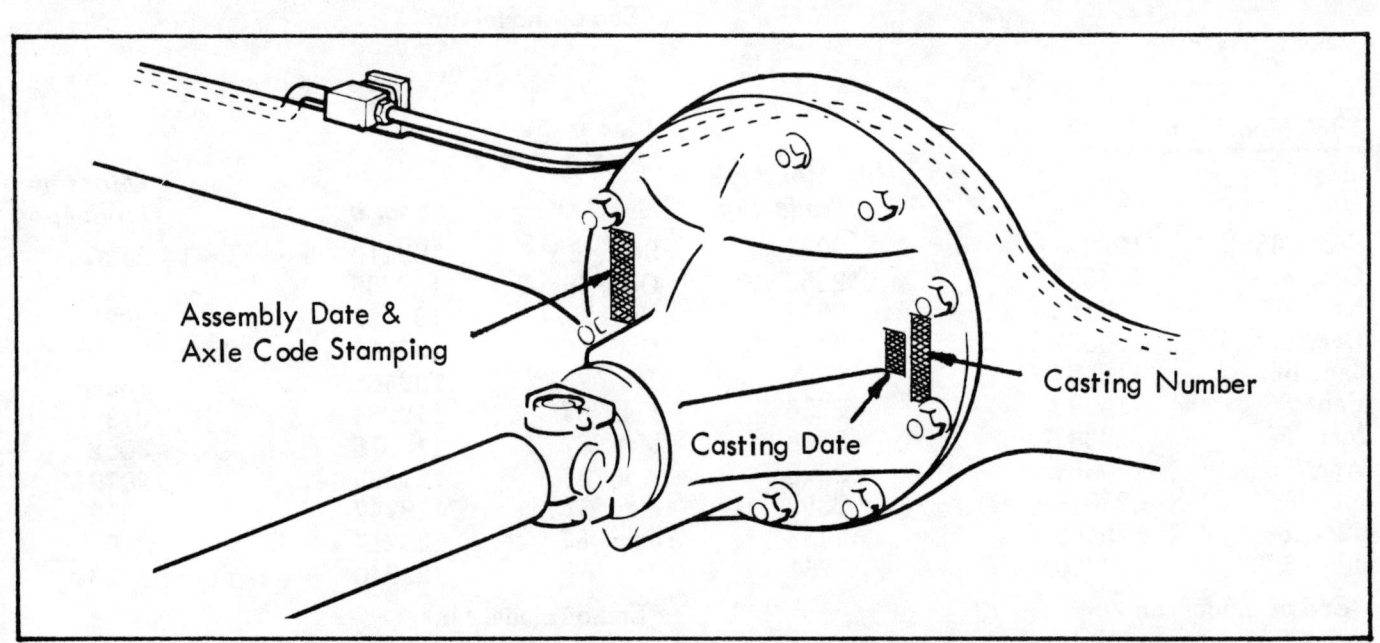

RPO numbers for each positraction axle ratio as had been used earlier. Positraction or "limited-slip" differentials from 1959 through 1962 were all ordered as RPO 675, regardless of the ratio. Each dealer desiring to order a different ratio specified that ratio on the order form. Yet, based on several window stickers that I have examined, when the sticker was printed showing all options, a single digit letter code was suffixed to the RPO 675 number when it appeared. For example, 675M, 675F, etc. In examining the cars represented on the window stickers I have seen, it appears that this letter suffix corresponds with the second letter used in the code on the accompanying chart, presented here. Therefore, a 1962 with RPO 675M on the window sticker would have a 3:70 positraction and metallic brakes, while a 675F printout would indicate a 4:56 positraction axle, etc.

So now, you've just crawled underneath your car, checked the rear axle code, and found out that it is incorrect. Was your car originally equipped with positraction? It is easy to tell. Check the fill hole at the back of the housing to see if it has the large round positraction tag affixed to it? That's not too reliable. Next, check the spare tire cover to see if it has a positraction warning label affixed? Again, that's not completely reliable.

You can pull the axles out and see if they use roller bearings (positraction did!), or ball bearings (non-

positraction used these)? Too difficult?

Instead, check the driver-side axle tube. On the top, if the car used positraction originally, there will be a small vent fitting with a tube running across to behind the axle carrier. *That* is the easiest and most reliable way to detect positraction.

Rev. Michael Ernst
P.O. Box 36
Bowler, WI 54416
Phone: 715/793-4608

Positraction Identification

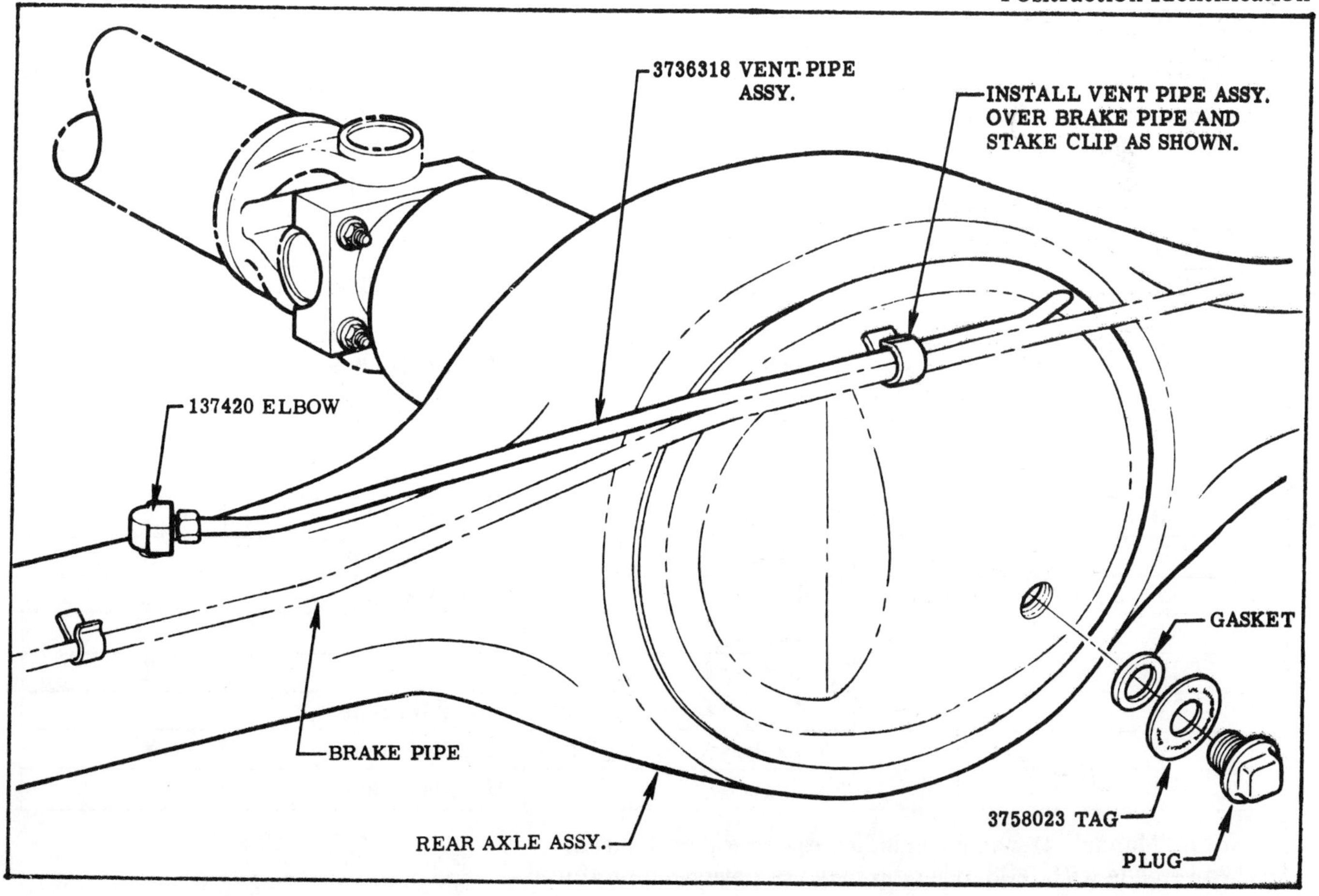

225

1961 CORVETTE AXLE CODES

AXLE CODE	RATIO	TRANSMISSION	EQUIPMENT (if applicable)	POSITRACTION
AC	3.36	3-speed		
AE	3.55	Powerglide		
AF	3.36	3-speed		X
AH	3.70	4-speed		
AN	3.70	4-speed		X
AP	4.11	Manual		X
AQ	4.56	Manual		X
AS	3.70	4-speed	H.D. Brake/Susp.	X
AT	4.11	Manual	H.D. Brake/Susp.	X
AU	4.56	Manual	H.D. Brake/Susp.	X
FJ	3.70	4-speed	Metallic Brakes	
FK	3.70	4-speed	Metallic Brakes	X
FL	4.11	Manual	Metallic Brakes	X
FM	4.56	Manual	Metallic Brakes	X

Note: "Manual" transmission indicates either 3 or 4 speed.

1962 CORVETTE AXLE CODES

AXLE CODE	RATIO	TRANSMISSION	EQUIPMENT (if applicable)	POSITRACTION
CA	3.36	Manual & Powerglide		
CB	3.36	Manual & Powerglide		X
CC	3.55	4-speed	Special Cam	X
CD	3.70	4-speed	Special Cam	X
CE	4.11	4-speed	Special Cam	X
CF	4.56	4-speed	Special Cam	X
CG	3.70	4-speed	Special Cam	
CH	3.36	Manual & Powerglide	Metallic Brakes	
CK	3.36	Manual & Powerglide	Metallic Brakes	X
CL	3.55	4-speed	Metallic Brakes	X
CM	3.70	4-speed	Metallic Brakes	X
CN	4.11	4-speed	Metallic Brakes	X
CP	4.56	4-speed	Metallic Brakes	X
CQ	3.70	4-speed	H.D. Brake/Susp. & FI	X
CR	4.11	4-speed	H.D. Brake/Susp. & FI	X
CS	4.56	4-speed	H.D. Brake/Susp. & FI	X
CT	3.08	4-speed		
CU	3.08	4-speed & Powerglide*		X
CV	3.08	4-speed & Powerglide*	Metallic Brakes	
CW	3.08	4-speed & Powerglide*	Metallic Brakes	X
CY	3.70	4-speed	Metallic Brakes	

Note: "Manual" transmission indicates either 3 or 4 speed.
*Powerglide with 3.08 axle ratio may not have been produced.

1963-1967

VEHICLE IDENTIFICATION PLATES 1963-1967 STING RAY

By Joe Clark

While researching our last article on the gas tank build orders, we uncovered a great deal more than originally expected. The same applies to the present project, with a lot of questions turning up unanswered.

In any documentation of originality, accuracy is the name of the game. Those owners of cars in good or excellent original shape have a fairly easy time of confirming originality by checking on engine number, optional equipment codes, plus confirming the color and trim as to factory specs.

Much of the checking is often done by locating the original owner or selling dealer and collecting any documentation that might still be available. (i.e. window sticker, dealer order, invoice, etc.).

However, for the owner of the average car — the car that has had no special care — and lots of owners — the task of documentation is harder, but by no means impossible.

On pre-1963 cars, the lack of a data plate (such as found on the Sting Ray series), factory color, trim and optional equipment are more difficult to verify, barring the presence of a dealer order or window sticker.

A friend of ours recently purchased a 1962 Corvette from a high volume Baltimore Chevrolet dealer. The car was about average and had come in on trade. Upon close examination the new owner noticed several variations that set this car apart from other '62's. Checking further, he was able to confirm that the car was originally a factory fuel injected vehicle that had been re-engined. He later even located the plugged holes that had held the factory FI emblems.

Unfortunately, nowhere on the straight axle series was there factory documentation of color, trim or equipment — except engine suffix (presuming the original engine is still with the car).

Starting with the 1963 series, Chevrolet began affixing to each new Corvette, two very informative little plates. They were riveted to the crossmember beneath the glove box door.

The plate on the right was the typical V.I.N. plate containing the car's year, type (coupe or convertible), serial number and plant of origin (and in some cases Dealer Delivery Date).

Taking a sample of each year, let's look at a few examples for interpretation.

3	0867	S	100042
Year	Model	Plant	Sequence
1963	Convertible	St. Louis	42nd Unit

4	0837	S	122224
Year	Model	Plant	Sequence
1964	Coupe	St. Louis	22,224th Unit

19467	5	S	100035
Model	Year	Plant	Sequence
Convertible	1965	St. Louis	35th Unit

19437	6	S	100520
Model	Year	Plant	Sequence
Coupe	1966	St. Louis	520th Unit

19467	7	S	122939
Model	Year	Plant	Sequence
Convertible	1967	St. Louis	22,939th Unit

While these examples may seem repetitive to the seasoned owner-restorer, there are subtle variations in each plate that can be noted year to year. Further, many owners have been unable to interpret the plates until they realized the significance of each printed character.

If the serial number plate is quite a simple and direct source of information, the accompanying plate, by comparison, is rather puzzling, while at the same time presenting some valuable information.

PLATE I

```
       Chevrolet Division General Motors Corp.
                  Detroit, Michigan
J3
Style 67-467                              S7753 Body
Trim 418BA                               980AA Paint
                  Body By Chevrolet
```

From Convertible 194677117736.

PLATE II

```
       Chevrolet Division General Motors Corp.
                  Detroit, Michigan
H06
Style 67-437                              A1092 Body
Trim 420                                   988 Paint
                  Body By Chevrolet
```

From Coupe 194377S113718

PLATE III

```
       Chevrolet Division General Motors Corp.
                  Detroit, Michigan
A10
Style 64-867                               315 Body
Trim 490AB                              936AA Paint
                  Body By Chevrolet
```

From Convertible 40867S100464

PLATE IV

```
       Chevrolet Division General Motors Corp.
                  Detroit, Michigan
K23
Style 67-467                             A-4763 Body
Trim Std.                                  972 Paint
                  Body By Chevrolet
```

From Convertible 194677S122849

These examples from actual cars are given to assist the reader in his or her own data plate interpretation.

Plate I is the author's own 1967 Convertible (467). Starting with the upper left corner we see a J.3 for the time built code. This code will usually appear in the upper left and will contain both a letter and one or two numbers.

The "J" refers to May; 3 to the 3rd. To arrive at the above, the months are given in alphabetical order, starting with August production represented by "A",

(continued)

September production by "B", etc. To assist the reader, the accompanying chart is provided:

Letter Code	Month
A	August
B	September
C	October
D	November
E	December
F	January
G	February
H	March
I	April
J	May
K	June
L	July

Thus E-12 equals December 12th
K-15 equals June 15th, etc.

Continuing with Plate I, the *style* is a '67-467, that is, a 1967 convertible (model 467).

Trim is a 418 BA. Here is where some of the mystery begins to develop. The 418 designation probably refers to vinyl and the BA may refer to color of dash pad, seats and carpet (in this case, Elkhart Blue).

Body is a St. Louis product (thus the "S") and it is the 7,753rd St. Louis body in 1967.

Paint is a number 980 and is Elkhart Blue. Here again, however, the letter suffix "AA" is not able to be ascertained at this writing.

The second car, (Plate II) is a 1967 Aerocoupe. It was built March 6th and the *style* numbers verify it as a 1967 — model 437 — coupe. *Trim* is a number 420 meaning vinyl ? in a saddle shade? Note here the absence of any letter suffix. What this means is subject for speculation. The car has an original saddle tan interior.

Body number indicates that this car has an "A" body. These were bodies built by A.O. Smith Company for Chevrolet in Smith's Ionia, Michigan plant. The bodies were shipped to St. Louis for final trimming and assembly. This particular body is the 1,092nd body built by A.O. Smith in 1967.

The *Paint* number 988 is Marlboro Maroon — note here again the lack of letter suffixes.

Plate III is an early car, a 1964, built August 10, 1963, as a convertible — as confirmed by the *style* code.

Trim number is a 490AB. 490 is a code for vinyl, AB must refer to color combination — red in this case.

Body is a very low number, 315. Note here the lack of an "A" or "S" prefix. This, for a change, is easy to explain.

The contract for outside bodies with A.O. Smith did not start until February, 1964. The prefix "A" or "S" commenced with 1964 car #109,678, and continued through the 1967 model year run. Thus, all cars built prior to 1964 — #109,678, were St. Louis Chevrolet bodies — excepting of course, the Flint "First 300" in 1953.

Lastly, the paint on this car is a 936 Ermine White, but the meaning of the "AA" is not known.

Car #4 is another 1967 convertible, built June 23rd — a very late car. *Trim* is Std. This we know to be black vinyl in 1967. The body is an A.O. Smith, number 4,763. This gives a rough idea of A.O. Smith production for the year 1967 as this car is very close to the end of the run (91 cars).

Paint is 972 Ermine White. Note again no suffixes.

Adding to the confusion, the oft mentioned color and trim combination chart #3843115 seems to be somewhat less than an accurate source. This table only represents the 1964 model run and in some cases the numbers and suffixes given simply do not check out — even on 1964 cars! In matching up documented original cars to the table, numbers and letters, especially in the trim area, were not in agreement.

A cautionary word is in order here. When looking at any identification plate, keep in mind the possibility of a misprint or a wrong letter or number. In that, at the moment, there is no absolute interpretation of all data plate codes, information given on these plates is subject to question until a absolute meaning can be assigned to each of the letters that are now a mystery. There have also been errors discovered in known codes, such as *Time Built* codes — wrong days, and even wrong months being stamped on the I.D. plates.

1965 car serial number one lists a paint code of 900 ZZ. Nowhere is ZZ explained and number 900 is normally the code for Tuxedo Black. (The car was factory painted silver).

There is a way we can start to solve this problem. I emphasize *we* because it is going to require some effort on the part of you, the reader.

What we would like you to do, is grab a pencil and paper, go to your car and copy down your data plate information — every letter, number and code, — serial # included.

If you will send this to me along with the *original* body and trim colors of your car, we can probably put together a chart of letter codes and their meanings.

This project depends on volume of response to get a broad idea of letter code meanings. If we have enough response the results will be published in an upcoming *RESTORER*.

Responses to:
J.M. Clark
Box 353
Havre de Grace,
Maryland 21078
301-939-2467

7017380 FUEL INJECTION UPDATE

by Gene Dressen

The first two articles I wrote for the *RESTORER* delt with the 7017380 fuel injection unit used in 1964 and 1965 and the fuel injection air cleaner used from 1963 through 1965. In those articles I mentioned a few things that I would like to readdress in this article.

In the article on the fuel unit I mentioned that in 1964 the St. Louis Assembly Plant started stamping the car serial number on the plenum chamber of the fuel injected cars. The procedure of identifying a Corvette to it's engine was actually started in 1960. This same year the serial tags were spot welded to the steering column instead of being attached to the body with screws. Apparently someone thought it wise to make it as difficult as possible to steal a Corvette and get away with it by just changing a body tag.

The procedure of stamping the serial number on the engine didn't slow many people down. When they stole a Corvette for it's engine they just obliterated all possible identification points on the engine and the injection unit if so-equipped. As you have examined fuel injection units, how many of them have you noticed with the serial/model number tag missing from the left front of the plenum chamber? These tags don't just fall off, but they come off very easily with a chisel.

Someone came up with the idea to start stamping the plenum chamber with the car serial number stamp; the same procedure used to stamp the engine and transmission case. I have been unable to locate the exact date on which the word came down to stamp the fuel unit. I do have serial numbers on four 1964 Corvettes, though that were stamped. The serial numbers of the Corvettes and the serial number of the plenum chamber are shown in the accompanying chart. Of all the 7017380 units I have documented, these four are the only ones used on 1964's that I have found to be stamped. It is also quite ironic that the first three units belong to cars that were possibly produced the same week, since there is less than 250 cars between them. The presence of the stamps on these units and the absence of stamps on a great number of the units in the 2200 and 2300 unit-serial-range that I have documented, indicates to me that the observed absence of a serial number stamp on the plenum chamber after these 14,000 serial number cars must have been due to human error.

The person stamping the engines when the first three cars on the chart were built remembered to stamp the fuel units. Of course I haven't seen every fuel injected 1964 built, and I'm sure that a great number of those after 14,000 *are* stamped. What I am saying is that they *all* should be stamped, but *aren't*. I'm not considering the small number of service units that shouldn't be stamped. The enclosed photo shows the stamping on unit serial 2094, car serial 4114842 (1964).

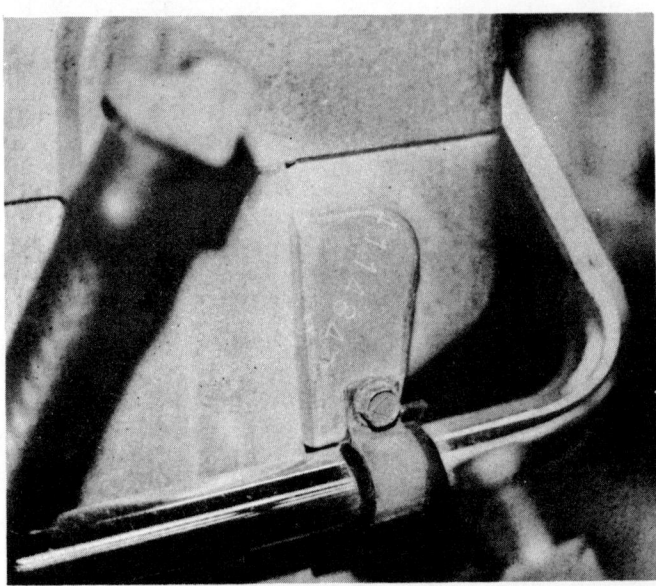

It is extremely difficult to get some of this information. Some of it slowly pieces itself together after a long time of studying it. It is also extremely difficult to locate unmolested cars from which to get the information. As things work out I never seem to have a piece of paper when I *do* find something that's interesting. This happened at the concours at 1978 Bloomington. Some of you will remember a 1964, factory fuel, red convertible with white interior. This was an example of an unmolested car. Things were just like they were when the car left the factory. I am going from memory on this but the car was a very late car, with an "RX" motor built in June of 1964. The unit serial was 2138 or 2139. I looked all over this unit for a serial number stamp, but there was none. I owned a unit, number 2338, which came off of a very late 1964. It had the 1111063 distributor. This unit was pulled from a car and put in a box. It was not stamped either. I will make a guess and say that the person who stamped the units in the 14,000 series was not the same person who didn't stamp the units late in the 1964 production year.

Now that I have stuck my neck out, I would like to hear from all owners of factory fuel injected 1964 Corvettes who know for sure that the unit on their car actually belongs to the car. Possibly we can find a breaking time when the units were no longer stamped. This could have occurred quite easily if a new person came onto the line and was not told that he had to stamp the fuel cars one additional time. We should also be able to tell when the stamping started.

There was also a time when the location of the plenum chamber stamping was changed. It could have been the size of the area available, the movement involved to get into location to stamp, any number of reasons that changed the stamping location from the front of the unit to the right side. The earliest unit from a 1965 fuel car that I know of being stamped on the right is 943. Something happened with 5101463. This unit is stamped on the front, just like the 1964 cars were. A photo is shown.

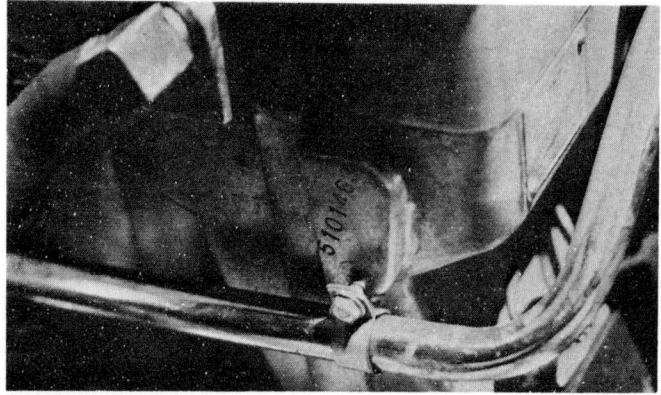

Another photo shows the location of the stamp as it should appear on the 1965 cars. I said *should.* I have seen units that have been stamped all over this area. Most of them are on the heavy boss extending

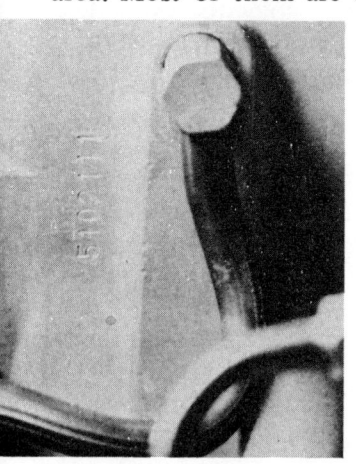 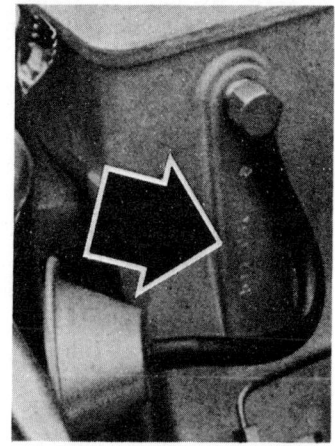

toward the plenum runners. There were, again, apparently a number of different people who stamped the engine because of the varied locations on this right rear side. It would seem that after finding a location that worked, the worker would stamp the next one in the same location. The latest factory 1965 unit that I know of, and I have examined it and believe it to be original, was stamped twice. The first stamp was on a surface that was concave, so only the two end stamps are readable. The second was moved to the heavy boss, where it took.

To show you the value of this stamping on the unit, I helped identify a stolen 1965 fuel car that had been totally denumbered. Everything was missing except the car serial number on the plenum chamber. GM, you did a good thing.

In the article on air cleaners, I mentioned that there were two numbers that were appearing for the rubber hose that connects the cleaner to the fuel unit. I did some digging in the 1963, 1964, and 1965 assembly manuals. What a valuable tool! The 1963 manual states that the part number for this hose is 3825656. This is the thick heavy hose. The part number appears on the hose. In examining the 1964 manual it states that on Sept. 17, 1963 the hose was changed from 3825656 to 3853879. This is the light rubber hose currently available from GM. It is difficult to tell exactly when the change did take place — in the 1965 manual a note relating to fuel injection fender emblem modification was added on October 18, 1964, but the change still hadn't been made on my car built on November 13th. It probably took a good month for the changes to go into effect, and longer to use up all the old numbered parts.

1964 Corvette serial 7889 has the early hose on it. I'm sure that it's original. The late 2338 unit I had also used the thick early hose. The unit from 4114842 and the air cleaner were removed by the original owner and just recently sold to a friend of mine. A photo he sent shows that the air cleaner has the later thin hose still in place. Here is an example of both hoses showing up during the entire year on the 1964's. I don't know the answer to this one other than that they put on the part they picked up out of the bin. Information on the hose application on your 1964 would also be appreciated. Hopefully this type of information can be expanded to the point that it can be used in judging events.

Currently I have serial numbers on approximately 70 1965 factory fuel injected Corvettes. On only a few of them do I have complete information. May I also request any of you who own 7017380 units or 1965 fuel cars to contact me. I would very much like to know about your car. Send for questionnaire to Gene H. Dressen, 753 Wayne, Pocatello, Idaho 83201.

PLENUM CHAMBER STAMP LOCATIONS

	Car serial number	Unit serial number	Stamp location
1964	4114605	1746	front
	4114842	2094	front
	4114848	1745	front
	4116068	2234	front
1965	5100943	2245	side
	5101463	2252	front
	5102111	2158	side
	5102442	1924	side

CORVETTE MODELS
With Dr. Michael Zimmerman

This issue's column deals primarily with the Corvette SR-2, a racing/street car produced in several versions in 1956. My model is based on the cutaway drawing on pages 54-55 of Ludvigsen's *Corvette: America's Star-Spangled Sports Car*. The major features setting the SR-2 apart from the stock '56 Corvette are the large head rest and fin, the racing windshield, air ducts for the rear brakes, and an extended body nose. Using parts from four kits (AMT's '62 [#2205] and '63 [#A-163] and 2 Monogram '57's [#2227]), almost all of these modifications can be reproduced rather easily. The exception is the extended nose, which isn't absolutely necessary on a 1/24th scale.

To follow along with the numbered directions for the 2227 kit, these alterations must be made:

1. Cut off the tabs for the front bumper overrider assembly.
2. The SR-2 dual mufflers are tubular rather than the flat, stock, oval mufflers. They can be made from the edge of the part's tree and glued in place after removing the thin section of the exhaust pipes. The exhaust system should be painted gray or silver after painting the fram black. The optional rear axle is used.
3. It may be necessary to file grooves in the floor pan to clear the mufflers. Be sure to scrape the paint off areas to be glued.
4. The SR-2 uses aluminum Halibrand knock-off wheels, and parts from 3 kits are required to duplicate them. The "mag" wheels from the '62 are the right style but are too small for the '57 tires. I removed the center portion from the '57 mag wheels with a hot knife and sandpaper rolled around a dowel, glued in the '62 wheels, shortened the axle portion, drilled out 1/8th inch holes for the axles, added the knock-off spinners from the '63, painted the wheels to the axles. You might be able to fit in

the bearings supplied with the kit but after having my '41 Continental roll off a "flat" table top I prefer non-functional wheels.

5. Engine modifications are fairly simple, the only alterations being the heavy duty transmission and the intake manifold and dual 4 barrel carbs from the '62 (left over if you build the '62 with fuel injection).

6. No change.

7. The inner fenders are flat black and the red interior should receive a thin layer of Dull-Cote. Omit the silver and beige trim, painting only the hardware silver.

8. Scrape the plating off the steering wheel rim and paint with dark brown. The dash is Dull-Coted red with black instruments and chrome trim. This section demands the most extensive modifications, to the body. The fuel injection symbols and deck lid catches should be cut off and these areas sanded flat. The head rest, from the '62 kit, is rounded off on top by applying plastic putty and sanding smooth. The headrest fits well behind the driver's seat, with only minimal filling—in with putty required. A cardboard pattern for the fin, the really distinguishing feature of the SR-2, should be made and the fin made from a scrap piece of flat plastic and glued on. The coves on the doors are prepared by cutting them out of the body of the second '57 model. The right is used on the left side and vice versa, so that the inside of each cove piece is now on the outside. These small pieces are sanded to fit into the door depressions and glued into place.

9. The major problem is modeling the SR-2 (or a '58 Corvette) is the hood louvers. I found a very effective solution by cutting the heads and points off straight pins and glueing them onto the hood. The pins must be slightly bowed in the center, as the hood surface has a slight curve. The hinge should be placed as far forward as possible and the hood painted with several coats of red, which both covers and seals in the pins. The effect is quite pleasing, as can be seen in the photos. The body should also be painted red at this time, the coves brush painted silver (use a *good* brush), and the flags the usual silver, red and black. A final coat of Gloss-Cote improves the finish.

10. Scrape the paint off junction points between body and frame. I found that I was able to slide the hood in after putting the body on the frame; taping the hood in as suggested in the instructions tends to remove some of the paint.

11. No change.

12. The SR-2 uses '58 style tail lights which can be

(continued)

made from the custom tail lights in the '62 kit and glued into the '57 rims. The rear bumper and license plate are omitted and the bumper mounting holes in the rear pan filled in the touched up in red.

13. The stock grille and headlights are used, with the front bumpers and grille overrider omitted. The large parking lights are made by reversing the air cleaners for the '57 dual carbs (part #66). The center is cut out and a piece of clear plastic inserted and the upper half of the rims filed down to fit on the fender. The back of the lens is painted silver. To make the lens use the rim as a pattern to scribe clear plastic (I used the window for the hard top) and break with pliers. The plastic breaks just like glass and can be sanded to fit.

14. The custom windshield for the '62 fits very well and is used without a frame. The stock rear view mirror is used and the antenna and roll bar omitted.

15. 1/16th inch and 1/4th inch white striping tape are used for the *piece de resistance*. The tape does not stretch, so allow a little slack on the hood for the depressions between the louvers. Be careful to match up the various panels. Pulling off the tape for repositioning pulls off paint.

Buying four kits to make one car may seem like a bit of overkill, but the '62 and '63 models can still be built and a 4:1 price ratio is very cheap compared to the cost of building a real race car on a road car base. And you don't have to worry about brake and gear box failures with the SR-2 model.

If I may be permitted a brief post-1967 digression, I have also recently completed Monogram's 1/8th scale 1978 Corvette (#2603). I have yet to see a perfectly designed model, but Monogram's are generally of the highest quality and the '78 maintains this reputation. The directions do not match the quality of the kit, being diagrammatic and occasionally unclear.

Specific points of difficulty are the installation of the lower radiator hose (the pattern is too long) and the tie rod (the tires must be flexed and it is *very* easy to install the rod backwards). The positions for the latches on the T-tops are not marked and the directions are misleading, making installation a trial and error process.

The directions for installing the wheels are simply incorrect. If, as indicated, you do not glue the wheel bearings to the axle shafts, the wheels fall off. If you glue the brakes to the inner wheel halves, again as indicated, the wheels will not turn.

The painting instructions are also rather remarkable. I don't think there was ever a Corvette with a brown engine and shocks or black exhaust manifolds. The mainfolds should be flat orange and the engine blue. The light tan interior is greatly appreciated, either left this color or painted over. The relief for the interior door handles is low and difficult to paint. The instrument panel decals are excellent in detail and should be applied with a decal solvent.

The various exterior chrome pieces, including the

rocker panel strips, exhaust extensions, and T-top trim should be installed last. If put on during the building, they are continuously being pulled off in later stages. The rear Corvette nameplate would be better moulded as a separate chrome piece and the rear license plate frame doesn't fit flush.

Two left over parts are the bumper support bars from Monogram's '65 kit. These pieces are the clue that Monogram is saving some money by using the same chassis parts for both kits. This economy move is surprising in a kit this expensive, as it leads to some inaccuracies, such as the battery being positioned under the hood.

Final assembly is greatly simplified by screws holding chassis to body, an approach that should be more often used. The finished kit is a beautiful model. Decals are supplied to build a Pace Car version but, as in real life, I chose to avoid Pace Car hysteria.

Corrections

The text pages appearing in The Best of The Corvette Restorer are reproduced exactly as they originally were printed. This information represents the best knowledge available at the time, but errors are always possible. This is especially true of a subject as complex as auto production, since factory exceptions, changes, and modifications are common. Often, publishing data is the only way to force some of these errors or omissions to surface.

The following corrections are those known to the NCRS at the time of the printing of The Best of The Corvette Restorer. As a general statement, you should ignore the addresses given for authors. Many have changed, and all correspondence should now be sent to THE NATIONAL CORVETTE RESTORERS SOCIETY, Box 81663, Lincoln, Nebraska, 68501. Also, any prices or values given in the text should be ignored as well for obvious reasons.

Volume 1, Number 3, text page 23: After printing the production figures for different fuel injection units, it was realized that the numbers applied not to units, but to horsepower/engine combinations. Refer to text page 94 for the corrected information.

Volume 2, Number 1, text page 35: The article reveals that the location of the Flint Corvette plant was at Van Slyke and Bristol roads. The plant was actually located at Van Slyke and Atherton.

Volume 3, Number 1, text page 66: For additional important information on 1956–1957 headlamps, see text page 87.

Volume 3, Number 3, text page 85: The article states that the pump castings should be cadmium plated. This is incorrect. The castings should be zinc-chromated.

Volume 4, Number 1, text page 95: The projected total column of 1957 engine production should be ignored.

Volume 4, Number 2, text page 103: The right center photo of the fast steering adaptor is printed up-side-down. Stand on head when viewing.

Volume 5, Number 1, text page 173: After this article was published, reader response indicated that later 1960 Corvette #987730 radios were build using pushbuttons with curved finger indentations.

Volume 5, Number 3, text page 195: 1965 convertible production is shown at the bottom of the page to be 15,276. This should be 15,376.

Volume 5, Number 4, text pages 227–229: The "time built codes" refer to the month and day that the **body** was built at either Chevrolet St. Louis, or A. O. Smith in Ionia, Michigan. They do not necessarily refer to the date the vehicle reached final assembly in St. Louis. This is especially true of A. O. Smith bodies built from January 1964 through the 1967 model year. Also, the letter code shown on page 229 may not actually represent the month indicated. Further investigation continues.

NCRS MEMBERSHIP REQUESTS

To receive information regarding joining the membership ranks of the National Corvette Restorer's Society, just return one of the coupons or a facsimile to the NCRS, Post Office Box 81663, Lincoln, Nebraska 68501. You'll be sent a handsome information package free of charge.

Yes, please send me complete NCRS membership information

NAME _____
ADDRESS _____
CITY _____ STATE ____ ZIP ____

Mail request to:
N.C.R.S.
P.O. BOX 81663
LINCOLN, NE 68501

Yes, please send me complete NCRS membership information

NAME _____
ADDRESS _____
CITY _____ STATE ____ ZIP ____

Mail request to:
N.C.R.S.
P.O. BOX 81663
LINCOLN, NE 68501

Yes, please send me complete NCRS membership information

NAME _____
ADDRESS _____
CITY _____ STATE ____ ZIP ____

Mail request to:
N.C.R.S.
P.O. BOX 81663
LINCOLN, NE 68501

Yes, please send me complete NCRS membership information

NAME _____
ADDRESS _____
CITY _____ STATE ____ ZIP ____

Mail request to:
N.C.R.S.
P.O. BOX 81663
LINCOLN, NE 68501

NCRS INFORMATION COUPON

NCRS INFORMATION COUPON

NCRS INFORMATION COUPON

NCRS INFORMATION COUPON

GREAT CORVETTE BOOKS

from Michael Bruce Associates. Buy from your favorite local book store, Corvette dealer, or order direct from the publisher: Michael Bruce Associates Inc., Post Office Box 396, Powell, Ohio 43065

CORVETTE! AMERICA'S ONLY

This is the contemporary Corvette book, the book that every Corvette enthusiast can relate to. It has the proper balance of what happened in 1952 when the Corvette dream was first forming, to what happens today. It opens previously closed doors of GM Styling and Engineering, yet includes the exterior world of Corvette concours shows, auctions, and swap meets.

Its 144, 7½" X 9" pages open horizontally for maximum subject display. There are over 160 photos and styling renderings, many in full color. Chapters are titled The Creators, The Racers, The Stylists, The Mania Explosion, and The Favorites. A special Facts section lists options, option costs, number codes, and numerous other details.

The standard version is hardbound in silver metallic with blue and red embossing. A deluxe hardbound leather edition is also available. The deluxe book is hardbound in black calfskin with gold embossing, and is a strictly limited offering of just 300 copies, each sequentially numbered.
PRICE: $22.50 ($50.00 for leather edition)

CORVETTE! SPORTSCAR OF AMERICA

Corvette! Sportscar of America combines a large (10¼" X 8⅜") horizontal page format with striking photography and fine layout design to produce a truly beautiful auto publication.

Coverage includes a section on great Corvettes of the past, interviews with personalities who played direct roles in shaping the Corvette's destiny, an incredibly detailed account of Corvette factory production during its first three years (1953–1955), an informative look at the scores of labels used on Corvettes through the years, a chapter devoted to the literature, films and other items used by Chevrolet dealers to promote the Corvette, and much more, all lavishly illustrated in over 250 photos and illustrations, many in full color.

Corvette! Sportscar of America is hardbound in black with silver embossing, and is protected by a coated paper dust jacket. A deluxe package is also available which has the same book but substitutes a hard slip case for the dust jacket, and includes a set of eight 8" X 10" selected prints for framing.
PRICE: $34.50 ($44.50 with hard case and framing prints)

THE BEST OF THE CORVETTE RESTORER

You know about the National Corvette Restorers Society. From a humble beginning in 1974, this organization grew to be the largest of its type anywhere. These are the great nit-pickers of the Corvette world. NCRS members have ferreted out the most nitty-gritty information imaginable. From Chevrolet sources, dealers, and heaven-knows where else. All of this found its way into The Corvette Restorer, the excellent NCRS quarterly magazine. The NCRS never reprints individual issues, but they've granted Michael Bruce Associates the rights to reprint the best of the first five volumes of The Corvette Restorer in one handsome package. We call it The Best of the Corvette Restorer.

Officially, the NCRS limits its interests to 1953 through 1967 models, but there's fascinating reading here for every Corvette enthusiast. The publication is soft-bound with a beautiful full color cover. It's 240 pages will keep you busy a long time.
PRICE: $14.95

THE DELUXE CORVETTE BLACK BOOK

The Corvette Black Book is that little book you've been waiting for. Nothing frustrates the Corvette enthusiast more than not being able to find information when needed. The Deluxe Corvette Black Book is a **new updated version** of the famous Corvette Black Book published by Michael Bruce Associates. It jams loads of facts about every Corvette year from 1953 through 1980 into 120 pages that measure just 4½" X 7¼". Included are options, option costs, colors, codes, ID numbers, labels, photo/illustrations, and much more. This isn't just a conglomeration of someone else's charts and figures. We assembled the whole thing. You'll not find such information presented so clearly and correctly anywhere else.

Pains were taken to make this as accurate as possible. Prior to printing, proofs were sent to several leading Corvette experts in the country for examination. Change after change resulted in a thing of beauty, factually speaking, to behold. All this, and quality paper and printing too. You need this.
PRICE: $7.95

Notice: This publication is not in any way connected with the **"Black Book"** published by National Auto Research Publications, Inc.

Check or money order enclosed for:

☐ Corvette! Sportscar of America @ $34.50 ($44.50 deluxe) $ _____ . _____
☐ Corvette! America's Only @ $22.50 ($50.00 Leather) _____ . _____
☐ The Best of The Corvette Restorer @ $14.95 _____ . _____
☐ The Deluxe Corvette Black Book @ $7.95 _____ . _____

Michael Bruce Associates, Inc.   Postage/Handling   1.00
P.O. Box 396 Powell, Ohio 43065   **TOTAL ENCLOSED** $ _____ . _____

NAME _____
ADDRESS _____
CITY _____ STATE _____ ZIP _____

Check or money order enclosed for:

☐ Corvette! Sportscar of America @ $34.50 ($44.50 deluxe) $ _____ . _____
☐ Corvette! America's Only @ $22.50 ($50.00 Leather) _____ . _____
☐ The Best of The Corvette Restorer @ $14.95 _____ . _____
☐ The Deluxe Corvette Black Book @ $7.95 _____ . _____

Michael Bruce Associates, Inc.   Postage/Handling   1.00
P.O. Box 396 Powell, Ohio 43065   **TOTAL ENCLOSED** $ _____ . _____

NAME _____
ADDRESS _____
CITY _____ STATE _____ ZIP _____